P9-CME-055

Leo Rosten, a writer of exceptional range and versatility, has been delighting readers for more than four decades with stories, articles, and columns in magazines like *The New Yorker, Saturday Review*, and *Look*, as well as with books that have become American classics: *The Education of H*Y*M*A*N K*A*P*L*A*N, Captain Newman, M.D.*, and *The Joys of Yiddish*. He has also written ten movies, several mysteries, books about travel, and works of social and political commentary.

He has a Ph.D. from the University of Chicago, is an honorary fellow of the London School of Economics and Political Science, and has taught at Yale and Berkeley.

LEO ROSTEN

The Joys of

YINGLISH

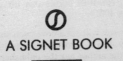

A SIGNET BOOK

WARRANTY TO THE READER

If, after reading this *opus*, you are not completely delighted, just return the book to me—enclosing the receipt for the exact amount you paid.

I promise to return your receipt within five days.

—LEO ROSTEN

—————————

SIGNET
Published by the Penguin Group
Penguin Books USA Inc., 375 Hudson Street,
New York, New York 10014, U.S.A.
Penguin Books Ltd, 27 Wrights Lane, London W8 5TZ, England
Penguin Books Australia Ltd, Ringwood, Victoria, Australia
Penguin Books Canada Ltd, 10 Alcorn Avenue,
Toronto, Ontario, Canada M4V 3B2
Penguin Books (N.Z.) Ltd, 182-190 Wairau Road,
Auckland 10, New Zealand

Penguin Books Ltd, Registered Offices:
Harmondsworth, Middlesex, England

Published by Signet, an imprint of New American Library,
a division of Penguin Books USA Inc. This is an authorized reprint
of a hardcover edition published by McGraw-Hill Publishing Company.
Also available in a Plume edition.

First Signet Printing, September, 1992
10 9 8 7 6 5 4 3 2 1

To
the memory,
evergreen,
of
my father, who enriched me
with the gift of laughter,
and
my mother, who fired me with
ambition and confidence and her
ferocious sense of honor:

Aleyhem ha-sholem

"fer klempt A
hearts"

= It tugs at my
heart, I'm so upset!!

Contents

Acknowledgments

I want to acknowledge the invaluable assistance (and instruction) of the experts, living and dead, who so generously helped me during the writing of *The Joys of Yiddish*, *Hooray for Yiddish*, and the present volume:

Maurice Samuel
Dr. Shlomo Noble
Rabbi Seymour Siegel
Prof. Nathan Susskind
Rabbi Solomon D. Goldfarb
Dr. Felix Kaufmann
Dr. Gershon Winer
Rabbi Bernard Mandelbaum
Prof. Joshua Fishman
Prof. Joseph Landis

None of the above should in any way be held responsible for whatever errors may be found in my text. The mistakes are mine—all mine: I refuse to share credit for them with anyone.

My greatest debt, as always, is to my wife, Zimi, whose spirit, wit, patience and amused understanding of a writer's *mishegoss* sustained me in the writing of this long book—as they have of everything I have published in the past thirty years.

—*L.R.*

To My Reader

This is an entirely new book. It is freshly conceived and freshly written, from this page to the last. It is built upon the foundation of *The Joys of Yiddish*, which was published in 1968, and *Hooray for Yiddish*, which appeared in 1982.

The speed with which Yiddish words, phrases and phrasings have become a part of demotic English, and the speed with which distinctly Jewish styles of humor and wit, irony and paradox, sarcasm, derision and mockery have infiltrated every level of English, is little short of astonishing.

I once remarked that no one can spend twenty-four hours in any major city in America or Great Britain without encountering a surprising number of words and phrases and inflectional stresses that have been plucked directly from the language called Yiddish—if not in the English spoken, then surely in the newspapers and magazines the residents read, the radio programs they listen to, the movies they see and adore, or the television fare to which they are addicted. I cite but a handful of headlines from England's most illustrious papers and magazines:

> A BOBS-WORTH OF NOSH
> MISH-MASH IN DOWNING STREET
> HOME LOAN HOO-HA
> ENOUGH IS ENOUGH ALREADY
> SOME CALL IT CHUTZPA
> SHOULD-SCHMOUD, SHOULDN'T-SCHMOUDN'T

Television has, of course, become the most powerful lever of language and the most prolific disseminator of neologisms the world has ever seen. Let a sitcom or a talk show use some new, colorful word or phrase that is totally alien to English (*cockamamy*, *megilla*, *maven*, *shlep*, *shtick*, *shlemiel*) and it is only a matter of hours before that locution is being bandied about with delight.

At least three to four hundred individual words from Yiddish are now part of colloquial English. (What do I mean by "Yiddish," and how does it differ from "Jewish"? See the entry YIDDISH in the lexicon that follows.) As for Yiddish idioms and syntax: before I started writing this tome I kept a casual record of translated Yiddish I read or heard in English. And before three weeks had passed, my notes bulged with linguistic gems such as these:

That no-goodnik!
Don't be a *yenta*.
On her, it looks great.
That's not chopped liver . . .
Get lost.
Big deal!
Go fight City Hall.
She's a *maven* on Picasso.
How come you went?
Al*right* already!
What's the bottom line?
Again with the temper?
Could be.
It's okay by me, bubbee.
Wall Street is taking a bath!
His acting needs more heart and less *shmaltz*.
Don't *shlep* that heavy case!
Calm down, boychik!
So have a *nosh*.
Say, listen: a dummy, he's not!
I should have such *mazel*.
Fat-shmat, she'll be married before you!
Who *needs* it?
You want an example? I'll give you an example.
Go do her something.
It's a *nothing* of a skirt.
Go know she was a cop!

Eat your heart out.
Say, that's some fancy-shmancy outfit.
Excuse the expression.
Aggravation? I could bust.
Don't ask!
The whole *shmeer* wasn't kosher.
Look who's talking!
We had a nice, long *shmooze*.
Is he some kind of crazy?
So make with some laughs, *shtarker*.
Come on—*live* a little!
That was some boo-boo!
I need it like a hole in the head.
What a *klutz*!
That's like putting ham on a *bagel*.
Nu?

You will find each and all of these fourteen-karat Yinglish-isms in their alphabetical place in the pages that follow.

—————————

I should stress the fact that Yinglish, that bright, brash, colorful, utterly unique amalgam of English and Yiddish, was born (and growing prodigiously) long, long before there was a television set in America. In historical sequence, more or less, here are the channels through which Yiddish words—and, more important, Jewish modalities of laughter—infiltrated our noble tongue:

Comic Strips

Jewish cartoonists were among the most skillful practitioners of this new form, which became the most popular part of any metropolitan newspaper—even more popular than the sports pages. Nationwide syndication of comic strips made it possible for such talents as Harry Hirshfeld ("Abie the Agent"), Bud Fisher ("Mutt and Jeff"), Rube Goldberg, and Al Capp ("Li'l Abner") to corral fans from coast to coast. George Herriman's immortal "Krazy Kat," beloved by intellectuals, was lovingly described as "half Dickens, half Yiddish."

Vaudeville

What student of the popular arts would question the massive influence of vaudeville during the first half of the twentieth century? And which *maven* of "variety acts" would deny that the ranks of the most popular comedians contained an inordinately high number of Jews? One need only recite the names that still strike sparks of recognition: Potash and Perlmutter, Smith and Dale ("Dr. Kronkheit"), Jack Benny, Lou Holtz, Eddie Cantor, Willie and Eugene Howard, George Burns, the four Marx Brothers, Milton Berle, George Jessel, the Avon Comedy Four, the Ritz Brothers . . . Their comedy routines and risible one-liners were written by many gag writers—most of whom, by a huge margin, were Jews.

Tin Pan Alley

This prolific incubator of Yinglish spread romantic sentiment and unabashed *shmaltz* throughout the nation via the lyrics of popular songs and that wholly American invention: jazz. The song writers, whose names adorned millions of copies of sheet music, have become legends: Irving Berlin, Billy Rose, Dorothy Fields, Harry Ruby, Howard Dietz, Larry Hart, Ira Gershwin . . .

Broadway

The most popular vaudeville performers attained increased stardom in the comedies and musical comedies that sent road companies, as well as "the original Broadway cast," across the length and breadth of the land. And every hit play, whether drama or comedy, was rewarded with a prolonged national tour and sprayed forth the Jewish wit, humor and verbal pyrotechnics of playwrights such as George S. Kaufman, Morrie Ryskind, Ben Hecht, Oscar Hammerstein II, Moss Hart, Abe Burrows, Alan Jay Lerner, Neil Simon . . .

Movies

The overwhelming majority of pioneer movie producers were Jews: Lasky, Goldwyn, Zukor, Mayer, Fox, Laemmle, Warner. And the number of Jewish writers in Hollywood, especially after the advent of sound, is simply countless. A roll-call would include every writer so far listed, plus platoons who had never written for vaudeville, the Broadway theater, or radio.

Radio

When radio was born, guided by the remarkable talents of David Sarnoff and William Paley, both Jews, the medium swiftly enlisted the most popular performers of the stage, vaudeville and movies: Ed Wynn, Eddie Cantor, Jack Benny, Burns and Allen (Gracie was not Jewish). New stars were made or enhanced by radio shows that were networked across America. Soon, there was not a hamlet unfamiliar with the particular talents of, say, Milton Berle and Gertrude Berg ("Molly Goldberg"). The writers of radio comedy, forerunners of television's sitcoms (in which many played a significant part), include humorists such as Mel Brooks, Carl Reiner, Nat Perrin, Milt Josefsberg, Woody Allen . . .

Nationally Syndicated Columns in Newspapers

The immense popularity of "gossip columns," another invention of the twentieth century, created vast audiences for Jewish journalists: Walter Winchell (a gifted creator of new words and picturesque phrases), Leonard Lyons, Louis Sobol, Irving Hoffman, Sidney Skolsky (sometimes called "Hollywood's Samuel Pepys"). Famous non-Jewish columnists, such as Damon Runyon, O. O. McIntyre, Dorothy Kilgallen and Jimmy Cannon, lived and worked in New York, and their columns were heavily steeped in Jewish modes of banter and raillery.

Magazine Cartoons

Aside from the comic strips, which won such immense affection from American readers, remember the "single-frame," plotless cartoons, with or without captions or "balloons" that verbalize a character's thoughts. For decades, cartoons of this school have been featured in the *Saturday Evening Post*, *Collier's*, the *New Yorker*, *Esquire*, *Look*, *Liberty* and some women's magazines. The names of the leading cartoonists include Steinberg, Hirshfeld, Soglow, Steig, Hoff, plus dozens of other visual humorists who were and are Jewish.

Novels and Short Stories

Volumes can (and should) be written about the prominence of Jewish writers—essayists, short story writers, novelists, poets—in American literature ever since the turn of the century. Certain names leap to the fore: Edna Ferber, Fannie Hurst, Irwin Shaw, Norman Mailer, Herman Wouk, Philip Roth, Jerome Weidman, Saul Bellow, Joseph Heller, Bernard Malamud, Herbert Gold, Mark Harris, Isaac Bashevis Singer, Wallace Markfield . . . American humor was galvanized by the Jewish slant of writers for the *New Yorker*, such as S. J. Perelman, Arthur Kober, "Leonard Q. Ross," Samuel Hoffenstein, and Dorothy Parker.

Musical Comedies

A moment's reflection is enough to realize that in the dialogue and lyrics of Broadway's glittering musical plays, an irresistible stream of Yinglish poured into our vernacular—for any Broadway success soon came to national attention via radio, sheet music, movies and television. Consider the leading writers of the triumphs of the musical stage: Ira Gershwin, Oscar Hammerstein II, Larry Hart, "Yip" Harburg, Frank Loesser (*Guys and Dolls* is a glittering parade of Yinglish), Alan Jay Lerner, Jerry Bok, Sheldon Harnick, Joseph Stein, Stephen Sondheim . . .

Television

The most influential shapers of speech, in America or Britain, China or Turkey or Russia, are the writers for television. In the night-after-night impact of talk shows, and under the week-after-week percussion of situation comedies, English speech and slang and other vivacities of language are formed with a speed, and on a range, hitherto unknown in human history. When Johnny Carson quipped, about a guest's huge fee for a performance in Las Vegas,

"That's not chopped liver!"—that Yiddishism was heard at luncheon tables from Beverly Hills to Bombay in the weeks ahead.

The shows that *launched* television as a mass medium were mostly written by Jews: *The Milton Berle Show*, *The Jack Benny Show*, *Your Show of Shows* (with Sid Caesar and Imogene Coca), Burns and Allen, *The Texaco Hour*, *The Fred Allen Show*.

The earliest gems of television sitcoms were written by platoons of gag writers, dominantly Jewish: Phil Silvers' *Sergeant Bilko*, Jackie Gleason's *The Honeymooners*, Lucille Ball's *I Love Lucy*, *The Carol Burnett Show*. The most recent and most popular classics in this *genre*, *The Mary Tyler Moore Show*, *All in the Family*, *The Odd Couple*, *M*A*S*H*, and *Barney Miller*, feature Jewish names in the credits, designated as Story Consultant or flanked by "story by," "written by" or "story supervision." Such categories sweep in comedy wizards like Norman Lear or Larry Gelbart.

In all of the above, the comic ingredients and stratagems, the styles of irony and persiflage, the character-types (the *shlemiel*, the *klutz*, the *nebech*, the *shlimazel*, the *plosher* or *k'nocker* or *luftmensh*, the *yenta* or *kibitzer* or *narr*) bear the unmistakable scent and style of Jewish humor.

Yiddish is an exceptionally beguiling tongue. I have called it the Robin Hood of languages. It developed a phenomenal variety of comic uses, an extraordinary range of observational nuances, a striking skill in delineating psychological insights, and remarkable modalities of sarcasm, irony, paradox and mockery.

Since the culture of the Jews exalts reasoning, no less than faith, it is not surprising that so much Jewish wit hinges on logic to celebrate illogic. I have always thought that a liberating kind of lunacy dances through Jewish jokes. A mind-boggling example of this is found in a letter Groucho Marx once sent me:

Dear Junior:
Excuse me for not answering you sooner. But I have been so busy not answering letters lately that I have not been able to get around to not answering yours in time.

I have never been able to improve upon my description of the special characteristics of Yiddish in the introduction to *The Joys of Yiddish*. Permit me the luxury of quoting myself:

> Steeped in sentiment, Yiddish is sluiced with sarcasm. It loves the ruminative, because it rests on a rueful past; it favors paradox, because it knows that only paradox can do justice to the injustices of life; it adores irony, because the only way the Jews could retain their sanity was to view a dreadful world with sardonic and astringent eyes. In its innermost heart, Yiddish swings between *shmaltz* and derision.

I do not mean to suggest that Jewry—in Germany, England, France, the Middle East, America—found Yiddish as admirable as I do. On the contrary: from the beginning, worldly, Sephardic and assimilated Jews (in England, Germany, France, the Americas) *despised* Yiddish. They sneered at its "bastard origins," its "vulgarity," its "hybrid" vocabulary. Hebraicists dismissed it as "uncivilized cant." German Jews branded it a "barbarous argot" or, more vehemently, a "piggish jargon."

Each of these haughty and condescending enclaves seemed to forget that English, French, German, Italian, Russian, Polish, Romanian (etcetera) *all* began as "vulgar" tongues—that is, as the vernacular of the uneducated masses. The nobility and the priests used Latin and Greek. Not too long ago aristocrats all over Europe spoke French, the refined, proper language, the verbal currency of decorum and taste and elitist elegance. The *national* language was spoken by serfs and servants, peddlers and thieves.

One thing is certain: it was with Yiddish that the Ashkenazim, the Jews of central and eastern Europe, created the unique and radiant culture, a triumph over excruciating adversities, of the now-vanished *shtetl*. And it is in Yiddish that that civilization—so poor, so fearful, so savaged, so brave, so raucous, so gallant, so pathetic, so pious, so sardonic, so sentimental, so resigned and embittered and impassioned and admirable—has been preserved.

It is nothing short of astonishing, even miraculous, to me that so small a population as the Ashkenazim, mired in such poverty, tormented by such persecutions, shut out of so many professions, decimated by so many pogroms, subjected to so many enslavements (up to twenty-five years of Czarist military service, in the most abhorrent and humiliating tasks), nevertheless, and within a short period of history, produced such a galaxy of writers, playwrights, poets, novelists, journalists, literary critics, historians, translators, scholars, philologists, philosophers and thinkers.*

In this volume I have dropped many entries that will be found in *The Joys of Yiddish* and *Hooray for Yiddish*. Why? For the simple, undeniable reason that they have failed to establish a firm, lasting foothold, or wide circulation, in English. Examples include *geshmat, chaussen, lump, yekl, letz, kapore, fress, frosk, edel, tzitzit, yachne, gilgul, tachlis, gridzheh* . . .

This pruning is not without rewards: in place of the dropouts, I offer you a cornucopia of entirely fresh or brightly renewed Yinglish words, phrases, phrasings, idioms and acrobatic syntax—each of which *has* won a secure place, and ever-widening deployment, in contemporary (especially colloquial) English.

Jewish folk sayings, with which I fell in love when I was a child, are no less distinctive, insightful, and memorable than Jewish jokes. I published a large volume, my *Treasury of Jewish Quotations* (1972), from which I offer you the most scintillating of samples: I know of no epigrams that surpass them:

> When a young man marries, he divorces his mother.
> Out of snow, you can't make cheesecake.

*The briefest catalogue would include I. L. Peretz, Sholem Aleichem, Mendele Moiche Seforim, Sholem Asch, I. J. Singer (older brother of Isaac Bashevis Singer); playwrights Shlomo Anski, Peretz Hirshbein, Abraham Goldfaden, H. Leivick; poets Sholem Abramovich, Morris Rosenfeld, H. N. Bialik, Abraham Reisen, Moishe Halperin, Jacob Glatstein. No English journalist surpassed Abe Cahan, the genius of the Jewish *Daily Forward*, for analytic acuity and polemical power.

The man who marries for money will earn it.

A rabbi whose congregation doesn't want to run him out of town isn't a rabbi; and a rabbi whose congregation does run him out of town isn't a man.

When you go to a restaurant, choose a table near a waiter.

The folk sayings were not only sardonic; some stop the heart:

I felt sorry for myself because I had no shoes—until I met a man who had no feet.

The rich have heirs, not children.

Pity was invented by the weak.

When you add to the truth, you subtract from it.

No one is as deaf as the man who will not listen.

Dear God: if You forgive us, we will forgive You.

It occurred to me that witticisms achieve the greatest longevity of any writer's output. How few of us have read a page by the authors of lines we remember with that special gratitude we accord the wickedly apposite:

If triangles had a God, He would have three sides.

The doctor who treats himself has a fool for a doctor— and a fool for a patient.

No one forgets where he buried the hatchet.

Conscience is the inner voice that tells us that someone is watching.

An idealist is one who, upon observing that a rose smells better than a cabbage, concludes that it will also make better soup.*

———

Whatever their experience or ethos or faith, people ultimately voice the bitter conclusion that life is unjust, fate blind, fortune heartless. And I began to understand that all mortal beings, whether Zulu or Christian or Jew, desperately try, through the reiterated sorcery of words, to fortify their faith in a passionate necessity to believe that virtue *will* be rewarded, that evil *will* be punished, that truth *will* somehow triumph in the end.

—LEO ROSTEN

*The authors, successively, are Voltaire, Hieronymous Anonymous, "Kin" Hubbard, H. L. Mencken, and again Mencken.

The Jew has made a marvelous fight in this world, in all the ages; and has done it with his hands tied behind him. The Egyptian, the Babylonian, and the Persian rose, filled the planet with sound and splendor, then faded to dream stuff and passed away. The Greek and the Roman followed, and made a vast noise, and they are gone.

Other peoples have sprung up and held their torch high for a time, but it burned out, and they sit in twilight now, or have vanished. The Jew . . . is now what he always was—exhibiting no decadence, no infirmities of age . . . no slowing of his energies, no dulling of his alert and aggressive mind.

—MARK TWAIN, *Harper's Monthly*,
September 1899

Life is a dream for the wise, a game for the fool, a comedy for the rich, a tragedy for the poor.
—SHOLEM ALEICHEM

The Jews are just like everyone else—only more so.
—ANON.

If God lived on earth, people would knock out all his windows.
—FOLK SAYING

The pursuit of knowledge for its own sake, an almost fanatical love of justice, and the desire for personal independence—these are the features of Jewish tradition which made me thank my stars that I belong to it.
—ALBERT EINSTEIN

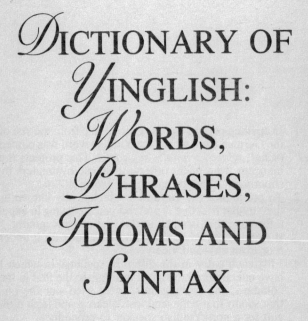

DICTIONARY OF YINGLISH: WORDS, PHRASES, IDIOMS AND SYNTAX

Helpful Hints

1. In spelling certain words, I drop the *c* from the *sch* of the German from which the Yiddish word was cloned (*schul*, *schlep*, *schmalz*, *schwartz*). This protects the innocent, who might otherwise startle bystanders by shouting, "Look at that stupid *sklemiel!*"
2. To pronounce the guttural *kh* (technically known as the "uvular fricative") pretend you are trying to expel a fishbone that is stuck in the roof of your mouth.
3. If you do not find an entry under *ch*, look for it under *h* or even *kh*—and vice versa.
4. I list each entry in the different spellings in which I have encountered the word in English: the first in the column is the spelling most often used—or the one that seems to me the simplest, clearest and least difficult for a non–Yiddish speaker to pronounce.
5. If you question my English transliteration of certain Yiddish or Hebrew words, please consult the brief, emphatic mazes in the Appendix.

—L.R.

A

abracadabra

The Aramaic name for the devil. Used by Hebrew cabalists.

1. Hocus-pocus.
2. Meaningless, mystical mumbo-jumbo.
3. Gibberish.

Abracadabra comes from ancient cuneiform and obsolete Hebrew scripts.

The rich, exotic cabalistic literature, and the lush writings of "Ari" (Isaac Luria: 1534–1572) and his cult, burst with dire proscriptions regarding a horde of evil spirits: Mevet, Lilith, Belial, Azazel, and—of course—Satan, the Evil One.

To fight the omnipresent *dybbuks* and devils, mystics conjured up a battalion of heroic angels (Gabriel, Michael, Raphael, *et al.*), each of whom had his own esoteric alphabet, studded with "sacred" signs and secret names for God, recited as charms against diseases, as magical incantations, and in special combinations designed to drive off the demons of darkness . . . One of these devils was named (in Aramaic) Abracadabra.

The great *Oxford Dictionary of the English Language* states that the origin of *abracadabra* is unknown—although not to my mavens (see above). The word first appeared in

English 'way back in 1696: how, then, can I claim it to be Yinglish, which did not even begin to scratch a foothold in English soil until two hundred years after 1696?

Well, I do not claim *abracadabra* to be Yinglish, but descended to us through Hebrew. The true point, I confess, is that I find *abracadabra* too alluring a word to banish from my banquet. Besides, it is the perfect lead into one of my favorite stories, and illustrates that special mode of deflating scorn that distinguishes Jewish/Yiddish responses to the pretentious or the phony.

Groucho Marx's friends, praising a local psychic's powers of divination, begged Groucho to attend a séance. Groucho sat quiet and cynical as the swami stared into a crystal ball, intoned, "Abracadabra," called up departed souls from the Beyond, and answered questions from his paying guests—question after question—in an eerie monotone.

After a prolonged spell of omniscience, the sorcerer intoned, "My medium . . . is growing tired . . . There is time for . . . one more question."

Groucho asked it. "What's the capital of South Dakota?"

accentuating disagreement, or forcefully dismissing an assertion, by tacking sh- or shm- onto a crucial word, then repeating the sardonic compound

Yinglish at its most mordant and its most effective: A priceless ploy to convey mockery, scorn, corrosive contempt.

"Art–shmart, I call it garbage!"
"Fat–shmat, he is having the time of his life."
"Teacher–shmeacher, she has the manners of a mule!"
"Lady–shmady, she acts like a *yenta*!"
"Locked–shmocked, that door never *did* stay closed."

The most familiar (and ludicrous) form of this airy congé is, of course, the black-humor joke:

"Mrs. Notkin, did you hear the terrible news about Mr. Glassman?"
"No! What happened?"

"He has cancer!"

"Heh," shrugged Mrs. Notkin. "Cancer-shmanzer, as long as he's healthy!"

SCENE: **A Hotel in Tel Aviv**

MR. STOLZ (picks up phone): Hello. Operator? . . . Give me, please, the manager of your Room Service. (waits)

MANAGER: Room service.

MR. STOLZ: This is room four-oh-eight, Mister Room Service. I want to order mine breakfast.

MANAGER: Certainly, sir. What would you like?

MR. STOLZ: I would li-ike a glass orange juice—but it should be stale and taste bitter . . . Then toast, it should be burned 'til it's practically black! . . . And coffee, but make it cold and sour—

MANAGER: One *mo*-ment, sir! We can't fill an order like that!

MR. STOLZ (pityingly): Can't–shman't: You did *yes*terday!

See also CONTEMPT VIA CONFIRMATION . . . , CRITICIZING A PERSON . . . , SH-.

accentuating scorn or disdain by moving an adjective to the front of a sentence

"Fronting" adjectives, which professional linguists call "topicalization," is a prime example of the irony so easily achieved in Yinglish. (The device is also found in the colloquial dialogue written by English authors with sensitive antennae, *viz.* Dickens.) Consider these exquisite examples:

"What," asked Rappaport, "do you think of his wife?"
"Interesting, she's not."

OR

"Beautiful, she isn't."

OR

"Lucky, you can't call her."

The bold transposition of predicate adjectives (or nouns, as in "A dummy, he's not") is particularly loved by speakers of Yinglish. "Bert isn't a hero" is a juiceless character-ization—compared with "A *hero*, Bert isn't," which suggests that although Bert may be kind, good-looking, even honest, of one thing you can be sure: Bert is no *shtarker* (*q.v.*).

A pioneer linguist has published a study of one hundred college students to demonstrate that Jews are much more likely than non-Jews to accept the fronting of certain "indefinites." (See Mark Feinstein's "Ethnicity and Topicalization in New York City English," *International Journal of the Sociology of Language*, 26).

A.C.E.

Initials for "After the Common Era," used instead of A.D., for "*Anno Domini*" (Year of our Lord").

In many Jewish encyclopedias, histories, scholarly jour-nals and magazines, "B.C." is given as B.C.E. ("before the Christian era began"), and A.D. is rendered as A.C.E. ("after the beginning of the Christian era.")

Jewish scholars and historians, writing for technical jour-nals or historical compilations, faced an uncomfortable problem *vis-à-vis* "B.C." and "A.D." Given their convic-tions about the Messiah of the Jews, they could hardly accept Jesus as "our" Lord.

The reason for this was best explained by the great Mai-monides: the Messiah will come down to earth in order to restore the State of Israel, gather in all the Exiles, rebuild the Temple; after *that* will come the Resurrection, then the Day of Judgment. Now, since the Nazarene did not restore the State of Israel nor gather in the Exiles nor rebuild the Temple, the contemporary rabbis of Palestine could not think him their Messiah.

Ever since those days, Jewish historians have not been at ease with "B.C." and "A.D." Fortunately, *common* begins with the same initial as *Christian*—hence: "Before the Common Era," and "After the Common Era."

See also B.C.E., C.E.

Accusing someone of idiocy by denying the obvious

This deadpan ploy, typical of Jewish sarcasm, is making headway in Yinglish.

Q: How would you like an all-expenses-paid trip to
   Hawaii?
A: I prefer to spend the winter in a foxhole in the Bronx.
   (Meaning: "How can you even *ask* such a stupid ques-
   tion?")

Q: Listen, how would you like to win the ten-million-dollar
   lottery?
A: I would *hate* it. Think of the *taxes*!

Q: How would you like to get out of this cold weather for
   a month free—all expenses paid—in a fine hotel in Santa
   Monica?
A: On the ocean? I'd rather spend the winter in a boxcar
   in Alaska.

Adam

Hebrew: *adam*: "man."
The first man, created by God from the dust of the
earth (*adamah*), progenitor of the entire human race.

Have you ever wondered why the Lord made only *one*
man? I mean, why did He not create ten, a thousand, a
million? The answers are profound—and fascinating:

Why did God create only one man? So that no one
could say that virtue and vice are hereditary.
—TALMUD: *Sanhedrin*, 4a

Why did God create but one man? So that no one
should be able to say, "My father is better than your
father." (Or "My race is superior to yours.")
—adapted from *Sanhedrin*, 37a

Why did God create Adam alone? In order to teach us
that whoever destroys a single life is as guilty as
though he had destroyed the entire world. . . .
—TALMUD: *Sanhedrin*, 4:5

Further: have you ever wondered why the Lord waited
until the last day of His initial labors before creating our
common forebear? If so (and even if not so), the reason
strikes me as staggering:

Why was man created on the last day? So that he can
be told, whenever pride takes hold of him: Do not
forget that God created the gnat before thee.
—adapted from TALMUD: *Sanhedrin*, 37a

Konrad Lorenz, that admirable ethologist, may have had Adam in mind when he called man "the missing link between apes and human beings."

Mark Twain decided that Adam was created at the end of the week—when God was tired. (And because He was disappointed in the monkey.)

ADAM (to Eve; flabbergasted): "What do you *mean* the boys don't look like me?!"   —Red Buttons

See also EVE.

Adjectives converted into nouns for purposes of emphasis or ridicule

Yinglish to the core.
"She's a crazy."
"Have you heard any new funnies?"
"Their kid is some ugly!"

Using an adjective as a noun demonstrates the delightful inventiveness of Yinglish: "a mental," "a cheap."

Please note: I am *not* talking about nouns like *smarty, toughie, softy, sharpy*, which are simply adjectives made into nouns by adding *-y* or *-ie*. I am discussing adjectives which, *entirely unchanged*, are colloquially used as nouns.

In the *Oxford Dictionary of the English Language*, for instance, *skinny* is described only as an adjective, never as a noun. And authorities such as William and Mary Morris (*Dictionary of Contemporary Usage*) and Harold Wentworth and Stuart Berg Flexner (*Dictionary of American Slang*) cite no usage that would contradict my claims.

Long, long before the turbulent sixties, when youthful rebels latched onto "the crazies" as a proud characterization of themselves—or of the more extreme advocates of their movement—American Jews were converting adjectives to nouns with complete equanimity. Early in this century, on the Lower East Side, in Brooklyn, in the Bronx, in the Jewish enclaves of Chicago, Detroit, Los Angeles, our grandparents were coining nouns such as "a fat" . . . "an ugly" . . . "a crazy."

Jewish comedians were particularly fond of such transmutations: "He certainly knows how to deliver a funny!" or "She is some piece of dull!"

Jewish children seemed drawn to such linguistic jewels as "My father is no cheap," or "Watch out for him; he's a real tricky."

I think the direct conversion of adjectives into nouns appealed to those who enjoy the mischief of colloquial English, the humor of unorthodox syntax, or the sheer surprise of novel usage.

Julius Baylis had moved from Brooklyn to New Jersey. One day, on the commuter train, Baylis ran into Simon Laskin, a distant cousin.

"Say, look, Shimmel!" Mr. Baylis sang out.

"Well, well, some surprise," smiled Mr. Laskin. "Listen, I just heard you moved way out in the suburbs."

"Absolutely."

"Tell me, Julius, wasn't the change pretty tough for you and Millie?"

"At foist, it was moider!" said Mr. Baylis. "You know, a big house, a lot of grass, no place to go at night, not even a corner newsstand . . ."

"I can imagine!"

"I don't mind telling you, Shimmel, that I was practically ready to move back to Brooklyn. Then I got myself a par-amour—" he beamed. "What a difference that made!"

"A—*paramour*?" gulped Laskin.

"That's right."

"Does—Millie know?"

"Sure she knows," said Baylis.

Laskin blinked. "And she doesn't raise hell, Julie? What is she, some kind of *dumb*? Doesn't she even *mind*?"

"Why should she mind?" echoed Mr. Baylis. "Why should she care *how* I cut the grass?"

Dr. Jason Feldsher, the well-known psychiatrist, shook the new patient's hand. "Sit down, Mr. Konig, sit down. Now, what is your problem?"

"My problem," sputtered Mr. Konig, "is *people*. No matter what I say or do, they—" his voice rose in agitation, "they call me a loony! A kooky! A crazy! A—"

"Mr. Konig," said Dr. Feldsher gently, "why not slow down? Relax . . . Perhaps you ought to start at the beginning . . ."

"Okay," sighed Mr. Konig. "In the beginning, I created the heavens and the earth. And the earth was without form . . ."

adjectives fronted, for purposes of emphasis or impact

This enchanting Yinglish ploy has added matchless nuances of forcefulness, irony and intensity to our tongue:

Beautiful, she isn't.
Smart, he is.
Lucky, they never were.
Happy, I am.

I do not think anyone can deny that this metathesis (as professional linguists would characterize the rearrangement of words) focuses attention, distributes emphasis and emanates humor in a way that is far beyond the expressive range of conventional sequences:

She isn't beautiful.
He is not smart.
They never were lucky.
I am happy.

Mrs. Feinstock hurried to the door of her son's room. "Bernie! It's late. Get up!"

Her son grumbled, "I don' wanna get up."

Mrs. Feinstock flung the door open. "Bernie! You have to wash, dress, eat, go to school!"

"I don' wanna go to school," her son mumbled.

His mother recoiled in horror. "What's gotten into you, Bernie! *Crazy*, you are?"

"I *hate* school!" cried Bernie. "The teachers don't like me. Four-eyes, the kids call me. They throw spitballs at me! They—"

"Bernie Feinstock, stop that at once! *You—must—go—to—school!*"

"Why?"

"For two reasons: First, you're forty-six years old—"

"Ma . . ."

"—and second, you're—the—principal!"

Adonai

Adoni (singular)
Adonim (plural)

Pronounced *ah-doe*-NOY. Hebrew: "My Lords." (Note the plural.)

The name of God. It is usually rendered in English as "Lord."

The singular form of *Adonai* is *Adoni*; the plural of *Adoni* is *Adonim*; and *Adonai* is the plural plus the possessive *i*—thus, "My Lords" or "My Masters."

You will (or should) ask at once: "Why is the Hebrew word for God a *plural*?" Bear with me—and the conjecture of experts. The very ancient Hebrews (*i.e.*, those who lived prior to the second millennium B.C.) were polytheists. They sacrificed animals. They spoke of the "gods," not of God. And after the world-shaking events on Mount Sinai, Hebrews simply did not change their nomenclature. (If this explanation does not satisfy you, don't blame me: I merely record the consensus of the best-informed philologists and historians.)

Adonai may be called the holy name of God, as contrasted with *Adoshem* (*q.v.*), which is used in informal, everyday discourse.

A pious Jew will never utter the sacred *Adonai* except during prayers—with his head covered and after washing his hands.

It is worth noting that "Jehovah" or "Jahevah," which are the English renderings of the four sacred Hebrew letters denoting the Almighty (*Y H V H*), are entirely incorrect! *Yahvah* or *Jehovah* are *not* God's name; and they never were. (See JEHOVAH.)

Very pious Jews never write or type the word "God" in full: instead they write or type "G–d."

Please remember that *Adonai* is only one of the Hebrew names used to indicate the Lord's divine attributes. The great Maimonides listed seven of these: namely, Y H V H, El, Eloha, Elohim, Elohai, Shaddai, Y H V H Tsevaot.

Furthermore, *Shaddai* indicates God's contentment with the world after He had created it. The Lord said *"Dai!"* (the Hebrew word for "Enough!")—and at once the entire universe stopped growing as it had been doing from the moment *Adonai* had created it.

Shaddai, accordingly, represents one of the divine attributes, namely: Plenty.

It intrigues me to think that contemporary cosmologists, debating the "Big Bang" versus the "Steady Growth" hypotheses, might find that regal and conclusive *"Dai!"* a delightful bit of evidence supporting the Steady Growth (and not the Big Bang) explanation of the early days of the Cosmos.

Clever readers will of course pounce upon the possible connection between *Adonai* and *Adonis*. Their pounce is not foolish: Adonis happens to be the Greek form of the Semitic *adon*. Adonis was the Syrian god of agriculture. And in ancient Greece, a magic-ridden cult worshiped Adonis.

No area of faith, and no aspect of divinity itself, is spared cynical deflation in the humor that Jews bring to bear upon even holiest matters. Jewish jokes have always proceeded on the assumption the Lord does not mind being the subject of amusement . . .

"Of *course* God has a sense of humor: after all, He created the human race." I felt no fear of the wrath of the Almighty when I said that, or later remarked: "Don't blame God: He's only human."

Jewish folk sayings about God may be distinctive, among the religions of our world, for their irony, their irreverence, and their bitterness. Here are a few:

If God lived on earth, men would knock out all His windows.

Dear God, I know you will help Your people; but why don't You help us *until* you help us?

What the Lord does is certainly best—probably.

God may love the poor, but He helps the rich.

Oh, Lord: help me. If You don't, I'll ask my uncle in New York.

God is closest to those whose hearts are broken.

Dear God: You help total *strangers*—so why not me?

Dear God: Please help me get up; I can fall down by myself.

———

The saying I find most haunting—indeed most tragic—since the Holocaust, is this one: "Oh, Lord; please do not inflict upon us all that You know we can endure."

———

"But how can you be so *positive* that God does not exist?" asked the rabbi.

The atheist huffed: "A man has to believe in *some*thing!"

———

Stephen Kugelman, the new young rabbi in Hillsdale, was a golfaholic. One Saturday morning, after prayers, the rabbi was so possessed of the desire to play golf that he donned huge sunglasses, stole into his car, and drove miles and miles from his synagogue to an obscure golf course in a faraway town. Before he teed off, he briefly prayed to the Lord to forgive him for breaking the holy Sabbath.

Up in heaven, to the right of God's golden throne, sat Father Abraham. Suddenly Abraham exclaimed, "No, *no!* I cannot believe my eyes!"

The Lord looked at Abraham. "What excites such wrath in you, my son?"

"On Your holy Sabbath," moaned Abraham. "That new rabbi in Hillsdale . . . Not praying, not studying Your Holy Torah—but playing *golf!*"

The Lord looked down upon the earth and what He beheld brought a frown to those divine features. "Dear Me," He sighed. "Yes, you are right . . . A desecration of My Holy Day . . . scandalous . . ."

"Lord, You must punish him!" said Father Abraham.

Solemnly, the Almighty nodded. Then He cupped His hands, and just as Rabbi Kugelman hit the ball off the second tee, the Lord let out a long, cosmic "*whoosh*" . . . The divine wind caught the rabbi's ball, lifted it two hundred yards, swerved it between two trees, where it struck a big rock, bounced and—*mirabile dictu*—dropped into the cup!

"A hole in *one*?" gasped Father Abraham. "*That* you call a punishment?"

The Lord winked, "So tell me: whom can he *tell?!*"

See also JEHOVAH, YAHVEH, Y H V H.

Adoshem

From Hebrew: formed from the first syllable of *Adonai* and the last syllable of *Ha-Shem:* "the Name." Pronounced *ah-doe*-SHEM. Rhymes with "follow them."

The spoken name, used by pious Jews, for God, instead of the sacred *Adonai.* Orthodox Jews never utter the name Adonai, except during prayer in a synagogue.

Different names are used by pious Jews when discussing the Lord, depending upon which aspect of Him is intended. When God's justice is involved, the Lord is *Elohim;* the Creator of the World is *Bore Olam;* when God's mercy is involved, the Lord is called *Ha-Shem;* when the Ruler of the World needs a designation, it is *Ribon*—more commonly, *Ribono shel Olam* (in Yiddish: *Riboyne shel oylem*). And *yah,* which may be written but is never pronounced, is formed from two Hebrew letters, *yud* and *hei.*

These happen to be the first and last letters of the holy tetragrammaton (from the Greek "four-letter word"), Y H V H or J H V H, which is vocally rendered as either "Yahweh" or "Jehovah." The tetragrammaton is the symbol and the secular synonym for the holy and ineffable Name. (See Y H V H.)

———————

Solly Fishbein went off alone one day to scale the sheerest face of Mount Carmel. Up and up he moved, until he dug his boot onto a ledge that gave way! Solly fell 150 feet—managing, by a miracle, to grab hold of a branch on a gnarled bush.

"Help! Help!" yelled Solly. "Oh, God, help—*save me!*"

A great voice far, far above intoned: "My son, do you have full faith in Me, your Lord and Master?"

Solly almost turned to stone as he heard the voice of God Himself. "Oh, Lord, yes! *Yes!* With all my heart and soul do I believe in You!"

"Do you trust Me without reservation?"

"Oh, yes, Lord!" cried Solly.

"Then—let go of that branch!" came the Voice of the Lord.

"*What*?!" gulped Solly.

"I said—let go of that branch!"

A long pause; then Solly quaked: "Excuse me, Sir; but—is there anyone else up there?"

Rabbi Norkin asked, "Now, children, who can tell me why there is only one God?"

Little Susan waved her hand energetically.

"Yes, Susan?"

"There is only one God because He is *everywhere*, so there's no room for anyone else."

The great throng of Hebrews patiently waited at the foot of the mountain for hours and hours now. Only the night before, Jahweh had appeared in a cloud before Moses, who had come down from the mountain with the sacred tablets on which were inscribed the commandments . . . And Moses had gone back . . .

Suddenly the tip of a white staff was seen moving down the mountain—and the fluttering of a white robe . . . A great murmuring possessed the throng. At last they beheld—Moses.

A cheer rang out. And Moses stood before the assemblage and in a commanding voice said: "Children of Israel, I bring you tidings from our God. For six hours I have been with Him, recounting the petition you assigned me to convey to Him. And I can now give you His answer!"

A weighty silence fell upon the Hebrews.

"The answer of our Lord God, King of the Universe, to your petition about the Commandments contains—good news, and bad news." Moses spread his arms to still the throng. "The good news is that I managed to persuade the Lord to cut the list from fourteen to ten!"

Cheer after cheer rose from the congregation.

"What is the bad news?" someone cried.

Moses stared at the throng. "The bad news . . . He would not budge. Adultery is still in."

See also HA-SHEM.

advertising one's forebearance by repeating a question without any comment whatsoever

A most subtle Yinglish ploy.

Q: "Did you know she was going to ask you to let her use your house in the country for a yard sale?"
A: "Did *I* know she was going to ask me to let her use my house in the country for a yard sale?"

The crosstown bus was jam-packed at rush hour. A very large, very fat woman got in and, as the bus started up, gazed about angrily.

Yissel Nossbeim, hiding behind his newspaper, slunk lower in his place.

In a loud, grating voice the fat woman declared, "Isn't there *one* polite man here who will offer me his place?!"

Yissel sighed, lowered his paper, and rose. "Is there one polite man? Yes, lady, I'll make a small contribution . . ."

Agadah

Pronounced *ah*-GOD-*a*.

That part of the Oral Law that is distinguished from Halakha (*q.v.*)—and therefore does not deal with the laws that govern the daily activities of observing Jews.

But the Agadah complements the Halakha—explaining laws through parables, songs, satire, informal sayings, moralisms, stories, quotations from the prophets, words of consolation and comfort, etc.

Louis Ginzberg's classic *Legends of the Jews* arranges this vast kaleidoscopic body of Agadic material according to the events and persons in Scripture.

See also HAGGADA, HALAKHA.

again . . . ?

Choice Yinglish. The common English adverb transformed into an accusatory, sarcastic challenge.

Directly translated from the Yiddish *vider* ("again"), or *shoyn vider?* ("again already?").

Spoken Yiddish is particularly rich in expletives added to sentences, or particles tacked onto words, to infuse them with color and force. *Again* may be used in many contexts:

1. I don't believe it! ("You mean to say that *again* you want to eat out?")
2. Can you beat that? ("*Again* she had caviar for breakfast?!")
3. You must be crazy! ("You want me to apologize *again*?")
4. *What?!* ("*Again* she hung up on me!")
5. So soon? ("*Again* he wants a loan?")
6. Don't *tell* me! ("*Again* he can't pay the bill?!")
7. Do you mean to say . . . ("*Again* he married a woman twelve years older?!")
8. For God's sake! ("*Again* you ran into a parked car?!")
9. Once more. ("*Again* I'll have to explain the rules to her.")
10. Over and over. ("I suppose that as usual he'll be late *again* . . .")

A prize example of the power of *again* is this story:

Barney Minsky, a timid man, stood before the desk of his boss, Mr. Askerman, and stammered: "Mr. Askerman, I j-just have to ask you for a raise! My wife says we can't *live* on my salary . . ."

"How much of a raise were you thinking of?"

"Uh—my w-wife says twenty dollars—"

"Certainly!" Mr. Askerman stood up. "I think twenty dollars is absolutely fair."

An overjoyed Minsky hurried home.

His paycheck that Saturday contained the twenty-dollar raise. But when Minsky opened his pay envelope the week after that he could not believe his eyes. He rushed to Mr. Askerman's office. "Mr. Askerman, Mr. Askerman!"

"Calm *down*, Minsky! What's the matter?"

"My r-raise," sputtered Barney Minsky. "What ha-happened to my *raise*?!"

Mr. Askerman's jaw dropped. "Your *raise*? Are you crazy? *Again* you want twenty dollars a week more?!"

See also AGAIN WITH . . . ?

again with . . . ?

From Yiddish: *shoyn vider mit?*: "already with . . . ?" This interrogatory phrase adds the preposition *with* to the already complaint-drenched *again?*

"Lou, you're my oldest friend," said Sol Jablon, "so I want to tell you something very personal."

"Certainly, Max."

"Well, in April my wife asked me to increase the household money I give her by—ninety dollars a month!"

"*Ninety dollars*?" gasped Lou Weiss.

"And that's not all! In July, she asked me for ninety dollars a month more!"

"Migod, Max!"

"And last week, it was *again* with the ninety dollars . . ."

"Max, *Max*. I don't understand it! What does she *do* with all that money?"

"Who knows?" sighed Jablon. "I never give her a penny."

agreement deployed to maximize contempt

Expert embroiderers of the nuances available in Yinglish especially enjoy using nominal, placid agreement with a foolish question to convey a blistering contempt for the questioner.

Q: But won't you feel terrible if the doctors tell you you have to have surgery to remove that little tumor from your brain?

A: Oh, *yes*. As you so shrewdly foresee, I'll feel quite unhappy if the doctors tell me I have to have surgery to remove a tumor from my brain.

A variation of this icy stratagem lies in altering the adjectives, as above, or the nouns, as below:

Q: I'll bet you feel nervous about having to have your leg cut off at the knee.

A: Oh, yes—I would probably feel a bit uneasy if I only had to have my arm cut off at the wrist.

I now give you the briefest of jokes, with an opening and banal dialogue that has been bandied about for thousands of years—but a punchline that has, to my astonishment, never been so much as murmured in all those centuries:

MRS. ELKIN: I see you're pregnant, Mrs. Toplowitz!
MRS. TOPLOWITZ: It's true. It's true.
MRS. ELKIN: So *mazel tov*!
MRS. TOPLOWITZ: Thank you.
MRS. ELKIN: Are you hoping for a boy or a girl?
MRS. TOPLOWITZ: Certainly.

———

Lev Bryshkov stood before the three judges in Uzbek.
"—And your punishment is ten years of hard labor in Siberia! . . . Have you anything to say?"
Lev cleared his throat. "Comrade Judges, the United States is a terrible, decadent country. It savagely exploits the proletariat. Hunger, unemployment and racism defile every corner of that reactionary land. Is that not right?"
"Right!" the three judges assented as one.
"Then why not send me there?" asked Bryshkov.

Aha!

Widely used Yinglish expletive to express an astonishing range of emotions: surprise, pleasure, sudden illumination, delight, triumph.

Please do not assume that this exclamatory jewel is the Yiddish equivalent of the English "Ahh . . ." Nor should you assume that *Aha!* is a simple clone of *Hoo-ha!* (*q.v.*).
"Aha!" is a unique, versatile, juicy expletive that covers a considerable gamut of feelings:

1. Astonishment.
   "You mean scientists still can't explain electricity?"
   "That's true?"
   "*A-ha!*"
2. Delight.
   "I'm the winner of the jackpot? *Aha!*"
3. Triumph.
   "Aha! So you admit I'm right?!"

4. Surprise.
   "She isn't a woman—she's a *man*. A-haaa . . ."
5. Sudden illumination.
   "*Aha*, so that's why they canceled the party!"
6. Resignation.
   "You mean I'll have to pay for all the damages? . . .
   Ah . . . ha . . ."

Aha! is distinctly Yiddish in its nuances and its overtones—second, in these ways, only to *Oy!* or even *Nu?*

For twenty years Mr. Rabinowitz had been eating at the same restaurant on Second Avenue. On this night, as on every other, Mr. Rabinowitz ordered chicken soup.

The waiter set it down and started off. Mr. Rabinowitz called, "Waiter! Eh—eh!"

"Yeah?"

"Taste this soup."

The waiter said, "*Hanh?* Twenty years you've been eating the chicken soup here, no? Have you ever had a bad plate—?"

"Waiter," said Rabinowitz firmly, "taste the soup."

"Listen, Mr. Rabinowitz, what's gotten *into* you?!"

"I said, 'Taste the soup!' *I'm* the customer, you're the waiter. You are supposed to please *me*. Taste the soup!"

"All right, all right," grimaced the waiter. "I'll taste—where's the spoon?"

"*Aha!*" cried Rabinowitz.

See also AI-AI-AI, FEH!, HOO-HA!, MNYEH, OY, PSSSSH!

ai-ai-ai
ai-yi-yi

Quintessential Yiddish. Pronounced *ay-ay-*YI or AY-*yay-yi.* Rhyme it with "my, my, my."

This eloquent exclamation, a form of dialogue with the self, should not be confused with the classic *oy-oy-oy.* A folk saying goes: "To have money may not always be so *ai-yi-yi,* but *not* to have it is *oy-oy-oy!*"

Ai-ai-ai may be cried, crooned, or sung out in a juicy

repertoire of shadings; it is sent forth *forte* or *pianissimo*; it can run up or down the tonal scale; it is counterpointed by a variety of facial expressions—according to the vocalizer's histrionic talent. It often verbalizes reverie.

The three syllables should not be clipped, as Spaniards do in mouthing their stern Iberian *ay-ay*. Nor should the syllables be barked out, as the Japanese do in grunting their hoarse, harsh "Hai!" (which means "yes" but sounds as though it came out of a robot greatly in need of oil). Nor should the syllables be uttered as in the fine old British naval "Aye, aye, sir."

The Yiddish *ai-ai-ai* is of an altogether different genre: it ties the consonantal *y* into the compliant *ai* in a liquid linkage that enhances both euphony and meaning.

1. Sung out happily, up the scale (*ai-yi-*YI!), with a beam or laugh, it expresses admiration, envy, surprise, all-other-words-fail-me.
   "Did I see a wonderful movie! Ai-ai-*ai!*"

2. Uttered sadly, with a dolorous expression, a shake of the head, or in hollow *diminuendo* (AI-*yi-yi*), it emits monosyllabic pellets of dismay, pity, lamentation or regret.
   "Did she suffer! Ai, ai, ai!"

3. Uttered sarcastically, or garnished with a glare, a snicker, a sneer, *ai-ai-ai* is a scathing package of scorn.
   "So he'ʳ on the committee for the annual picnic. *Ai-ai-ai.*"

4. Delivered in commiseration.
   "During this terrible heat-wave you have to stay in the city? *Ai-ai-ai.*"

5. Uttered with regret.
   "Your daughter is not yet married? *Ai-ai-ai.*"

6. In anguish.
   "It hurts so much I can't walk to the corner. *Ai-ai-ai.*"

7. Delivered as a warning.
   "I'm telling you. Don't get him angry! *Ai-ai-ai!* What he does when he gets angry!"

8. Declared in reprimand.
   "Stop complaining! Don't make such an *ai-ai-ai!*"

These feeble ground rules are not to be interpreted rigidly. My mother (*aleha ha-sholem*), a virtuoso of the *ai-ai-ai*, could make it jump through hoops beyond the eight delineated above.

Many an accomplished complainer can trill an *ai-ai-ai* up the scale as if it were a dirge, which is no small feat, and some can pronounce a down-scale *ai-yi-yi* with so joyous and percussive a first syllable that the rest sounds not like depression but exhaustion from too much delight.

When Mr. Jacobs returned from Europe, his partner in Windsor Men's Clothes hung on his reminiscences.

"And I even was in a group who went to the Vatican," beamed Jacobs, "where we had an audience with the pope!"

"*Ai-ai-ai!* The pope! . . . What does he look like?"

"A fine man, big chest, well-built, size forty-four, short."

See also AHA!, FEH!, HOO-HA!, MNYEH, PSSSSH!

A.K.

A code term prized by Yinglish *mavens*. Initials for the vulgar (and taboo) phrase: *alter kocker*: "old defecator."

1. An old man.
2. A person who is constipated.
3. A crotchety, ineffectual old person.
4. (Affectionately) Old codger.

My mother (*aleha ha-sholem*) would *never* tolerate the use in our home of such an uncouth, vulgar phrase as *alter kocker*. Yet that phrase, along with its discreetly camouflaged A.K., is a testimonial to the ineradicable earthiness of Yiddish.

A.K. is, of course, the English rendering of the initials. It should be noticed that A.K. is often used with fondness no less than in ridicule, or it may be merely descriptive:

Clinically:

"He has a lot of intestinal problems. After all, he's quite an A.K."

Descriptively:

"What do you make of Mr. Blattberg's condition?" asks Dr. Melnick.

"There's not much we can do," replies Dr. Antman. "It's not serious. Keep in mind that Mr. Blattberg is an A.K."

Affectionately:

"Don't be too hard on the man. After all, he's a pretty old A.K."

Derisively:

"Sadie, stop your *kvetching* [complaining]. You're beginning to sound like an A.K."

Philosophically:

"With all his grumbling and eccentricities, he's really a lovable A.K."

I make no special plea for *alter kocker*, but I certainly prefer A.K. to its English equivalent, *old fart*.

———

Two A.K.'s had sat in silence on their favorite park bench for hours, lost in thought. Finally, one gave a long, heartfelt "Oy . . ."

The other one sighed, "You're telling *me*?"

———

Two A.K.'s sat next to each other observing a prolonged, silent communion.

At last one ventured, "So *nu*, Fischel. How are things with you?"

"Eh!" shrugged the other. "And how about you?"

"Mn-yeh . . ."

Then the A.K.s rose. "Well, good-bye, Harry!"

And Harry said, "It's always a pleasure to have a real heart-to-heart talk."

———

Have you heard about the A.K. who bought a cocker spaniel so that he could call him Alter?

———

Back in the 1930s, *Variety*, the unique "Bible of Show Biz," introduced *A.K.* to the world of Broadway and Hollywood and newspaperdom in general. Many readers thought that A.K. were the initials for "ass kisser."

But *Variety*'s editors, who are famed for their wit (and excellent journalism), solemnly alleged that A.K. were the initials for (of all things!) "antedeluvian knight."

Yinglish, by the way, has a proper pair of initials for those who want to say "He's an ass-kisser" but believe it to be, as it undoubtedly is, a rank vulgarism. The initials are T.L. (*q.v.*).

If you don't want to suffer in your old age, hang yourself while you are young.

—Jewish folk saying

OLD MR. PITCHIK (answering phone): Hel-lo-o.
WOMAN'S VOICE: Is this 555–4861?
MR. PITCHIK: No, lady. You got the wrong number.
WOMAN: Are you *sure*?
MR. PITCHIK: Listen, lady, I am eighty years old. Did I ever lie to you before?

The board of the synagogue was astounded when their rabbi, a widower aged seventy-eight, announced that he was going to get married again—to a twenty-nine-year-old girl!

"How can you *consider* such a scandalous thing?" exclaimed one member of the board.

"It will be a disgrace to our congregation!" cried a trustee.

"It could be *dangerous* for you, *Rebbe*!" cried a doctor. "Do you realize that marriage at your age, with—sex, there can be a heart attack . . . maybe even death . . ."

The A.K. nodded, sighing: "That is in the hands of the Lord, blessed be His Name. After all, if in His infinite wisdom, He decides on death—I certainly will miss her!"

Two old Jews who had not seen each other in over forty years met on the Grand Concourse in the Bronx. With cries of astonishment and delight they embraced, hugging each other, patting backs, kissing cheeks, clucking and gurgling their joy.

Then one man pulled away, stared at the other and said, "Eh—you know something terrible? . . . I don't remember your name!"

"Hanh?!"

"I—don't—remember—your—*name*! Tell me your *name*!"

The second man cleared his throat. "Eh . . . how soon do you have to know?"

alav ha-sholem   (masculine)
aleha ha-sholem   (feminine)
aleyhem ha-sholem   (plural)
alavasholem   (colloquial)

Often heard in Yinglish. Hebrew; rhymes with "olive-a roll 'em." The two words for the masculine are pronounced as if they were one, usually dropping the *h* sound. Pronounce the feminine form *ah-*LEV-*a ha-*SHO-*lem* (Yiddish) or *sha-*LOAM (Hebrew).

1. Literally: Unto him [her], peace.
2. May he [she] rest in peace.

This invocation is obligatory whenever you mention someone who is no longer breathing. The English equivalent, of course, is "May he [she] rest in peace."

Whenever you hear, say, "My Tante Besse, *aleha ha-sholem* . . ." it would be scandalous to ask, "And how *is* your Aunt Bessie?"

When I was growing up, I was puzzled by the negative embroidery that blithely surrounded *alavasholem: e.g.,* "Charley? That no-good! *Alavasholem.*"

In time I learned the emotional acrobatics involved. Those who are named, even negatively, are dead, and one *must* wish the dead well. The *pro forma* invocation is really a ritual, and rituals offer sanctioned outlets for the discharge of conflicting emotions. The obligatory phrase takes care of ambivalence simply by eliminating choices. In this odd way you can rage, "That rotten, worthless bum—" adding the immediate "—*alav ha-sholem.*" This not only assuages any pangs of conscience but drafts custom to your side as an ally. Invoking mercy wipes the guilt off malediction—but only after hostility has been vented.

Jews are at home with such strong and complex emotions and express them with panache and confident hedging.

SCENE: Café Royale (alav ha-sholem)

The ever-impudent waiter, one of the Royale's veteran servitors, brushed some crumbs off the tablecloth and asked the two customers, "So now, gentlemen. What'll it be? Coffee, seltzer, tea?"

The first customer said, "I think I'd like tea."

"Okay," the waiter nodded. "And what about you, mister?"

"I'll have tea, too," said the second man, "but waiter," he added sarcastically, "be sure that the glass is clean!"

"Right!" The waiter snapped, and went off.

Soon enough, he returned with two glasses of tea. "Tea for two," he quipped. "Now, which one of you asked for a clean glass?"

When I was ten, a bearded old man once patted my head and smiled, "Such a nice boy. You should live to be a hundred and twenty-one!"

When I reported this to my father, *alav ha-sholem*, he explained, "Jews use that phrase of affection because Moses is supposed to have lived to the age of a hundred and twenty."

"Oh—but why did the old man say 'a hundred and twenty-*one*'?"

My father chuckled. "I guess he was making a wish you shouldn't die suddenly."

Jews even employ *alav ha-sholem* for comic effect. Thus:

"My doctor is a regular genius. Such important patients! For instance: Nathan Popper, *alav ha-sholem*; Jenny Finegold, *aleha ha-sholem*; Professor and Mrs. Rosenkranz, *aleyhem ha-sholem* . . ."

"So, Jennie," said Sadie, "Goldie tells me you have had a very hard time."

"What do you mean, 'had'? Do you think everything *now* is hotsy-totsy?"

"So—what happened, Jennie?"

"What happened is plenty. Like last June, my dog was run over. In July, my daughter got a divorce. In August my darling husband, *alav ha-sholem*, dropped dead. And you know what? Next week—" Jennie winced—"the painters are coming."

aleichem sholem
aleykhem shol'm

From Hebrew. In Yiddish, pronounced *a*-LAY-*khem* (gargle the *kh*) SHO-*lem*. In Hebrew, the accent is on the final syllable (*sha*-LOME) and is Englished as *shalom*.

1. The usual response to the customary greeting, "Sholem aleichem," which means "Peace unto you."

When two Jews meet, one usually hails the other with a cheerful "*Sholem aleichem*," and the other usually replies with a smile, reversing the order: "*Aleichem sholem*" (Peace unto you).

It gives me great pleasure to tell you that an Israeli, asked why Jews do this, shrugged and explained, "Because in Israel we usually don't know if we're coming or going."

2. (As an ejaculation) Thank goodness!

SCENE: Obstetrics Ward

WOMAN: How come you obstetricians are so busy—*sholem aleichem!*—these days?
DOCTOR: Because so many men—*aleichem sholem!*—are working for us.

See also SHOLEM ALEICHEM.

aleph baiz
aleph bez

Pronounced OL-*lif* BAZE; rhyme with "Ma Riff haze."
Hebrew: The first two letters of the Hebrew alphabet.
The alphabet—*i.e.,* the "abc's."
"He is learning his *aleph-baiz.*"

Aleph is the name of the first letter in the Hebrew alphabet, *beth* is the name of the second. The similarity of *aleph-beth* to "alphabet" is obvious.

The Hebrew alphabet, incidentally, came from the inhabitants of Canaan, which was the part of Palestine the Greeks called Phoenicia.

Hebrew was most probably the language spoken by the Phoenicians/Canaanites (Isaiah mentions "the language of Canaan"), who almost surely created the letters that formed the Semitic alphabet (from which all the alphabets in Europe descended). Hebrew is the first recorded alphabet in history.

Hebrew was one of a cluster of related languages (Aramaic, Ugaritic, Akkadian, Arabic) known as Semitic. Today, the only Semitic languages are Hebrew, Arabic and Abyssinian.

One of the most endearing customs I know involved a Jewish boy's first day in Hebrew school, or *heder* (*cheder*). The teacher, by tradition, would show the boy the alphabet on a large chart, and before (or after) the child repeated the teacher's *"aleph,"* the father or mother would place a drop of honey on the child's tongue. "How does that taste?" the boy would be asked.

"Sweet."

"Ah, but learning is sweeter."

aleykhem shol'm

See ALEICHEM SHOLEM.

Alice Island

The way a vast number of Jewish immigrants pronounced "Ellis Island," the great port of entry in New York harbor.

See also CASTLE GARDEN, ELLIS ISLAND.

aliyah
alyah
aliot   (plural)

Rhymes with "Maria." Pronounced: *a*-LEE-*yah*. Hebrew: "going" or "ascending."

1. The honor of being called to the lecterns during a

synagogue service, to read a portion of the Torah; or to recite the blessings before and after. (More properly called *aliyah ha-torah*.)
2. Migration to the State of Israel.
3. A visit or a pilgrimage, usually to Jerusalem.

To read aloud from the Hebrew text takes considerable skill, because no vowel sounds are indicated, and there are no punctuation marks (!) or signs for oral accent.

Today, the one "called up" often does not read at all (rabbis do not want to embarrass the members of their congregation who don't know Hebrew); instead, the text is chanted by an appointed reader or elder. (*Autres temps, autres moeurs.*)

Don't say "I went on an *aliyah*," but "I made *aliyah*."

———————

Mr. Grossman, an accountant from New Jersey, had longed to make *aliyah* to Jerusalem.

Shortly after he arrived, he went to an optician. "I'm having trouble reading, Doctor. Maybe I need stronger lenses."

The optician placed a large chart before Mr. Grossman, saying, "Read the letters on the bottom line."

Mr. Grossman squinted and squirmed. "I can't."

"What about the next line up? The letters are larger."

Mr. Grossman stared and shook his head. "I can't."

The optician cleared his throat. "Excuse me, mister. Are you *blind*?"

"Oh, *no*, Doc. I just never learned Hebrew."

alkay

Pronounced *all*-KAY; rhymes with "fall day."

1. Okay.
2. Everything's all right.

This neologism is one of the most common malformations of colloquial English by colloquial Jews.

My father, who became quite fluent in English, always said "alkay" when he meant "okay."

I often said, "It's 'okay,' Pa, not '*alkay*.' "

"They don't mean the same thing?"

"Yes, they do mean the same thing, but *alkay* is wrong."

My father explained: "*I* don't use *okay* when I *mean* *alkay*. Take our car. If you ask, 'How are the tires?' I say, 'Okay.' If you ask, 'How is the battery?' I'll say, 'Okay.' But when I want to say that everything—the whole motor, lights, brakes are *all* working fine, I say '*alkay*!'"

Little did I dream that my papa was performing a feat of what is now called psycholinguistics.

Space engineers and cosmonauts have coined the expressive "A.O.K.," meaning "all systems working."

Had my father been alive to hear this, he would, I think, have smiled, "Ufcawss! Like me, they mean *alkay*."

GOLDMAN: Have you heard the joke about the two Jews who—

SILVERMAN: Hold it! Why does it always have to be a joke about two Jews? Can't a story be just as funny if told about two Spaniards? Or two Eskimos? Or—

GOLDMAN: *Alkay*, enough. So this joke is about two Eskimos . . . Well, two Eskimos met at a B'nai B'rith meeting, and the first Eskimo said, "Isadore, when is your boy going to be Bar Mitzva?" So the second Eskimo said, "Moe—"

SILVERMAN: Okay, stop. Go back to the two Jews.

already

Much used for comic effect in Yinglish. From Yiddish: *shoyn*. Vintage Yinglish. Widely used for comic effect on countless TV shows.

1. It's about time. ("So come on, already.")
2. Premature. ("Already he's arguing?")
3. With no further ado. ("Enough already!")
4. By now. ("He hasn't agreed already?!")
5. I *mean* it. ("Stop! I'm already fed up!")

When using *already* this way—as in "Come *on*, already!" or "Eat, already!"—you are using true Yinglish.

Jews of the Lower East Side, the West Side of Chicago, etc., adapted English words to Yiddish patterns to create new idioms. The amusing, or simply expressive, ring of such neologisms swiftly led writers and comedians (and later, talk show regulars) to adopt the Yinglish modes.

Abraham Bloom, a waiter at a restaurant famous for the independence (not to say insolence) of its waiters, died.

Some of his friends decided to hold a séance, in hopes of communicating with him. So they went to none other than:

ROSE LEVITS
ORACLE
SPIRITUAL INTERMEDIARY

Now, ten of Abe Bloom's friends sat around the table, under a shaded lamp, as Madame Levits went into a deep trance, intoning hollowly, "Abie . . . Abie . . . are you happy? . . . I will rap three times, then you should answer . . ." Mme. Levits rapped—slowly, solemnly—three times.

The friends sat, hushed.

"Abe . . . Abe . . ." crooned the oracle, "*please* pay attention. Are you in heaven? In bliss? . . . I will knock *four* times." And four times—loudly—did Mme. Levits rap on the board.

But the room stayed silent as the grave . . .

"Abe! Abe Bloom! What's the *matt*er? We want to hear you already!" Now the seeress firmly knocked five times—in vain. "Abe!" cried Mme. Levits. "I know you're there! . . . *Why don't you answer?*"

The disembodied voice of Abie the waiter replied, "Because . . . you're . . . not . . . my . . . table."

"Doc," said Mr. Warshauer, "You know I'm seventy-nine. You know how with me making love maybe once a *month* is good already. Well . . . I have a friend who is eighty-one. And last week he told me, man to man, that he makes love three times a week! . . . Doc, what should I *do*?"

"Tell him the same thing," said the doctor.

See also AGAIN, ALRIGHT ALREADY, ENOUGH ALREADY, YET.

alright already

Yinglish: used in parody or for comic characterization. From the Yiddish *shoyn genug*, which means "already enough," or *genug shoyn*, which means "enough already."

"*Alright* already," a thriving export from the Bronx, is simply a form of "enough already!"

"Alright already" and "*Alright* already!" are commonly heard in many of the sitcoms on television.

1. Enough!
2. For God's sake!
3. Please shut up!
4. I can't *stand* any more!

"Alright already!" also signifies exasperated agreement:

5. Okay, okay, just stop nagging!
6. You win!
7. I give up: you shut up.

"Alright already" is not always deployed in disgust. It can be uttered in agreement—to cut off further discussion:

8. Okay, okay; let's get on with it.

SCENE: **A Bible Class for Children, Long Island**

ACT 1

TEACHER: Georgie, who blew down the walls of Jericho?
GEORGIE: Don't look at me, ma'am; *I* didn't.

ACT 2

TEACHER: Mr. Fardroos, I must talk to you about your boy, Georgie. When I asked him who blew down the walls of Jericho, he answered, "Don't look at me; I didn't!"
MR. FARDROOS: Miss, let me assure you: if my boy said he didn't do it, he didn't do it!

ACT 3

PRINCIPAL: Miss Shorskie, I hear that Georgie Fardroos,

when asked who blew down the walls of Jericho, answered, "*I* didn't." Is that true?

TEACHER: Absolutely. And his father vouches for the boy's honesty!

ACT 4

PRINCIPAL: Mr. Binter, as chairman of the board of trustees of our synagogue you will be interested in something that involves Mr. Fardroos. When his boy's teacher asked who blew down the walls of Jericho, the lad replied: "Not me." Mr. Fardroos has assured the teacher that his son could be trusted. I asked the teacher what she thought, and she said that—

CHAIRMAN: Alright, *alright* already! I'm a busy man. Get the wall fixed and send the bill to me.

See also ENOUGH ALREADY.

alrightnik   (masculine)
alrightnikeh   (feminine)
alrightnitzkeh   (feminine form, parodied)

Pure Yinglish.
From the English *all right*, with the incomparable Slavic -*nik* added.

Alrightnik was introduced to Yiddish readers by Abraham Cahan, the great editor of the *Jewish Daily Forward*.

1. One who has succeeded, *i.e.*, done all right, and shows it by boasting, ostentation, crude manners, gaudy dress.
2. *Nouveau riche*, with trimmings—but not well-read, well-mannered, or respectful of learning.

As is true of many Yiddishisms, the pungent suffix -*nik* is enlisted in the service of scorn.

Alrightniks are materialists; they parade their money; they lack modest, sensitive qualities. They talk loudly, dress garishly, show off.

Alrightniks may be envied, but they are not admired, for they have "succeeded" without gaining taste, breeding or spiritual values. Above all, they are not devoted to learning, hence cannot be respected.

Joe E. Lewis, the nightclub entertainer, once monologized: "Show me a Jew who comes home in the evening, is greeted with a great big smile, has his shoes taken off, has his pillows arranged for him, is served a delicious meal—and I'll show you an alrightnik who lives in a Japanese restaurant."

Mrs. Furthman, a widow and an attractive alrightnikeh, was deeply depressed by the suburb into which she had recently moved.

One day she telephoned a neighbor and said, somewhat embarrassed, "Shirley, you're the only person I can ask. Would you give me some—confidential advice?"

"Gladly, Ann."

The alrightnikeh blushed. "Well, how—how do you go about having an affair in this town?"

"I," beamed Shirley, "always start with 'The Star-Spangled Banner.' "

An alrightnikeh (or alrightnitzkeh) called a decorator to her new apartment. "I want you to fix up this place, from top to bottom. Money is no object."

The decorator asked, "Do you want to make your apartment look modern?"

"Modrin? . . . N-o."

"French?"

"French?" echoed the alrightnikeh. "Never!"

"Perhaps provincial?"

"God forbid!"

The decorator sighed, "Madame, you must tell me—what period *do* you want?"

"What period? I want my friends to walk in, take one look, and drop dead! Period."

The underlying creed of alrightniks is best stated in folk sayings like this one:

If the rich would only hire the poor to die for them, the poor would earn a very good living.

And the poor (and the envious) have this to say of alright-niks:

You can live like a king and still die a fool.

If you rub elbows with the rich, you'll get a hole in your sleeve.

The rich have heirs—not children.

Whenever there is too much, something is lacking.

See also -NIK.

A.M.

The acronym for *able momzer* ("able bastard")—not the English abbreviation A.M. for *ante meridiem* (before noon). Recent addition to Yinglish.

1. Verbal shorthand for *able momzer*, someone very clever and competent.
2. Code name, among the young, for a smart, resourceful but not likable person.

Dr. Kosoff turned to his patient with a smile. "You're in *splendid* health, Mr. Fratkin: heart, blood pressure, lungs, the works. You're seventy-six years old—and in as good shape as a twenty-year-old!"

"That's great," said Mr. Fratkin.

The doctor and his patient stood up and shook hands. "See you next year, Mr. Fratkin."

"Okay, Doctor."

Mr. Fratkin went out of the office.

In a moment, Dr. Kosoff heard a loud crash outside his door. He leaped to the door and opened it and beheld—on the floor, stretched out and motionless, lay Mr. Fratkin. Bent over him, pale as a sheet, was Dr. Kosoff's nurse, stammering, "He fell like a *rock*, Doctor!"

The doctor quickly knelt beside the motionless body, felt Mr. Fratkin's pulse, listened for Mr. Fratkin's heart-beat and exclaimed, "He's dead!" He put his hands under the dead man's arms. "Nurse, quick. Take his feet!"

"F-feet? Wh-why?"

"For God's *sake*, Nurse. We've got to turn him around! Make it look like the man was coming *in*!"

(Can there be any doubt that Dr. Kosoff was an A.M.?)

See also k'NOCKER.

Amen
Awmain
Omeyn

Hebrew: "So be it." Pronounced *aw*-MAIN or *aw*-MINE or even *oo*-MAIN.

In Yinglish this benedictory word is usually vocalized as "awmain."

Amen.

1. This is one of the most widely known words in all the world: Jews, Christians and Muslims share its usage, which occurs at the end of a prayer and signifies an affirmation of what preceded it.

When services were held in the Temple in Jerusalem, a longer formula than *amen* was used as the response of affirmation made by the people during the liturgy that was recited by the priests and the Levites. After the Temple was destroyed (A.D. 70), *amen* was retained in the Jewish liturgy.

The Talmud has ruled that *amen* is to be recited "with the full power" of the voice.

A forceful enunciation of *amen* was (and is) believed by the credulous to help open the doors of paradise.

It is worth remembering that the loud, emphatic utterance of *amen* became connected with the expression and confession of repentance, which is very strong in Judaism.

The Great Synagogue in old Alexandria was said to have been so huge that worshipers in the rear could not hear the cantor and therefore could not know when a prayer was ended. To enable these unfortunates to participate in a mighty, responsive "*Amen!*" at the right moment, an attendant standing next to the rabbi would raise or drop a huge flag, the signal for all the faithful to thunder in one great affirmation, "AW-MAIN!"

2. An interjection used as a response to a good wish.
   "I hope your daughter gets well real fast."
   "*Awmain.*"
3. An expletive uttered in support of someone else's malediction, to co-wish misfortune upon someone

who is heartily disliked, or to co-wish disaster upon someone hated.

"May every bone in his body be broken by gangsters!"

"Awmain."

"She should have an ache in every tooth and a fire in every toe!"

"Awmain."

"May his brains turn to sauerkraut and his tongue to ashes!"

"Awmain."

"Like a beet he should flourish—with his head in the ground."

"Awmain."

4. An admission of wrongdoing. The forceful reiteration of "Amen" became attached to the voicing of repentance, a feeling of great power in Judaism.

5. A caustic way of emphasizing a point, underlining a hope, or rubbing in a truth.

The best illustration of the last usage, a virtuoso deployment of *amen*, seems to me the climax of this delicious tale:

Old Mr. Tichnor was sleeping in his apartment, deeply and soundly, when his telephone rang and rang. Annoyed, he picked up the phone, grumbling, "Hel-lo."

"Is this Mr. Tichnor?" asked a female voice.

"Yeah."

"Mr. Tichnor in apartment Three-B?"

"That's right."

"Well, this is Mrs. Epstein, in Two-A. And I just want to tell you that it's half past three in the morning and your damn dog's barking is driving me absolutely insane!" And the woman slammed the phone down so violently that Mr. Tichnor's ears afflicted him with a headache.

The next night, at exactly 3:30 A.M., Mrs. Epstein's phone rang and rang and awakened her out of a pill-induced sleep. "Hello, hello," she mumbled.

"Hello. Is this Mrs. Epstein?"

"Yeh."

"Mrs. Epstein in apartment Two-A?"

"Yeh! Yeh!"

"Mrs. Epstein, this is Mr. Tichnor, in apartment Three-B."

"What?!"

"And I'm calling to tell you something."

"At half past three in the *morning*!"

"Yeah. Mrs. Epstein, I don't *own* a dog."

"What? Hanh? You crazy—"

Sweetly, sweetly came Mr. Tichnor's "Aw-main."

America gonif!
America gonef!
America gonev!

From Hebrew: *ganov*: "thief."

1. (Literally) America, (you) thief!
2. Wonderful America!
3. Where, except in America, could such a thing *happen*?
4. A tribute to anything exceptionally clever, ingenious or resourceful.
5. Isn't that astonishing?!
6. Can you beat that?
7. Wow!

Immigrant Jews never ceased to marvel over one or another aspect of life in America. Into the declamatory "America *gonif!*" they poured all their awe and wonder, all their gratitude and admiration. The phrase was a celebration of their good fortune in being in this blessed land, this land of limitless opportunity.

A similar tribute was expressed in the phrase "Only in America!" But at least in my family's circles in Chicago, where I was raised, "Only in America" was a pallid tribute compared with "America *gonif!*" A dozen times a week my father (bless his soul), reading the morning paper or listening to the radio, would exclaim, chortle, announce, cry out or shout, "America *gonif!*" *No* one I ever met loved or appreciated this country more.

———

On little Moishe's first day home from school, his proud mother ran out to meet him.

"So, Moisheleh, what did you learn?"

"I learned how to write," said Moishe.

"Already? On the first day? America *gonif!* So tell me, Moisheleh, what did you write?"

Little Moishe shrugged. "I don't know."

"What do you mean you don't know?! How is that possible?! *You* wrote it, didn't you? So?"

"I don't know how to read!"

See also GONIF.

anger converted to nominal exoneration, employing "just," "only," or "merely" for sarcastic reinforcement

Yinglish buffs love this ploy, very common in Yiddish, which is just as effective when deployed in English:

> "Mind? Why should I mind? Your recklessness only cost me five hundred dollars."
> "How friendly of you to answer my call—just because I phoned you thirteen times, leaving my number . . ."
> "Annoyed? Why should I be annoyed? Because your directions took me a mere two hundred miles out of the way? . . ."

a nothing

> Yinglish to the core, and at its most devastating. From the Yiddish *gornit* or *gornisht*: "a nothing."

The use of the article *a* is what makes this phrase Yinglish, meaning:

1. A dummy, a cipher.
2. Someone who simply does not matter.
3. A person with no respected qualities.
4. A *shlemiel* in spades.

In Yiddish, the concept of "a nothing" is magnified by doubling the obloquy: "He is a *gornisht mit gornisht*," literally, "He is a nothing with nothing" meaning "He is of absolutely no consequence."

5. In fashion, chic.

Among the *cognoscenti* of the world of fashion, where understatement sometimes reigns, "a nothing of a dress" or "a little nothing of a shirt" is often bandied about. You may be sure that when a woman uses this phrase, she expects you to know that the dress is very *chic*: simple but quite expensive.

"Coco" Chanel herself introduced the famous—and by now classic—"little black dress." It swept the ranks of fashion in Europe, the United States and wherever *haute couture* dominated taste.

French designers and *boutiques* adapted the phrase "*un petit rien*" ("a little nothing").

It surprised me greatly (since I assumed "a nothing" was colloquial and of modern vintage) to learn that "I am a nothing" is found in the Talmud! (*Berakot*, 17A.) The phrase occurs in a paraphrase, at the end of the solemn Amida prayer recited on the most awesome of Jewish holidays, Yom Kippur.

———————

Reciting the Yom Kippur Confession, which is an array of no fewer than fifty-six categories of sin, Adam Hamburger, a prosperous manufacturer of kiddies' clothes, a man quite well known for his philanthropies and community service, swayed back and forth, beating his breast for each sin, and moaning, "O Lord, forgive me, forgive me— for I am a nothing, a *nothing*!"

And seated right next to him, a poorly dressed *shnorrer* (beggar) swayed back and forth, too, beating his breast and moaning, "Oh, Lord, oh, Lord! Forgive me—I am a nothing, a *nothing*!"

Mr. Hamburger gasped, shot a glance toward heaven and, pointing a finger at the *shnorrer*, complained to God: "Look, look! Look who has the *nerve* to call himself a nothing!"

See also NAYFISH, SHLIMAZEL, SHMO.

A-1
A—Number One

Yinglish, even though the component parts are English.

1. Incomparable.

2. Tops.
3. Without either peer or superior.
4. Wholly admirable.

The phrase consists of three English words, of course; but the usage is distinctively Yinglish. You may hear the phrase used a hundred times a week by Jews in the discourse of business, but will not often hear it employed by gentiles. In this respect, "A–Number One" is akin to the Jewish use of *customer (q.v.)*.

Mrs. Tarsher stormed into the A-1 Laundry and Cleaners ("We pick up and deliver, too") and demanded to see the owner.

Mr. Keplis appeared behind a curtain. "So, lady, I'm the owner. You have maybe a complaint?"

"A *complaint*?" echoed Mrs. Tarsher. "Do you have the *nerve* to call yourself an A–Number One Cleaner?! Well, take a look." She flung something on the counter. "Just take a look at that sample of your work!"

Mr. Keplis picked the object off the counter and studied it closely. "Lady, there's not a thing wrong with this lace."

"Lace?" echoed Mrs. Tarsher. "Lace, you call it? When I brought it to be cleaned, it was a *sheet*!"

"Baskin!" sang out the editor of the *Jewish Megillah*. "Step into my office."

The young reporter hastened into Mr. Gluckman's office.

"Baskin," said Mr. Gluckman. "You've been working here for six months, right?"

"Yes, sir."

"Well, I want to tell you you've been doing a very good job. A–Number One!"

"Thank you, Mr. Gluckman."

"Baskin, how much are we paying you?"

"A hundred and fifty a week."

Mr. Gluckman nodded. "I'm glad."

Same Story, Different Ending

"How much are we paying you?"

"A hundred and fifty a week!"

Gluckman nodded. "That's good."

appeal

English used as Yinglish with a special meaning; a noun, not a verb.

1. A meeting, rally, concert, recital, lecture or program that raises money for any worthy cause.
2. An extended and intensive campaign to solicit funds not only for a charity but for any cause: political, welfare, social, reform.

Jewish communal life glitters with a remarkable number of "affairs" or "appeals," always energized by the Judaic concept of charity as a sacred *duty*. So profound and penetrating is the idea of "giving" that, in fact, there is no Yiddish word for charity. Then how is the idea of "charity" conveyed? By the Hebrew word *tsedaka*, which means not "charity," but "justice" or "moral obligation."

Anyone raised in a Jewish immigrant home became accustomed to the incessant parade of appeals: for aid to poor immigrants, widows in need of succor, orphans, the blind, for planting trees in the Holy Land, for relief for the victims of pogroms around the world, etc.

No month went by without raffles, bazaars, recitals (piano, violin, vocal), lectures, debates. My mother (*aleha ha-sholem*), a woman of indomitable will and astonishing energy, organized many a committee for many a crying cause.

It was rare to find an immigrant home without a row of tin cans, each with a slot in the top for depositing coins, on the kitchen windowsill. These cans bore labels like:

For the Blind.
For the Lame.
For the Aid of Orphans.
Needy Widows.
To send a rabbi on a trip to the Holy Land.
For the Home for the Aged.
For hot school lunches for Jewish children in Lodz.

Each can, called a *pushke (q.v.)*, was emptied when a representative of one or another worthy group made his biweekly or monthly rounds.

The *pushke* was the exclusive province of the Jewish wife. It represented her savings out of the household money her husband provided. Religious women would always drop a few coins into one or another can every Friday night, just before lighting the Sabbath candles.

DEBBY: Mama, you have to come to the appeal tomorrow night!

MOTHER: I went already to *two* appeals this month.

DEBBY: But this one is very special—Professor Paul Yarmolinsky is going to give us a fascinating lecture: "Sex in Marriage."

MOTHER: Uh, Debby . . . that lecture I don't have to hear!

DEBBY: Why not, Mama?

MOTHER: I already gave.

Israel Slotnick
120 East 56th Street
New York, N.Y.

Dear Iz:

Knowing of your interest in the work of our committee, I am putting your name down for a pledge of $1,000 in our current appeal for funds. I am the chairman of the drive.

Yours,
"Chick" Bender

Les Bender
906 Seventh Avenue
New York, NY

Dear "Chick":

Thanks for advising me that you put me down for a pledge of $1,000 in your current appeal for funds.

I am the chairman of another appeal. So I am putting *you* down for a $1,000 pledge there.

In this way, Les, no money has to pass between us.

Yours,
Iz

See also BENEFIT.

appetizing

In Yinglish, a noun: the part of a delicatessen, specialty food store or supermarket devoted to appetizers.

The first time I saw this outlandish designation ("appetizing," not "appetizers") I stood as if struck by thunder. (One cannot, of course, be struck by thunder; then how does one explain "thunder-struck"?) I had never seen "appetizing" used as a noun in any city in which I had resided: Chicago, Washington, Los Angeles.

I first encountered the peculiar adjective-as-noun in New York, every so often in the 1950s and frequently in the 1970s. But Stuart Berg Flexner (*I Hear America Talking*) says that Russian Jews have been talking about "an appetizing store" since the 1890s. Perhaps in New York and Brooklyn . . .

In the past two decades, American cities have witnessed the remarkable diffusion of *appetizing* as a noun—to designate that part of a delicatessen (or supermarket) devoted to such delicacies of Jewish cuisine as chopped liver, *gefilte* fish, smoked whitefish, lox, herring in sour cream, *shmaltz* herring, *et alia*.

A fancy, very popular delicatessen in New York has this proud slogan emblazoned on its shopping bags:

THE *ultimate*
IN
GOURMET APPETIZING

I would not call this the ultimate in gourmet English.

Ashkenazi
Ashkenazim (plural)
Ashkenazic (adjective)

Pronounced *osh-keh-*NOZ-*zee*. Hebrew: *Ashkenaz*: "Germany." Originally, *Ashkenaz* referred to a minor kingdom in ancient eastern Armenia.

The name applied, since the sixteenth century, to the Jews of central and eastern Europe—ancestors of the vast majority of Jews in the United States. (Before that, "Ashkenazi" was the Hebrew appellation for a German.)

Medieval rabbis dubbed Germany *Ashkenaz* after a passage in Jeremiah (51:27), ruling that after the Flood, one of Noah's great-grandsons, named Ashkenaz, had settled in Germany. I have no idea what evidence persuaded the learned men to do this.

The two great branches of world Jewry are the Ashkenazim and the Sephardim—the Ashkenazim being much larger in numbers. The Sephardic Jews mostly came from Babylon (Iraq today), the Greek islands, Africa, Portugal, Spain, southern France, the Orient. The Ashkenazim moved around to Syria and Greece, then Rome, then to northern France, then to Germanic cities down the Rhine (around the eleventh century), then to central and eastern Europe—where they found settlements of Jews who had emigrated there long, long before, after the destruction of the Kingdom of Judah, in the sixth century, B.C.

Ashkenazic Jews are distinguished from Sephardic Jews in many significant ways: the Yiddish they speak, their style of thought, their pronunciation of Hebrew, aspects of their liturgy, many customs, food habits, ceremonials and, for want of a better (or even equally good) characterization, their *Yiddishkeit* ("Yiddishness"). This is not surprising, given the considerable differences in history and experience across a span of a thousand years.

The Ashkenazim followed the religious practices and traditions of the scholars of Palestine; the Sephardim continued and elaborated the practices and traditions of the Jews in Babylonia and spread throughout the diaspora in Greece, Turkey, the northern coast of Africa and the Iberian peninsula.

Yiddish, sometimes called Judeo-German, is entirely the creation of the Ashkenazim. It is their *mama-loshn* (mother-tongue), the language of the home, of the street, of social and business discourse. Hebrew was and is "the sacred tongue," reserved for prayer, rituals, discussions of the Talmud.

Sephardic Jews cannot understand a word of Yiddish—unless that occasional word happens to be a Hebrew name for a holiday or religious rite. The vernacular, equivalent to Yiddish, of the Sephardic Jews is Ladino (or Judesmo), a dialect that consists of Castilian, Spanish and Portuguese components. Ashkenazim are as baffled by Ladino as Sephardim are by Yiddish.

———

The style and self-esteem of Sephardic Jews in Europe contrasted in the sharpest manner with that of the Jews in central and eastern Europe.

The Sephardim were cosmopolitan, sophisticates, philosophers, scientists, mathematicians, astronomers, bankers, a vanguard of emerging rationalism and the Enlightenment. They were advisers and financiers to kings and princes and bishops. They were admitted to the innermost councils of the court, where they acted as physicians and state treasurers and diplomatic advisers. To this day, streets in Toledo, Madrid and Barcelona bear Jewish names.

Compared with such worldliness, such pomp and wealth and influence, the Ashkenazim were for the most part peddlers, peasants, proletarians, fundamentalist in faith, steeped in poverty, bound to orthodox tradition and medieval superstition and fervent and desperate Messianic dreams. They resisted the secular world and scorned secular knowledge.

Their intellectual world was bounded by the Torah at one end and the Talmud at the other. They held to dogged piety, incessant praying and boundless compassion. They were resigned to the horrors, the humiliations and brutality of the world around them. They considered themselves (please note) God's hostages for the redemption of mankind!

And the Ashkenazim created an entirely distinctive civilization—in a Yiddish literature that Sephardic Jews could not understand, about a kind of person the Sephardim had never *seen*, celebrating passions and visions Sephardim could comprehend only by considerable effort—effort that very few Sephardim had either the occasion or the desire to expend. It was in the Ashkenazic world that *Yiddishkeit* ("Jewishness") reached its golden age; it may never return.

From 1880 to 1910, about one-third of the Jews in eastern Europe migrated—over ninety percent of them to the United States.

———

There has been no significant conflict in the New World between Sephardic and Ashkenazic Jews. The Ashkenazim adopted some Sephardic rituals with no difficulty, and marriages between Ashkenazic and Sephardic Jews have not been uncommon.

All this was markedly different from the hostility that later came to characterize the feeling among *German* Jews toward East European Jewry. To the prosperous, Americanized, bourgeois German Jews, the new immigrants from Russia, Poland, Hungary, Romania—poor, gaunt, bearded, earlocked, black-hatted, dressed in long black caftans— looked like "medieval apparitions."

To the *Deutsche Yehudim* (German Jews), the Ashkenazim were religious fanatics or—doubly puzzling—"agitators," union organizers, socialists, radicals. And the German Jews simply *loathed* Yiddish, which they thought a vulgar and despicable corruption of their own language.

It is the Ashkenazim who coined such dry, caustic, sad and sardonic observations as the following:

"Thou hast chosen us from among all the nations"— but why did You have to pick on the Jews?

When a Jewish farmer eats a chicken, *one* of them is sick.

If a Jew breaks a leg, he thanks God he did not break both legs; if he breaks both legs, he thanks God he did not break his neck.

When trouble comes, Jews feel it first; when fortune smiles, Jews feel it last.

Every Jew has his own brand of madness.

A Jew on a desert island will build two synagogues—so that he will have one he does not want to go to.

If a group of Jews on a long journey are overtaken by barbarians who say, "Give us one of your number, or we shall kill you all," let all be slain: for no Israelite may deliberately be delivered to barbarians.

—TALMUD: *Sanhedrin*, 84a

The real "Jewish Question" is this: From what can a Jew earn a living? —Sholem Aleichem

We are God's stake in human history.
—A. J. Heschel

Stephen Birmingham's lively *Our Crowd* contains many revealing anecdotes and pungent comments by descendants of the Teutonic patricians about the German Jews' strong sense of responsibility—and ambivalence—toward their poorer, less worldly co-religionists.

For more scholarly explorations of Ashkenazic–Sephardic tensions, see Jacob Rader Marcus's *Early American Jewry* and Nathan Glazer's perceptive "Some Characteristics of American Jews," in *The Jews: Their History, Culture and Religion*, edited by Louis Finkelstein. Glazer's *American Judaism* (University of Chicago) is an invaluable analysis.

Were I asked to cite the works that best portray the culture of the Ashkenazim, I would name the following: *The Brothers Ashkenazi*, by I. J. Singer, a stupendous novel, fit to rank with Dickens and Balzac (be sure to read the translation by Maurice Samuel); *Yoshe Kalb*, also by I. J. Singer; *The Dybbuk*, by S. Anski; *Three Cities*, by Sholem Asch; the matchless stories of "Mendele" (Mendele Mokher Seforim); and, of course, the rollicking tales of Sholem Aleichem.

Recently discovered memoirs with surprising and memorable material are *The Samurai of Vishgorod* (Jewish Publication Society) and *The Journeys of David Toback* (Shocken).

For sociological-ethnological studies, I recommend *Life Is with People*, by Zborowski and Herzog; *Studies in Judaism*, by Solomon Schechter; *The Jews: Their History, Culture and Religion*, edited by Louis Finkelstein; *The Jews of Poland: A Social and Economic History*, by Bernhard D. Weinryb; *On the Edge of Destruction*, by Celia Heller; the essays in *The Golden Tradition*, edited by Lucy Davidowitz; and the recent, perceptive *The Jews in Polish Culture*, by Alexander Hertz.

See also SEPHARDI, YIDDISH.

assent enthusiastically enlarged, to denote mockery

Mockery, a prized aspect of Yiddish discourse, is transferred to Yinglish quite easily.

1

"Do you think she really is a virgin?"
"Oh, absolutely. I'm *sure* of it! And so is her baby."

2

"I hear that Joe's new wife is pretty."

"Pretty? She's positively gorgeous—all three hundred pounds of her."

3

"Listen, Schneiderman! What about that hundred dollars you owe me?"

"I know. First thing tomorrow morning, I'll—"

"Tomorrow morning?" growled Fisher. "Tomorrow, tomorrow! I'm sick of your tomorrows! Last month you told me you couldn't repay me. The month before that you said you couldn't pay. And last *year* you said—"

"Enough!" exclaimed Schneiderman with a pained expression. "Didn't I—each time—keep my word?"

automatic and sarcastic repetition—to avoid the obvious and to maximize conviction

This automatic, sarcastic response is about as widely diffused in English as any Yinglishism.

"I'll tell him, I'll tell him."

"I'm coming, I'm coming."

"I know, I know." (Usually "I know, I *know*.")

"You'll like it, you'll *like* it."

The latter has, of course, won international attention as an advertising slogan: it was enormously effective.

Repetition is a staple of Jewish communication and illustrates the propensity of Yiddish to use irony to banish the banal.

The difference between "You'll like it" and "You'll like it, you'll *like* it" is as monumental as the difference between "I don't know," which is bloodlessly phatic, and "I don't know, I don't *know*!" which is a defiant—even proud— confession of ignorance.

". . . And *then* I went to see the doctor—Maury, *Maury*!"

"Mmh?"

"Maury, are you listening to me or reading the newspaper?"

"I'm listening, I'm listening."

"I *said*, this afternoon I went to see the doctor!"

"Mmh." Maury turned the page. "So how is he?"

automatic apposition

A familiar, satirical Yinglish usage: the deliberate removal of conventional, syntactically coordinated pauses in spoken English—equivalent to the removal of appositive commas in written English. Apposition is automatically conferred:

"My son the doctor . . ."
"My daughter the novelist . . ."
"My uncle the mathematician . . ."

This construction is spoken boldly, as if "son-the-doctor" were one word. The particular pleasure-*cum*-pride of Jewish mothers is by this stratagem transferred, kit and kaboodle, into the English vernacular.

Query: Is apposition without the customary pause employed when the speaker is speaking about disreputable relatives? Do mothers, that is, say:

"My son the forger . . ."
"My daughter the call-girl . . ."
"My nephew the grave-robber . . ."

Generalization is difficult here. Ordinarily, Jewish mothers avoid like the plague any reference to felonious or even shady relatives. But when a reference is unavoidable, the speaker may say, "My son, who no-good informers *framed* . . ." or "My daughter, who was absolutely *forced* to confess something she never in a hundred *years* could do . . ."

I can vouch for one case where a Mrs. Latznik, let us call her, returned from a visit to her son in the county prison. Her neighbors were, of course, all agog to hear how Mrs. Latznik would report the experience. Mrs. Latznik did not let them down:

"This morning I went to visit my Marvin," she said. "He is waiting to get his pardon, you know, in the—county—jail. And, ladies, let me tell you something! Never in your *life*, never even on TV, did you see such a *beautiful*, clean, attractive jail! You could eat off the floor! And the food—my Marvin tells me you would not find better in the most expensive restaurant!''

Awmain

See AMEN.

B

badchen
badhan
badchanim (plural)

Hebrew: *bodhan* or *bodkhan*: "jester." Pronounce the word BOD-*khen*, with the Scottish/German *kh*. Rhymes with "cod ken."

A professional entertainer or fun-maker—especially at Jewish weddings or anniversaries.

During the Middle Ages, jesters and clowns, traveling musicians and masquers were common figures throughout Europe. Rabbinical wisdom had urged Jews to make merry during family celebrations. The perceptive sages knew how important it was for people to enjoy periodic catharses after the burdens and sufferings and fear they so long and so often endured.

The Jews loved their jolly jokesters, who would first recite a poem to the bride and groom, would orate on the sanctity of marriage, would extol the parents and the guests—and then would lampoon everything, teasing the nuptial couple, spoofing the ceremony itself, extemporizing poems, perhaps donning a mask, clowning and ad-libbing, leading the whole company in jolly songs and dances.

A *badchen*'s verses and jocularity were often original, and often extemporized on the spot. Many Yiddish folksongs and witty doggerel came down the centuries via the *badchanim*.

American families rarely employ *badchanim* anymore.

The *badchen* is, of course, the direct ancestor of the Borsht Belt *tummler*.

———————

Jewish folk sayings arose from *any* human situation, showering laughter or ironic warnings; weddings were no exception.

If you dance at every wedding, you'll weep at every funeral.

To a wedding, walk; to a divorce, run.
　　　　　—Sholem Aleichem

Laughter is heard further than weeping.

When a man faces his Maker, he will have to account for those pleasures of life which he failed to enjoy.
　　　　　—TALMUD J.: *Kiddushin*

See also BORSHT BELT, TUMMLER.

bagel

Eighteen-karat Yinglish. Rhymes with "Mabel." From German: *Beugel*: "a curved or round loaf of bread."
　　A shiny roll, hard, crusty and glazed on the outside, but soft (one hopes) and chewy in the center, shaped like a tiny life preserver.

Bagels are called "doughnuts with a college education," "doughnuts in *rigor mortis*," "Brooklyn jawbreakers," and "alligator teething rings."
Bagels were especially prized among poor Jews, who usually ate coarse black bread; to them a roll made of white flour was a rare luxury.
Bagels are baked in a special way: unbleached, high-gluten flour, seasoned with a sprinkling of malt, sugar and salt, "raised" with yeast, of course—then plunged into boiling water before they are baked. The best bagels are baked in a hearth.
I suppose that you, like most people, think that a plain or toasted bagel, with cream cheese and lox (smoked salmon), is the traditional Sunday morning breakfast for Jews. It is certainly widespread, and a delectable delight, but the threesome is not traditionally Jewish: the combina-

tion is an inspired gastronomic achievement first created by Jews in America.

Bagels and hard-boiled eggs were once the traditional offering to mourners after a Jewish funeral, in the home of the deceased. Why? Because eggs and bagels, being round, were believed to symbolize the unbroken continuation of the process of life and death.

For the same reason, bagels were widely believed by Jews to have such magical attributes that they could guarantee good luck to those who ate, chewed, fondled or *wore* them. Do not snicker; the sophisticated Greeks thought so, too, since a circle, having neither beginning nor end, was celebrated as the "perfect" form. (This idea also accounted for the confident assumption that all the celestial orbits must be round—a widespread concept that stymied the finest astronomers, from Thales to Kepler.)

Bagels were once favored as a present to a woman after she gave birth to a child. They were widely used by European mothers as teething rings. In some countries, little bagels were strung out on strings and used as amulets for children, in the form of necklaces or bracelets.

The first printed mention of bagels, by the way, is to be found in the Jewish Community Regulations of Cracow, Poland, for the year 1610, where it was stated that bagels would be given as a free gift to any Jewish woman who was pregnant.

It has been estimated (or, more likely, guessed) that nine million bagels a day are consumed in the United States. There is scarcely a supermarket today that does not stock bagels, fresh or frozen. On St. Patrick's Day, some bakers smilingly sell *green* bagels! This is a feat of cross-cultural fertilization.

American bakeries, delicatessens and supermarkets sell as many as sixteen varieties of bagels: containing pumpernickel, rye, raisins, honey, cinnamon, etc., their crusts sprinkled with poppy seed, onion, salt, sesame seed, etc., etc.

Some "fast food" eateries feature bagels and burgers, French toast bagels, pizza bagels, hoagie (!) bagels, taco bagels and, for all I know, bacon on bagels.

———

I am told that bagel bakeries may be found in Nome, Alaska, in London and Manchester, in Tokyo and, most obviously, in Tel Aviv. Over three hundred bakeries in New York produce bagels.

One Lyle Fox, originally from Chicago, sells six thousand bagels a day in Japan—mostly to young Japanese women who consider bagels chic and spread them with dried fish or soy sauce(!).

The very thought of slices of tender lox, topping a layer of sweet butter on which cream cheese has been lathered, the whole enclosed by a toasted bagel is so delicious that, to stop the watering in my mouth, I am going out to lunch.

INTERMISSION

The proverbial man from Mars entered a Jewish bakery. "Hey, what are those small wheels?"

"They're not wheels," said the *baleboss*. "They're bagels. Here, try one."

The Martian did. A beatific smile crossed his lips. "Wow! These would go *great* with cream cheese and lox!"

On January 15, 1981, Teddy Kolleck, mayor of Jerusalem, shared the pulpit, wearing the red robe of an Episcopalian cleric, at the Cathedral of St. John the Divine in New York.

After the service, the Right Reverend James P. Morton, dean of the cathedral, invited the audience of seven hundred "to an informal reception with loaves and fishes—otherwise known as bagels and lox." (*New York Times*, January 16, 1981)

America *gonif!*

Sir Roland Tetherington, visiting New York, went into the famous Stage Door Delicatessen and, among other things, ordered, "A bagel, please."

"How would you like it?" asked the waiter.

"Um—" Sir Roland pondered, then said, "On rye."

See also BIALY, CHALLA, DELI, GEFILTE FISH, KOSHER.

baleboss   (masculine)
balebosteh (feminine)

> From Hebrew *baal* ("master") and *bayis* ("house").
> Pronounced, respectively, *bol-e*-BAWS, to rhyme with
> "Allah loss," and *bo-leh*-BUS-*ta*, to rhyme with "Walla
> puss, ma." *Balebosteh* is a Yiddish coinage.
>
> 1. The head of the household.
> 2. The owner of a store or shop.
> 3. Manager or superintendent.
>
> Considerable admiration was accorded the immigrant
> who escaped "working for a boss" by saving up enough
> money to become his own *baleboss*. Many Jewish
> women "worked in the store" (grocery, stationery,
> meat, fish, cigar, notions) alongside their husbands.
>
> 4. A conscientious, immaculate housewife-cook-laun-
>   dress-cleaner.

The highest compliment paid a *balebosteh* is "She keeps
a home so clean, *you could eat off the floor!*" No one I
knew ever did, in fact, eat off anyone else's floor, but I
cannot count the number of times I heard the phrase—
or the number of times that the symbolic riband of the
Jewish *Légion d'Honneur* was pinned upon my mother's
apron.

I was greatly impressed, as a child, by the obsession with
cleanliness in our household, and the scorn with which
untidiness was castigated. Cleanliness was not second to
godliness; it was second to nothing. The Talmud *bursts*
with urgent rules and warnings about personal hygiene.
(See chapter VIII of Rev. Dr. A. Cohen's *Everyman's Talmud*, Dutton).

A Texas oil magnate was touring Israel in a rented Cadil-
lac. Driving across a long, barren stretch of desert, he
beheld a small house. As he drew nearer he spied a man
leaning on the fence.

The Texan pulled to a stop. "Hiya, neighbor."

"*Shalom*," smiled the man.

"You live here, suh?"

"Sure."

"What in the world do you do, way out here in the middle of nowhere?"

"I raise chickens," the man replied.

The Texan surveyed the barren environs. "How much land do you own?"

"My lot is sixty by a hundred."

"Miles?"

"Oh, no, Mister. *Feet*."

"Well, well," the Texan grinned. "You know what, suh? Back home, I've got me a spread where I get in my car at nine A.M. and I drive and drive—and I don't even get to see the fence at the back of my property until four-thirty that afternoon!"

"My, my," sighed the *baleboss*. "I used to have a car like that."

On Houston Street, the window of Shimmel Kolach's hardware store contained this sign:

EVERYTING
FOR THE KICHEN

A passerby read the sign and promptly went in. "Where's the *baleboss*?"

"You are looking at him," said Mr. Kolach.

"There are two mistakes in English spelling in your window sign!"

"I know."

"Really?" frowned the passerby.

"Certainly. You think I'm a dummy?"

"Then why don't you correct the spelling?"

"Why should I correct it?" shrugged Kolach. "At least ten people a week come in to tell me about the mistakes— and at least *six*, once they're in, buy something!"

An immigrant entered a kosher restaurant on Delancey Street. The waiter who poured his water was—GOT-TENYU!—Chinese! And the Chinese servitor proceeded to rattle off the menu in fluent Yiddish, even unto the idiomatic grunts, sighs and *nu*'s.

When the immigrant had dined and was paying his bill, he asked the cashier, in Yiddish, "Are you the *baleboss*?"

"Who else?"

"Well, I certainly enjoyed the food—but even more, the fact that your waiter speaks such excellent Yiddish!"

"*Sha!*" hissed the proprietor. "He thinks we're teaching him English!"

––––––––

"My wife is such a great *baleboosteh*," boasted Frackman, "that she vacuums every room every day and puts a completely clean, empty bag in the Hoover every night!"

"Humph," said Kolchak. "I've got a wife who, whenever I get up in the middle of the night to go to the bathroom, changes the sheets."

Bar Mitzva
Bar Mitzvah

Part and parcel of modern Yinglish. Pronounced *bar*-MITZ-*vah*, to rhyme with "car *hits* ya." From the Hebrew: "son of the commandment" or more broadly, "man with [many] duties." *Bar Mitzvah*, a proper noun, is often used (inexactly) as a verb: "Allen was *bar mitzvahed* yesterday."

The ceremony, held in a synagogue or temple, in which a thirteen-year-old Jewish boy reaches the status and assumes the duties of a "man"—*i.e.*, becomes committed to lifelong adult religious and ethical obligations, among them being his eligibility to be counted as one of the ten males needed for public prayer (a *minyan*). Orthodox rabbis tend to insist that the *Bar Mitzva* be commemorated/celebrated on the boy's thirteenth birthday, according to the Hebrew calendar. Among Conservative and Reform rabbis, the date for the *Bar Mitzva* may be set according to the time the boy's parents expect the largest turnout of family and friends.

The *Bar Mitzva* ceremony, which did not exist until the fourteenth century (!), is *not* a sacrament; it is not a religious ritual; it simply signals the arrival of a Jewish boy at the age when, presumably, adult responsibilities commence.

The thirteenth year, in many cultures, is considered the beginning of puberty and is celebrated with initiation rites. Ancient rabbinical sources contain the alarming notification that after his thirteenth birthday a Jewish boy is responsible for observing no fewer than six hundred thirteen (!) holy commandments. (I must record my doubt that a careful accounting of this is kept, even in heaven.)

In Reform Judaism, there has arisen, in *addition* to the *Bar Mitzva*, a ceremony of confirmation—that is, the boy confirms his faith. (Orthodox Jews regard Jewishness as something that does not require confirmation.) In America the custom arose of delivering a *Bar Mitzva* speech that begins, "Today I am a man." When a rosy-cheeked thirteen-year-old announces this in a piping tenor, you may expect broad smiles, of both pride and polite dubiety, to dance through the congregation.

Today, the boy usually delivers a prayer, in Hebrew or English, and pledges himself to live up to the ideals of Judaism. He thanks his father and mother for all they have done for him. (At this point, parents' and grandparents' eyes well up.) The boy is called to the altar to read the week's section from the Torah.

To Jewish parents, the *Bar Mitzva* is a proud landmark of high symbolic meaning, *i.e.*, their son's dedication to the lofty precepts of an ancient people and tradition. Papa, Mama, sisters, brothers, grandparents, in-laws, friends, friends of friends, *all* of Papa's business associates, many of Mama's neighbors—all are present. The parents and grandparents beam and *kvell* (*q.v.*) to the bursting point. The father gives the boy a *tallis* (prayer shawl) of his own. A *Bar Mitzva* feast follows the service.

If you want to know more about *Bar Mitzvas*, go to one. They're charming, innocent and always put a lump in my throat. (For the equivalent ceremony for girls see BAS MITZVA.)

———

At the last *Bar Mitzva* I attended, I heard these stories and witticisms:

Two Martians who had landed in Haifa happened to run into each other.

"What's your name?" asked the first Martian.

"4286. And yours?"

"3359."

"That's funny, you don't look Jewish."

Joel Plintik was quite a ladies' man—and a wit. He took a lovely girl to dinner and, as they were having demitasse, said, "You know, Sally, I've enjoyed this so much I—well, I'd like to have breakfast with you!"

The girl smiled. "I'd like that, too . . ."

"Great!" Joel chuckled. "So tell me, what will I do: phone you or nudge you?"

You have a wonderful head on your shoulders; too bad it's not on your neck.

You have the manners of a perfect gentleman: whose are they?

I don't know what I would do without you—but I'd rather.

Our club is having a membership drive—to drive him out of the club.

He hasn't been himself lately: let's hope he stays that way.

> —The above are lifted from Henny Youngman
> and Joey Adams.

See also BAS MITZVA.

baruch ha-Shem
barukh ha-Shem

Hebrew: "Blessed be the Name [of the Lord]."

Pronounced *bah*-RUKH *ha*-SHEM. Use the guttural *kh* of "*Ach!*" Rhymes with "Ma Ruth ha Ben."

If you talk to a pious Jew or a devout rabbi of whatever denomination (Orthodox, Conservative or Reform), you will hear "*Baruch ha-Shem*" uttered often, just as you hear "God willing" or "If it please the Lord" from a devout Christian.

A recent telephone call with a rabbi friend of mine ran this way:

"How have you been?" I asked.

"Pretty well—now—*baruch ha-Shem*. I was in the hospital for three weeks. Had an automobile accident. But I'm fine now, *baruch ha-Shem*. How have you been?"

"I can't complain," said I.

"*Baruch ha-Shem*," said he.

Bas Mitzva
Bas Mitzvah
Bat Mitzva

Hebrew: "daughter of the commandment." Pronounced *bahs*-MITZ-*vah*, to rhyme with "Joss fits ya."

The "confirmation" or "coming-of-age" ceremony for girls, akin to the *Bar Mitzva* for boys.

In recent years, some Reform and Conservative congregations have introduced a *Bas Mitzva* ceremony, which is a *Bar Mitzva* for girls when they reach the age of *twelve*. (Boys become *Bar Mitzva* at the age of thirteen.) Girls mature earlier than boys.

Many an Orthodox Jew still shudders at the idea of a *Bas Mitzva*; others give a girl a *Bas Mitzva* at home, but not in the synagogue.

Bas Mitzva services are sometimes held for groups of girls from twelve to eighteen years of age.

———————

At my niece's *Bas Mitzva* I heard the following joke:

Mr. Lapidus approached a young man on Collins Avenue in Miami saying, "Excuse me, my boy . . . Are you Jewish?"

"No, I'm not," said the young man.

"Are you sure?"

"Of course I'm sure!"

"You're not—eh—just teasin' me?"

"No. Why should I tease you?"

Mr. Lapidus sighed. "I don't know. Stay well . . ." He started off.

"Wait." The young man glanced around and, lowering

his voice, said, "I'll tell you the truth, mister. Not a *soul* in Miami knows it! I'm a Jew."

Mr. Lapidus chortled, "Well, well. That certainly is funny! You don't *look* Jewish!"

See also BAR MITZVA.

B.C.E.

Initials for "Before the Common Era," used instead of B.C.

Jewish scholars and historians faced an uncomfortable problem in the use of B.C. and A.D. They could hardly accept Jesus as "*Our* Lord": Maimonides and earlier sages had held that the Messiah would restore the State of Israel, gather in the Exiles, rebuild the Temple—and after all that would come the Resurrection and then the Day of Judgment.

Since the Nazarene did not restore the State of Israel, gather in the Exiles or rebuild the Temple, the folk and rabbis of Palestine could not think of Yeshua (Jesus' name in Hebrew) as their *meshiach*.

Fortunately, *common* and *Christ* both begin with a *C*, so B.C. and A.D. are rendered in Jewish/Hebrew works of scholarship and reference as B.C.E. ("Before the Common Era") and A.C.E. ("After the Common Era").

Language is rarely so beneficent.

See also A.C.E., C.E.

begin already!

Yinglishmen have taken this phrase to their hearts. From Yiddish: *Fong shoyn on* (or *oon*). Exasperated entreaty: "Be*gin* already!"

This impatient, sarcastic, altogether annoyed outburst is Yinglish at its most expressive.

Nothing comparable to "Be*gin* already!" existed in conversational English before this direct translation from Yiddish was invoked by desperate Jews.

A delightful exercise in word-play concerns a Chinese man, named *Fong Oon* ("begin"), who had a father named *Oonfong* ("beginning"). *Oonfong* was an extremely impatient sort who would often explode to his dilatory son, "*Fong oon fun oonfang, Fong Oon!*"

A Hadassah group from Milwaukee touring England arrived at Runnymede Meadow, about nineteen miles west of London.

The Cook's Tour guide was chatting with several of the women when Bella Blaustein, the group leader, snapped, "Mr. Wetherby! We're always running late. So please, *begin* already!"

The guide sighed and addressed the assembled ladies: "We are standing on *very* historic ground, ladies. We are in Runnymede Meadow where, legend has it, under that very oak tree, King John signed the first real Declaration of Human Rights in all of human history!"

"When was that?" asked one woman.

"Twelve fifteen," replied Mr. Wetherby.

Mrs. Blaustein looked at her watch, then glared at Mr. Wetherby; "Missed it by twenty-three minutes!"

belittling someone simply by echoing his or her question—plus tonal embroidery or eloquent expressions

> Yiddish is incomparably rich in verbal devices to convey contempt, scorn, derision or incredulity. A much-used linguistic ploy, this technique is gaining wide usage among Yinglishmen.

> BELSON: How would you like two free round-trip tickets to Palm Beach?
>
> ICKELHEIM (glancing toward heaven): How would I like two free round-trip tickets to Palm Beach?!

> The seemingly innocent repetition of a question is rendered more powerful when accompanied by visual reinforcements: a dropped jaw ("I don't be*lieve* it!"), narrowed eyes ("You *can't* be serious!"), a gasp of surprise ("Are my ears *hear*ing correctly?") or unconcealed disgust ("What sort of fool do you take me for by asking me such a cockamamy question?").

"How much will such an extraction cost me, Doctor?" asked Mrs. Gittler.

"Fifty dollars," said the dentist.

"Fifty dollars!" exclaimed Mrs. Gittler. "Isn't that a lot of money for a few minutes' work?"

"Isn't that a lot of money for a few minutes' work?!" the dentist repeated, forcing a smile. "For you, Mrs. Gittler, I can pull it out very, *very* slowly."

See also DEFLATION . . . , EXPOSING ABSURDITY . . .

ben
bene (plural)

> Hebrew: "son." Rhymes with "hen."
> Son, or son of.

A Jew is considered a *ben b'rith*, or "son of the covenant [with God]."

Before family names were common, a Jew was known by his given name plus the name of his father, *e.g.*, Yochanan *ben* [son of] Zakkai. Sometimes the form used was *bar*, which is Aramaic: Shimon bar Kochba. For a girl, one said *bas*: Rivka bas Bethuel.

The old form—*i.e.*, Yitzchok ben Shmuel—is still used on some wedding certificates and in the synagogue when a man is called up to read a passage from the Torah.

Many European Zionists, emigrating to Palestine/Israel, changed their names to Hebrew; thus, David Gruen became David Ben-Gurion. Jewish actors sometimes did the same: Jacob Shieron became Jacob Ben-Ami. Israel is full of *ben*s.

Hebrew names ending in the letter *i* mean "son of . . . ," "son of the tribe . . . ," "son of the clan of . . ." Such identifications were imperative because the Hebrews did not have family names. A legal document might be signed "Simon ben Avrum" (Simon son of Avrum) or even, when the names were too common, "Simon ben Avrum ben Yitzkhok."

benefit

Yinglish, without the slightest doubt, this metaplasm puts a straightforward English word to new uses.

A sponsored performance—of a play, a recital, a concert, a lecture—in which the proceeds are used for the benefit of the subsidizing organization.

The benefit (no need to add "performance") was underwritten by a Jewish fraternal society, guild, *verein*, trade union, or organization composed of immigrants from the same city in the Old Country (Warsaw, Vilna, Odessa, Bialystok). Hundreds of such communities of *landsman* flourished in New York and other cities with large Jewish populations.

The organization would put up the money for the production, paying the theater or producers in advance, then sell the tickets to its membership—and to the public at large. The price of the tickets represented a profit to the sponsoring group, which used the money for its educational or philanthropic program.

As a child in Chicago, I was often taken by my parents to meetings of the Workmen's Circle (Lodzer Branch) and to endless benefits, concerts, recitals, choral groups, Yiddish-theater parties.

In an old theater on Blue Island Avenue I saw admirable performances in Yiddish by New York companies in such classics as *Yoshe Kalb, The Dybbuk, The Golem*. It was theater in the grand style and European tradition.

Bes Midrash
Bet Midrash
Bes Medrash
Beth Ha-Midrash

Pronounced *bess*-MID (or MED)-*rosh*, to rhyme with "less bid (or red) fish." Hebrew: "House of Study." Yiddish pronounces the terminal *t* as *s*. Sometimes used as another name for a synagogue.

House of Study, usually part of a synagogue.

The *Bes Midrash* was originally the place where male Jews met to study; since prayers were frequent there, the name came to be used for synagogue, too.

Study and prayer, or (better) study-prayer, was the most potent mortar in Jewish life and history. It lent meaning and purpose to the most desperate of existences. It illuminated life. It ennobled, inspired, redeemed. It admitted even the humblest Jew to the company of sages, prophets, scholars and saints.

Virtually *all* of male Jewry used to participate in a perpetual seminar—on the Torah and the Talmud. Even the cobblers. Even the tailors. The drovers and diggers, farmhands and carpenters. The peddlers and beggars and shopkeepers.

It is a fact of tremendous importance that every male Jew past the age of six (except for mental deficients) could read and write! They were all arguers and dialecticians and amateur theologians. W. E. H. Lecky, the Irish historian, summarized the Jewish ethos during the Middle Ages in this singular passage:

> While those around them were grovelling in the darkness of besotted ignorance; . . . while the intellect of Christendom, enthralled by countless superstitions, had sunk into a deadly torpor in which all love of enquiry and all search for truth were abandoned, the Jews were still pursuing the path of knowledge, amassing learning, and stimulating progress with the same unflinching constancy that they manifested in their faith. They were the most skilful physicians, the ablest financiers, and among the most profound philosophers. Jewish communities all over Europe automatically established study groups, communally supported.
> —*The Rise and Influence of Rationalism in Europe*,
>   vol. 2, p. 271

In 1887 in the small town of Kroz, *nine* separate study societies thrived. Kroz had only two hundred Jewish families, but supported twelve teachers (two women, to teach girls), and two bookbinders!

> In almost every Jewish home in Eastern Europe, [wrote Abraham Joshua Heschel] even in the humblest and poorest, stood a bookcase full of volumes. . . . Almost every Jew gave of his time to learning, studying the Talmud. . . . At nightfall, almost everyone would leave the tumult and bustle of everyday life to study in the *beth ha-Midrash*. And in the House of Study, every Jew sat like (an) intellectual magnate. . . . When a problem came up, there was immediately a host of people pouring out opinions, arguments, quotations. . . . The stomachs were

empty, the homes barren, but the minds were crammed with the riches of the *Torah*.

—*The Earth Is the Lord's*, pp. 42–44

Once I noticed [writes a Christian scholar, who visited the city of Warsaw during the First World War] a great many coaches on a parking place but with no drivers in sight. In my own country I would have known where to look for them. A young Jewish boy showed me the way: in a court-yard, on the second floor, was the *shtibl* [room] of the Jewish drivers. It consisted of two rooms: one filled with *Talmud*-volumes, the other a room for prayer. All the drivers were engaged in fervent study and religious discussion. . . . It was then that I found out . . . that all professions, the bakers, the butchers, the shoemakers, etc., have their own *shtibl* in the Jewish district; and every free moment which can be taken off from their work is given to the study of the *Torah*. And when they get together in intimate groups, one urges the other: "*Sog mir a shtickl Torah*—Tell me a little *Torah*."

—*Ibid.*, p. 46

Many, many Yiddish words are related to study and scholarship.

See also MELAMED, TALMUD, YESHIVA.

Beth Ha-Midrash

See BES MIDRASH.

Better you [he, she] should . . .

Metaphrase, from Yiddish: *Beser zolst du*: "Better should you . . ."

The Yinglish version of "It would be better if you . . ."

The phrase has appeared more often in novels, plays, and short stories (by Jewish writers) than it does in life. I am glad this is so: "Better you should" makes me shudder.

Minnie Gerber was plain, shy, thirty-two—and unmarried, and her mother grieved sorely over her plight.

One day, Mrs. Gerber said, "Don't get mad, Minnie—

but I have a good idea. To end this sitting around, night
after night, hoping *maybe* some nice man—from where?
from the clouds? from a star?—will come along—''

"Mama!"

"Better you should put an ad in the newspaper . . .''

"Mama! You have to be joking!"

"I'm not joking.''

"But the *shame*—''

"What shame? You don't give your *name*. Like this.''
Mrs. Gerber handed her daughter a slip of paper, on which
she had printed:

> JEWISH GIRL FROM FINE FAMILY,
> EDUCATED, GOOD COOK,
> BIG READER, AGE 27, WOULD LIKE TO MEET
> INTELLIGENT, REFINED JEWISH GENTLEMAN.
> OBJECT: MATRIMONY.
> —BOX 703.

Minnie stammered and gulped protestations, but her
mother insisted, "What's to *lose*? And just think of what
could happen!"

And so the advertisement appeared. And each morning
the girl known as Box 703 hastened down three flights of
stairs to meet the postman.

On the fifth day, she came running up and burst into
the apartment: "Mama! An answer! Forwarded from the
paper!" With flushed cheeks, Minnie ripped open the envelope, devoured the contents—and burst into tears.

"Minnie!" cried Mrs. Gerber. "What's wrong?!"

The girl gasped, "It's from Papa.''

———

Old Chaim Preisinger, on his deathbed, was dictating his
last will to his old friend and lawyer. "So—my first son,
Simcha, he should have fifty thousand dollars. My daughter, Rosie, she should have one hundred thousand dollars.
And my son Josiah, he should have fifty thousand
dollars . . ."

"Just a minute," said the lawyer. "Your whole estate
comes to four thousand dollars, Chaim. How do you expect
your loved ones to get fifty thousand dollars, one hundred
thousand dollars—''

"That's their business," croaked the old man. "Better
they should work their heads off for it, the way I did!"

bialy

As much part of Yinglish as *bagel, lox* or *alrightnik*.
A slightly underbaked roll shaped like a rubber wading pool, with baked onion sprinkled in the declivity.

The name *bialy* is the affectionate diminutive for Bialystok, the city in Poland where Jewish bakers perfected this extraordinary confection. If you ask me, the bakers made Bialystok immortal.

Bialys have become almost as much a part of New York breakfast cuisine as *bagels*. They can also be toasted, lathered with butter, cream cheese and lox. I *love* them.

Jonah Ehrlich bought a large home in Westchester. His wife staffed it with English servants and invited three couples out for their first Sunday brunch of the season: the Benders, the Strausses and the Brechers.

On Sunday morning, Mrs. Ehrlich noticed that the table was set for twelve. "Henshaw!" she called.

"Yes, madam," said the butler.

"You have set the table for twelve."

"Yes, madam."

"But I told you *three* couples were coming. Plus me and my husband—that makes eight in all."

"Yes, madam."

"Then *why* did you set plates for twelve?"

"Well, madam, Mrs. Bender phoned just an hour ago. She told me she is bringing the Bagels and the Bialys."

Late one fearful night—the rain pouring down, the storm blowing in fury—Mr. Salov was about to close his delicatessen when a man staggered through the door. "A bialy!" he gasped.

"One bialy. And—?"

"That's all."

"That's *all*?" Mr. Salov could hardly believe his ears. "No cream cheese—"

"No."

"A piece lox?"

"No."

Mr. Salov stared at the dripping stranger. "On a terrible night like this, you came out for—one—bialy?"

"That's what she wants."

"*She*?!" echoed Salov. "Your wife?"

"Certainly, it's my wife! Do you think my *mother* would send me out for one lousy bialy on a night like this?"

"*Hanh*?" exclaimed Mrs. Harnish. "You're asking a dollar a dozen for your *bialys*?!"

"That's right, lady."

"But Fenshel's, right across the street, is asking only ninety cents!"

"So, lady, go buy them across the street."

"Across the street *today*," mourned Mrs. Harnish, "he hasn't got a bialy in his store!"

"When *I* don't have a bialy in my store," said the *bale-boss*, "I charge only *sixty* cents a dozen!"

See also BAGEL.

big deal

Yinglish, *par excellence*. Directly from the Yiddish: *A groyser kunst!*: "Some big art!" (meant quite sarcastically). Pronounced with the emphasis strongly on *big*.

1. A derisive dismissal of someone's statement, boast or proud appraisal.
2. An emphatic put-down.

Although it would seem that "big deal," consisting of two perfectly ordinary English words, is an English expression, the fact is that that locution, as a sneer or jeer or gibe, was introduced into English quite recently: in the 1940s, according to the authoritative *Dictionary of American Slang*, edited by Harold Wentworth and Stuart Berg Flexner.

"I just closed a big deal," is *not* the usage I am talking about. My entry celebrates "Big deal!" as a retort, a put-down, a dry deflation of anyone's claim of an achievement:

"You know what I [he, she, they] just did?"

"What?"

"Won third place in our town's fashion contest!"

"*Big* deal . . ."

Unlike so many words or idioms, the provenance of "Big deal!" can be given with exactitude. The comedian Arnold Stang, who always portrayed the classic *shlemiel*, made "Big deal!" his trademark or *shtik* (*q.v.*)—first, on the Henry Morgan radio show, then on Milton Berle's enormously popular television series.

The colorful, cutting phrase was so effective that it was picked up by other entertainers. It seemed perfectly at home on the *Jack Benny Show*, for example.

"Big deal" has by now become a standard wisecrack on television's sitcoms, talk shows and comedy skits. It will surely endure—because of its built-in sneer and ironic impact.

In Yiddish, a similar retort, conveying the utmost scorn, is the exclamation *khokhma!* (use the Scottish or German sound as in *loch, ach!*) with the emphasis on the final syllable.

At a suburban train platform, just as a train starts to close its doors, Mr. Shamish frantically runs alongside it.

The train starts to pull out.

Mr. Shamish, huffing and puffing, stops his chase and in a burst of defiance hollers at the train: "*Bi-ig* deal!"

This delightful vignette has been embroidered down the years. The version I like best is this:

The old Jew shouts at the departing train, "*Khokhma!*" and shakes his fist at the train.

Nearby, a woman asks, "Mister, why are you so mad?"

"Because I missed that damn train by two *seconds*!"

"Humph!" the woman scoffed. "The way you're carrying on you could have missed it by two *hours*!"

Bite your tongue!

Yinglish, from the Yiddish *Bays di tsung*, or *Bays dir di tsung*: "Bite your tongue!"

"Say no more!" "Stop right there!"

Why is this Yinglish? Because in English we say either "*Hold* your tongue!" or "Bite your *lip*!"

This colorful imperative is particularly pictorial: Biting your tongue is a foolproof way to stop acting the fool, or revealing something embarrassing.

SCENE: A Park Bench, Brighton Beach

After sitting for a while in silence, Mrs. Elkin sighed to her friend, "Nellie . . ."

"Yeh, Sophie?"

Sophie shrugged, shook her head and sighed, "Oy-y."

Nellie nodded. "Oy-oy-oy."

Sophie murmured, "Oy-y-y-y-y!"

Said Nellie sharply, "Enough! Bite your tongue! Didn't we agree not to talk about our children?!"

blintz (singular)
blintzes (plural)

Nearly every English dictionary contains *blintzes*. From Ukrainian: pancake.

A pancake folded around pot cheese (or strawberries, cherries, blackberries, potatoes, apples, peaches) and fried to a crisp golden brown. Also known as Jewish *crêpes suzettes*. A feature of Jewish Sunday breakfasts or brunches.

Jews adore blintzes slathered with sour cream.

Latter-day converts to this confection have taken to capping blintzes with brown sugar, honey or jam. The only justification I can see for not using sour cream is that you don't have any—not that blintzes in any form, stuffed or topped however you want, are not altogether delicious.

The historic victory of Israel in the Six-Day War was hailed by the wits in Tel Aviv as a *Blintzkrieg*.

There is no shortage of wits in Tel Aviv. When I was there, I sometimes felt I was caught behind the lines—in a *Vitskrieg*.

The old Lindy's Restaurant, the renowned hang out of Broadway's actors, singers and vaudeville comedians, and

Sardi's, a favorite water-hole for "show biz" luminaries from Hollywood (and even London), were unfailing sources of humor—for writers and columnists like Damon Runyon, Walter Winchell, Leonard Lyons, O. O. McIntyre, etc. I cannot recall how many funny anecdotes, jokes and ad-libbed one-liners I heard, down the years, at Lindy's or at Sardi's, but that was hardly surprising, considering the "regulars" one was sure to encounter in those hang outs every night after 11:30 P.M., when the theaters completed their performances, and after 12:30 or 1:00 A.M., when the nightclub routines finished.

What with the journalists, actors and stand-up comedians, jocularity would rock the walls from the wit (or ghostwit) of masters like Phil Silvers, Milton Berle, Jackie Gleason, Red Buttons, Bob Hope, one or another Marx Brother, the immortal Smith and Dale ("The *Sunshine Boys*"), Fred Allen, Jerry Lewis—the list seems endless.

But we were talking about blintzes:

SCENE: **Lindy's**

CUSTOMER: Tell me: how are the *blintzes* tonight?
WAITER: How *are* they? They're the best we've had in *years*.
CUSTOMER (grimacing): I'll wait for a fresh batch.

bluffer (masculine)
blufferkeh (feminine)

You can't get more Yinglishy than this neologism coined from the English *bluff*. Rhyme with "duffer" and "duffer-keh."

Please note that the following uses of *bluffer* are *not* like the English words, which describe a strategy or strategist in the game of poker:

1. A congenital boaster.
2. One who exaggerates in a flattering or conceited manner.
3. A man or woman given to hyperbole.
4. A cheat; a con man.
5. A chronic deceiver.

"He's nothing but a *bluffer*" is tantamount to saying "He's nothing but hot air."

"Watch out for her—she's a seductive *blufferkeh*."

When extra forcefulness is sought, speakers of Yinglish will add prejudice to disparagement:

"Don't trust that Galitzianer *bluffer*!"
"I wouldn't lend a penny to a Litvak *bluffer* like that!"

———————

Lottie Moss, a salesgirl at the perfume counter of a fancy lingerie shop, rang up record sales because of her ingenious sales pitch: lowering her voice and narrowing her eyes, she'd murmur, "Listen, madam, I am warning you: *Don't* wear Purple Passion scent if you're only bluffing. See what I mean?"

B'nai Brith

Modern Hebrew: "Sons of the covenant." (The *-th* ending never appeared in classical Hebrew.) Pronounce it to rhyme with "Hooray Smith."
   The world's largest organization of Jewish men, organized in 1843. It devotes itself to many educational, vocational guidance, philanthropic, community and inter-faith activities. It supports the Hillel Foundations on two hundred forty college campuses.

The organization founded the superb nonsectarian National Jewish Hospital in Denver. Perhaps B'nai Brith's best-known division is the Anti-Defamation League, established in 1913, which has long studied and fought discrimination, prejudice, and anti-Semitism.

B'nai Brith has over 500,000 members in over forty countries, and many component agencies. B'nai Brith Women, organized in 1897, engages in a wide variety of programs: adult education, human rights, public affairs, and invaluable services to Israel. There are around 120,000 members.

bobbe

See BUBBE.

bobbe-maise

See BUBBE-MAYSE.

bobbe-mayse

See BUBBE-MAYSE.

bobkes

See BUPKES.

boo-boo

Yinglish origin, now widely accepted as English slang. Origin: see below.

1. A boner; an embarrassing *faux pas*.
2. A verbal blunder; a Freudian slip.
3. A malapropism.
4. Euphemism for accidental loss of bowel contents by a child or baby.

The use of *boo-boo* for "boner" or "mistake" rocketed to public attention around 1949–1950 as a trademark of the comedian Jerry Lewis in nightclub and television skits with his partner, Dean Martin. *Boo-boo* became popular among radio and television performers; it was (and is) a funny-sounding, indispensable label for any *faux pas*.

"In front of the whole class? What a boo-boo!"

The august *Oxford English Dictionary* states that *boo-boo* comes from the English *boob*. That may be true in England–if *boo-boo* is used to name a foolish utterance by a boob. But a *boo-boo*, as used today, especially on television (the greatest, swiftest disseminator of idioms, solecisms, paronyms, neologisms, syncopes and verbal blunder) is not necessarily committed by a boob. The wisest of men, and the biggest of brains, can "make a boo-boo." All malapropisms or spoonerisms are known to the great mass of Americans as boo-boos.

Boo-boos are a delightful source of laughter to anyone with an appreciation of accidental wit or humorous incongruity.

The most memorable of all unintended revelations, to my mind, was the one committed by some cable operator who sent the following message from a man at a convention in Paris to his wife in Cincinnati:

> HAVING WONDERFUL TIME.
> WISH YOU WERE HER.
>
> CHARLEY.

I think Sigmund Freud would have burst into laughter at that insightful *boo-boo*.

———

As straight malapropisms, boo-boos appear every day—and many deserve preservation. Here are some favorites from radio:

> ". . . the President of the United States, Hoobert Heever."
> "It strikes me as funny, don't you?"
> "I present to you the distinguished Virgin of Governor's Island."
> "Do you wake up feeling tired and lustless?"

Other famous boners may not classify as malapropisms, technically, but a few more laughs may enliven your day and lower your cholesterol. The following gems appeared in high school examinations:

> "The language spoken in Latin America is Latin."
> "Sid Caesar was a Roman emperor."
> "Montreal is the capital of Spain."
> "The Grand Canyon is one mile high and two miles deep."

———

Boo-boo, or "boom-boom," as a euphemism for *bowel movement* began as a parent's or nurse's code word (like "B.M.," for a child's "accident" in diapers or panties).

Among non-Jews in the Bronx and other boroughs of New York, the tympanic "boom-boom" served as the code word or genteel designation for a child's bowel movement.

———

Alex Spindel, a Hollywood producer in New York to see the plays, met an extremely beautiful (if dim-witted) chorus girl. After a giddy two-day courtship, Alex married the girl.

Back in his home in the Hollywood Hills, Alex decided to give a dinner party, to introduce his bride to his friends.

"Lily, you're going to meet some of the brightest writers and directors in the movie business—"

"Oh, sweetie," frowned Lily, "I have to tell you, I'm as nervous as a *cat*. All those educated, high-brow types—what can a girl like little ol' me *possibly* have to talk to them about?!"

"Doll, there's not a thing to worry about. *They'll* talk your ears off! All you have to do is smile and nod and say, 'That *is* amusing,' or 'How interesting!' . . . They'll adore you."

Alex was right. The new Mrs. Spindel charmed one and all, listening, wide-eyed, smiling. . . . Only after the dessert did she make a boo-boo.

As Alex stood up at the table, saying to the guests, "Shall we have coffee in the library?" his lovely Lily trilled, "Honey, do you think it's open this late at night?"

See also BOOM-BOOM.

boom-boom

Yinglish: genteel expression for a baby's bowel movement, akin to the long-used English "B.M."

Those who remember that marvel of television humor, the weekly serial, *All in the Family*, will have no trouble recalling what "boom-boom" referred to: little Joey's big, diaper-filling bowel movements.

Boom-boom bears a sonic relation to *boo-boo*, to be sure, but I think it unlikely that Bronxians coined the former out of the latter. A large explosion of stomach gas was called a "boomer," as was a large deposit in a baby's diaper.

borsht
borscht

Pronounced BOAR-SHT; from the Slavonic (and, possibly, Turkish).

Beet soup.

I see no reason to spell it *borscht* instead of *borsht*: In Yiddish, the *sh* sound is conveyed by one letter, the *shin*; there are no *sch* spellings. To use the *sch* cluster in *borsht* is to give it an entirely false Germanic provenance. On restaurant menus, *borsht* is sometimes spelled *borscht* (!) or even *borshch*(!)—this I encountered in a Russian cafe.

Beet soup is served hot or cold (delicious!), often with a slab of sour cream (superb!), sometimes with cucumber slices or chopped egg floating on it (a *mechaieh*!).

Borsht was a great staple among Jews, because beets were so cheap and plentiful. (In fact, they were cheap *because* they were plentiful.) "You don't need teeth to eat *borsht*." Another Jewish saying goes, "*Billig vi borsht*": "Cheap as *borsht*."

Borsht Belt

That sizable suzerainty in the Catskill and Pocono Mountains, ninety miles from New York City, the vacation paradise of summer (and now winter) resorts that cater to, and once were almost exclusively patronized by, Jews. Grossinger's was perhaps the most renowned. The best-known today in "the Jewish Alps" are the Concorde, Kutscher's, Brown's, Nevele.

The "Borsht Belt Riviera" was famed for staggering, monumental amounts of kosher food, superb dill (new) pickles, sublime chicken soup with mounds of matzo balls or noodles (or both), delicious rolls and breads of infinite variety, cakes and cheesecakes and chocolate concoctions galore.

From this legendary mountain Valhalla came (and still come) some of the most brilliant comedic talents (actors, actresses, writers, directors) in American vaudeville, movies, radio and television. Many acted as entertainment *tummlers* around the clock. The briefest of lists would include Smith and Dale ("The *Sunshine Boys*"), Fanny Brice, Moss Hart, Gallagher and Sheen (!), Jack Benny, George Jessel, Jerry Lewis, George Burns and Gracie Allen, Sid Caesar, Martha Raye, Phil Silvers, Danny Kaye, Milton Berle, the Ritz Brothers, The Avon Comedy Four, Red Buttons, Joey Bishop, Shecky Greene, Buddy Hackett—but need I go on?

SCENE: A Hotel Restaurant in the Catskills

MR. MENDEL: Waiter, I'll have the *borsht*.
WAITER: Take my advice; have instead the chicken soup.
MRS. MENDEL: I'll have pea soup.
WAITER: Don't take the pea soup—take the barley.
  The soup is brought, the customers served.
MR. MENDEL: This chicken soup is marvelous! The best I
  ever tasted!
MRS. MENDEL: Waiter! Why didn't you recommend *me*
  the chicken soup?
WAITER: *You* didn't ask for the *borsht*!

———

SCENE: The Long Porch of a Catskills Resort

The women were rocking back and forth, gazing at the
lovely sunset.
"And how many children," asked Mrs. Alpert, "do you
have?"
"No children," sighed Mrs. Minkoff.
"*No* children?!" blinked Mrs. Alpert. "What do you do
for aggravation?"

———

From a Borsht Belt menu:

Today's Special
Barely soup

———

On another menu:

Dreaded Veal Cutlet

———

The three ladies at the lunch table in Toplinski's Catskill
Paradise hotel ("Absolutely Kosher, 100%, Certified *Scho-
chet* on Premises!") fell to discussing their children with
customary pride.
"My son," said the first woman, "is a famous doctor,
who already is secretary of the Medical Association in
Flemington, New Jersey!"
"*That's* nice," said the second mother. "*My* boy, Al-
fred, is already a professor in Columbia University Law
School!"
"Oh, *my*!" said the third woman, "*My* son, Harold, is
in Buffalo, the rabbi of the finest temple—"

"A *rabbi*?!" cried the other two. "What kind of career is that for a Jewish boy?!"

___

SCENE: **A Dance Hall in the Borsht Belt, 1925**

YOUNG MAN: Are you dencing?
YOUNG LADY: Are you esking?
YOUNG MAN: I'm esking.
YOUNG LADY: I'm dencing.

___

Why is it that the walls in a Catskills hotel room are very thin when you try to sleep and very thick when you want to listen?

bottom line

Yinglish phrase, so familiar that very few realize it is a direct metaphrase from the Yiddish: "*untershte shure*." "What's the bottom line?" means:

1. "What does this all boil down to?"
2. "What does it add up to?"
3. "Cut all the trimmings; how much will it *cost*?"
4. "What is the absolutely minimal commitment required to conclude this deal [negotiation, bargaining, contract, merger, lawsuit]?"

Within the past decade, "What's the bottom line?" has taken a firm place in English. The phrase has spread with uncommon swiftness simply because it is impossible to misunderstand. It has the quality of exactitude for which there is no substitute.

But this phrase has long, long been familiar to speakers of Yiddish, or Jews who understand Yiddish. For instance: a public speaker (and in Jewish circles, lectures are a common part of the cultural-political scene) often concluded his speech with this phrase, "*Di untershte shure iz—*"

In one or another setting, a long-winded lecturer, or a participant in a discussion, would often be interrupted by impatient listeners: "So, *vos iz di untershte shure?*"

Sol Steinmetz's careful study, *Yiddish and English* (University of Alabama), suggests that the phrase may have first taken off in New York's financial-commercial community "where one frequently hears accountants, stockbrokers, salesmen and merchants use Yiddish words and expressions." Steinmetz cites the appearance of "the bottom line" in *The New Yorker, Saturday Review*, and *TV Guide*. To this group I would add *The Wall Street Journal*, the business section of the *New York Times, Barrons, Forbes, et alia*.

————————

"Did that economist paint a picture of the months ahead!"
"What was the bottom line?"
"The bottom line? No depression."

boychik

Pure, popular, toothsome Yinglish: a paronym from conventional English: "boy" plus the Yiddish/Slavic diminutive *-chik*.

Many and varied are the connotations of this delightful word:

1. Little boy.
2. Affectionate/admiring term for a male, young or old.
3. A mischievous, charming scalawag.
4. A shrewd corner-cutter; a clever operator.
5. A condescending appellation; a put-down.

This neologism is deployed with various shades of meaning:

Proudly: "You know my brother? Some *boychik*!"
Fondly: "Take my word, *boychik*; she's not your type."
Ironically: "Pushing seventy, he's chasing after girls. Some *boychik*!"
In warning: "When you deal with that *boychik*, leave your wallet at home."
As a put-down: "Look, *boychik*, I know what you're up to."

Boychikel diminutizes the diminutive—for enhanced fondness or sarcasm:

"Listen, *boychikel*, I can give you lessons in brains!"
"You know, you're not a *boychikel* anymore, Moe. Go slow."

Here is Freud's favorite story, the one he used to crown his analysis of the manipulation of reason in Jewish jokes. This is the way I tell it:

> Two traveling salesmen, competitors, meet in a railway station. They exchange *sholem aleichems*. They eye each other.
> "So—eh—where are you going?"
> "I'm going to Pinsk."
> "Pinsk? . . . Listen, *boychik*: when you tell me you're going to Pinsk, you expect me to figure you're going to Minsk. But I happen to know you *are* going to Pinsk—so *why are you lying?*"

"And another thing, Harry, the reason you are not popular is that you are such a smarty pants—always know the answer, always ready with criticism. *Boychik*, you are just too pretentious!"
"Pre*ten*tious?" echoed Harry. "*Moi?*"

Two elderly Jews sat side by side on a bench overlooking a lake in the Catskills. They were watching a girl in a bikini on a surfboard that was being towed at great speed across the surface of the water behind a motorboat.

The men watched the boat pull the surfboard the full length of the lake, then turn in a great, foaming arc, and speed the girl back—to the other end of the lake, where the sweeping, white-crested turn was repeated.

After studying this action, one of the men stood up saying, "*Boychik*, I think I'll start back to the hotel."

"Wait, wait," said the other. "What's your hurry?"

"I'm not in a hurry."

"So why don't you stay and watch those two?"

"What for? Can't you see she'll never catch him?"

bread (slang)

From Yiddish: *broyt*. A loan-word converted to a new, ancillary meaning. Yinglish as all get-out.

1. Among jazz musicians: money.

Yiddish makes widespread use of *broyt* as a substitute for *money;* "*a shver shtickl broyt*" ("a hard little piece of bread"); "*Er hargert zikh zu makhen a shtickl broyt*" ("He kills himself to earn a piece of bread").

Jazz musicians and nightclub entertainers, of whom many were Jewish, began to use *bread* to mean money, or "a living." Black musicians quickly adopted this usage, which spread through black urban culture.

I distinguish the Yinglish use of *bread* from the straightforward English, as in Conan Doyle, say, where a blackmailer tells Sherlock Holmes, "Here's how I make my humble bread."

2. Among rock-and-rollers and in the drug culture, *bread* is sometimes inside cant for "the wherewithal," the loot (from a mugging), the cash with which to purchase "the stuff," "the candy," or "the fixin's."

bris
Brith Milah

Bris is Yiddish; *brith*, or *brit*, is Hebrew. In Hebrew, *milah* means circumcision: *Brith Milah*: "covenant of circumcision." (There was no *-th* ending in Hebrew, originally; only a few hundred years ago did biblical scholars, both Hebrew and gentile, replace the terminal *-t* with *-th*.)

The ceremony, on the eighth day of a Jewish boy's life, which attends his circumcision, "the cutting of his foreskin."

The Lord (in Genesis 17:10) declared it His covenant that every Hebrew "man-child" should be circumcised. This slitting and removal of the prepuce imprints into the male body a life-long sign that Israel will be perpetuated through his seed. (Among the early Christians, baptism was called "sealing.")

I have many memorable things to tell you about circumcision, but the most astounding concerns Abraham (or Abram), the patriarch to whom the Hebrews (and many Arabian people) trace their ancestry. (By tradition, in fact, Arab legends hold that he laid the foundation of Mecca.)

This Abraham, a great and very brave man, circumcised himself—at the age of forty-nine.

Jesus of Nazareth was circumcised on January 1; some Christian creeds still celebrate that momentous event.

Circumcision is formally described as "the covenant of Abraham our Father." Tradition has it that Abraham sits at Hell's gate, and will not allow any circumcised Jew to be incarcerated there. (I cannot tell you what a comfort this is.)

Now, to return to the *bris* and the details of circumcision. The operation was always performed by a *mohel* (pronounce it MOY-*el*) who is *not* a rabbi, but a specialist in slitting with a double-edged knife of maximal sharpness. The cut is very swift and cannot be interrupted.

Orthodox and tradition-bent Jews still insist on a *mohel*'s performing the operation. A great many modern Jews ask an M.D., sometimes the obstetrician himself, to do the cutting. (Males who convert to Judaism are obliged to undergo circumcision.)

Before the circumcision, the baby is carried to the waiting males, who, as the boy is handed to the *Sandak* (godfather), recite this blessing in Hebrew: "Blessed be he that cometh."

After the baby is placed on the *Sandak*'s knees, a formal religious service begins. Indeed, throughout and before and after the circumcision, prayers ascend to heaven. The most significant, immediately after God's seal has been effected, is this one:

> May this lad grow in vigor of mind and of body to a love of the *Torah*, to the *chuppa* [wedding canopy] and to a life of virtuous deeds.

A name is now given to the boy; a blessing is offered over a small glass of sacramental wine—of which a drop is placed on the baby's lips.

Now comes the *bris*, or celebration with wine and, usually, sponge cake.

Many and horrendous were the punishments Jews have suffered down the ages for circumcising their boys: Hadrian forbade the rite (which in part led to Bar Kochba's rebellion); Antiochus Epiphanes, a friend of Caligula, instituted the death penalty (!) for circumcision; a monarch of the Visigoths named Sisebut, about whom I know no more than his startling name, demanded that Jews replace circumcision with baptism. No monarch succeeded in stopping the Jews from fulfilling God's commandments.

Circumcision is far from a uniquely Jewish rite: nor did the ancient Hebrews invent it. Herodotus tells us that the Phoenicians, Syrians and Ethiopians performed the cutting of the foreskin. Among Muslims, circumcisions (called "purification") is mandatory—no pun intended. Eskimos and American Indian tribes practice circumcision.

In a good many cultures, women refuse sexual union with an uncircumcised *bravo*. Circumcision rites have been noted by anthropologists in Africa, Indonesia, Australia.

Centuries ago circumcision was regarded as hygienically desirable; slitting the foreskin of the penis was considered preventative of penile infections and possible damage to the kidneys or urinary tract.

When the alleged medical and hygienic value of circumcision became generally known, hordes of non-Jews had their baby boys circumcised—so much so that it is no longer possible to tell Jews from *goyim* in the showers of gymnasia. (My research in this area has not been systematic.)

About three decades ago, American doctors began to question whether any possible advantages were offset by the pain and possible psychological trauma inflicted upon the baby boy. A committee appointed by the American Medical Association was instructed to research the problem.

The American Academy of Pediatrics, the world's largest organization of pediatricians (37,000 members), declared in 1971, and several times thereafter, that there were "no valid medical indications" for the performance of routine circumcision. In many states, Blue Cross–Blue Shield health insurance groups stopped paying for circumcisions, considered "unnecessary for medical purposes."

But on March 5, 1989, the academy announced that, according to extensive research conducted at Brooke Army Medical Center in Texas, comparing the records of 427,698 babies born in hospitals from 1975 through 1984, uncircumcised boys suffered eleven times more often than circumcised boys from urinary tract infections during the first year of life! The American Academy now announced that there were "potential medical benefits and advantages" to circumcision.

Lawrence K. Altman's report in the *New York Times* for March 6, 1989, cautions that the results may have been skewed by the army's reviewing process. Still (or even "Nu?"), the difference in official attitude from 1971 to 1989 is of considerable significance.

One of my favorite stories about a *bris* involves the one where Mr. Kotcher patted a swaddled baby held by Mr. Samuels and beamed, "Say, you sure have a beautiful little boy there!"

Mr. Samuels frowned. "First, Kotcher, it's not a boy. And second, will you please stop squeezing my finger!"

See also MOYL.

broche

Pronounced BRAW-*kheh*, making that *kh* a long, throat-clearing sound, as in *Mad* magazine's "Yecch!" Hebrew: "benediction." Plural: *broches*. This word is often encountered in English writings by Jewish authors.

1. Blessing; a prayer of thanksgiving and praise.
2. To "make a *broche*" is to offer a blessing.
3. A Jewish girl's name.

Broches are recited, by Orthodox Jews, during prayers: three times daily, with special *broches* on *Shabbes* and in festival services. The silent prayer that precedes and follows communal praying contains nineteen *broches*. In the morning prayer, there are three *broches* associated with the *Shema*; in the evening prayer, four *broches* are associated.

The formula for a benediction must include "*Shem U' Malchus*," which is the name of God affirmed as King.

To a tradition-observing Jew, the occasions that call for a *broche* include:

the first act upon arising
upon eating and/or drinking at any time, even between

meals (there are separate *broches* for different foods and drinks)

upon washing one's hands—which is strictly enjoined (this must be done as soon as one gets out of bed in the morning, before praying, before eating)

the last act before retiring

upon returning from a hazardous journey

upon recovering from a grave illness

upon the arrival of a new season

upon seeing the new moon

upon donning a new garment

upon smelling a fragrant odor

upon seeing natural phenomena, such as lightning, majestic mountains, a magnificent sunset, etc.

upon seeing a strangely shaped person or animal

upon receiving bad news

upon seeing a scholar or sage

Etcetera, etcetera, etcetera . . .

Mrs. Gidwitz told her benevolent old Orthodox rabbi, "My grandchildren are driving me crazy this year: they want to have a Christmas tree! Rabbi, could you maybe make some dispensation, a special *broche*, over such a tree . . . ?"

"Never!" said the rabbi.

So Mrs. Gidwitz consulted a more lenient rabbi, a Conservative. "No," he said. "I'm sorry."

So poor Mrs. Gidwitz went to the young new Reform rabbi.

"I'll be *glad* to!" he smiled. "Only tell me, Mrs. Gidwitz: what's a '*broche*'?"

See also DAVEN.

bubbe
bobbe
buhbeh

From Slavic: *baba*: grandmother; midwife. Pronounced: BUH-*beh* or BAW-*beh*. (There is a Hebrew word *baba*, but it means "little doll" and shouldn't be confused with

the Yiddish for grandmother; *baba* means grandmother in Japanese, too—but do not jump to conclusions.)
  Grandmother.

I was mystified once in Edinburgh, to hear the distinct use of *baubee* in a context that could have no possible connection with "grandmother." What the Scot was referring to, it turned out, was a half-penny.

Jenny Lieberman and two classmates were discussing Darwin and the revisionists' criticism of the theory of evolution.
  Jenny's *bubbe* said, "Heredity . . . environment . . . Young girls, already you worry about such things?"
  "It's a complicated subject, Gramma."
  "Complicated-shmomplicated. *If* the baby looks like his father, that's heredity. *If* he looks like a neighbor, that's environment!"

Jerry Asher wanted to give his old *bubbe* a birthday present. And when he heard about a pet shop that had a mynah bird who actually talked Yiddish, Jerry hurried over.
  It was true: Herman's Pet Shop had a mynah bird that talked Yiddish. "Why not?" shrugged the bird in Yiddish. "My father was Jewish, my mother was Jewish. I went to a *cheder.*"
  Herman wanted three hundred dollars for the mynah bird. "Think of the hours and hours your lonely *bubbe* will spend talking to this pet, unburdening herself of sorrows, recalling old times—"
  "I'll take it!" cried Jerry. "Deliver it tomorrow, her birthday. To Mrs. Abe Silberberg, Two Seventy West Ninety-third Street."
  The next afternoon Jerry called his grandmother. "Happy birthday! And you should have a hundred more!"
  "*Alevay* I should have *one* more," sighed Grandma.
  "*Bubbe*! Did you get my present?"
  "Certainly I got your present."
  "And how did you like it?"
  "De-*li*-cious!" cried *Bubbe*.

P.S. I always thought this an unimprovable joke. Then I heard this surprising topper:

The grandson sputtered. "D-delicious? *Bubbe*, that bird—*spoke—Yiddish*!"

Bubbe chuckled. "You're such a joker."

"I'm not joking, *Bubbe*! That bird spoke perfect Yiddish!"

"Don't be silly . . . If he could talk, why didn't he *say* something?"

See also BUBELEH.

bubbe-mayse
bobbe-mayse
bawbe-myseh
baba-myseh
bobbe-maise

A compound noun cherished by Yinglishmen. Pronounce it BUB-*eh* MY-*seh* or BAW-*beh* MY-*seh*.

1. (Literally) Grandma's story.
2. An absurd account or explanation.
3. An old wives' tale.

This compound noun is used with zest to pulverize an account, excuse or explanation:

"Imagine that man trying to get away with such a *bubbe-mayse*!"

———

I pass on to you a memorable piece of doggerel:

A pharmacist named Abe Leisen,
So loved his bubbe *from Meissen,*
*   That to ensure her fame*
*   And immortalize her name,*
He invented the drug Bubbemycin.

———

Bubbe-mayse seems, obviously, to mean what it literally says: grandmother's tale—or old wives' tale. But historian-linguists trace the phrase back to the Italian *Story of Bovo* (or *Buovo*), a romantic tale of the fifteenth century chronicling the adventures of a hero yclept Bovo.

The fantastic adventure became immensely popular among Jewish women after a leading Jewish scholar and poet, Elijah Bochur, translated it into Yiddish in 1507. The story has been published in over a hundred editions. One can, in fact, study the linguistic history of Yiddish by noting the successive changes in the text.

buhbeh

See BUBBE.

bubeleh
babeleh (Galician/Slovakian Yiddish)
bubee (entirely Yinglish: affectionate, diminutive)

Any Yinglishman worth his self dotes on *bubee*.

Hebrew: *buba*: "little doll." Rhyme with "foot mullah." Be sure to pronounce the *u* as in *put*, and not as in *cut* or *stuck*.

Little grandmother.

Although this word is usually considered to be of Hebrew/Russian origin, the surface resemblances are misleading: my experts say that the Yiddish *bube* or *bubbe* or *bubeleh* arose independently.

1. The affectionate form of *bubbe, baba, bobe, bawbe*.
2. "Little grandma" (when said to a child).
3. Term of endearment enjoying wide, recent usage, fondly used between a husband and wife, parent and child, relatives, friends.
4. Synonym for "dear," "darling," "honey."
5. A delicious fluffy pancake; a Passover treat.

Jewish mothers call both female and male babies *bubeleh*. This carries the expectation that the child in the crib will one day be a grandparent. It also honors the memory of the mother's mother: in calling a baby "little grandmother," a mother is addressing the child in the way the child will in time address *its* grandmother—and its child.

In theatrical (and advertising) circles, where hugs, kisses and terms of endearment luxuriate in all seasons, *bubeleh* and *bubee* (pronounced to rhyme with "goody") have become familiar Yinglish words:

"Well, *bubee*, how *are* you?"
"*Bubeleh*, where have you *been*?"

"*Bubeleh*, couldn't you tell me, your own father, about it?"

Hollywood and television talk shows have become veritable hothouses of *bubeleh*. Even the Waspiest of actors and the blackest of singers cleave the air with threnodies of Yinglished affection. I suspect that natives of Alabama, Utah and even Bensonhurst think the glamorous folk are calling each other "little boobs."

Do not quail before the many-splendored uses of this neologism, which conveys the shmaltzy love Jews bestow on both their grandmothers and their grandchildren. (It is no greater than the mooning, moist miasma in which Italians swathe *their* grandmothers or offspring.)

The classic story about *bubeleh* concerns the proud mother who was sending her six-year-old boy off to school for the very first time. "So, *bubeleh*, you'll get off the school bus carefully and hang up your clothes on a hook, don't throw them on the floor. And to the teacher you'll always say 'Yes, ma'am' or 'No, ma'am.' And you'll be a good boy and do everything she says. And when it's time to come home, I know you'll button up good, *bubeleh*, so you won't catch cold . . ." (on and on).

When the lad returned that day, his mother smothered him with kisses. "You liked school, *bubeleh*? You learned something?"

"Yep," said the lad. "I learned that my name is Irving."

Old Mrs. Sophie Spelnick, long widowed, marched into the travel agency and said, "I want to go to a place in Burma called—" She placed a piece of paper on the desk of the agent, Noel Grant:

SHINGBWIYANG

"I'd better call our central office." Mr. Grant made a phone call. "Give me a readout on a place in Burma spelled S-H-I-N-G-B-W-I-Y-A-N-G . . . Air India? . . . Change in Calcutta? . . . Hold on . . . Mrs. Spelnick, there *are* flights, but then you would have to hire a guide and ponies to take you up a mountain—"

"Do it. Forget expense."

As the old lady started out, Mr. Grant said, "Please excuse me, madam, but . . . *why* are you taking such a long, costly, *very* hard trip?"

"I am going to a holy cave, where is the most world-famous swami!"

Within forty-eight hours, Sophie Spelnick was on Air India's flight to Calcutta. A waiting travel representative put her aboard a local plane to Shingbwiyang. And there a native, with two ponies, waited. The old lady got on one pony, and a guide on the other, and the two started up the mountain.

Up, up, up they rode, passing saffron-clad monks and sackcloth-wearing pilgrims by the dozen. At last the indomitable woman reached the entrance to the cave.

The guide helped her down from her pony. The cave was filled with pious worshipers, murmuring. The swami wore a gold turban and saffron robe, and sat cross-legged, his pale hands in his lap, mumbling: "Oom—oom . . ."

Mrs. Spelnick pushed through the seated acolytes, and in a clear, commanding voice declaimed: "Sheldon, *enough*! Come home, *bubeleh*!"

bummer (masculine)
bummerkeh (feminine)

> Pure Yinglish: This redolent, pejorative metaplasm is a good example of the embellishment of an English, not a Yiddish, word: "bum."

1. A real "low-life," a disreputable character.
2. A freeloader, a sponger.
3. One unlikely to repay a debt.
4. A dissolute person; of low morality.
5. A promiscuous male or female.
6. An untrustworthy man or woman.
7. Someone with a shady reputation.
8. An unsuccessful and costly business deal, involving a loss—due to deception, broken promises, or tricky dealings.
9. (Drugs) A bad "trip," one with prolonged, painful or frightening after-effects.

This neologism offers a striking example of the dexterity with which Jews can take an English word and embroider it with evocative meanings simply by adding a suffix or particle. We see the same linguistic process in the English word *bluff* being neologized into *bluffer* (*q.v.*).

I commend to you this intriguing and thought-provoking dialogue:

"Hello, Nat?"

"Speaking."

"This is Freddy Adelman. Listen, Nat, can you join our poker game on Wednesday night?"

"I'll look at my calend—nope, Freddy. I can't make Wednesday. Vladimir Gurfinkel is giving a concert in Lincoln Center."

"Oh. So how's about Saturday? At Joey Guber's place?"

"Wait . . . let's see. No, Freddy, Saturday night Gurfinkel is playing at Carnegie Hall."

"Then—next Tuesday! That'll be a *great* game. At my—"

"Aw, Freddy, I am sorry. *Tuesday* night Vladimir Gurfinkel is a sell-out at Town Hall!"

"Mi*god*, Nat," exclaimed Freddy, "you have become a real music nut! Do you follow this Gurfinkel around—"

"No, no, Freddy. I never even laid eyes on the guy!"

"B-but—"

"Whenever Vladimir Gurfinkel gives a recital, I visit Alma."

"*A*lma? Who's Alma?"

"His wife."

I ask you: is not Nat a *bummer*? And is not Alma Gurfinkel a *bummerkeh*?

Aaron Ofsevitz, age eighty-one, was vacationing at a fine hotel in Sarasota, Florida.

One night, in the restaurant, he beheld a thin, small, white-haired man at a table with a most beautiful girl. The next night Mr. Ofsevitz noticed the same man with *two* beautiful girls.

And every day this cheerful marvel dived into the swimming pool from the high platform, twelve feet above the water's surface, and swam ten swift laps without pausing.

And every night after dinner, the skinny, white-haired bummer was dancing with different chicks until the wee, wee hours.

After weeks of observing this extraordinary and strenuous schedule, old Mr. Ofsevitz could not help accosting the subject of his envy. "Excuse me, sir. I don't mean to seem pushy—but I have been watching and admiring you for *weeks* now. I can't get over your energy, your—your living it up—the beautiful *tchotchkes* you date . . . May I ask you, please, one question?"

"Sure," grinned the white-haired marvel.

"Well," asked Mr. Ofsevitz, "in the strictest confidence—you can trust me not to tell a *soul*—how *old* are you?"

The white-haired man shrugged. "Twenty-seven."

Charley Bronstein sat in the Ten Palms Country Club, balefully staring at Maxwell Konofsky, who was at the bar. Konofsky was a notorious ladies' man, a compulsive Don Juan. Charley Bronstein rose and firmly strode to Maxwell Konofsky's stool. "Konofsky," he said in a steely tone, "I'm going to ask you a question—and I want a straight answer!"

"What's your question?" smiled Konofsky.

"My question is—did you sleep with my wife last night?!"

Maxwell Konofsky regarded Bronstein with the greatest pity. "On my word of honor, on my dear mother's grave—"

"*Did you sleep with my wife last night*?!" cried Bronstein.

Konofsky scowled: "Not a wink, Charley. As God is my witness: *not—a—wink!*"

Charley beamed. "Thanks, Max."

bupkes
bobkes
bubkes
bopkes

From the Russian for "beans" and the Yiddish for "goat turd." Pronounced BUP-*kes* or BAWB-*kes*.

Yinglish expletive used in show business circles to dismiss or register outrage over:

1. An offer or percentage that is so small, or so "insulting," that it should be dismissed out of hand.
2. An outrageously inadequate price or proposal.
3. Insignificant quantity, bordering on nothing.
4. A heated *demarche*, equivalent to "Nuts!" "Forget it!" or "Drop dead!"

Bobkes, bupkes, or *boukes bopkes* are often encountered in books or articles by Jewish critics, writers and novelists:

"Do you know what they had the nerve to offer me for a complete screenplay? *Bupkes!*"
"What do I think of the storyline? It's strictly from hunger. To put it in a nutshell, pal: I say, '*Bupkes!*'"
"Four weeks he worked on the sketch, and what did they offer him? *Bupkes* with *bupkes!*"

In Hollywood and New York theatrical circles, *bupkes* occupies a potent place in the protocol of outrage. It is a word that bristles with scorn and seethes with resentment. When one's *amour propre* is defiled, "*Bupkes!*" rides to the rescue of pride.

Bupkes may be uttered with scorn or sarcasm, indignation or contempt. The expressive expletive takes over where "Nonsense!" or "Baloney!" stop for a rest.

I know of no English word that carries quite that deflating or embittered aroma.

by (for "at")

Yinglish, regrettably.

In Yiddish one says, "She's by Molly," more often than "She's *at* Molly's [house]." I see no reason for using such diction in English. The phrase was a favorite of immigrant Jews. "By" is used instead of "at" for comic purposes today.

SCENE: **Restaurant**

"Hello, friend!" sang out Mr. Gurvitz.

"I don't think I know you," said the condescending man Gurvitz had accosted.

"We both ate here last night," said Mr. Gurvitz.

"Really . . .?"

"I wouldn't of recognized you, mister—except for the umbrella by your side."

"Hmph!" sneered the stranger. "Last night I wasn't carrying this umbrella."

"I know," said Gurvitz. "I was."

by me [you, him, her, them] instead of "to me [you, him, her, them]"

Metaphrase, from Yiddish: *bei mir.* Wholly Yinglish.

1. To me.
2. In my opinion.
3. In my [our] house [or circle].

I must record my distaste for this phrase. I must also confess that when deliberately used in sardonic disparagement ("By him, he's a master of English!") it is deadly.

"By him, he's a wit."

"By her, I'm a millionaire."

"By us, it's brunch every Sunday at noon."

———————

This barbarism won popularity in theatrical circles through a story told about the late Samson Raphaelson, playwright and screenwriter.

Having struck it rich early in his career, with the phenomenally successful *The Jazz Singer*, Raphaelson bought a yacht. Dressed in blazer, white flannels and cruising cap, he proudly came to his mother.

"Look, Mama!" He pointed to the braided "Captain" above his visor. "How do you like your son the Captain?"

Mrs. Raphaelson surveyed her son's splendor, read the gold braiding and replied, "Sammy, by *me* you're a captain. By *you* you're a captain. But tell me, by a *captain* are you a captain?"

Mr. Raphaelson assured me that this anecdote, too good to be true—is.

————

An *avant-garde* art gallery was having a showing of the ultra-abstract paintings of Zoltan Ferruci.

Mrs. Jenny Engel sauntered about the gallery and stopped before a small, oblong white panel, in the center of which was a tilted black prong. She studied this *objet d'art* for a while, then signaled to the gallery owner. "I find myself interested in this one. . . . *Very* provocative. I may buy it, for my husband."

"Madam—"

"What does the artist call it?"

"The artist doesn't call it anything—"

"What would *you* call it?" asked Mrs. Engel.

The owner of the gallery said, "By me, it's a light switch."

C

Cabala
Kabala
Kabbalah

Pronounced *ka*-BAH-*la*. Hebrew: "tradition."
    The intricate, esoteric body of thought of Jewish mysticism.

The cabalists insisted that God and His exalted mysteries could never be comprehended by reason alone: mysticism, numerology, cryptic formulas and occult thought—all were part-and-parcel of Scriptures, they claimed, and the only true link to the meaning and mind of God.

Before the Middle Ages, cabalism was a minor stream of mystical Jewish thought, steeped in superstitions and drenched with divinations. Not until the thirteenth century did a coherent text appear, in Spain: *The Book of Splendor*, or *The Zohar*.

Isaac Luria (1534–1572), the outstanding cabalist (he was known as "Ari" (the "Lion"), a visionary who claimed to speak with the Prophet Elijah, presided over a circle of fervent disciples to whom he expounded arcane formulas and invocations; their prayers contained many hidden Names of God, upon which the faithful were exhorted to meditate. Minatory rituals were ordained. Elaborate manipulations of numbers attended every conceivable interpretation of passages from the Torah and the names of prophets.

It is not so hard to understand why supernatural doctrines attracted so many Jews. Given the wretchedness, the poverty, the abiding terror under which they lived, many devout souls became convinced that they would be delivered from the terrible tribulations of their plight only by the Messiah, who would come down to earth to usher in the Day of Judgment.

One may ask: What else except the miraculous was there to place hope in? Heaven is the poor man's last hope—and only reward.

The authority to consult is Gershom Scholem, *Kabbalah.*

See also MESCHIACH.

cantor
chazzen
hazzen
chazzonim (plural)

In Yinglish/Hebrew/Yiddish: *Chazzen,* pronounced KHOZZ'*n*, using the *ch* of Scottish (*loch*). Rhyme with "parson." From Hebrew: "a seer."

The singer who assists the rabbi in religious services.

The *chazzen* sings long passages of the liturgy. His recitation is not a chant or singsong, as is that of ordinary Jews in prayer: It is virtuoso singing, especially in the falsettoes, which are singularly sweet.

The melodies that cantors trill are not written down, but they *are* standardized; anyone familiar with the liturgy can enter a synagogue or temple and know from the cantor's melodic line whether it is an ordinary service, a Sabbath, Passover, or Rosh Hashanah.

The cantor (who *can* be any member of the congregation) sings out the opening words of a prayer, which the congregation takes up. The cantor starts a new prayer by intoning its initial phrases.

Emotion is expressed by a cantor with intensity, because the cantor speaks for the congregation (he is known as the "emissary of the congregation") in intoning the emotions embedded in Hebrew texts: suffering, contrition, compassion, despair—and always gratitude to the benevolent (!) God.

The Hebrews thought vocal music a divine art, one that could effect a special *rapport* between man and the holy.

The use of instruments in synagogues was discontinued after the destruction of the Temple (where harp, cymbal and horn *had* been used) in A.D. 69.

Toward the end of the Renaissance, in a radical departure from tradition, congregations began to employ professional cantors. (Few congregations could afford to pay them very much, so cantors also taught Hebrew to the young; some even served as sextons.)

By the middle of the eighteenth century you could hear music (a choir, an organ) in the synagogues of well-to-do congregations across Europe—in England, France, Germany, Italy, but not ever in eastern Europe, where the idea was anathema to the pietists.

In time, a special *bravura* style of rendering the prayers won over even the fundamentalists of Poland. The cantors were important in altering the monotonous sing-song of services that were part-praying, part-mumbling and much wailing.

After Franz Liszt went to hear a famous cantor in Vienna, he wrote: "Seldom were we so deeply stirred by emotion as on that evening, so shaken that our soul entirely surrendered to . . . participation in the service."

Chazzonim were never accorded the respect given a rabbi. It was once said that when you inform a *chazzen* of a calamity, he whips a tuning fork out of his pocket, taps it, gets the key, then cries, "*Gevaaaalt!*"

Modern *chazzonim* are often university graduates and hold teaching certificates. A growing number of cantors in Conservative or Reform temples are women. The contralto voice is superb during worship . . .

"Our new *chazzen*!" said one Jew. "What beautiful singing!"

"Eh!" scoffed the other. "If I had his voice, I'd sing just as good!"

casting doubt on the sanity of another by stressing one word in a sentence repeated as a question

Yiddish bulges with linguistic devices to express emotions—ranging from astonishment to scorn to flabbergasted incredulity. The economy and power of such ploys are what has brought them into the mainstream of Yinglish.

BRENDA: I may marry Jason.
FATHER: You may marry *Jason*?!

LOUIE: I expect her father to pick up the check.
FRED: You expect *her* father to pick up a *check*?

Castle Garden

Pronounced "Kessel Goddin" by immigrants.
The port of entry, in New York City, for many millions of immigrants.

"Castle Garden" was often used as a synonym for Ellis Island, but that was incorrect. Castle Garden was a huge music hall/cabaret on a little island just off the tip of the Battery in Manhattan (the water has long since been filled in). From Ellis Island, newcomers to America could easily read the large electric sign, its many bulbs creating an archway over the music hall, that read:

CASTLE GARDEN

Castle Garden was converted to an immigration port of entry around 1855. Each week, thousands of newcomers poured into the island. The processing was beset by dreadful "cattle car" congestion and sanitary nightmares. Corruption, bribery and blackmail were visited upon bewildered aliens who could not speak a word of English.

These immigrants packed their few household belongings, much of which would be lost or pilfered on the way, and forsook their native towns and villages to embark on the greatest journey of their lives. They parted with loved ones, seemingly forever, and made their way by foot, coach, and train to the bewildering port cities of Western Europe.
At a cost of thirty-four dollars . . . crammed into steerage for as long as three weeks, Jewish immigrants were confined to herring, black bread, and tea by their dietary laws. It was "a kind of hell that cleanses a man of his sins before coming to Columbus' land" . . .
—Moses Rischlin, *The Promised Land: 1870–1914*

In 1892 the huge tide of immigration, and the abominable conditions, led the federal government to take over: Ellis Island, in the bay, superseded Castle Garden.

Among some Jews, the "Golden Portal" became known as *Trer'n Indz'l*, "Isle of Tears." I give you one harrowing incident:

> Among the last to pass through the gates are a Russian Jew and his son. "Why did you come?" the inspector asks abruptly. "We had to" is the reply. "Are you willing to be separated; your father to go back and you to remain here?" The two look at each other with no visible emotion, for the question came too suddenly. Then . . . something in the background of their feelings moves, and the father, used to self-denial through[out] his life, says quietly, without pathos and yet tragically, "Of course." After casting his eyes to the floor, ashamed to look his father in the face, the son repeats, "Of course." Thus the healthy youngster is permitted to enter America, and the physically depleted father is detained, "for this was their judgment day."

> —Stanley Feldstein, *The Land That I Show You*

See also ALICE ISLAND, ELLIS ISLAND.

C.E.

Initials for "Common Era."
Jewish encyclopedias and reference works usually avoid A.D. and B.C.

Columbus discovered America in 1492 C.E., for which Jews have been grateful ever after.

Columbus, by the way, took several Jews along on his historic voyages—as interpreters. He assumed that any Indians or Orientals he would encounter would probably be primitive, and would therefore speak God's language: Hebrew.

See also A.C.E., B.C.E.

chai

Pronounced KHY, rattling the *kh* as if you are trying to *yech* a breadcrumb out of the roof of your mouth. Rhyme with "sky." Hebrew: *chai*: "life."
Life.

It has become fashionable for young upwardly mobile Jews (and alrightniks) to wear a gold Hebrew letter (ь) on a necklace. This does not mean that the wearer is religious, orthodox, or even an observing Jew: it only identifies the wearer as Jewish.

A bizarre numerology grew up, down the centuries, in connection with the Hebrew word *chai* ("life"). Each letter of the Hebrew alphabet served as a number. (This alphabet predated the Arabic numeral system.) Thus, the first letter of the Hebrew alphabet, *alef*, serves as a one, *bet*, as two, and so on through *yud*, which is ten. The next letter, *kaf*, is twenty; *lamed* is thirty, etc.

Since the Hebrew letters forming the word *chai* add up to the number eighteen (*ches* serves as eight; *yud* as ten), this number became charged with magical attributes.

Tradition-observing Jews give money to charity in amounts that are multiples of eighteen—in gratitude for a relative's recovery from illness, in honor of a child's birth, a *Bar Mitzva*.

In time of either stress or rejoicing, the Jew had one automatic response: give to charity.

Chaim

Chaim (pronounced KHY-*im*), Hebrew for "life," a common boy's name.

It was sometimes hastily bestowed upon someone during a serious illness—as a talisman against death. It was actually believed that a changed name might confuse the Angel of Death, who would be looking for the victim under his original handle. Instead of finding Moshe Skolnick, say, the Angel of Death would find only Chaim Skolnick in bed.

It is doubtful, in my opinion, that such cunning ruses had any effect on the vital statistics.

See also L'CHAIM.

chairlady

Yinglish, one hundred percent pure.
A female presiding officer.

The women in my mother's circle were pioneer feminists. In our living room, meetings of "the ladies" were often held in answer to her summons: to form a committee to send clothes to Poland; to raise funds for free milk for schoolchildren. It was in our living room that I first heard the clarion "Mrs. Chairlady!"

Now this was a linguistic invention of some consequence. These feminists rejected "Mrs. Chairman" out of hand; they gave short shrift to the oxymoron "Madame Chairman"; easily, effortlessly, they said, "Chairlady."

———————

At a PTA meeting the chairlady said, "—and now let's discuss the petition about raising teachers' salaries—on a strictly merit basis."

Up rose a hand.

"Yes?"

"It shouldn't matter if they're merit or single. They should be treated the same."

challa
challah
khale

Becoming a staple of Yinglish. Pronounce it KHOL-*leh*, with a German or Scottish *kh*. Hebrew. Rhymes with "Scala."

The very soft, braided white bread, glazed with egg white, that is a Sabbath delicacy. For *Shabbes* it is always made in a braided form. On holidays it may be kneaded into other shapes: circular, ladderlike, etc.

Children especially adore challa—for its almost-like-cake texture, its braided top, its crisp crust and ever-so-soft inside. If you have never tasted challa, stop reading and rush to a Jewish bakery.

———————

Two challas, uncut, are on the table of observing Jews on Sabbath eve; they are not cut until after the *broche* (blessing). This practice perpetuates the memory of the wilderness, where God dropped a double portion of manna on Friday (and none on the Sabbath). Or, say some, it recalls the Temple, where two rows of bread were lined up before the altar. (The home, which is of limitless importance in Jewish life, is in fact called in Hebrew *migdash mehad*—"a small temple.")

Like the bagel and the bialy, challa has become part of American cuisine. Scarcely a supermarket or bakery I know of is bereft of challas—not only on Fridays, when Jews traditionally buy them for the Sabbath ceremony, but every day of the week.

In suburbia, challas have become quite popular for sandwiches—even ham sandwiches, be it noted.

A beggar came to Mrs. Isaacson's back door. "Lady, I'm absolutely starving!"

"You poor man. Come in. On the table is bread. Challa and dark bread. Start while I get you some food."

The beggar fell upon the soft, sweet challa.

"Eh, mister," murmured Mrs. Isaacson. "There's *black* bread, too."

"I know." More slices of challa were wolfed down.

"Mister . . . the *challa* is much more expensive!"

"Lady," observed the beggar, "it's *worth* it!"

See also BAGEL, BIALY.

---

chalutz (masculine)
halutz
chalutzim (plural)

Often encountered in essays or fiction by Jewish writers. Pronounced KHA-*lootz* (with the guttural *kh*) to rhyme with "ma loots" or *kha*-LOOTZ. Hebrew: "pioneer."

1. Pioneer.
2. (More particularly) A young man or woman who went to Palestine (today, Israel) to settle the land.

The *chalutzim* went to Palestine early in this century to live under the most primitive conditions. They had to build roads, drain swamps, plant trees, reclaim desert that had been uncultivated for centuries.

Many of them live cooperatively in *kibbutzim*. Many

chalutzim were well-educated Europeans who gave up professional careers in order to "live the ideal: to build Zion" with the sweat of their brow and the toil of the hands. The first formal *halutz* group was founded by David Ben-Gurion in 1915—in the United States.

See also KIBBUTZ.

Chanukah
Chanuka
Channukah
Hanuka
Hanukkah

> Established in Yinglish. Rhymes with "Monica." Pronounce it KHON-*eh-keh*, with the Scottish *ch* of *loch*, not with an English *ch*. Hebrew: "dedication."
> "The Feast of Dedication," more colloquially known as "The Feast of Lights."

One of the less solemn Jewish festivals—a secular, *not* a religious, celebration. Chanukah, the only Jewish holiday connected with a war, commemorates the extraordinary victory of the Jewish Maccabees over Syrian despots (167 B.C.) in a rebellion for religious freedom. The victory rescued Judaism from complete annihilation.

The Jewish rebellion was led by a Hebrew priest, Mattathias of the Hasmoneon family, and his son, Judah the Maccabee ("the Hammer"). It continued for three years of guerrilla warfare against the armies of Antiochus IV, known to his minions as Epiphanes, "the risen god." Antiochus planned to force the Jews to accept Greek polytheism. He ordered them to build altars and shrines for idols and to stop circumcising male babies. The great Temple was desecrated by a huge statue of Zeus; Jewish courts were used for orgies.

The Maccabean uprising seemed hopeless. Guerrilla groups of Jews, unaccustomed to fighting and equipped with primitive weapons, fought the well-armed Seleucid soldiers—and they won out at Emmaus. They returned to Jerusalem—to find a sacked, burned Temple, which they began at once to restore. On the twenty-fifth day of the Hebrew month of Kislev, in 165 B.C., Judah the Maccabee lit the lamps of a great menorah (candelabrum) to begin a week-long festival. According to legend, a cruse of oil in the synagogue miraculously burned for eight days and nights.

Each Chanukah, Jews light candles for eight days in their homes: one on the first evening, and adding one light each night on a nine-branched menorah. A special ninth candle, called the *shammes* (servant), stands taller than the rest in the menorah, and is used to light the others. (This is interpreted as showing that one can give love and light to others without losing any part of one's own radiance.) Each Chanukah the prophecy of Zechariah is read: "Not by strength, not by power, but by my spirit, sayeth the Lord." (The repugnance of the Israelites to violence actually prevented King David himself from rebuilding the Temple—because he had been "stained by the blood of war"!)

———

Chanukah became popular with American Jews after they saw their children, especially in the suburbs, envying the celebrations and gift-giving of Christmas. So Chanukah was revived and enlarged, as a "Jewish Christmas"—for which it had never been intended.

The Hanukkah Anthology, edited by Philip Goodman, is a treasure trove.

———

One Chanukah, Mrs. Michaelson gave her son, Milton, a present: two beautiful neckties.

Milton ripped off the tie he was wearing and, after a swift examination, replaced it with one of the ties his doting mother had brought him. Then he turned to her proudly: "Look Mama? Isn't it a *beauty*?!"

Mama looked, looked puzzled, then inquired, "What's the matter, Milty? You don't like the other one?"

———

In a well-to-do suburb of New York (or Chicago, or Detroit, or Los Angeles—wherever the story is repeated), during the school's celebration of Christmas, one of the kindergarten's Jewish children was heard singing the old and endearing carol in this understandable way:

"God rest ye, Jerry Mandelbaum."

Chasid

See HASID.

chaucham

See HACHEM.

chazzen

See CANTOR.

cheder

See HEDER.

checkmate

> From Arabic, German and Yiddish (*not* Hebrew): "*Esh shach mot*" means "The King (or *sheik*) is dead!" The *mot* is German (*matt*) and Yiddish, meaning: "Weak, exhausted." Dr. Nathan Susskind declares that this use of *mot* is derived from the Arabic "through the mediation of Spanish and French."
>
> "Checkmate" in the game of chess signifies that this particular contest is over: the player who utters the phrase has fatally trapped the King of the other player, who cannot move without being "taken."

The Persians seem to have invented chess, and taught it to the Arabs, from whom the Jews learned the game— which they played with great enthusiasm.

Rabbis and theologians condemned chess because it demanded so much concentration and intensity that it became a serious distraction from the study of the Talmud and the endless religious argumentation in which Jews spent so much time.

Many of the greatest names in the history of chess are those of Jewish grandmasters; *e.g.*, Steinmetz, Lasker, Botvinnik, Reshevsky, Fine, Fischer.

Old Rabbi Bagan was playing chess with young Rabbi Frolich, newly arrived in the community of Cracow. After ten minutes of play, the old man leaned forward and sighed, "*Rebbe, Rebbe* . . . I have something to tell you that—that weighs heavily on my heart . . . !"

"Please, rabbi, tell me."

Rabbi Bagan said, "I have heard a rumor—about you—that—"

"Oh, rabbi!" laughed Rabbi Frolich. "I know all about that rumor—and I can tell you, flatly and unconditionally, that there is not a single grain of truth in it!"

The old man leaped to his feet, his features dark with anger, and swept the pieces off the chessboard. "*True* it should be yet?" he thundered. "*Isn't it bad enough that there is a rumor*?!"

Chelm

> Pronounced KHELM (not *Ch*elm): give it the guttural *kh* of "*Ach!*" Rhymes with "helm."
> The legendary town inhabited by half-wits, simpletons, and fools.* The Jewish equivalent of England's Gotham, whose "wise men" were idiots.

How Chelm achieved its reputation for bumbling gaffes, cockamamy reasoning and hilarious *non sequiturs* I do not know.

Chelm would enjoy no special name or fame, and surely no place in this lexicon, were it not that in Jewish folklore it has become the archetypical incubator of amiable nitwits, the equivalent of Holland's "Kampen," Italy's "Cuneo," and Germany's "Schildburg"—all famous for boneheads, dunces and nincompoops.

There must be a thousand tall tales about the unbelievable Chelmites. I give you my favorites.

The wisdom of Chelm has decreed: "Sleep faster; we need the pillows!"

The current craze in Chelm, I am reliably informed, is a game called "Guess Who?" It is a simple game, but the Chelmites roll on the floor in laughter as they play it.

What are the rules of "Guess Who?" There is only one:

---

*Chelm is used as the name of a mythical place, but there were two real Chelms—one, forty miles east of Lublin, with a population of around four thousand; another, just east of Tarnow.

A player leaves the room: the rest of the group try to guess who it was.

———

In Chelm, the citizens go to a dentist to have wisdom teeth put in.

———

At their weekly meeting, the council of wisemen in Chelm discussed this profound philosophical question: "Which is more important to mankind: the moon or the sun?"

The debate waxed eloquent and went on for an hour. Then Rabbi Shmerl raised both hands, and a silence fell upon the elders; for when Rabbi Shmerl raised both hands it meant that he had reached a definite conclusion, which he would announce with definitive reasoning.

And this is what the saintly rabbi of Chelm now proclaimed: "The answer is obvious, *baruch ha-Shem*, for it follows the teaching of our beloved Talmud. . . . The moon, my children, *has* to be more important than the sun! Why is that so? Reflect: The sun shines only in the daytime, which is *when we don't need it*. But the moon shines at night, when we do!"

"Oh!" "Yes!" "Awmain!" cried the Council, thankful that the Lord had sent them so brilliant a teacher.

———

Of all the tales—tall, wild, weird, wonderful—told about hapless Chelm, my *favorite* favorite is this:

Things were getting worse and worse in poor Chelm. Jobs were virtually non-existent. Food was running low.

To find *some* solution, the elders met. After prolonged discussion they decided that the best hope for Chelm was for the town to develop and sell a new brand of—beer.

After considerable experiment, they produced a liquid they thought excellent. What to do now?

Rabbi Shmerl had the answer: they would send a gallon to a famous brewmaster in Munich, with this letter:

O Worthy Brewmaster:
   Seeking to help our poor, we have produced a beer that we want to sell everywhere.
   We are humble folk, not known, so it would help our cause greatly if a famous brewer such as you praised our potion.

May the Holy One, blessed be His Name, speed your answer.

                                   The Elders of Chelm

A week later came this answer from Munich:

Your horse has diabetes.

chotchke

See TCHOTCHKE.

chutzpa
chutspa
hutspa
khutspa
khutspe

As indisputably a part of Yinglish as *maven, kibitzer, shlep.*

Pronounce this KHOOTS-*pah*, rendering the uvular fricative *kh* as in the German *Bach.* Do not ever, ever pronounce it with the *ch* you use for "chicken," "choo-choo," or "Chippewa." From Hebrew: "audacity," "insolence."

Unbelievable, unmitigated, astounding, brazen gall; unforgivable presumption; incredible effrontery; rooted in arrogance and bristling with effrontery.

Chutzpa may well be crowned the peerless, quintessential Yinglish word, unequaled by English pejoratives like *nerve, effrontery* or *brassy.*

The best definition of *chutzpa,* by all odds, is this: *chutzpa* is the quality demonstrated by the defendant in a courtroom who, having murdered his mother and father, threw himself on the mercy of the judge because "I am an orphan . . ."

No other Yiddish word has carved out so large a role in English. It is in any English dictionary worth the price. It is found in a good many legal briefs and judicial rulings. (I receive six or seven letters a year, plus legal rulings, from lawyers.)

Groucho Marx was the very personification of *chutzpa.* His calculated derangement, abetted by that rasp of a voice and that wall-eyed contempt, expressed what the rest of us simply have not the wit, much less the audacity, to utter.

When a woman said, "I made a stew last night," Groucho leered, "Anyone I know?"

Once, leaving his house after dinner, I paused at the door. "I'd like to say good-bye to your wife."

Said Groucho, "Who wouldn't?"

Driving back into California from a casual trip to Tijuana, Mexico, he was stopped, as are all returning tourists, by U.S. immigration officials.

"Are you an American citizen?"

"Yes," said Groucho.

"Where were you born?"

"New York."

"What's your occupation?"

Groucho leaned forward and whispered, "Smuggler." (*That's* chutzpa.)

———

Chutzpa Galore:

Steven Borrok, a shrewd and experienced Broadway producer, had a new play, *Roses for Rita*, by Mort Gumpel.

"We'll open on December thirty," said Borrok.

Gumpel was surprised. "December thirtieth? Isn't that a strange date for an opening?"

Borrok shrugged. "You'll see."

Roses for Rita opened. The critics slaughtered it.

So on January 1 a big ad appeared in the New York papers:

SECOND YEAR
ON
BROADWAY!

(That surely was *chutzpa*.)

———

SCENE: **Swimming Pool of a Hotel in Hawaii**

"Madame Morganstern," said the lifeguard sternly, "the management has instructed me to tell you to command your son—not to urinate in the waters of the bathing pool!"

Retorted Mrs. Morganstern, "It is well known that every child will, from time to time, urinate while bathing."

"That is true, madame, but not from the *diving* board!"
(*That* is chutzpa!)

The Internal Revenue agent walked into Feinberg's
Fancy Deli on Delancey Street and asked for the owner.
"I am Milton Feinberg," said one of the men behind the
counter.

The IRS agent flashed his identification. "I have a question about your income tax returns."

They sat down at a corner table, where the IRS man
opened his briefcase, pulled out a folder, spread its contents
before Feinberg, and said, "I call your attention to this
section—Professional Expenses, tax deductible."

"My expenses are very big," said Feinberg.

"But not *this* big," said the revenue agent. "Look. Right
here, under 'Business Expenses' you list five trips—to Israel!"

"Right."

"Five trips to *Israel?* Those you call '*Business* Expenses'?!"

"Certainly."

"How can a small delicatessen justify—"

"What do you mean 'justify'?" Feinberg drew himself
up. "We de*liver!*"

The very summit of *chutzpa* is reached in the conduct of
Bernie Shloss, a *paskudnyak* beyond peer, in the tragic tale
I now give you.

Henry Ratner, a traveling salesman, came home a day
early from a week-long trip out of town. Eager to surprise
his wife, he tiptoed through the house. His darling Ruby
was not in the kitchen, not in the dining room, not in the
living room.

Henry Ratner flung open the door to their bedroom with
a huge grin on his face and a buoyant "Surprise!" nascent
on his lips.

The joyous word was never uttered, for the surprise was
on Henry Ratner: what he beheld in the big double bed
was indeed his darling Ruby—moaning with lust as lusty
Herman Yanklov, Henry's closest friend, was making impassioned love to her.

"Oh, Ruby, *Ruby!*" came from Henry Ratner's quiv-

ering lips. "You—my wife—my sweetheart—my only love
. . . You, the woman I have treasured all these years—the
sweetheart of my dreams, the acme of all my hopes . . ."
Suddenly Henry Ratner's eyes became slits of steel, and
the anguish in his tone turned to a bitter barb of rage. "And
you, Hermie Yanklov—can't you stop while I'm *talk*ing?!"

cockamamy
cockamamie

Yinglish: gorgeous, colorful—and *sui generis*. Pronounced cock-*a-may-me*. Not Hebrew, not Yiddish, but
undeniably Yinglish, Manhattan division.

1. Implausible, ludicrous.
2. Far-fetched, so absurd as to offend credulity.
3. Imitation; fraudulent.
4. A contrived, confusing *mish-mosh*.
5. A foolish excuse, *ad libbed* as an explanation or defense.
6. (As an epithet) Absurd! Ridiculous!

The number of definitions suggests the utility of this concoction, a linguistic gem born on the Lower East Side,
cherished in Brooklyn, pampered in the Bronx, and now
indispensable to the Yinglish argot of urban life or suburban
persiflage.

I never heard *cockamamy* in the Midwest, the South,
the Southwest or California. I first encountered (and was
momentarily baffled by) *cockamamy* in New York City. At
first I thought it a scatological spin-off from the Yiddish
kock ("to defecate"). I later savored its pungent, pejorative
aroma in an essay by S. J. Perelman; it was one of his
favorite Yinglish adjectives.

7. Decalcomanias: dye pictures transferred to the back
   of the hand after wetting, rubbing and peeling off the
   paper.

This etymology seems inevitable: How many children on
Broome Street or Flatbush Avenue could pronounce the
forbidding *decalcomania*? True, the word became short-

ened to "decal," but how could "decal" hold a candle to *cockamamy?*

Wentworth and Flexner's *Dictionary of American Slang* defines "cockamamie" [*sic!*] as "quixotic, crazy . . ." and cites a first use as occurring in 1931. I heard it almost a decade earlier. I should add, in the interest of cultural pluralism, that I do not for a moment doubt that the Italian, Irish and Slavic kids who were brought up in the Bronx or the Lower East Side cried "*Cockamamy!*" too.

In the lobby of Miami's Excelsior Park Hotel, Mr. Leffovitz beheld a man smoking a very large—and very smelly—cigar. Said Mr. Leffovitz, "That's some *cockamamy* cigar! It must cost all of five cents."

"It cost me sixty."

"Sixty cents! How many of those stinkers do you smoke a day?"

"Ten, fifteen."

"And how many years have you been smoking that garbage?"

"Fifty."

"Well, did you ever stop to think that if you hadn't thrown away all that money on cigars, you could own a hotel as big as this!"

The stranger paused. "Do *you* smoke?"

"Absolutely not!"

"So, do you own this hotel?"

Said Mr. Leffovitz, "Certainly."

In the movie *Teacher's Pet*, Clark Gable delivered "*cockamamy*" with scornful relish, describing an idea from Doris Day as totally absurd, desperately invented.

Cohen

See KOHEN.

computernik

Yinglish. Someone who is mad about computers, large or small; an electronic nut.

The mathematical wizards crowded before the great computer at the Technion Institute.

"It's a mistake!" exclaimed one scientist.

"No question of it."

"The computer made a mistake!"

The assembled *meyvinim* (in Yinglish, *mavens*) passed the readout tapes around, calculating, frowning, scrutinizing.

And after a full hour of communal bafflement, the chief of the laboratory, observing the dismay on the faces of his colleagues, exclaimed: "Gentlemen, don't be discouraged. Do you realize it would take forty-two hundred mathematicians, working twelve hours a day, over three hundred sixty-three *years* to make a mistake like this?"

The Technion Institute in Israel perfected an electronic translator, a machine that could, with blinding speed, render the text of any one of forty languages into any one of the others.

The marvelous machine was returned to the laboratory for improvement when this sentence from the New Testament was fed into it:

The spirit is willing, but the flesh is weak.

—and this answer, in Russian, popped up:

The vodka agrees, but the meat smells.

See also -NIK.

concurrence as a vehicle for sarcasm

Yinglish shrewdly employs nominal agreement as a vehicle for blistering deflation:

JACK: I suppose you're a little depressed, going in for major surgery tomorrow.

MILT: Oh, sure. I suppose I am a *little* depressed — going in for major surgery tomorrow.

The most surprising "punchline" in jokedom may be this:

"Sophie," said Mrs. Winograd, "is it true that you're going to have a baby?"

"It's true, it's true."

"That's *won*derful, Sophie! Do you want a boy or a girl?"

"Certainly," said Sophie.

contempt by nominal concurrence

Yinglish.

Q: "Won't your toothache drive you stark, raving mad unless you hurry to the dentist?"

A: "Oh, yes, I will go stark, raving mad unless I rush over to the dentist."

———————

Asher Benjamin, first mate on the Israeli S.S. *Hatikva*, received a cable that he was now the father of a fine, eight-pound boy. Asher went on a glorious binge.

The next morning, as he took the helm, he read in the ship's log: "First mate Benjamin was drunk last night."

When the captain came into the cabin, Asher said, "Sir, I wish you would remove that entry in the log. I've *never* in my life been drunk before. But . . . last night, I received this cable!" He showed the captain the cable.

The captain read it. "Congratulations, Benjamin. But the entry stays in the log. After all, you *were* drunk."

"Yes, sir, but—"

"There are no ifs, ands or buts. Facts are *facts*!"

The next morning, the captain found this entry in Asher Benjamin's handwriting, in the ship's official log:

"The captain was sober last night."

contempt via confirmation —by adding the searing *sh-* prefix

Yinglish has fattened and flourished on this deft, simple device for mockery.

"I don't deny that he's clever. But clever-shmever, he's still a crook!"

"Who says she's not a good cook? But cook-shmook, the lady is a slob."

"On the cello he's a genius? Genius-shmenius, why doesn't he pay his bills?"

The contemptuous prefixing of *sh*-, a derogatory syllable (and one that begins many taboo/obscene/offensive Yiddish words, *shmuck* being the most prominent) is a peerless example of Yinglish. I know of no English equivalent for so scornful a dismissal of an assertion, an allegation, a conclusion, or a challenge.

I fortify this claim with a memorable example:

Jake Chadish came into the office of his boss. "Mr. Brankoff," quavered Chadish, "can I maybe take tomorrow off?"

"What's tomorrow, a national holiday?"

"No, no, Mr. Brankoff. It's—for me and my wife—our golden anniversary!"

"Golden-shmolden! Am I going to have to put up with this *mishegoss* every fifty years?!"

See also ACCENTUATING DISAGREEMENT . . . , CRITICIZING A PERSON . . . , SH-.

Could be

One hundred percent Yinglish. Directly from Yiddish: *Es ken zayn* (pronounced *'s ken zyn*): "It could be."

1. It may be; it *may* come to pass.
2. Anything is possible.
3. Wait and see.
4. *Who* knows?

"Could be" might not have come into wide English usage (aside from use 1, above), were it not for its persistent use by Jews. English, to be sure, has no problem with "*It* could [might] be . . ." or "*It* could [might] be that . . ." But that's the point: "*It* could be . . ." is nowhere as crisp or effective as "Could be."

When not used as a neutral statement, "Could be" contains innuendos beyond the boundaries of "It could be that . . ." "Could be" is astringent: a doubt, a caveat about probability, a reminder of the surprises that may transform the unlikely into the actual.

The Jewish propensity for skepticism is beautifully

served by this truncated form of "Perhaps that's so—but don't forget: maybe it isn't."

Sagacity is attributed to doubters, that is, to those who (in a world profusely populated by *fonfers, ploshers, k'nockers, shacher-machers, trombeniks,* etcetera) do not take things at face value, do not fall for constantly optimistic asserverations, do not believe every promise and, in general, use so many grains of salt per annum that they might as well buy it by the barrel.

JOE: I don't think Howie will have the *nerve* to show up at tomorrow's meeting.
AL: Could be.
JOE: "Could" be *what*? You think he will, or you think he won't?
AL: Could be yes, but could be no.

JOE: Do you think Joanie is telling the truth?
AL: That gossip? But—could be.

JOE: Who do you think will win the pennant?
AL: It's too early in the season to say.
JOE: How about the Red Sox?
AL: Mmh . . . Could be.
JOE: Or the Giants.
AL: Also could be.

JOE: I wonder if Marshak will pay my bill?
AL: Could be. How long do you expect to live?

"So, listen, Morrie. Could be . . . I'm not the perfect wife for you. Could be . . . I don't like your friends. Could be . . . I'm just too—outspoken!"

"By who?" asked Morrie.

crazy-doctor

Note the all-important hyphen. Pure Yinglish.
     A psychiatrist, psychoanalyst or psychological therapist.

A *crazy-doctor* is not a doctor who is demented: he is a doctor who treats crazy people.

Jews are quite at home with ideas of insanity, hallucinations, schizophrenia, paranoia. Jewish history is studded with dramatic instances of one or another *meshuggener*. The Bible itself is surely a chronicle of extraordinary irrationality, of one sort or another, possessing many ancient characters. And in the history of psychiatry and psychoanalysis, Jews have played a conspicuous, often commanding, role.

Remember the old, well-known, unchallenged Jewish folk saying: "Everyone has his own *mishegoss*."

And the remarkably prescient: "An *einredenish* [obsession] is worse than a disease." (Literally, *einreden* means "to talk one's self into something.")

And: "Love is the best medicine."

———

Here are some memorable observations:

A psychoanalyst is a Jewish doctor who hates the sight of blood.   —Anon.

A psychotic thinks that 2 plus 2 equals 9. A neurotic knows that 2 plus 2 equals 4—but he just can't *stand* it.
                                                           —Anon.

A neurotic builds castles in the air. A psychotic thinks he lives in them. The psychoanalyst collects rent from both.   —Anon.

The depressed person builds dungeons in the air.
                                                           —Anon.

A hysteric knows the secret of perpetual emotion.
                                                           —Anon.

Anyone who goes to a psychiatrist ought to have his head examined.
                                                —Samuel Goldwyn

———

Anecdotes to treasure:

Two psychoanalysts meet while strolling on Park Avenue. It's a matter of choice which one will greet the other thusly: "You're fine; how am I?"

———————

Two psychiatrists enter an elevator.

The attendant calls, "Good morning, gentlemen."

The psychiatrists get off on their floor. One asks the other: "What do you think he meant by that?"

———————

DR. MESSER: God, I'm tired. All day long, every day, all I hear are stories of suffering, marital strife, parental crises, anxiety, rage, guilt, sexual hang-ups . . . Tell me, Al, how do you manage to look so serene after listening *all day*?

DR. HYMAN: *Who* listens?

———————

"Hello, Dr. Mishkin," said Mrs. Rangelman, on the phone, "I would like to come and see you, because I am terribly depressed. In fact, I think I have gone *meshugge*!"

"Well," said Dr. Mishkin, "suppose you come in next Thursday—"

"Wait, Doctor. Before I come in—how much do you charge for a consultation?"

"Seventy-five dollars."

"*Hanh*?" gasped Mrs. Rangelman. "Good-bye, Doctor. *That* crazy I'm not."

See also MESHUGGE.

criticizing a person or a policy simply by uttering the name as a back-formation with a prefatory fricative of disdain

An economic, albeit eloquent, way of expressing disagreement, disparagement, disdain or disgust—in a manner not available in conventional discourse.

This has become a very popular ploy in Yinglish. I love it.

"Hitler-Shmitler, the man was a psychopath!"

"Tariffs-shmariffs, they are bound to hurt American consumers."

"Smoke-shmoke, you're talking about *cancer*!"

"Atheists-shmatheists, when they face death they're not so certain."

See also ACCENTUATING DISAGREEMENT . . . , CONTEMPT VIA CONFIRMATION . . . , SH-.

customer

Yinglish; *not* a simple synonym for a buyer, client or prospective purchaser.

1. A person who fits the characteristics required, sought or described.

"You want Charley to join the delegation? Well, he's a willing customer."
"You asked Nelly to give the opening speech? You chose a good customer!"

In colloquial English, *customer* means a potential buyer, or it is used with an adjective for characterization: "She's a steady customer," or "He's a tough customer."
But in Yinglish, *customer* takes on a wholly different meaning: *i.e.*, someone whose characteristics are not described (as in the examples above) but take on meaning from the preceding conversation, as below:

2. Sarcastic disagreement with a choice or recommendation.

"You asked him to be an impartial arbitrator? How could you choose such a customer?!"
"You're complaining to *me* about my daughter's bad behavior? I'm the wrong customer."

———

An illuminating use of the unique Yinglish denotation of *customer* is found in the following episode.
Some years ago, Dr. Harvey Novick, a fine surgeon, was being considered for a tenured professorship at a certain medical school.
The faculty committee rejected him because, as a member of that committee confided, "They just don't want a full professor who is—well, a Jew."
After a sleepless night of anger and frustration, Dr. Novick wrote the following letter to the chairman of the committee:

Dear Dr. Hastings:

May I recommend for the Robertson Professorship in Surgery a man I have known for over 15 years. He is absolutely honest, dependable, does not drink or use drugs of any nature. His name is Michael McKeon.

Mr. McKeon, I should add, is not an M.D., and has never practiced medicine or surgery. But he fits the basic requirement of your committee. He is the perfect customer for the prestigious professorship in question: McKeon is a *goy*.

Yours truly,
Harvey Novick, M.D.

P.S. Mike McKeon is the janitor at 447 Commodore Avenue, where I live.

———

The waiter lifted his pencil and his notepad. "So what would you like to eat?"

"Waiter," frowned the diner, "I gave my order at least half an hour ago!"

The waiter nodded. "Well, *that* waiter can't serve you. I—"

"Tell me," scowled the customer, "did he leave much of a family?"

(That customer was a *customer*.)

D

dairy

Yinglish
    Abbreviation for dairy foods.

The conversion of an adjective to a noun is a familiar propensity of Yinglish speakers: "Danish" has become an acceptable way of asking for a Danish pastry (unknown, incidentally, in Denmark, where such confections are called Vienna buns).

The designation of dairy foods, to distinguish them from meats, takes on special importance among "observing" Jews—that is, Jews who follow the kosher laws (*q.v.*).

SCENE: A Dairy Restaurant

"Waiter, waiter!" called Mr. Lenski. "This fish is awful!"

The waiter scowled, "But, Lenski, you ate here last week and said the fish was delicious."

"That was *last* week!" said Lenski.

"I give you my absolute word," said the waiter, "this is *the same fish!*"

Bernard Rolich appeared before the Pearly Gates.

The admitting angel hummed to himself quite merrily as he consulted a golden volume of records. "Rolich . . . Rolich . . . Bernard Rolich . . . Tell me, mister, it says here you were a strict vegetarian. Is that true?''

"Absolutely. I was so healthy because I ate strictly dairy for twenty-seven years!''

"Hmm . . . My . . . Well! . . . How do you like this?!'' The angel looked up. "Mr. Rolich, you're not due to be up here for another twelve *weeks*! Tell me, who is your doctor?''

daven
davenen

These are strictly Yiddish, not Hebrew, words.

Pronounced DAH-*ven*, to rhyme with "robin," and DAHV-nen, to rhyme with "sob men."

Daven may be remotely descended from the French *l'office divin*, "divine service," or even from an old Persian word, *divan*: "a collection of poems." To complicate matters more, the suffix -*nen* is Germanic. The incomparable Max Weinrich, examining every possible etymology in his definitive *History of the Yiddish Language* (page 680), declares the origin of *daven* to be unknown. Incidentally, *daven* is a word used only by East European Jews, and their descendants.

To pray—*i.e.*, to pray the prescribed prayers of the liturgy.

Daven refers only to formal prayer, alone or in a congregation—and not to personal, impromptu, meditative entreaties or invocations. A traditional Jew *davens* three times a day (*shachris, minchah*, and *mairev*)—and adds supplementary prayers on the Sabbath and festivals.

Orthodox and some Conservative Jews wear a prayer shawl (*tallith*; "*talis*" in Yiddish) and phylacteries (*tephillin*) when praying—except on the Sabbath. Reform Jews do not wear phylacteries.

A devout Jew will not read from the Torah, or recite the *Shema* (*q.v.*), or pronounce the sacred Hebrew name of God, unless his head is covered. The Orthodox never leave their heads uncovered; they wear either hat or *yarmulka*—or both.

There is no law in the Bible pertaining to the custom of covering the head, nor is the custom mentioned in the writings of the rabbis. (This practice was, of course, not limited to the Jews: the use of a turban, fez, or other head covering is considered a sign of respect in many parts of the Orient and the Middle East.)

Christians bare their heads in church; the practice originated with Paul who wrote (I Corinthians) that a man who covered his head while "praying or prophesying . . . dishonoureth his head." I believe that Paul (originally, Saul) was overreacting to his boyhood indoctrination.

An observing Jew will recite the *Shema* four times daily: "O Israel: The Lord, our God, the Lord is One." Then comes this passage from the Bible: "Thou shalt love the Lord thy God with all thy heart, with all thy soul, and with all thy might."

The Silent Devotion, an extraordinary prayer of eighteen (really nineteen) benedictions, is also offered four times daily by Orthodox (and many Conservative) Jews. Recited or murmured or chanted while standing, it involves three thoughts: Wisdom, Learning, Immortality. It extols God's glory; it offers a hope for the welfare of the one who prays, his family, and the community at large; and it thanks God for His blessings.

About praying, as on all other matters, not excluding the Lord Himself, Jews have delivered themselves of a rich, juicy catalogue of discontents, ironies, sardonic comments and lamentations: yet

A place is reserved in Heaven for those who weep, but cannot pray.

Prayer is the service of the heart.
   —TALMUD: *Ta'anith* 1:1

Even when the gates of Heaven are closed to prayer, they are open to tears.   —TALMUD: *Berakoth* 32a

I love the yarn about the old Jew who found himself in a strange place, and when it was time for him to say *mairev* he found that he had lost his prayer book. So he addressed the Lord: "Dear God, I have bad news for You. I don't have my prayer book. Even worse, I am getting old and forgetful, so I cannot recite the evening prayer by heart.

But I have a solution, Almighty One: I will just call out the letters in the alphabet, and You, please, put them together in the right way."

———

Morris Meltzer confided to his rabbi: "My wife—we're going to have a baby."

"*Mazel tov!*"

"It's our first child, *Rebbe*. And my Lily isn't so young. When she goes into labor, at our home, would you make a special prayer for her?"

"I'll do more than that! I'll bring along a whole *minyan* to *daven*!"

When the labor pains began, Meltzer telephoned the doctor—and the rabbi: "*Rebbe*! The delivery has started!"

The rabbi arrived with nine alert males, and then prayers began. And what loud, vigorous prayers they were!

Outside the bedroom, Morris paced and paced. Soon the cry of a baby was heard. The doctor stuck his head out the door: "It's a boy!"

Morris ran to the head of the stairs and announced to the swaying bodies below, "It's a boy!"

"*Mazel tov!*" yelled the *minyan*.

"Praised be the Lord of Israel!" cried the rabbi.

Back to the bedroom door ran Morris. It opened. Soon "A girl!" called the doctor.

Morris sped to the stairway. "Twins! A girl! I have *twins*!"

Now the *Mazel tovs* shook the very rafters.

Back to the bedroom raced Morris Meltzer.

Out popped the head of the doctor. "Another girl!"

"What?!"

"Triplets!"

Morris Meltzer fairly flew to the stairway, down which he now bellowed, "Hey, all of you down there! For God's sake, *stop praying*!"

———

If praying did any good, they would hire men to do it.
                                        —Folk saying

Pray only in a room which has windows (to remember
    the world outside).   —TALMUD: *Berakoth*, 34b

I love to pray at sunrise—before the world becomes
    polluted with vanity and hatred.
                              —The Koretser Rabbi

And now, dear God, farewell: I am going to America.
—Polish Jew, after finishing a prayer

See also TEFILLIN.

dayan
dayyan
dayen
dayanim (plural)

Pronounced *die*-ON, to rhyme with "try on"; pronounce the plural *die*-AW-*nim*. Hebrew: "judge."
A rabbinical judge.

In the rabbinical literature, *dayan* meant "sage," a student of the Law, the leading rabbi of the community. (God is called *Dayan Emes*, "the righteous judge.")

Every *dayan* was a rabbi, trained in interpreting the Torah and Talmud; but not every rabbi was a *dayan*. His decision was known as a *Din Torah* (a verdict of the Torah).

In countries where Jewish communities were forced to live apart from the general population, the governments often granted judicial authority (in cases involving only Jews) to the *dayanim*.

My grandfather was a *dayan* in Lodz, and to his home Jews came with a multitude of problems. He held himself quite superior to rabbis, who came to him with their problems. He also preferred to conduct religious services in his home: he seemed to consider the synagogue a place for less illustrious worshipers—hence, his followers would make up a *minyan*, over which he presided, in his own library!

deflation by grossly magnified
mock concurrence

Yinglish employs a versatile battery of linguistic devices for the puncturing of pomposity, the pricking of pretension and the drastic lowering of foolish expectations.

One such device is the deflation of rosy predictions by seeming (but sarcastic) agreement with them:

"If you ask me, the judge will award you a million dollars!"
"If the judge asks you, he'll award me *twenty* million dollars!"

———

I know of no more withering reply than the one old Mr. Nesselbaum gave to the barber who whipped the white cover around his neck and asked, "So, mister, a haircut?"

"No," said Mr. Nesselbaum. "I just dropped in for an estimate."

See also BELITTLING SOMEONE . . . , EXPOSING ABSURDITY . . .

deli

Yinglish to the hilt.

Truncated form of *delicatessen*, which is from German via French via Latin—*delicatus*: "giving pleasure"—plus German—*essen*: "to eat." (French: *delicatesse*: "delicacy.") Pure Yinglish, without a shred of doubt.

1. Cooked meat, fish, relishes, salads, cheese.
2. The store where such foods are featured.

Need I extol the glories of this urban institution, never more popular than today, when there seems to be a delicatessen in the most rural places?

You can get pastrami, chopped liver, lox, pickled herring, *et al.*, in remote parts of Arizona, New Mexico, Utah—and Alaska.

The length of the word *delicatessen*, difficult to get on a small sign or window, caused some unknown genius to invent *deli*. I salute him.

———

SCENE: **Shmalky Rubin's Fancy Deluxe Deli**

DINER: Vaiduh! Vaiduh! Come look!
WAITER: I'm looking.
DINER: In my soup! What's that *fly* doing in my soup?
WAITER: Well, I *think* it's the breast stroke.

———

Abby Riegelman entered the King David Deli on Broadway and ordered the Special Whole Smoked Whitefish Platter.

The platter came and, indeed, looked delicious. But as

Abby picked up his knife and fork, the cold, small, beady eye of the smoked whitefish stared at him in so bitter and reproachful a manner that Abby simply could not bear it. A wave of guilt swept over him, a wave so powerful that Abby laid down his knife and fork and hurried out of the King David Deli.

A week later, Abby Riegelman found himself near Delancey Street, where he entered Yosha Krimmer's Famous. He sat down at the counter and ordered, "Bagels and cream cheese, a bottle of Dr. Brown's Seltzer, and a nice whole smoked fish."

When the waiter placed the order before Abby, the cold, glaring eye of the whitefish transfixed Abby as, in an icy *sotto voce*, the fish murmured, "What's a matter, mister? You don't eat at the King David anymore?!"

See also APPETIZING.

demolishing a statement with an outlandish remark

Yinglish, which includes psychological overtones no less than words, phrases and syntax.

Jews are so appreciative of wit, sarcasm, innuendo, and so annoyed by the obvious or the banal, that it is not surprising that their humor prizes swift and deflating observations.

The following is a true anecdote, about a twelve-year-old boy who was given to romanticizing, and his wry seventy-year-old grandfather, who often cautioned him not to be so gullible.

BOY: Listen, Grampa, it says here that it cost the United States almost ten billion dollars to put a man on the moon.

GRANDFATHER: Well, well. And does that include meals?!

destroying a proud claim with an irrelevant and wholly unexpected declaration

A Yinglish tactic directly modeled on a common Jewish gambit.

"And ladies," Mrs. Forkin addressed her Current Events group, "we will all have to learn to adjust to this fantastic new world—in which an American astronaut has circled the world over a hundred times!"

"*Mnyeh*," sniffed Mrs. Pasternak, "If you have money, you travel."

Diaspora

From Greek: *diaspora*: "scattering." The Hebrew equivalent is *galuth*: "exile"; the Yiddish is pronounced *golus*.

The dispersion of Jews around the world.

Many Jews (and more gentiles) seem to think that the Diaspora, or exile of the Jews from the Holy Land, began when the Romans tore down the Great Temple in Jerusalem, in the year A.D. 70. This is erroneous.

The enslavement and exiling of Hebrews goes back at least to 721 B.C., when the Assyrian king, Sargon II, destroyed the northern Israelite kingdom of Samaria (*i.e.*, the kingdom of ten of Israel's twelve tribes); the inhabitants vanished.

In 701 B.C., the Assyrian Sennacherib defeated the army of Judah and then recorded (in cuneiform) how he had transported 200,150 people, with halters around their necks.

In 586 B.C., Nebuchadnezzar destroyed Solomon's Temple in Jerusalem and deported huge numbers of Hebrews to serve as slaves in Armenia, Georgia, the Caucasus.

King Cyrus of Persia defeated Nebuchadnezzar's son in Babylon in 538 B.C. Under a historic proclamation, he allowed all Jews to return to Judea. Some did, and they rebuilt the Temple. Most of the exiles did not return. They remained scattered throughout one hundred twenty-seven provinces of the Persian Empire.

There was a thriving Jewish colony in Egypt in the fifth century B.C. Alexander the Great widened the area of Jewish settlement. By the second century B.C., the Hebrews were to be found all over Syria and Asia Minor and Greece—and westward to Rome.

The Roman conquest brought the Jews into the imperial sovereignty, and the Jews settled in many Italian cities, soon following the Roman legions along the northern coast of Africa, into Spain, into northern France—and at outposts along the Rhine. (All during this period, the Jews spoke Greek and Latin.)

During the Middle Ages, the Diaspora sent Jews into north and west Europe and into England.

The Crusades, the virulent wars by Christian kings and princes against the Muslims to capture Palestine and the Holy Grail, took a terrible toll among Jewish communities. The first Crusade (1096–1099) simply slaughtered huge numbers of Jews in Worms, Cologne, Mainz—and eastward in Prague and Salonika. When Jerusalem was captured in 1099, the Jews there were massacred.

The subsequent Crusades constitute an Age of Horrors for medieval Jews; wholesale depredations by the crusaders in York (England), in southern France, in northern Spain.

After the fury of the successive crusades abated, the Jews of western Europe began to move eastward, to central and eastern Europe. They found small communities of Jews there, with whom they assimilated. They also began to speak Yiddish.

I cannot complete my comments on the Diaspora without giving you W. E. H. Lecky's unforgettable account of one occurrence in the fifteenth century, in Spain:

> History relates very few measures that produced so vast an amount of calamity. In three short months, all unconverted Jews were obliged, under pain of death, to abandon the Spanish soil. Multitudes, falling into the hands of the pirates who swarmed around the coast, were plundered of all they possessed and reduced to slavery; multitudes died of famine or of plague, or were murdered or tortured with horrible cruelty by the African savages.
>
> About 80,000 [Jews] took refuge in Portugal, relying on the promise of the king. Spanish priests lashed the Portuguese into fury, and the king was persuaded to issue an edict which threw even that of Isabella into the shade. All the adult Jews were banished from Portugal; but first all their children below the age of fourteen were taken from them to be educated as Christians. Then, indeed, the

cup of bitterness was filled to the brim. The serene forti-
tude with which the exiled people had borne so many and
such grievous calamities gave way, and was replaced by
the wildest paroxysms of despair.

When at last, childless and broken-hearted, they sought
to leave the land, they found that the ships had been
purposely detained, and the allotted time having expired,
they were reduced to slavery and baptized by force. A
great peal of rejoicing filled the Peninsula, and proclaimed
that the triumph of the Spanish priests was complete.

—*History of Rationalism in Europe*, vol. 2

See also GALUS.

dismissing an idea with scorn simply by framing it as an indignant question

"You think *I* should invite *her* to our wedding?!"
"*I* would be better off in Scarsdale?"

Whenever a question is framed "*I* should" or "*I*
would"—instead of "Should I" or "Would I"—you may
safely conclude that you are being told, not asked.

Do me [him, her] something

Yinglish. A literal translation of the Yiddish *Tu [ti] mir
eppes*.

I know of no language other than Yiddish from which
this awkward but expressive phrase could have come.
It is given extra flavor when phrased "*Go* do me something."

1. There's not a thing you can do!
2. I don't care what you feel or say.
3. It's done, and that's that.
4. I know you disapprove, and I knew you would disapprove, but that's what I wanted to do, and I did—so
   accept it.

Mr. Wishner told his new secretary, "Please check these
sales figures. And to be sure, add up the column three
times."

At 4:30 the secretary said, "Here you are, Mr. Wishner."

"Did you check your results?"
"Yes, sir. Three times—"
"Thank—"
"—and here are the answers."
(Go do her something.)

See also GO FIGHT CITY HALL, SO SUE ME.

donstairsikeh   (feminine)
donstairsiker   (masculine)

Yinglish—in fact, there is no other broken language this
metaplasm could be from. Pronounced *don*-STARE-*zi-keh*.

The neighbor who lives downstairs:

"Am I lucky! My *donstairsikeh* is an angel."

A *donstairsikeh* lives below an *opstairsikeh*.

A Yiddish curse runs: "May you have an inconsider-
ate *opstairsikeh [opstairsiker]*!"
Another folk saying, however, goes: "Love thy *donstairsiker*—even if he plays the bugle!"
"You can know someone better by the comments of
his neighbor than by the praises of his mother."
"If you mix with your neighbors, you'll be surprised
by how much you'll learn about your own home."

The mourners filed past the coffin, some sobbing, some
sighing, and Mrs. Eisenstadt murmured, "Look at him. My
donstairsiker. So relaxed, he looks . . . so tanned . . . so
healthy . . ."
"Why not?" replied the widow. "He just spent three
weeks in Arizona!"

See also NEXDOOREKEH.

Don't ask!

Charming—or pungent—Yinglish, used for comic impact.

From Yiddish: *Freg nit [nisht]*. "Don't ask *me*" is
English; "Don't ask" is canonical Yinglish.

1. The answer would dishearten you.
2. I would have to say "No."
3. Things are very bad.
4. I *hate* to give you the answer.

This laconic imperative contains a veritable symphony of signals:

"Don't ask me to answer [whatever it was you want to ask me] because I know the answer will upset you!"

OR

"Were I to answer your question, instead of putting you off with 'Don't ask!' it would depress me so much you'd be sorry you inquired!"

OR

"Take a hint: desist!"

"How is your brother?
"Don't ask." ("He's in bad, bad shape.")

"How was the movie?"
"Don't ask." ("It was so awful, words fail me.")

"How's business?"
"Don't ask!"
"Really? . . . You know, for *this* time of year, that's not so bad!"

Don't mix in

Expressly Yinglish, particularly as parody, from the Yiddish phrase: *Mish zikh nisht [nit] arayn [arein]*.

1. Don't butt in.
2. Stay out of this, please.
3. Mind your own business!

"Don't mix in" is the precise Yinglish equivalent of "Stay out of this" or "Don't interfere" or the brusque "This is none of your business!"
Jews of earlier generations would translate directly from

the Yiddish to exclaim, "Don't mix *yourself* in!" But the reflexive "yourself" of Yiddish sounds in English like the object of the verb *mix*; this amusing relationship is the comic basis upon which vaudeville performers once used to get laughs in their German or Yiddish dialect routines. (The Amish of Pennsylvania, I am told, say "Throw the cow over the fence some hay.")

Reflexive verbs, incidentally, are mandatory in Yiddish, as they used to be in English: "I wash," without adding an object, can mean "I wash the clothes," "I run a laundry," "I need to wash myself up," "I wash the windows," "I'm going to wash the vegetables," etcetera.

In Tel Aviv, one dark night, Special Agent 6-Z-4 looked up and down the street, then darted into the apartment building. He slipped the Colt into his outer pocket, knocked on the door of 2D twice, paused, knocked once, paused, knocked twice again.

From inside, a voice inquired, "Who's dere?"

"Goldblatt?" whispered 6-Z-4.

The door opened; a bald-headed little man in pajamas said, "*Sholem aleichem*."

"The ostriches," murmured 6-Z-4, "have arrived in Greece."

"*Ha-anh*?" goggled Goldblatt.

"The ostriches," repeated 6-Z-4 slowly, "have arrived in Greece . . ."

A light entered the eyes of the bald-headed little man. "Ah-*aha*! Mister, I don't want to mix in—but I am Goldblatt, the piano teacher. You want Goldblatt the spy. Upstairs, 4B."

It was old Mr. Eizenstat's first ocean voyage. And the third day out, the ship ran into a terrible storm. The heavings and lurchings and rollings of the vessel forced ashen Mr. Eizenstat to the rail, where he retched in agony.

A voice from a kindly steward piped up, "Don't be too alarmed, sir. No one has *ever* died of seasickness."

"Oh, God," moaned Eizenstat. "Who told *you* to mix in!? That hope is all that's keeping me alive!"

doppess

I strongly recommend the infusion of this word into Yinglish—because there just is no English word remotely like it. Rhymes with "stop us." Possibly from German: *doppig*.

A commiserator—who does nothing but offer oral sympathy. What makes him or her a *doppess* is that the *only* thing he or she can (or wants to) do is make sympathetic noises. Apart from that, the *doppess* is entirely useless. (So is a *tsitser*, *q.v.*)

This admirable coinage describes a personality-type known in all cultures—and held everywhere in scorn. The word comes from New York's garment district, which is surely one of the world's richest cauldrons of linguistic alchemy.

A *doppess* is a special variant of a *shlemiel*, a *shmegegge*, a *klutz*, or a dope. I particularly call "dope" to your attention because (Hans Rosenhaupt wrote me) the natives of Frankfurt, Mainz and the surrounding terrain used the German slang word *doppess* to describe a clumsy (*doppig*) person. Dutch Jews use *doppess* to describe a fumbler or groper.

But the *doppess* I particularly cherish is something else again. He is unique—and is best described in the words of a Seventh Avenue *maven* I know:

> So think about a loft in the garment center. There stand a dozen men before the ironing boards, pushing their big, heavy steam-irons back and forth, back and forth.
>
> Okay? But every so often, one man runs his iron right off the board: *He*—is a *shlemiel*.
>
> The iron lands on the big toe of the next man. *He* is a *shlimazl*.
>
> And who is the *doppess*? The *doppess* is the *shmuck* who goes *Tsk! Tsk! Tsk! Tsk!*

See also SHMEGEGGE, TSITSER.

dotso

This Yinglishism is heard again and again in Jewish communities, though I have not seen it in print—even when, for example, in newspaper accounts, you may be sure *dotso?* or *dotso* was used instead of the proper phrases it clearly conveys. *Dotso* is a prime candidate for Yinglish. It stands for:

1. Is that so?
2. That's true.
3. Can you believe it?
4. I'll be darned!
5. I have to admit it.

My father, who had a peerless ear, believed his ears when he heard all around him:

"My daughter is getting married."
"Is *dotso?*"

"You know who called me up—right out of the blues? Milty Fink!"
"Is *dotso?*"

"Did you say you're flying to Texas?"
"Uh-huh. *Dotso!*"

I find *dotso* more crisp, amusing and memorable than "That's so" or "Is that so?"

———————

At a town meeting, Mr. Howland Thatcher, somewhat tipsy, exclaimed, "I'll have you know, Mr. Lodovitz, that I come from one of the first families of America! In fact, one of my ancestors signed the Declaration of Independence!"

"Is *dotso?*" murmured Lodovitz. "One of mine—signed the Ten Commandments."

———————

In the deli on Hester Street, Mr. Edelman called a waiter over. "Tell me, Waiter: what kind sandwich am I eating?"

"What you ordered, corn beef lean, on rye bread."

"Is *dotso?* I'm half way through and haven't hit even a *sliver* corn beef!"

"So try another bite," said the waiter.

Mr. Edelman took a bite. "Still no corn beef!"

The waiter, indignant, snapped "What do you expect? You went right past it!"

dreck

Yinglish *par excellence*. From the German for dung, excrement (vulgar).

1. (Literally) Excrement.
2. Cheap, worthless, trash.

Dreck is a well-known, widely used epithet in colloquial English and entertainment circles.

The driving *dr* and the emphatic *k* appeal to our indignation. "The play was *dreck*!" is much stronger than "The play was lousy." And *dreck* seems to purge the feelings more than does *junk*. *Dreck* is, in fact, just this side of taboo—like *crap*, its equivalent in English.

SCENE: **An Art Gallery**

TRABINSKY: Is that a painting? It says "Night Scene."
SAKORSKI: It should say "*Dreck* by Moonlight."
TRABINSKY: Why do they hang stuff like that?
SAKORSKI: Because they couldn't find the artist.

dresske
dresskeleh   (diminutive)

Yinglish, with a bang, not a whimper.
A little dress.

But the "little" does not stand for (or only for) "small." *Dresske* is obligatory and chic modesty; the dress may have come from Nieman Marcus.

The classic "throwaway" use of *dresske* was immortalized in Palm Beach when the mother of a famous radio tycoon, complimented on her new frock, replied, "*This* little *dresske*? It's *noth*ing! I use it only for street-walking."

Drop dead!

Bona fide Yinglish. From Yiddish: *Ver derharget*: "Get yourself killed."

1. Go to hell.
2. I wish you would die on the spot.

This expletive is a vigorous and acceptable version of the English "F—— you!"—all the more useful because its component words are perfectly respectable.

The phrase was used with enormous effect as the second-act curtain line in *Born Yesterday*. No one who saw Garson Kanin's comedy can ever forget the impact of the phrase as enunciated by Judy Holliday: "Du-rop du-ead."

The slow, sweet, studied rendition was stupendous. Waspish ladies have been tossing "Drop dead!" into their phones (to obscene callers) and as retorts (to abusive cabbies) ever since.

See also GAY IN DRERD!

dumkop

Commonly used in English, especially by Jews and Germans. From German: *Dummkopf*: "dummy" "dumbbell," "blockhead." ("Dummy," "dumbbell," "blockhead" are English analogues of this excellent word.) The Yinglish usage drops the *f*.

A stupid, foolish, silly person.

Dumkop does not mean mentally retarded (which, in Yiddish, is *opgeshtagn*), although that limitation may indeed be the cause of some *dumkops'* senseless or absurd conduct. "Lunkhead" is a good analogue.

———

The foreman came over to the new hand. "Nice day's work you've done, Klemmer. I see you marked and stacked all those crates neatly."

"Yes, *sir*!"

"Good . . . Did you stencil *This Side Up* on the top of each crate? That's *very* important."

"Oh, yes," said Klemmer. "And to protect them double good, I put the notice on the bottom, too."

———

"Now, Randy," the movie director said, "the next scene is crucial. You've been stranded on this desert island for over four years. One morning a beautiful, gorgeous blonde, wearing a life jacket, comes ashore. You help her take off the jacket. She comes into your arms. You start showering her with kisses—"

"Hold it," said Randy. "What's my motivation?"

(How can you answer such a *dumkop*?)

————

Hainich Tiznich, a refugee from Posnan, came to the United States and spent his first week wandering around and examining the marvels of the New World. He was particularly mesmerized by the supermarkets—where he beheld a thermos bottle. "What type special bottle is that?" he asked another shopper.

"That's a thermos bottle."

"Hanh?"

"It's a thermos bottle. It will keep hot water hot, and cold water cold—up to eight hours!"

The refugee was so impressed that he bought the thermos bottle and hurried down the street to the little diner where he had been eating. "Yissel," he said to the counterman. "Do you think you can get six cups of coffee in this bottle? I want to surprise my son and his family."

"Six cups? Easily," said the counterman.

"Great!" exclaimed Tiznick. He handed the bottle over. "So, please fill it up: one black, two with cream, one with two spoons sugar . . ."

dybbuk
dybuk

Strongly recommended for Yinglish. Pronounced DIB-*book*, to rhyme with "mid rook." Hebrew: "evil spirit."

1. An evil spirit that enters the body of a living person.
2. A demon who possesses someone—rendering him or her insane, violent, sinful and corrupt.

When someone went mad or hysterical or suffered an epileptic seizure, Jews would cry, "A *dybbuk* has entered into him [her]!"

A *dybbuk* is the closest thing in Jewish folklore to a vampire or an incubus—a migrating spirit who has to find a living body to inhabit. To protect women in childbirth from such demons, superstitious Jews once used odd amulets and fervent incantations. (Jews do not have a very vivid sense of the Devil, in the medieval Christian sense, as the supreme, cunning temptor.)

Those who believe in *dybbuks* believe they can be exorcised by a holy man, or *tzaddik*. One of the more charming details in the lore alleges that when a *dybbuk* flees a man or woman, a tiny, bloody spot, the size of a pinhead, appears in the pinky of the right foot. Either that, or a window develops a little crack.

S. Ansky, or An-ski (pen name of S. Z. Rapoport, 1863–1920), wrote a remarkable and compelling play, a classic of the Yiddish theater, called *The Dybbuk*, that is still performed around the world in many languages.

A splendid compendium to consult on matters concerning angels, demons, spirits, spooks and allied suprahuman beings both good and evil is Gustav Davidson's delightful *A Dictionary of Angels*.

A Dictionary of Demonology by Jacques-Albin-Simon Collin de Plancy (1793–1887) has long beguiled me. It catalogues spooky spirits from Adrammelch, "grand chancellor of hell" (who, learned rabbis said, took the shape of either a mule or a peacock) to Amduscias, a grand duke of hell, who is shaped like a unicorn and gives concerts.

My favorite in the bogeyman league is Tanchelin, who had such awesome powers that husbands begged him to sleep with their wives!

I am convinced that only a *dybbuk* could have perpetrated the Freudian slip that appeared in the following invitation to a wedding:

> MR. AND MRS. EDWIN GREENGLASS
> REQUEST
> THE PLEASURE OF YOUR PRESENTS
> AT
> THE MARRIAGE OF THEIR DAUGHTER
> GRACE
> TO MR. BERNARD A. SHLOSS

Dzhudesmo

See LADINO.

eat a little something

Yinglish, absolutely. I recommend that it be used, but only for satiric effect.

Do not for a moment think that the "little" is a hint for you to restrain your appetite: *au contraire*, the host's table may be sagging under the weight of the comestibles.

"Eat a little something" is the obligatory, *pro forma* Jewish invitation to start eating.

When this invocation is used on, say, Park Avenue, or in a mansion in Beverly Hills, it is used satirically, as if calling attention to its absurdity.

Is there anyone who has not heard the following exchange:

HOSTESS: So have some cookies, homemade.
GUEST: They're delicious! I already ate four.
HOSTESS: You already ate *five*—but who's counting?

eat fruit

Yinglish: often used for deliberate comic characterization, or in parody.

A Jewish mother (to her children) and surely a Jewish hostess (to her guests) would often sing out, "Eat fruit!"

In vaudeville and on Broadway (notably in plays by Clifford Odets), this invitation identified the hostess as Jewish.

But "Eat fruit!" was not simply a form of *politesse*. We must remember that to most Ashkenazim, fresh fruit was a rare and expensive luxury. My mother told me that the first time she ate an orange in Poland was on her tenth birthday: in fact, the orange was her birthday present.

In America, the abundance and low price of fruit made many an immigrant dizzy with pleasure. And the lesson drummed into Jews about the necessity, the *mitzva*, of generous hospitality created a steady flow of invitations to "have a piece fruit already!"

In the cabins of El Al planes, some wit suggested, the instruction lights should read:

> BUCKLE YOUR SEATBELTS
> NO SMOKING
> EAT FRUIT!

JASON: Did I hear you say you're a light eater?
MARCUS: Absolutely.
JASON: But, Mark, you must weigh two hundred pounds!
MARCUS: Two twenty.
JASON: Then how the hell can you say you're a light eater?!
MARCUS: As soon as it's light, I start eating.

eat your heart out

An indisputable part of the Yinglish canon. From Yiddish: *Es dir oys s'harts*: "Eat out your heart."

Be consumed by envy, jealousy, avarice, or cupidity.

This taunt is used for brazen, unabashed gloating: "He won, so eat your heart out!"

In Yiddish, the original meaning is less taunting and more descriptive, albeit exaggerated:

"Her children are so cold to her, she's eating her heart out."

"Your jealousy will make you eat your heart out one of these days."

Boris Solter taught his dog, Moishe, to stand on his hind legs for twenty minutes at a time. Then he taught the dog to wear a *yarmulka*. Then he taught him how to *daven*! Soon Solter got a prayer shawl and taught Moisheleh not to shrug it off his shoulders . . .

When the high holidays came around, Boris Solter took the dog with him to the synagogue. Boris had bought two tickets, and Moishe sat between Boris on one side and old Mr. Wolkoff on the other.

And at the right time, Moishe rose to pray—along with the whole congregation. True, his praying was not very clear, and was punctuated by muffled yips and heartfelt wails—but there could be no doubt about it: the dog was praying!

This led Mr. Wolkoff to exclaim, "Boris! Do my ears play tricks on me—or is your *hintele* actually *davening*?"

"He's *davening* all right."

"Boris!" cried Mr. Wolkoff. "You can make a fortune! This dog belongs on television!"

Sighed Boris, "Go eat your heart out. *He* wants to be a bookkeeper!"

-el (suffix; diminutive)
-eleh (more so)

Yinglish may employ the affectionate suffixes of Yiddish to diminutize a noun— *-eleh* being an extension, and greater affirmation, of *-el*. Thus:

cap	gun	kiss	pot
capel	gunel	kissel	potel
capeleh	guneleh	kisseleh	poteleh

The fond use of *-el* and *-eleh* is catching on in Yinglish, albeit more slowly than the use of the particle *-nik*.

The classic deployment of the ultra-diminutive always makes me laugh:

SCENE: Trautman's Delicatessen

MRS. SMOLLER: So, how much is that pickel?
MR. TRAUTMAN: That *pickel* is a *nickel*.
MRS. SMOLLER: So—eh—how much is this pickeleh?
MR. TRAUTMAN: This *pickeleh* is a *nickeleh*.

Ellis Island

About sixteen million immigrants, in all, passed through Ellis Island. The ancestors of some hundred million living Americans (!) came through the fabled Great Hall.

Some three thousand immigrants (of all nationalities) committed suicide on Ellis Island—after they were denied admission to the United States—because they had an eye disease, tuberculosis, an infection, seemed "subnormal" or had inadequate "papers."

See also ALICE ISLAND, CASTLE GARDEN.

enjoy!

> Emphatically Yinglish, widely used and accepted, and firmly settled.
> Enjoy! (Complete sentence.)

Dropping the hitherto essential object of the verb ("Enjoy *the food*," "Enjoy *yourself*," "Enjoy the *game*") has become a linguistic staple among Americans. The intransitive injunction has become familiar in TV comedies and in American advertising. "Enjoy!" is firmly and invulnerably established in our vernacular.

Americans seem to leap at the chance to abbreviate words and truncate phrases: Consider: "Have a happy"; "Order of ham and"; "A Danish"; "A burger."

England's conversations and humor are adopting the intransitive use of *Enjoy* at a noticeable rate.

Warning: I happen to dislike this metathesis. I *never* use the verb without an object: Go do me something. Sue me. Go fight City Hall.

Shepsel ("Slugs") Molinsky, a real no-goodnik, was gunned down by hit-men of the Callahan mob.

Bleeding from four bullet holes, "Slugs" staggered up the stairs to his mother's flat. "Mama!" he cried. "Mama!"

His mother flung open the door. "Shepseleh!"

"Slugs" clutched his bleeding abdomen: "Mama—I—"

"Don't talk!" beamed Mama. "First eat. Enjoy! Later, you can tell me everything!"

Little Gershon came home from school in considerable excitement. "Mama, Mama! In half an hour there is going to be an eclipse of the sun! Can I go out and watch it?"

"Why not, dollink?" replied Gershon's mother. "Enjoy! Only—don't stand too close!"

See also ENTITLED.

enough already!

Real McCoy Yinglish, with riffs and ruffles, from the Yiddish *Genug shoyn*.

1. Stop! Enough!
2. Say no more, *please*.
3. Change the subject.

Enough already is a peremptory, irritated imperative that has tickled the fancy of actors and entertainers in television circles, who, through endless sitcoms and talk shows, and incessant interviews, have introduced this Yinglishism to American (and English) populations everywhere.

The solecism is simply a colorful way of avoiding such clichés as "Let's change the subject," and is used for its jocular effect—which is the only usage I can recommend (or even bear).

"Now," smiled Dr. Wishner, "how can I help you?"

"Doctor," exclaimed the man across the desk, "I think I'm going crazy already. I just can't *remember* things!"

"What things?" asked Dr. Wishner.

"Any things! If you asked me what time I got up or went to the store or what I ate for my breakfast or even—where I just had *lunch*, I couldn't tell you one damn detail! Where, what time, where I'm going—"

"Enough already!" cried the doctor. "How long has this been going on?"

"How long has *what* been going on?" blinked the stranger.

See also ALRIGHT ALREADY, ENOUGH WITH . . .

enough with . . .

Yinglish galore. Metaphrase from Yiddish: *Genug mit*, which was widely used, in translation, in Jewish immigrant or first-generation circles.

1. That's enough about that.
2. Stop!
3. I don't want to hear any more about that!
4. *Please* change the subject.

Enough with is a less brusque, less abrasive way of saying *Enough already!*—which can be uttered only after enough annoyances have accumulated.

Like *Enough already!*, the solecism *Enough with* has spread like wildfire through the vernacular of the Yinglish speaking/comprehending world. As with *Enough already!* I urge that *Enough with* be employed only for deliberate sarcastic or mock-serious effects.

———————

Three elderly Jewish women sat on the porch, rocking back and forth, seemingly lost in memories.
At last, Mrs. Trakish sighed deeply "Oy . . ."
Silence.
A moment later, Mrs. Blumblut sighed "O-y-y-y."
Silence.
Then Mrs. Komsky scowled, "Enough with the children! Let's talk about cholesterol."

———

SCENE: **Aboard Israeli Warship during Mediterranean Maneuvers**

Ensign Louis Grossman, the communications clerk, knocked on the door and entered Captain Yala's cabin. There were a dozen men around the table, poring over a huge map.
Grossman snapped to attention and barked, "Urgent cable from Command, Naval Maneuvers!"

Captain Yala scarcely looked up. "Read it . . ."

Ensign Grossman cleared his throat:

To: Captain Yala
FROM: Admiral Notkin, H. Q.

Your last three tactical movements are undoubtedly the most stupid (repeat, stupid) I have witnessed in thirty years at sea!

A hush had fallen upon the assembled officers.

Captain Yala straightened up, cleared his throat, and said "Enough with secrets. Ensign, have that cable decoded at once!"

————

Louis J. Futterman, the movie magnate, telephoned his mansion in Bel Air. The butler answered.

"Put my wife on the line," said Futterman.

Silence.

"I said, put my wife on the line!"

"Sir, your wife is in the bedroom . . ."

"She's *sick*?"

"N-no. She's in bed—with a man!"

Futterman exploded. "*What*? Are you positive?!"

"Absolutely, sir."

"Now, listen. Listen carefully," seethed Louis J. Futterman. "Go into my study. There's a gun in the desk. Get it. Go upstairs. Open the bedroom door—and if you see my wife in bed with that man, shoot! *Kill them both!*"

"Oh, sir, I can't do that! I'm afraid—"

"You do that right now, do you hear? Enough with your fears! If you don't, I'm coming right home and *I'll* kill the two of them—and you, too!"

"Oh, Lord," moaned the servant.

"Now go and do what I told you! . . . I'll wait on this phone . . ."

In a few long minutes, the quavery voice of the servant returned on the line. "Okay, sir."

"Did you shoot them both?" asked Futterman.

"Yes, sir. And I was so *nervous*, I ran to the garden and I threw the gun in the swimmin' pool—"

"*Swimming* pool?" echoed Futterman. "We don't have a swimming pool . . . Listen! Is this Fairfax eight, seven, seven, two, four?"

entitled

Yinglish, pure and simple—and simple-minded.

An intransitive verb carved out of its proper transitive form, for colloquial economy and (presumably) wit, by deliberately omitting the object. Thus, "I'm entitled!" (instead of "I'm entitled to a rest") or "She's entitled" (eliminating "to a raise"). This usage parallels the popular "Enjoy!"

"I'll give you the refund. You're entitled."
"Let them go ahead of us. After such a long wait, they're entitled."

———————

"Mister Belzer," said the shoe salesman to his boss, "my wife says you have to give me a raise. She says I'm absolutely entitled!"

"So I'll ask *my* wife," replied Mr. Belzer, "if she thinks you're entitled."

See also ENJOY!

eppes

Used for comic effect. Honest-to-God Yinglish. Pronounced EP-*us* to rhyme with "deck us." From the Yiddish: *eppes*: "something, a little, a bit," by way of the German *etwas* ("anything, something").

Something; somewhat; a bit; sort of.

Eppes has such special aptness, distinctive flavor, and nuances that it was bound to be carried into English by Jews who prize uniqueness. *Eppes* is making great strides in Yinglish—and for ten good reasons, listed below.

Recent American slang has introduced the awkward "some kind of" to express special attributes—as if the speaker cannot find words to describe the extraordinary or do justice to his or her admiration:

"He is some kind of speech-maker!" ("He is a remarkably impressive orator.")
"She is some kind of cook!" ("She is an absolutely wonderful cook.")

Eppes does this, and achieves many other effects, with greater force and wider felicity.

1. Something. "Give him *eppes*."
2. Somewhat; a bit. "He is *eppes* strange." ("He is somewhat peculiar.")
3. Not much. "He is not *eppes* a genius." ("He is far from being smart.")

But *eppes* also conveys opposite meanings, such as:

4. Remarkable, prodigious. "He hit *eppes* a home run!" ("He hit a home run that belongs in a book of records.")
5. Extreme, large, notable. "Is she *eppes* a spender!" ("She spends an enormous amount of money."

And *eppes* can make a 180° turn, to mean

6. Perhaps; maybe. "Do you think he is *eppes* reliable?" "She could be *eppes* a snob."
7. Inexplicable: for some hard-to-explain reason.
   Q: "How come you're not eating much?"
   A: "All of a sudden, I'm *eppes* not hungry."

OR

8. Arguable, unsatisfactory, not established, not certain.
   "Do you think she's *eppes* a loser?"
   "I'm having *eppes* some doubts."
   "Is it *eppes* the whole story?"

OR

9. Sort of; some sort of. "There's got to be a way out. Who has *eppes* a solution?"
   "She was wearing *eppes* a hat—with feathers right out of a sleazy thrift shop!"

OR

10. Happily welcome, surprising, generous.
    "Did he throw her *eppes* a birthday party!"
    "Did she make *eppes* a windfall on that investment!"
    "Soon he'll be *eppes* a millionaire!"

"Clare, did my Billy give me *eppes* an anniversary! Two weeks in Portofino!"

"Portofino? Where's that?"

"Who knows? We flew there!"

The chief rabbi of a town was hauled before the High Court of the Inquisition and told, "We will leave the fate of your people to God. I'm putting two slips of paper in this box. On one is written 'Guilty.' On the other is written 'Innocent.' Draw."

Now this Inquisitor was known to seek the slaughter of all the Jews, and he had written "Guilty" on both pieces of paper.

So the rabbi put his hand inside the box, withdrew one slip of paper—and swallowed it.

"What are you doing?" cried the Inquisitor. "How will the court now know—?"

"That's simple," said the rabbi. "Examine the slip that's in the box. If it reads 'Innocent,' then the paper I swallowed obviously must have read 'Guilty.' But if the paper in the box reads 'Guilty,' then the one I swallowed *must* have read 'Innocent.' "

If you ask me, that was *eppes* a feat of reasoning!

Eskimo

"Code" name for "Jew."

I have no plausible evidence as to why the pejorative code word for "Jew" was/is/became "Eskimo." Code or "in" sobriquets offer any group a convenient, masked or frivolous way of referring to themselves or to a group other than themselves—therefore *infra dig*, if not inferior.

Blacks call whites "ofays." Jews call blacks "*shvartzers*," which is Yiddish for "blacks." Jews may ask, "Is she M.O.T. [member of our tribe]?" instead of "Is she Jewish?"

A few picturesque reasons have been offered for the use of "Eskimo" to mean "Jew": an Eskimo is obviously not an Anglo-Saxon; and *mo* may signal the Jewish name "Moe." (The most common names used to sneer a substitute for "Jew" are Abie, Ike, Moe.)

A joke, popular in the 1920s, had a punchline about Alaskans being Jewish: "Just consider the number of icebergs there!" (The verbal play was on "bergs.")

In Chicago, a stratagem such as "Eskimo" was heard

from gentiles, instead of, say, "kike," "sheeny," or "Yid." Not, I hasten to add, that such insults were ever in short supply.

———————

Old Mr. Cardohy, in room 109 of the old people's home, was as mischievous as he was spry. One day, reading about the wave of naked "streakers" around the country, he decided, on a sudden impulse, to undress and run through the dining room.

The room was packed when naked Mr. Cardohy appeared in the doorway, yelled "Eureka!" and ran around the tables and out.

The gaping silence was broken by old Shmuel Strudnick, a tailor: "Whatever that Eskimo was wearing, folks, he should never wear it again until he has it *pressed*, for God's sake!"

Eve

From Hebrew: *havvah*, or *havah*: "woman."
The first woman, created by the Lord out of Adam's rib.

You may ask, "What is Eve doing in a book about Yinglish?" That is a fair question. Eve is here because I want her here—and I am writing this book, not you. Besides, I have run into some fascinating data about our common mother.

The first mention of Eve, in the Masoretic text, calls her *ishah* (Genesis 3:20)—translated as "woman"—because she was taken from man: *ish*. But Adam is reported as having called his mate "woman" or "wife." No name.

Incidentally, the rabbis had no doctrine of Original Sin: the clear sin of Eve in the Garden was "removed" by the Israelites' "acceptance of the Law."

———————

The Old Testament's story of the creation of the first woman from the first man's rib is far from being unique. Similar tales are found among Polynesians, Burmese, Siberian Tatars, the Yuki and Salinan Indians of California, etc. . . . Eskimos think that Eve was made from Adam's thumb(!).

Such fables will enchant anyone who reads Frazer's *Golden Bough* or the astonishing inventory of origins and rituals compiled by Theodor Gaster in his *Customs and Folkways of Jewish Life*. But many myths, I think, may simply be echoes of biblical accounts *told* to the natives' great-grandfathers—by Christian missionaries.

* * *

Among the many Jewish folk sayings about Eve, the following sticks in my memory:

"If you know everything," said the cynic to the sage, "tell me what Eve did whenever Adam came home?"

"She counted his ribs," said the sage.

* * *

My favorite joke about Eve is this: "Adam," said Eve, "after we eat the apple, we're going to do *what*?"

See also ADAM.

excuse the expression
excuse my language
excuse the slang
etc.

Yinglish: a genteelism, déclassé, in poor taste and best avoided. When preceded by "You should . . ." the expression becomes a barbarism.

When used intentionally, this Yinglishism is designed to identify (and ridicule) the sort of people who use it: *i.e.*, those from a Bronx, Brooklyn or "lower-class" background.

The mannered phrase is never proper English for

1. "Forgive me for saying this . . ."
2. "If you will allow me to put it informally . . ."
3. "Excuse my use of such vulgar English . . ."
4. "I know that what I am about to say may strike you as improper [vulgar, unrefined] . . ."

* * *

Near the entrance of a very crowded bus, Lena Weisbord kept groping in her purse for a token. She zipped open another coin purse, fingered through it, closed it, tried another, fumbling about frantically.

The old man whom she was tightly jammed against said, "Lady, I'll give you a token—"

"Oh, thank you, but I have quarters—"

"I'll be *happy* to pay your fare," the old man declared.

"No, no," said Lena, groping in yet another purse removed from her bag. "I'll open *this* purse—"

"But *till* you get it open, lady," wailed the old man, "you already zipped and unzipped three times—excuse the expression—my pants!"

exposing the utter absurdity of a question by replacing obvious assent with acidulous disgust

In Yiddish and Yinglish, no sarcasm is more withering than that which negates the eminently desirable by pretending to prefer the transparently ludicrous.

ASHER: How would you and Bertha like to spend the winter in my condominium in California?

DENBOW: Do you think Bertha and I prefer to spend the winter in a cold-water flat on Delancey Street?

OR

Q: How would you like two tickets on the fifty-yard line for the Super-Bowl Game?

A: I'd rather stay home and paint my cellar.

See also BELITTLING SOMEONE . . . , DEFLATION . . .

expressing contempt by repeating someone's question in the precise form in which it was asked—but varying the intonation to express astonishment, indignation, resentment, umbrage or flabbergasted disgust

This conversational ploy, a much-favored form of sarcasm in Yiddish, is becoming a frequent enricher of persiflage in Yinglish.

Please note the various dramatic effects achieved by the mere shift of vocal stress, *seriation*:

1

Q: Have you sent in your contribution to the UJA [United Jewish Appeal]?

A: Have *I* sent in my contribution to the UJA? (Meaning: "Are you implying that I do *not* contribute to the UJA?")

2

Q: Have you sent in your contribution to the UJA?
A: Have I *sent* in my contribution to the UJA? (Meaning: "Do you think it takes a delegation to my house to argue me into contributing?!")

3

Q: Have you sent in your contribution to the UJA?
A: Have I sent in *my* contribution to the UJA? (Meaning: "Have I ever failed to send in *my* contribution?")

4

Q: Have you sent in your contribution to the UJA?
A: Have I sent in my *contribution* to the UJA? (Meaning: "Do you think it's nothing but a 'contribution'—when I consider it a basic obligation, a privilege, a thing *every* good Jew should do?")

5

Q: Have you sent in your contribution to the UJA?
A: Have I sent in my contribution *to* the UJA? (Meaning: "What kind of cockamamy question is that? Would I send my UJA contribution to the Council of Armenian Churches?!")

6

Q: Have you sent in your contribution to the UJA?
A: Have I sent in my contribution to the *UJA*? (Meaning: "How can you even suggest that I would send in a contribution to any charitable organization *before* I made my contribution to the UJA?")

However phrased, the deliberate repetition of a question to the questioner himself is a mode of sarcasm that puts the questioner on the moral (and guilt-laden) defensive.

F

Falashas

Falasha: (probably) "immigrant" in Old Ethiopic.
Some ten to fifteen thousand dark-skinned Jews who lived in Ethiopia, north of Lake Tana.

Probably descended from converts to Judaism, they claim to be direct descendants of the Ten Tribes ejected from Palestine. Romantic commentators think them descended from Solomon's son—by the lovely, legendary Queen of Sheba.

The Falashas know no Hebrew. They know only the Old Testament (in Geez) and nothing whatever of Talmud. They regard Moses' story as explicitly meant for them.

Very strict in morals and literal in observance, they fast every Monday and Thursday, at every new moon, and on Passover. They worship in synagogues and observe the laws of the Sabbath. They also practice rites that would make an American Jew's hair stand on end (an unchaste female, for instance, must leap into a roaring fire to purify herself).

The Falashas have Jewish monks. They believe in the evil shadow, rain doctors, and assorted soothsayers and raisers of the dead. About six thousand Falasha Jews have emigrated from this mountainous land to Israel.

For more about the Falashas' exotic ways and rites, see Jacques Faitlovitch's *The Falashas*, H. A. Stern's *Wander-*

ings Among the Falashas, M. Flad's *The Falashas of Abyssinia*.

fancy-shmancy

Pure Yinglish—and immensely popular as a "putdown" among Americans (and some Englishmen) of whatever ethnic or religious affiliation. A vivid reduplication, technically.

1. Overly ornate.
   "Did you ever see such a fancy-shmancy home?"
2. Affected.
   "When did she begin to use such fancy-shmancy language?"
3. Pretentious.
   "That fancy-shmancy Maurice Vermont: I knew him when he was Morris Greenberg."
4. Attempt at style that fails, hence is vulgar. "Their decorator is 'classy,' so their furniture is fancy-shmancy."

The sardonic *shm-* must have been among the earliest of what linguists call reduplications that was created or embroidered by Lower East Side Jews.

Fancy-shmancy came to the attention of cosmopolitan New York when it appeared in the very popular vaudeville sketches of Potash and Perlmutter, Smith and Dale, *et alia*.

The astringent phrase then graced the pages of *The New Yorker* in essays by the fastidious S. J. Perelman and stories by the ethnic humorist Arthur Kober.

See also SH-.

farchadat

Candidate for Yinglish. Pronounced *far*-CHAH-det, to rhyme with "char got it." Slavic: *chad*: "smoke," "daze."

1. Confused, dopey.
   "He is acting completely *farchadat*."
2. Smitten, beguiled.
   "You never saw any boy so *farchadat* by girls."
3. Shocked, surprised, stunned.

"That allegation is so *farchadat* I don't know how to answer it."

"Doctor, I have this terrible delusion that I am two people—two separate, independent people! I'm so *farchadat*! Do you think I need medicine? Should I go to a psychiatrist? Do you think I—?"

"Hold it!" said the doctor. "One at a time."

Rummaging through his desk, Morty Potemkin found a claim-check for a pair of shoes he had brought to I. J. Narkin's Shoe Repair—seven years ago!

That afternoon he went over to the shoe repair store. "Mr. Narkin, I know this is going to surprise you—and maybe this is all too late—but you were supposed to put new heels on a pair of my shoes—*seven years* ago!"

I. J. Narkin turned pale. "Seven yiss? Eh, you got to have a check!"

"I do," Morty handed Narkin the old, faded check.

Narkin, who was a bit *farchadat*, gulped, muttered to himself, disappeared behind a beaded curtain. After a bit, he returned, "Your shoes—dey are brown? And dey got a buckle, not laces?"

"That's right!" beamed Mr. Potemkin.

"They'll be raddy Tuesday."

See also FARFUFKET, FARMISHT, FARTOOTST, FARTUMELT, TSEDOODELT, TSEDRAYT.

farfufket
farfyufket   (playful pronunciation)

Recommended with pleasure for Yinglish. Pronounced *far*-FUF-*ket* or *far*-FYUF-*ket*. Origin uncertain (but the word is engagingly echoic).

1. All mixed up.
2. Befuddled.
3. Discombobulated.
4. Disoriented, unhinged.

If you are fond of *farfufket* you can enhance its phonetic appeal by using the mischievous *far*-FYOOF-*ket*, thus adding a liquid *y* for a gloss of affection.

Little Joey was over an hour late coming home from school. "Joey!" cried his mother. "What happened?"

"I was appointed Traffic Guard," said little Joey. "I have a white band across my chest. And I am supposed to stop traffic to let the kids cross the street!"

"So-o? You got so *farfufket* over that to be over an hour late?"

"Ma, you can't imagine how long I had to wait before a car came along I could stop!"

See also FARCHADAT, FARMISHT, FARTOOTST, FARTU-MELT, TSEDOOdELT, TSEDRAYT.

farmisht   (adjective)
farmishter   (masculine)
farmishteh   (feminine)

Yinglish would be enhanced by this echoic gem. From German: *vermischen*: to mix, to blend; and Yiddish: *farmish*, to confuse, to jumble, to befuddle.

1. Confused, mixed up.
   "He got me so *farmisht* I signed and ran!"
2. All balled up.
   "The plot is so *farmisht* no one can understand it."
3. Discombobulated.
   "The traffic lights got me so *farmisht*, I made a right turn instead of a left."

Farmisht and its derivatives are a colorful way of conveying the state of addlepated mix-up:

"A *farmishter* like Harry shouldn't be allowed to practice medicine."

"She is the most *farmishteh* member of the study group."

Mrs. Silberstein dialed her daughter's number and sang out, "Hello, darling. This is your mama. So how's everything?"

"Everything is just *awful*, Mama. The children are acting

crazy, the house is a mess, I have a bad back—and we are having three couples for dinner!"

"Stop! I'm coming right over," said Mrs. Silberstein. "I'll calm down the children, I'll clean up your place so every corner shines, and I'll cook a dinner for you and six guests no one will never forget!"

"Oh, Mama, you're an angel! That's just marvelous of you! . . . How's Papa?"

"What Papa? . . . Have you gone crazy? Your dear father—may his soul rest in peace—died seven years ago!"

A pause fell upon the line. "Er—what number are you calling?"

"Walton six, four, four, nine, one," said Mrs. Silberstein.

"This is Walton six, four, four, nine, *four*!"

"Omigod! I dialed the wrong number!" wailed Mrs. Silberstein.

"Wait! *Please*! I'm *farmisht*! Does this mean you're *not* coming over?!"

See also the delightful alternatives FARCHADAT, FARFUFKET, FARTOOTST, FARTUMELT, TSEDOODELT, TSEDRAYT.

farpatshket (adjective and verb)
farpotchket

Recommended for Yinglish. Pronounced *far-POTCH-k't*. From Russian: *patchkaty*: sloppy; Yiddish, *patshken*: to soil, to dawdle.

1. All messed up.
   "That's one *farpatshket* dish!"
2. Spoiled, ruined by over-decoration.
   "Only a woman of poor taste would want such a *farpatshket* living room."
3. Anything bollixed up, from a cruise to a cause.
   "The whole schedule was so *farpatshket* they had to throw it away."

There is an echoic splash to *farpatshket* that I admire. Words like this should be treasured:

"She tried to *improve* it?! That's a laugh. Why, she *farpatshket* it beyond belief!"

"You call that cubist expressionism? To me, it's a *farpatshket* piece of canvas."

See also FARFUFKET.

fartootst (verb and noun)
fartutst
fartootster (masculine noun)
fartootsteh (feminine noun)

Urged upon venturesome users of Yinglish. Pronounced *far*-TUTST, to rhyme with "far foots." From German: *verdutzt*: "confused," via Yiddish. A splendid example of echoic color and sonic humor.

1. Befuddled.
   "You look absolutely *fartootst*."
2. Bewildered.
   "All the technical jargon is *fartootsing* me!"
3. Distracted.
   "Keep your mind on the argument. Don't go off *fartootst*!"
4. Disoriented.
   "That *fartootsteh* doesn't know east from west—or vice versa."

When used as a noun, *fartootst* becomes *fartootster* (masculine) and *fartootsteh* (feminine). I recommend both of these buoyant nouns for the instant enrichment of your vocabulary.

Fartootst is one of a large clan of Yinglish synonyms to describe discombobulation's manifestations: *farchadat, farfufket, farmisht, fartumelt, tsedrayt, tsedoodelt*—all of which are included and embellished in this lexicon.

———————

The new secretary, Sherry Laskow, seemed eager to work.

Mr. Rackman, her employer, was pleased. As he went out to lunch, he said, "Miss Laskow, remind me to call Boris Yablon the minute I come back."

"Is his number on our office phone list?"

"No. Look him up in the telephone directory."

When Rackman returned from his lunch date, he said, "Miss Laskow, get me Yablon."

"Very soon, sir. I'm still working on it . . ."

"You're still working—on what?"

"His number," smiled Miss Laskow. "I'm already up to the *G*'s."

(Miss Laskow was—indubitably—*fartootst*. Does any English word describe her as well?)

See also FARCHADAT, FARMISHT, FARTUMELT, TSEDOODELT, TSEDRAYT.

fartumelt
fartummelt

A dandy word to recruit for Yinglish. Pronounced *far*-TOOM-*elt*. From German: *tummeln*: to rush around. Enrich your speech with this adjective.

1. Bewildered.
2. Dizzy.
3. Confused.

Shepsel, in the following story, and Yunich, in the next, were undeniably *fartumelt*.

Ezer and Shepsel were taking a walk. Suddenly the heavens opened and the rain poured down.

"Shepsel, open your umbrella."

Scoffed Shepsel, "My umbrella's not worth *bobkes*! It's full of holes."

"Then why did you bring it?"

"Did *I* know it was going to rain?" cried Shepsel.

———

"Battling Ike" Yunich went into the ring for the first time. In the second round he took a terrific blow to the jaw that sent him to the mat, flat on his back.

As he tried to wobble up to his shaky feet, his manager yelled, "No, no! Stay down! Stay down until nine!"

Ike nodded, *fartumelt* as can be, then asked blearily, "What—time—is it now?"

See also FARFUFKET, FARMISHT, FARTOOTST, TSEDOODELT, TSEDRAYT.

fartutst

See FARTOOTST.

faulting a virtue by repeating the word with a prefatory fricative of disapproval

This Yinglish ploy has caught on with great vigor, particularly in television sitcoms—which explains its wide dissemination in English conversation and newspaper columns.

"Neat-shmeat, he should go see a psychiatrist."
"Happy-shmappy, she makes *other* people miserable!"
"Good-shmood, why doesn't he go back to his family?"

Danny Gerhart's most fervent ambition had been to enter the Naval Academy at Annapolis. He wrote an excited letter home to his widowed mother:

. . . and I love *every* part of the Navy! I am making friends. There is not the slightest sign of anti-Semitism— not since Admiral Rickover, I guess. And next week, they're going to teach us how to use a *sextant*. I can hardly wait!!

> Love,
> Danny

The moment Mrs. Gerhart read this letter, she lunged for the phone and dialed her rabbi: "*Rebbe, rebbe.* Do you *know* what the Navy is now teaching our young men?!"

faygele

See FEYGELE.

Feh!

I recommend the wider use of this expressive expletive in Yinglish. Pronounced always with feeling, as FEH! Possibly from the German: *pfui*—or the Yiddish spoken in Austria (but that is of no consequence).

"*Feh!*" is the Yinglish replacement for exclamatory expressions of disgust, such as "Pee-yoo!" "Ugh!" "Phooey!" "Ecch!" and "Pfrr!" It strikes me as a crisp and exact delineation of disgust.

In crying "Feh!" you may bare your teeth and wrinkle your nose, in visual reinforcement of your conviction:

1. Expression of total disgust.
2. Epithet for indignant disapproval.
3. Forceful congé to signify rejection.

I recommend this blurted expletive as blissfully cathartic when

Stepping into dog-do.
Smelling a rotten fish, egg, minnow or whale.
Mentioning the candidate you voted against.
Describing the creeps who infest West Forty-second Street.
Appraising demented (or defiantly fraudulent) works of modern art.
Expressing any sight, or reliving any event, that arouses revulsion.
Railing against fate, misfortune, or the inevitable.
Delineating the character of the *paskudnyak* who ran off with your wife.
Describing the *chutzpanik* who thinks he's going to marry your daughter.
Recounting how a soprano murdered an aria.
Portraying strongly negative feelings about any sight, event, person, crisis, experience or emotion.

Feh!—I salute you!

I once wrote an entire story to illustrate the puissance of this incomparable expletive: "Mr. K*A*P*L*A*N and the Unforgivable 'Feh!' " You may find it, plus a happy plethora of Yinglishisms, in *The Return of H*Y*M*A*N K*A*P*L*A*N.*

"Old age! *Feh!*" snorted Mr. Binder. "So far, I found only one good thing about it."
"What's that?"
"I can brush my teeth and sing at the same time."

Sam Persky realized he had not seen his friend Herschel Bienstock for six months—in fact, not since Mrs. Bienstock had passed away. He hastened to Bienstock's apartment. "So how are you doing, Herschel?"

"Oh, Sammy," quavered Bienstock, "I barely get along. I'm so lonely . . ."

"Hersch, you know what would cheer you up? A nice game pinochle!"

"I would love it."

And so the two friends played pinochle.

After an hour or so, Sam Persky shot a look at his wristwatch. "*Feh!*" he grunted. "My watch stopped. Herschel, what time is it?"

"Who knows?"

"Give a look at your *zager* [watch]."

"I don't have a *zager*."

"So the bedroom, Hersch! On your bedside table."

"On my bedside table, I don't have a clock neider."

Sam Persky's jaw dropped. "You mean to tell me that in this whole apartment you don't have *one single* clock? For God's sake, Herschel, don't you ever want to know what *time* it is?!"

"Soitinly. When I want to know what time it is—I pick up my bugle."

"Your what?!"

"My bugle." Bienstock leaned over and from the floor lifted an old, battered bugle. "I'll show you." Bienstock went to a window, opened it, put the bugle to his lips and blared out a forceful "Ra-ta-ta-ta-*tah!*"

And from a dozen flats in the courtyard came this angry chorus: "What's the matter with you, you crazy, playing the bugle at a quarter to eleven at night?!"

See also AHA!, AI-AI-AI, HOO-HA!, MNYEH, OY, PSSSSH!

feygele
faygele

This euphemistic neologism is being used with greater and greater regularity in Yinglish because of usage 4 below. Pronounced FAY-*geh-leh*. Diminutive of the German *Vogel* and the Yiddish *foygl*: little bird.

1. A little bird.
2. A jailbird.
3. A young man of great delicacy, great sensitivity, or effeminate manners.

4. A male homosexual.

This euphemism was common in Jewish circles long before the English word *gay*.

In the Talmud there is a descriptive term, *tum-tum*, which gives you the general idea. But *tum-tum* more accurately referred to a shy, beardless adolescent—or a hermaphrodite.

"Mrs. Yastrow, is it true what I hear about your son?"
"What do you hear about my son, Mrs. Beckman?"
"That he announced—he's a practicing homosexual!"
Mrs. Yastrow moaned, "It's true, it's true."
"So where is his office?"

fifer

Recommended for the enrichment of Yinglish. Rhymes with "lifer." From German: *Pfeifer*: whistler.

1. Someone who whistles a lot, often unconsciously.
2. A loud, shrill, noisy person.
3. A boaster, a braggart.
4. Someone who talks adenoidally.
5. Someone whose way of speaking puts your teeth on edge.

A *fifer* is not necessarily a *fonfer*; the latter will talk your ears off.

To say "I *fife* on him" means "The devil with him!" or "I don't pay the slightest attention to his opinion!"

Mr. Dubin, a *fifer* who had just returned from his first trip to Europe, was regaling his friends with stories.

"And did you get to Rome?" one asked him.

"Naturally!"

"How did you like the Colosseum?"

Mr. Dubin made a blasé gesture. "Very nice—if you like modern."

The following episode involves a man (I call him Birnkraut) who may be a *fonfer* or a *fifer*: have it either way.

Julius Birnkraut had just moved into his new office. On the door gleamed:

GOLDEN OPPORTUNITY INVESTMENT COUNSELORS
PRES. J. O. BIRNKRAUT

There was a knock on the door. Birnkraut called out "Come in!" and lifted the phone, into which he briskly said, "Mr. Morgan, we bought ten thousand!" He waved the visitor to a chair. "I advise selling the potash and going into manganese . . . How much? Four million? . . . Thank you, Mr. Morgan!" Birnkraut scribbled a note and put the phone down. "Now, sir, can I help you?"

"Well," said the visitor, "I'm from the phone company. I just came to hook up your telephone."

See also FONFER.

fin

Thoroughly and long established in American slang. From Yiddish: *fin(i)f*: "five."

1. Five.
2. A hand (five-fingered).
3. A five-dollar bill.
4. A jail sentence of five years (criminal cant).

Fin is widely used, and known, in the vernacular—especially among sports fans, gamblers, Broadway types and gossip columnists. The slang word often appears in Damon Runyon's world, in stories by John O'Hara and S. J. Perelman, and in novels about detectives.

I do not support H. L. Mencken's contention (in *The American Language*) that *fin* is derived from the German *fünf* (five), which is pronounced somewhat like "*foonf*." The Yiddish version of the word is closer: *finif*. I believe that English speakers adopted the Yiddish, not the German, pronunciation because Anglo-Saxons simply cannot vocalize an umlauted *u* (*ü*). For example, *Führer* becomes "furore," "fyoorer," "fooroar," "furrer." But who can mispronounce *finif*—much less *fin*?

The Dictionary of American Slang, edited by Harold Wentworth and Stuart Berg Flexner, a reliable—nay, an invaluable—source-book, attributed *fin* flatly to Yiddish.

focusing irony by mere repetition

An effective sarcastic Yinglish rejection lies in the deliberate repetition, either blandly or bluntly, of an offer. Thus:

FRED: Will you take ten dollars for it?
GENE: Will I take *ten* dollars for it?

And that *tu quoque* is more contentious, therefore less ironic, than the steely echo, "Will *I* take ten dollars for it?"

Readers who wish to challenge my attribution of Yinglishness to this ploy of repetition are requested to see RIDICULE . . . or AUTOMATIC AND SARCASTIC REPETITION . . .

fonfer (noun)
fonfet (verb)

Recommended for Yinglish. Pronounced, respectively, FAWN (or FUN)-*fir* and FUN-*fit* or FAWN-*fet*. From Slavic: "to speak through the nose."

1. Someone who *fonfes, i.e.,* talks through his nose—unclearly or as if he has a bad cold. One of Sholem Aleichem's characters always pronounces "I am" as "I ab," and "You may" as "You bay." He was a *fonfer.*
2. A double-talker.
   "That *fonfer* can drive you out of your mind."
3. Anyone who is lazy, slow, "goofs off."
   "Don't be a *fonfer*—work!"
4. One who does not deliver what he promises; *i.e.,* he *fonfes* promises.
5. A shady, petty deceiver.
   "That *fonfer* will try to make you think black is white."
6. A constant excuse maker.
7. One who cheats.
   "He's a *fonfer*; watch his addition."
8. One who goes through the motions of a thing without intending to perform to his capacity, or your proper expectations.
   "It took him three hours to deliver that package? Did you ever hear of such a *fonfer*?"

  9. A boaster, full of bravado.
 10. A specialist in hot air, baloney—a trumpeter of hollow promises.
    "He should be selling lots on the moon, that *fonfer*."

———

BEIGEL: Did *I* get an order! From the J. C. Penney chain—for three hundred thousand dollars!
ROTH: Stop with the *fonfing*.
BEIGEL: You don't believe me? I'll show you the cancellation!

———

"I come from a famous fighting family!" *fonfet* Mrs. Donald Edson. "My great-great-grandfather fought the rebels at Gettysburg. My great-grandfather fought the Germans at Verdun. My grandfather fought the Japanese on Guadalcanal. And my father fought the North Koreans—"
    "*Mein Gott!*" exclaimed Mrs. Cooperman. "Can't your people get along with *any*body?"

See also FIFER, K'NOCKER.

for free

Yinglish, widespread—and undesirable, except when used for frivolous, comedic purposes. From Yiddish: *far gornit* (*gornisht, gurnisht*): "for nothing."
    For nothing; at no cost:

Q: Is there an admission charge?
A: No. It's for free.

The placing of the totally superfluous *for* before the totally adequate *free*, is an exact metaphrase from Yiddish. Hence, "for free" is a transplant into English by American Jews—but the transplant would long since have perished unless a wide stratum of Americans, mostly youths, found the phrase colorful, evocative, and amusing.

———

JANET: The rock-concert tonight is for free!
SUE: I don't think it's worth it.

ALFRED: The nerve of that Peter! He sees most movies for free!

JIM: How does he do that?

ALFRED: He waits for the show to end. Then, as the audience pours out, *he* walks in—backwards!

for-instance (noun)

Unequivocally, if lamentably, Yinglish. Used as a noun, and a single word—not a phrase.

1. An example.
   "Let me give you a for-instance."
   This usage, however ineloquent, appears to be firmly entrenched on the inelegant frontiers of Yinglish. It is used by many who know it is ungrammatical but are amused by its departure from the conventional.
2. Be specific (when preceded by "Give me a . . .).
   Secretary of State Dean Rusk once replied to a reporter, at a press conference, "Can you be more specific? Can you give me a for-instance?" Mr. Rusk is a Protestant, a Southerner but a Yinglishman nevertheless.

Why *for-instance* should replace *example* (for which it is meant to serve as an exact synonym) I cannot tell you—except that non-Jewish users find the words, phrases, metaphrases and oddities of syntax, of which Yinglish is chockfull, appealing, striking or amusing or (at least) a respite from the mundane.

"You say his lecture contained a few ungrammatical sentences?"

"Not a few. A *lot*."

"Well, give me some *for-instances*."

In this case, *for-instances* clearly attracts the eye and ear in a way that *examples* never can.

"Say, I can remember things you wouldn't *believe*."

"So, give a for-instance."

"A for-instance? Okay. I can remember before I was even born!"

"That's impossible!"

"Oh, yeah? Well, I remember going to a weekend party in Joisey with my father—"

"C'mon—"

"—and coming back with my mother!"

for real . . . ?

This brisk, cynical phrase is immensely popular in Yinglish circles—particularly among the financial community and Yuppies. Like *for free*, *for real* is a modified metaphrase from the Yiddish: *far emmes?*: "for true," "Is it really true?"

For real is an idiomatic substitute for:

1. "Is he [she, are they] really serious?"
2. "Is he crazy—or really this way?"
3. "Am I to take his action [statement, request, demand] seriously—or is he [she] just putting on an act?"
4. "That conduct is so bizarre that I wonder if it is meant to be taken seriously."
5. "Is he [she] putting us on?"

Samuel Goldwyn, a most distinguished producer, may have achieved as much immortality for his malapropisms as he has with his movies. Here are but the most dazzling examples:

"In two words: im possible!"

"The story is absolutely impossible—but it has possibilities."

"An oral contract isn't worth the paper it's written on."

"I have made up my mind: Include me out."

"Today, every Tom, Dick, and Harry is named Ronald."

Is it surprising that Hollywoodniks would often (somewhat dazedly) ask: "Is Goldwyn for real?"

SCENE: Sally's Sea Food Grotto

The waiter brought the "Today's Special" fish to the customer—who stared at it, then leaned over and began to whisper to the fish, then placed his ear close to the plate.

"Mister!" cried the startled waiter. "What are you *do-ing*?"

"I'm having a conversation with the fish."

"Talking to a *fish*? Listen, are you for real?"

"I happen to speak—and understand eight fish languages: Carp, Salmon, Pike, Herring—"

"But what did you just *tell* that fish?" asked the goggle-eyed waiter.

The customer said, "I asked him where he was from, and he answered, 'I am from Peconic Bay.' So I asked him 'How are things in Peconic Bay?' So he told me, 'How should *I* know? It's *years* since I was there!' "

For two cents plain . . .

A true Yinglishism, injected into colloquial English by Jews from the Lower East Side, who carried it to enclaves in Brooklyn and the Bronx.

A glass of plain seltzer (carbonated) water without syrup of any sort, served in a smaller glass than "for five cents plain."

This was a very popular drink, especially on spring or hot summer days, in the immigrant sectors of Manhattan and its attendant boroughs.

When I first visited New York I was pleasantly surprised to see many stores with their front (sidewalk) windows open, so as to serve customers on the street. Among the most popular of the things offered for sale were cigarettes, peanuts, candy bars, bottled soft drinks (Moxie, Root Beer, Orange Crush) and, from a fountain, seltzer in its many forms: plain, with chocolate, a cherry, a slice of fruit (a "float"), a spoonful of malt, etc.

The most popular (because cheapest) drink was "For two cents plain."

See also SELTZER WATER.

Forvits
Forverts

The Yiddish pronunciation of *forward*.

The great and memorable *Jewish Daily Forward*.

It is hard to exaggerate the role that this widely read, almost revered, Yiddish newspaper played in the lives of

Jewish immigrants. It was a newspaper, a schoolroom for English, a political forum, a bonding force. It reached a national audience, printing or distributing copies daily in New York, Chicago, Los Angeles. Its circulation built up steadily to a surprising national total of almost three hundred thousand.

The *Forward* was founded in 1897, as an official voice of socialism and the labor movement. It exercised an unrivaled influence on Jews in America. Its most important editor was the legendary "Abe" Cahan (1860–1951), inspired and indefatigable, with no peer as a polemicist. He had a lively intelligence, searing sarcasm, a muscular style. Not the least important of Abe Cahan's roles was that of opposing Communist influence in the American trade union movement, and of building a secular movement among American Jews, away from orthodox religious affiliations.

The *Forvits*, as it was universally called, played a memorable role in my life. Each night in Chicago, as soon as we finished dinner (we called it "supper"), my father would spread the *Forvits* across the kitchen table under the green glass gas lamps, and would proceed to read aloud to my mother and me.

And so, even as a boy, I snatched pieces of meaning from the *Forward*'s reports about the movers and the shakers of the world: breadlines in Warsaw, a debate in the Senate, a small pogrom in Romania, a large pogrom in the Ukraine . . .

After reading the news, my father turned to the "*Bintl Brief*" ("Bundle of Letters"), the popular "agony column": letters to the editor. Now I heard about raffish boarders making advances to respectable landladies; consumptive men forced to live on the pittances of in-laws; women begging some reader to take their children—who were starving; Socialist pressers who lamented their wives' indifference to the Class Struggle; tales of abandoned sweethearts (the *Forward* even publicized/traced husbands who had abandoned their wives or betrothed ones)—every conceivable experience in this sad, shimmering New World to which the immigrant hordes had come.

These letters to the *Forward* often asked for advice:

"Should I marry him?"
"Is such a girl to be trusted?"

"Will capitalism change only through revolution?"

"How can a mother's heart bear such shame?"

And famed Abe Cahan himself often answered the questions, in consoling, indignant or magisterial words. Many of the letters, and more of the answers, contained hallowed Jewish folk sayings, which my father read; the adages sank their roots into my mind:

"Out of snow, you can't make cheesecake."

"When you're hungry, sing; when you're hurt, laugh."

"When a father helps a son, both laugh; when a son helps his father, both cry."

"It's better to be embarrassed than ashamed."

"A man is not honest just because he never had a chance to steal!"

"A saloon can't corrupt a good man, and a synagogue can't reform a bad one."

"How is it possible that the clod who wasn't good enough to marry your daughter is the father of the smartest grandchild in the world?"

"The man who marries for money will earn it."

"When two divorced people get married, four get into bed."

"The longest road in the world is the one that leads from the pocket."

After the delicious heart-throbs of the *Bintl Brief*, our little kitchen heard the climax to each night's drama: the reading of a short story, a tale by Cahan himself or by I. J. Singer (Bashevis' older brother), Sholem Asch or the incomparable Sholem Aleichem.

To this day, I remember the textures, if not the plots, of those true-life dramas: yearning widows and shameless philanderers; men burning with idealism, men soured by life; the favors and fevers of love sought, love lost, love gained, love unrequited; *brises*, betrothals, betrayals, Bar Mitzvas; children who flourished, children who perished; the laugh in the doorway, the cry in the night—I can hear them all again, faint old music as from a calliope, playing its accompaniment to the kaleidoscope of memories of our plain but oh-so-rich kitchen and of the warmth of our feelings and the replenishments of our laughter and the gentle joys and fierce communion of the days when both I and my parents (*aleyhem ha-sholem*) were so very, very young.

from (instead of "about," "by," "of" or "with")

Yinglish, a solecism neither defensible nor desirable. I record, but in no way recommend, such Bronxian diction—which borders on barbarism.

1. About. "What does he know from hockey?"
2. By. "That's actually a story from Tolstoy."
3. With. "He's sick from the measles."

In English, the use of *from* in place of *of* is incorrect, indefensible, ungrammatical—so you should *never* ever use corrupt phrasings like

"Who knows from vacations?"
"My son doesn't know from barbers."
"He's the king from Jordan."

—unless, of course, you are a pip at parody:

Damon Runyon, a popular columnist and reporter in the 1930s, forged a wonderfully colorful dialect, Broadwayese—an amalgam of baseball, gambling, racing and pugilist lingos. What is especially marked is the explicit influence of Jews, or of Yinglish locutions, on Runyon's creative lingo. (But consider also the influence of writers Frank Loesser, Abe Burrows and George S. Kaufman, who directed *Guys and Dolls*, that *tour de force*.) The character Nathan Detroit produces a cascade of Yiddishized English whenever he opens his mouth: "I could die from [*sic*!] shame," "So sue me . . . shoot bullets through me," "So go ahead and . . .," "*Nu* . . ."

HUSBAND: Who are you mailing that to?
WIFE: The manager from my bank. I'm sending them a check for twenty dollars and sixty cents.
HUSBAND: Why?
WIFE: That's how much he said I'm overdrawn.

To celebrate his mother's eightieth birthday, Seymour Flick sent her a bottle of champagne and a jar of caviar.

That afternoon he telephoned. "*Mazel tov*, Mama!"

"Oh, Seymour! *Thank* you for the wonderful present!"

"You liked it, Mama?"

"The ginger ale I *loved*, dollink; but tell the store that those little black berries taste from herring!"

from hunger

Authentic Yinglish. From the Yiddish: *fun hoonger*. This locution has long been popular in theatrical, literary and critical circles. "Strictly" is often added to emphasize one's conviction.

1. Anything done out of severe necessity, rather than choice. "He wrote it without pleasure—but from hunger."
2. Second or third rate.

From that [this] he makes a living?!

Yinglish, and nothing can be done about it.

"Do you mean to say that *that's* what he does?!"

This is the climactic line from a famous joke: An elderly Jew asked his son, "Exactly what did Albert Einstein do that was so smart?"

"Einstein revolutionized physics," replied the son. "Why, he proved that matter is energy and that time is actually the fourth dimension! And that when light goes past the sun, it *bends* in the sun's gravitational field!"

The old man made a few obligatory clucks of admiration, shaking his head, then leaned over and asked, "So tell me: from *that* he makes a living?!"

From that, you could faint

From this, you could die.

Why is "From this, you could die" funnier than "You could die from this"? Because placing the phrase "from this" in front defers the revelation of the consequence and thereby heightens curiosity (or dread) by prolonging the tension.

See also I COULD BUST FROM . . .

Fuhr gezunderheit!
Fuhr gezunderhayt!
Fuhrt gezunderheit! (plural)

Pronounced *foor* (to rhyme with "moor," not with "door") *ge-zoon-der* HITE or *ge-zun-der* HATE or *ge-zin-der* HITE or *ge-zin-der* HATE. Yiddish, adopted from German. The pronunciation varies according to the geographical area from which the speaker (or his or her parents) came: Lithuania, Poland, Galicia, Russia, Romania.

1. Travel in good health.
2. May your journey not be shadowed by illness.

Jewish decorum is rich in benevolent salutations. Where the French sing out "*Bon voyage!*" or Americans "Have a good trip!" or Englishmen "Safe journey!" Jews declaim "*Fuhr* [or *fuhrt*] *gezunderheit!*"

Jewish greetings and salutations often enlist health in the service of amiability. Thus: "Wear it in good health!" or "Return in good health."

I hope "Go in good health!" takes root in Yinglish not only because of its felicity but because it lends itself to prodigies of sarcasm. The most memorable (indeed, unforgettable) story I know about this admirable phrase is the one about Ari Ben-Ruach, who became the commander of the S.S. *Simcha*, in the Israeli navy, in charge of the fleet maneuvers.

Admiral Ben-Ruach had an irrepressible sense of humor. Shlomo Gurelick, captain of the S.S. *Sabra*, a well-known worrier, was something of a *nudnik*.

With this background, I now give you an exchange of radio messages:

OPERATIONS CHIEF BEN-RUACH
S.S. SIMCHA
   FOG IS SETTING IN. VISIBILITY POOR. SHALL I HOLD COURSE OR RETURN TO HARBOR?

                    CAPTAIN GURELICK
                    S.S. SABRA

CAPTAIN GURELICK
S.S. SABRA
  YES.

                          OP CHIEF
                          S.S. SIMCHA

OP CHIEF
S.S. SIMCHA
  DOES YOUR "YES" MEAN I SHOULD PROCEED OR RE-
TURN?

                          CAPTAIN
                          S.S. SABRA

GURELICK
S.S. SABRA
  NO.

                          OP CHIEF
                          S.S. SIMCHA

OP CHIEF
S.S. SIMCHA
  AM THOROUGHLY CONFUSED! PLEASE CLARIFY!

                          CAPT. GURELICK
                          S.S. SABRA

GURELICK
S.S. SABRA
  GLADLY.

                          OP CHIEF
                          S.S. SIMCHA

OP CHIEF
S.S. SIMCHA
  URGENT! URGENT! SEND ME EXACT, EXPLICIT INSTRUC-
TIONS! REPEAT. SEND ME EXACT, EXPLICIT INSTRUC-
TIONS!

                          CAPT. GURELICK
                          S.S. SABRA

GURELICK
S.S. SABRA
  MESSAGE UNCLEAR. REPHRASE.

                          OP CHIEF
                          S.S. SIMCHA

OP CHIEF
S.S. SIMCHA
  UNLESS YOU GIVE ME EXACT, EXPLICIT ORDERS I WILL
HAVE TO MOVE IN CIRCLES!

                          CAPT. GURELICK
                          S.S. SABRA

GURELICK
S.S. SABRA
    FUHR GEZUNDERHEIT.

OP CHIEF
S.S. SIMCHA

Mr. and Mrs. Goldwyn were about to sail to Hawaii on a vacation. A group of friends came to the dock to see them off.

As the ship started to slip away, Goldwyn put his hands to his mouth and sang out: "*Bon voyage!*"

G

Galitzianer

Pronounced *gol-lit*-see-ON-er. Rhyme it with "Sol Itzy Honor."

A Jew from Galicia (not the Galicia of Spain; the Central European Galicia, north of the Carpathian Mountains, a part of the Austro-Hungarian empire from 1772 to 1919, when it was annexed by Poland).

As far back as the ninth century, there were Jewish settlements in central Europe's Galicia, which became a famous seat of Talmudic scholarship. Its Yeshivas produced a stream of noted rabbis and rabbinical authorities. By the twentieth century, ten percent of Galicia was Jewish.

The Jews in the Austro-Hungarian empire benefitted greatly from the enlightened Joseph II's 1780 decree, which established compulsory education for all his subjects.

Rivalry between Galitzianer and Litvak (a Jew from Lithuania) was pronounced; and Polish Jews were condescending to both; Russian Jews felt superior to all three—and German Jews (*Deutsche Yehudim*) shuddered at, and firmly distanced themselves from, all four.

In the United States, German Jewish families—Warburgs, Kahns, Schiffs, Loebs, Kuhns, Lehmans—formed an elite of noteworthy cohesiveness. The "pecking order" of this Establishment and its Pecksniffian patronage (of Russian, Lithuanian, Polish and Galician Jews) is well described by Stephen Birmingham in *Our Crowd: The Great*

Jewish Families of New York. San Francisco's Jews were a distinguished group of descendants of settlers dating back to the Gold Rush.

Yet for all the snobbery and distaste of the "assimilated" American Jews to their poor, ill-clad, often dirty, orthodox cousins from central and eastern Europe, the "family feelings" of responsibility, the awareness of a common heritage and an ancient religious faith, never-forgotten memories of persecution and catastrophe fostered ties of unity, fortified by an awareness of possible future crises, among the Jews in America.

See also ASHKENAZI, LITVAK.

galus
galut

Pronounced GOLL-*us*, to rhyme with "call us." Hebrew: "exile." (In Yiddish, the Hebrew *t* is pronounced *s*.)

1. Exile; the Diaspora; the dispersion of the Jews among the lands outside of Israel.
2. A state of alienation.
3. Residence among others, and in an insubordinate status.

See also DIASPORA.

Gan Eden

Pronounced *gon* AY-*din*, to rhyme with "wan maiden." Hebrew: "Garden of Eden."

1. The Garden of Eden.
2. Heaven.

Where was Eden? Popular theory placed it between the Tigris and Euphrates rivers. There Adam and Eve dwelt in innocent bliss, until their curiosity got the better of them—and all of us. This story was almost certainly borrowed from Babylonian mythology.

Now, Talmudists and cabalists are persuaded that there were *two* gardens of Eden: the luxuriant garden on earth; and one in the heavens, the eternal abode of all the righteous after death. The celestial *Gan Eden* was synonymous with Paradise.

Men's early images of paradise were singularly simple. The celebrated Talmudic savant, Rab (c. 352–427), said: "In *Gan Eden* there is no eating, no drinking, no cohabitation, no business, no envy, no hatred or ambition; but the righteous sit with crowned heads and enjoy the luster of the *Shekhinah* [Divine Presence]."

But the incomparable Maimonides remarked, "To believe so is to be a schoolboy who expects nuts and sweetmeats as compensation for his studies. Celestial pleasures can neither be measured nor comprehended by a mortal being, any more than a blind man can distinguish colors, or the deaf appreciate music."

The Talmud lists *seven* heavens. The recurrence of seven as a virtuous, lucky or magical number is, of course, familiar: *e.g.*, the Seven Against Thebes, the Seven Deadly Sins, the Seven Gifts of the Spirit, the Japanese Seven Gods of Luck, the Seven Years of Tannhauser, the Seven Virtues, the Arabs' Seven Vizers, etc. The ancient Hebrew scribes had Seven Names for God, which required special care in copying, and during the Middle Ages, the Lord was sometimes referred to as The Seven.

———————

It is worse to be in heaven with a fool than in hell with a sage.

A special place is reserved in Heaven for those who can weep but not pray.   —Folk sayings

A clown may be first in the kingdom of heaven if he has helped lessen the sadness of human life.
                              —Rabbi Baroka in TALMUD

———————

A rabbi once dreamed that he was in *Gan Eden*. There he saw all the sages, sitting and studying Talmud.

"Is this all there is to paradise?" he exclaimed. "Why, we do this on Earth!"

An angel answered, "Ah, you think the scholars are in *Gan Eden*, but you are wrong. It is the other way round: *Gan Eden* is in the scholars."

———————

The new arrival at the Gan Eden Resort near Haifa sat down in a beach chair. "I got up at dawn!" he boasted, "to see the sunrise."

"You soitinly picked the right time," said his neighbor.

Gay in drerd!

Yiddish. Vituperation.

1. (Literally) Go into the earth (*di erd*)!
2. Go to hell!
3. To hell with you!

A Jewish homosexual ordered the following inscription on his tombstone:

GAY IN DRERD

The pun deserves remembrance.

Crack troops of the Israeli army were working on survival techniques—ingenious methods of survival if lost on a desert, in a jungle, in a rowboat, on mountains.

In one lecture, the men were being taught about food that can be found in wood: termites, grubworms. "And grasshoppers," said the instructor, "are a tasty, nutritious food. In fact, King Solomon used to feed grasshoppers to his thousand wives!"

A voice from the ranks cut in: "*In drerd* with what he gave the women. What did *he* eat?"

See also DROP DEAD!

gefilte fish
gefülte fish

Yiddish, becoming Yinglish. Pronounced *ge-*FILL-*teh fish*. From the German: "stuffed fish."

1. Fish-cakes or fish loaf, made of various fishes that are chopped or ground and mixed with eggs, salt and lots of onions and pepper (sometimes with sugar).
2. Traditional Friday night fish treat, served at the Sabbath dinner.

Gefilte fish is becoming a staple in American cuisine. I have always found it delicious, hot or cold, and recommend that red or white *chrayn* (horseradish) be handy, to dip the fish into, to suit your palate.

Recipes for *gefilte fish* can be found in any number of cookbooks.

Gehenna

> Pronounced *ga*-HEN-*a*, to rhyme with "the henna," or *gay*-HEN-*a*, to rhyme with "say when a." Hebrew: *Gehinom*: "Hell." Literally: the Valley (*gay*) of Hinnom.
> Hell.

In the "valley of the sons of Hinnom," south of Jerusalem, says the Bible, children were sacrificed to the idol Moloch. For this reason, the valley was said to be accursed; *Gay-Hinnom*, or *Gehenna*, became synonymous with Hell.

Hell, according to early but apocryphal texts, is not located in the netherworld, but in "the third heaven"! (I should confide to you that lubricious angels who consort with human females are allocated to the second heaven, and are flogged each day.)

Purgatory, by the way, does not appear in any place in the Old or the New Testaments. The Catholic Church decreed the reality of Purgatory in 1274, 1439, and 1540. But the Church of England, in 1562, pilloried Purgatory as "vainly invented . . . grounded upon no warranty of Scripture [and] rather repugnant to the Word of God."

Anyone interested in angels or demons should wallow in the *Dictionary of Angels*, by Gustav Davidson.

> It is better to be in hell with a wise man than in heaven with a fool.   —Folk saying

---

Jerry Heldman was reading the obituaries in the morning paper when, to his astonishment, he read his own name!

As his eyes raced down the column, his stupefaction rose: the entire obituary was his—every date, place, fact of his life! He dashed to the phone and called his lawyer. "Hello, Erwin? Did you read this morning's paper?"

"Sure. Who is this?"

"What do you mean. 'Who is this'? It's me, Jerry! I want you to sue the paper—"

"*Jerry* Heldman?" cried the lawyer.

"Certainly! I want you to sue—"

"Hold it, Jerry!" said the lawyer. "Uh—where are you calling from?!"

gelt

Yinglish, often encountered in English stories, newspaper articles and feature columns. Rhymes with "felt." From German: *Geld*: "money."

1. Money.
2. Wealth.

Gelt, like *shekels* or *mazuma*, has long been a part of American slang.

"Where did he stash the *gelt*?"
"He'll do anything for *gelt*."

This may be a good place for a digression on *gelt* and lending it. "Money-lending" is a *sine qua non* of economic growth. However, the ethics of indebtedness have been interpreted in various ways. Roman law held that a debt was personal, so a note could not be transferred. In Germany, a man who owed money was obligated to pay it only to the original lender; hence, debts died when a creditor died! Even in enlightened England, up to the middle of the nineteenth century, some debts were not transferable. But the Talmud says a debt must be honored even if a creditor or debtor dies.

Christian Church fathers made the economically catastrophic error of considering any form of banking "usurious," no matter how useful, proper or modest the interest rate. (The Talmud forbids Jews to take "excessive" interest.) To build a cathedral or a ship; to buy tools, seed, livestock; to recover from a drought; to pay taxes; to tide a man over a disastrous harvest, accident or disease—for any of these, a loan was imperative.

Popes, kings and noblemen were driven to enlist (or preempt) the aid of Jews to finance their cathedrals and armies, their palaces and estates—in this way transferring the medieval sin of usury to those outside the Christian fold, *i.e.*, to souls already so doomed to perdition that an extra transgression did not matter.

Jews were *forced* to become moneylenders. They were forbidden to own land. They were forbidden to belong to certain guilds or practice certain crafts. Then they were despised for the hateful occupation of handling, managing or lending money. Oh, Shylock . . .

In eastern Europe, Jews were often murdered, in ones or twos or in the *en masse* orgy of a pogrom, to "cancel" the debts owed them by pious Russians or Polish nobles.

When Jews were forced out of banking, investment and money-lending activities, to be replaced by Christians (who had persuaded the authorities to push the Jews out), interest rates always rose, and economic growth was gravely stunted.

Seventeenth-century English monarchs earnestly asked the Jews to lend them money—to undercut the huge interest rates being charged by Christians. (William of Orange even knighted Solomon Medina, a Jewish banker.) William Pitt also enlisted the aid of Jews against English bankers, whose interest rates were simply crippling England's growth.

The role of the Talmud in the economic life of the West has been sparsely cited by historians. The Talmud laid down remarkably intelligent rules about property, contracts, insurance, real estate, equity, torts—and international law. Werner Sombart traces the beginnings of capitalism to Europe's Jews and W. E. H. Lecky stresses the part that Jews played in organizing trade between nations. David Ricardo, who wrote one of the most important and enduring works of economic theory, *Principles of Political Economy and Taxation* (1817), was a Jew.

———

The stereotype of Jews as good businessmen (they are certainly not better than Chinese, Arabs or Greeks) is not lessened by the delight Jews take in telling stories like these:

Mr. Jacobs is drowning: "Help! Help!" he screams.

A lifeguard swims to his rescue and shoves him toward shallow water. "Now—can you float alone?"

"Migod," gasps Jacobs, "is this a time to talk business?"

———

A week after the stock market plummeted to a new low, two brokers met. "Lord, what a horrible day!" groaned

Ted Solovsky. "And there's not a sign of relief in sight. Charlie, to tell you the truth, I can't remember when I last had one good night's sleep!"

"Really?" said Charley. "*I* sleep like a baby."

"*What?!* Do you *mean* that?"

"Absolutely," said Charley. "I get up every two hours—and cry."

Accounting Department
TO: Marcus Schwebel
FROM: Controller

I absolutely cannot and will not approve your latest Expense Account figures! They are outrageous!

Ray Wolf

P.S. How much would you take for the fiction rights?

Savor the following typographical error in a newspaper column:

The head of the investment firm would not say whether, in his own private holdings, he was more interested in stocks or blonds.

gendz

See GUNSEL.

Gesundheit!
Gezundhayt!

Pronounced *ge-*ZUND*-hite*, to rhyme with "the Bund kite." German: "Health."

1. Health. Someone once quipped that you can tell if a man is a Jew by how he answers the question: "How are you?" If he says "Fine!" or "Couldn't be better," he's no Jew. For Jews, by tradition, fear that boasting (of good health or good luck) may attract some jealous and punishing evil Spirit. In any case, the typical Jewish reply to "How do you feel?" is "Not bad" or "So-so" or "Can't complain" or "Oy, do I have a headache and chills and heart palpitations!—" etcetera.

2. The verbal amenity uttered when someone sneezes:
   "Kerchoo!"
   "*Gesundheit!*"

"*Gesundheit!*" is as obligatory a response to a heard sneeze as "*Aleichem sholem*" is to the greeting, "*Sholem aleichem.*"

The English phrase used after someone has sneezed is, of course, "God bless you." The creator of this custom in the West was St. Gregory.

In many societies, sneezing is believed to effect the expulsion of one or another evil spirit. This belief is strong among the Zoroastrian Parsees, Indian tribes of the Americas, and countless peoples in Africa and Polynesia. If you remember your Aristotle, sneezing was more empirically regarded—as a symptom of a pestilence.

The Romans cried *Absit omen!* ("Flee, omen!"). And the Spaniards, when a Cacique Indian of Florida sneezed, raised their arms to heaven and begged the sun to intervene against so evil an augury.

The range of Jewish sayings about health may be worth sampling:

Too much is unhealthy.
Your health comes first—you can always hang yourself later.
What a fat belly cost, I wish I had; what it does, I wish on my enemies.
When there's a cure, it was only half a disease.
                                                              —Folk sayings
Eat a third, drink a third, but leave a third of your stomach empty; for then, if anger overtakes you, there will be room for your rage.   —TALMUD: *Gittin*, 70a

---

Apocryphal, but not the less amusing:

When an El Al plane left New York, the pilot greeted the passengers in these words: "*Sholem aleichem*, ladies and gentlemen, and welcome to El Al airlines. This is your pilot, Itzchak Levin, wishing you a happy, restful trip. And if by some very remote chance we do run into some little trouble—God forbid!—do not panic. Your life-belt is under your seat. And if you must put it on, wear it in the best of health!"

Get lost!

Yinglish. From Yiddish: *Ver farvalgert!*: "Get lost!" Or *Farlir zikh!*: "Go lose yourself!" Or *Ver farfallen!*: "Go into hiding!"

1. Go away—fast.
2. Move on; don't hang around here!
3. Disappear!
4. (Slang) Scram!

Some linguists think "Get lost" is an Americanism and not of Yiddish origin. I maintain they are wrong.

Sidewalk barkers and hawkers were a common sight in Jewish neighborhoods. These hustlers were gifted in gab, tireless in their "sell," and hated to be watched by the gawking kids who always gathered to hear the pitch. To this undesired audience, a spieler would mutter, "Beat it!" "Why don't you go home?"

When none of these exasperated injunctions sufficed, the thwarted salesman might snarl, "*Farlir zikh!*" ("Go lose yourself!"). I was one of the urchins advised to get *farvalgert* ("Get yourself *really* lost!").

In Chicago during the 1920s, when Prohibition nurtured gangsters and violence galore, I heard the ominous "Get lost!" (to mean "Get away from here!"). The command was used by hoodlums who wanted no witness to their physical shenanigans. The striking phrase spread into street talk.

A Warner Brothers gangster movie—with James Cagney, or Edward G. Robinson—brought "Get lost!" to popular attention.

Gevalt!
Gevald!

Pronounced *ge*-VOLT! From German: *Gewalt*: "powers," "force." Rhymes with "revolve."

1. The Yiddish equivalent of "Help! Help!"—but somehow more heart-rending . . .
2. An exclamation of fear, astonishment, terror: "*Gevalt!* Fire!"

3. A desperate expression of protest: "*Gevalt*, Lord! *Enough* already!"

Gevalt is both an expletive and a noun:
He took one look and cried, "*Gevalt!*"
"Now take it easy, don't make a *gevalt*."

An old Jewish saying tells us: "Man comes into the world with an *Oy*—and leaves with a *Gevalt!*"

―――――――

Countess Mimi de Rothschild, so it is said, lay in childbirth in the magnificent bedroom of her magnificent mansion, moaning and wailing.

Downstairs her husband, the count, pacing back and forth, wrung his hands anxiously.

"She's not ready to deliver," said the obstetrician. "Stop worrying. Let's play cards."

They played cards.

Suddenly, they heard a piercing, shrill cry from the countess: "*Mon Dieu! Mon Dieu!*"

Up leaped the count.

"No, no," said the doctor. "Not yet . . . Play your hand."

They played on.

Soon the countess screamed. "Oh, God! Oh, *God!*"

Up leaped the husband.

"*No*," said the doctor. "Not yet . . . Deal."

The husband dealt . . .

And a little later, a long loud mighty "*Gevalt!*" was heard.

The obstetrician leaped to his feet. "Now."

―――――――

On the fairway of a golf course in Israel, Solly Graff was ambling along with his caddy when a ball struck him on the back of the head.

"*Gevalt!*" cried Solly, clutching his dome.

Mr. Hovitz, the golfer who had teed off, hurried up with apologies.

Solly cried, "You call yourself a golfer? You should be barred from this club! My head is *bleed*ing. I'll call my lawyer! I'll sue you for five thousand dollars!"

"B-but didn't you *hear* me?" protested Hovitz. "I yelled, 'Fore!' "

Solly paused, then said, "Okay, I'll take it!"

Irving Saperstein was considering his wife's suggestion that they move from Central Park West to one of the tonier parts of Long Island. "—and Irving, if we do that, I think we ought to change our name."

After some weeks the Irving Sapersteins became the Irwin Fremonts, and they bought a mansion in Oyster Bay and furnished it with antiques.

Their friendliness made friends for them easily, and their hospitality was so gracious, their cuisine so excellent, that the Fremonts soon shone on the social scene. Indeed, they were invited to become members of the emphatically non-Jewish Country Club.

The trustees gave a welcoming dinner at the club for the newly elected members: five couples: the Townsend Fillmores, the Clyde Watson-Setons, the Harley Hammonds, the O'Neills and the Fremonts.

The liveried servant serving Mrs. Fremont accidentally spilled an entire bowl of St. Germain soup in her lap.

"Oy, *gevalt!*" cried Mrs. Fremont—but swiftly and ingeniously rushed to add: "—whatever *that* means!"

gezundhayt

See GESUNDHEIT!

ghetto

Curiously enough, no etymology for *ghetto* is entirely satisfactory to experts. *Ghetto* is most often traced to Italian *barghetto*: "part of a city," because in Venice the *barghetto* was the foundry or arsenal section, to which Jews were confined.

1. The part of a city to which Jews were officially confined.
2. That part of the city in which Jews live, as a self-segregated group.
3. (As an adjective) Coarse, whining, too meek.

The Lateran Councils of the Roman Catholic Church in 1179 and again in 1215 issued fiats that forbade Jews from having close or continuing contact with Christians.

In Spain, from the thirteenth century on, Hebrews lived

in *juderias* that were gated and walled in—for their protection, it was said.

In 1555, Pope Paul IV ordered that the Jews in the several papal states be compelled to live in quarters separated from Catholics.

In Germany, laws forced the Jews to wear a special badge or a special (and comical) hat.

The Venetian ghetto was walled in, in 1516, and those walls were not torn down until 1797. For a vivid, detailed account of life in that ghetto from the fourteenth century to the twentieth, see Riccardo Calimani's *The Ghetto of Venice*.

Other laws, in Germany, Spain, the Ukraine, Austria, *et alia*, at one time or another forced Jews to attend "conversion" exhortations in churches, and cunning tortures preceded enforced baptism. Compulsory baptism, enforced with religious zeal, compelled many Jews thereafter to live secret lives as Marranos (*q.v.*).

It is worth noting that in Germany, from the thirteenth century to the mid-nineteenth, although Jews had to live in a separate area assigned to them, which they were not permitted to leave after dark, no use was made of the word "ghetto"! A partition divided the Jewish from the non-Jewish part of town. The Jewish section was called *Judengasse* (Jews' street). But among Jews, the segregated area was called The Street or The Place.

Yet there was considerable concourse between Jews and gentiles: servants and maids often came into Jewish homes, as did gentile merchants, scholars, preachers.

Until the Nazis, of course.

———

In 1892, the novelist Israel Zangwill (1864–1926) called London's East End, where many poor Jews lived, the ghetto.

Zangwill also created the phrase "the melting pot" and introduced many Yiddish/Hebrew words to English readers.

give!

Yinglish, absolutely.
   Slang, imperative for

1. Talk!
2. Tell me (us)!
3. Open up!

This colloquial command is familiar to any moviegoer:

"Who paid you, Lefty? C'mon, *give*!"
"Who killed her, pal? . . . *Give*!"

give a . . .

Yinglish, taken directly from the Yiddish: *geb a* (familiar) or *get a* (formal).

Where Americans say "Take a look," and the English say "Have a look," speakers of Yinglish say "Give a look." (In Yiddish, *geb a kuk*.)

It is my firm conviction that the only time to say "Give a . . ." is for jocular effect.

1. Give, make. "If anyone bothers you, give a scream!"

"Give a . . ." eliminates prepositions that are obligatory in English:

2. Give [me]. "If you want to chat, give a call."*

Captain Glantz of the Israeli navy asked the new lookout, "Misha, suppose one of our sailors falls into the sea. What would you do?"

"I would give a holler: 'Man overboard! Man overboard!' "

"Good. And suppose an *officer* falls overboard?"
Misha hesitated. "Which one?"

glatt kosher

Often seen on Jewish butcher stores. Hebrew: *glat*: smooth; *kosher*: clean.
Wholly and certified kosher.

---

*Modern Hebrew has adopted this Yiddish locution, much to the surprise (or chagrin) of purists.

You will see the sign *Glatt Kosher* on the windows of butcher shops or restaurants that strictly observe the dietary laws.

The reason for using *glatt* (smooth) is interesting: certified Jewish slaughterers carefully examine every animal. If the lungs show any sign of disease, notably tuberculosis (evidenced by nodules), the meat is declared unkosher (*trayf*). When the lungs are totally free of any sign of disease, the meat is certified as *glatt* (smooth).

See also KOSHER, TRAYF.

glitch (noun and verb)
glitsch

From German: *glitschen*: "to slip," and Yiddish, *glitch*: "slide."

1. (Originally) A slide: to slide or skid on a slippery surface.
2. A risky undertaking or enterprise: "Be careful. It could be a *glitch*."
3. (In engineering, aircraft and computer circles) A mechanical defect; a "gremlin."

During World War Two, two delightful neologisms for a mishap entered the language: "gremlin," from England, and "glitch," from aeronautical wizards in the aircraft companies of southern California.

After all the passengers were belted in, and the aircraft reached its flight path, through the sound system came the pilot's voice:

"Good morning, ladies and gentlemen. Thank you for flying Eagle Airlines. We shall be flying at a height of twenty-two thousand feet. Our present ground speed is six hundred miles per hour. So lean back and relax . . . This plane, the JX-80, is the latest, *safest* aircraft anywhere in the world. Our operations are governed by the finest computers—which guarantee that nothing can go wrong . . . nothing can go wrong . . . nothing can go wrong . . ."

(*That* is a *glitch* of monumental stature.)

———

Glitch was used, in the most matter-of-fact way, in a story about a telephone breakdown in the House of Representatives, in the *New York Times* on June 24, 1988, page 13.

glitz   (noun)
glitzy   (adjective)

Pure Yinglish. German: *glitzern*: "glitter." *Glitz* and *glitzy* are not, as is commonly assumed, a combination of "glitter" and "ritz" or "ritzy," though they appear to be. They are new coinages, to mean:

1. Gaudy, ostentatious.
2. Overly adorned.
3. Superficially attractive.
4. Kitsch.

Glitzy has simply soared in usage during the past few years. It is a favorite of the fashion and interior decoration pages of English newspapers. Its mimetic qualities have added greatly to its popularity.

Go (verb, without the conjunction "and")

Yinglish, without a doubt.

In English, one says, "Go *and* see [look, ask, tell]. . . ."
Using an imperative without any link to a conjunction is pure Yiddish, no doubt derived from the biblical phrase, translated literally: "Go tell . . ." "Go praise the Lord . . ." (In English this becomes "Come, let us praise the Lord.")

"Go see who's at the door."
"Go give him a hand."

Please note that in this Yinglish construction there is no comma or oral pause after the verb, as there would be in English, where a conjunction might be absent but is understood, as in:

"Go, tell him the bad news."
"Go, see if she's the one we want."

In Penn Station, Lucy Mendelson was delighted to hear what her cousin, Violet, told her about the big penny scale. "Go step on it. I'll drop the penny. You'll see."

Lucy got on the scale. She watched the needle rise, then stop, leaned closer, then studied the chart. "Vi! Go look: I should be five inches taller!"

Go fight City Hall

Yinglish. From the Yiddish: *gai*, "go."

This rueful phrase is well known in colloquial English. It often is used by writers or reporters to signal that the user of the phrase is Jewish.

1. What can one *do*?
2. What's done is done! (The law is the law.)
3. It's hopeless to try to change that.
4. Don't waste your time!

This expression can be used philosophically or bitterly, in resignation or in disgust.

Where does this eloquent locution come from? The best explanation I have managed to find, after consulting a formidable panel of *mavens*, is this: The conclusion of a Yom Kippur hymn, forcefully exclaimed, goes "*Gay shray khay v'kayom!*" which literally means, "Go cry out [to the living Lord]," but the declamatory phrase is taken to mean, with a certain skepticism, "Go complain to God: what *good* will it do?"

Any better explanation of "Go fight City Hall" will be warmly welcomed.

Go figure

A Yinglish variation of the Yiddish *Gey vays* ("go know").

1. An expression of surprise that something unexpected happened.
   "Go figure the engine would explode!"
2. A confession of ignorance.
   "So go figure he was a crook!"

3. How could I have anticipated something as crazy as that?!
   "Go figure her brother was a prize-fighter!"
4. Could anyone in the *world* have been expected to make allowances for such an improbability?!
   "Go figure the whole building would sink right into the bog!"

See also GO KNOW . . .

go for (instead of "going to be")

This metaphrase, directly translated from Yiddish, has become Yinglish, as used by persons raised in the Bronx or on the Lower East Side or influenced by parents/relatives who were. It is unacceptable English, even when used as Yinglish.

1. Studying to be.
   "Are you going for doctor?"
2. Aiming toward.
   "Is she going for a career or for marriage?"

I deplore this usage. To emphasize my discontent, let me use a classic Bronxism: "Don't fail to avoid it if you can."

Go know . . .

From Yiddish: *Gey vays*.

A wry or heartfelt disclaimer. Picturesque Yinglish.

1. How could *I* know?
2. How could you *expect* me to know?
3. How could *anyone* know?
   "Go know that beautiful girl was an undertaker!"
   This vivid disclaimer is matchless as a stratagem of self-exculpation: "Go know my telephone was tapped!"
4. A sarcastic gloss.
   "Go know you were a deadbeat."
5. Don't be a fool.
   "Go teach a dog how to bark."
   "Go show Picasso how to paint."

Scene: **Hotel in Tel Aviv**

Mr. Chertok picked up the phone. "I would like some Seven-Up. Room 307."

"Seven-Up? Yes, sir."

The Seven-Up never arrived. But the next morning Mr. Chertok was awakened—at precisely seven.

(Go know he had talked to the night operator, not room service!)

———

Go know someone would create this marvelous story:

Stephen Douglas was busy electioneering in Illinois. He noticed a tall, thin, rawboned young fellow in overalls—always sitting in the first row, listening with the utmost intensity to the orator's words.

One day, after a rousing peroration, Douglas signaled to the lanky lad, who shuffled up to the podium. "Young man," said Douglas, "I notice that you are in the front row of every speech I deliver."

"Yes, sir."

"May I ask you—why?"

"Well, Mr. Douglas," the young man blushed, stretching his suspenders, "I'm kind of hoping I'll be up there on that platform one day, debating you—m'self."

Stephen Douglas chuckled. "I admire ambition. How do you earn your living, young man?"

"I split logs."

"And what's your name, friend?"

The young man blushed again. "Abe."

"Abe what?" asked Stephen Douglas.

"Kapinsky," said the tall, thin, rawboned young man.

———

Little Vera marched into the library, went to the return counter, and slid a book across the top.

The librarian picked up the volume: *Pandas*. "Well, Vera, how did you like this book?"

"Not much," said Vera.

The librarian looked surprised. "Didn't you like the wonderful descriptions of panda life?"

"Oh, yes."

"Weren't the pictures marvelous?"

"Oh, *yes*."

"Aren't pandas the most darling little things?"

"Yes, ma'am, they sure are."

"Then why did you say you didn't *like* the book?"

Go know the tot would reply, "This book tells you more about pandas than I care to know."

golem

A direct analogue from the Yiddish/Hebrew. Pronounced GO-*lem*, to rhyme with "dole 'em," or GOY-*lem*, to rhyme with "boil 'em." From Hebrew: "matter without shape," "a yet-unformed thing" (Psalms, 139:16).

1. A robot, an automaton, a lifeless figure in human form.
2. A simpleton, a fool.
3. A clumsy man or woman, a clod.
4. A graceless, tactless type.
5. Someone who is subnormal.

"He looks like a *golem*. He walks like a *golem*. He is as slow-witted as a *golem*. He barely gets around, poor *golem*. He's not normal; he's a *golem*."

The *Talmud* poetically speculates:

"How was Adam created? In the first hour, his dust was collected; in the second hour, his form was fashioned; in the third, he became a shapeless mass [*golem*]; . . . in the sixth he received a soul; in the seventh hour, he rose and stood on his feet. . . ."
                                                              —*Sanhedrin*, 65b

Golem appeared in Jewish folklore around the twelfth century—and recurs ever after. German Hasidim thought a *golem* was created by the mystical, ecstatic manipulation of Holy Names.

The most famous of these imaginary creatures was the Golem of Prague. In the seventeenth century, a legend grew around Rabbi Judah Löwe (or Low) of Prague, a renowned scholar; he was supposed to have created a *golem* to help protect the Jews. The *golem* helped Rabbi Löwe bring criminals to justice; he exposed spreaders of anti-Semitic canards; he even discovered in the nick of time that the Passover *matzos* had been poisoned!

Rabbi Löwe, the story went, removed all life from the *golem* every Friday, for he would not allow the creature any mobility that might desecrate the Sabbath.

A well-known play, *Der Goilem*, written in Yiddish, by the Jewish poet Leivick Halpern (1888–1962), who wrote as H. Leivick, was performed for years to huge audiences all over Europe and America.

The story of the *golem* has been made into a movie several times: in French, German, Yiddish.

I am inclined to believe that Mary Shelley may have gotten the idea for Frankenstein from one of the *golem* legends.

Would you believe that volume 4 (F–G) of the great *Oxford English Dictionary* has no entry for "*golem*"? Nor the *Encyclopaedia Britannica*? Nor the *Encyclopedia Americana*? Heavens.

When the scientists at the great Weizmann Institute in Rehovoth, Israel, built their first electronic computer, they dubbed it, with some relish, "Golem I."

gonif
gonef

Quite common Yinglish. Pronounced GON-*if*. From Hebrew: *ganov*: "thief."

1. A thief, a crook.
2. A tricky, clever person whom one should not trust.
3. A mischievous, bright child.
4. An amusing, ingenious person.

It is almost impossible to pronounce *gonif* without some accompanying expression that signals the usage you intend. Thus:

Uttered with dismay or a frown or in anger, the meaning is disagreeable: "That *gonif* should be arrested!"

Voiced with admiration, a grin or an approving cluck, the title *gonif* is clearly a form of praise: "That *gonif* is good for a laugh any time of day or night."

Whenever a grandparent calls one of his or her tribe a *gonif*, you may be sure a compliment, appreciation or cheerful praise is being accorded: "You have to be on your toes to beat that *gonif*!"

———

H. L. Mencken, whom I have long enjoyed and admired, spells this juicy word *ganov* and defines it as "gun"—as in "gunman." I have no idea where Mencken found this. Perhaps one of his informants confused *gonif* with *gunsel* (*q.v.*).

My favorite Yiddish observation on *gonif* is this paradigm of cynicism: "Don't say a man is not a *gonif* if he never had a chance to steal."

———

"Have you anything to say before I pass sentence on you?" asked the judge.

"Yes, your Honor." The prisoner took a deep breath. "How can I be convicted of forgery when—when I *can't even write my own name*!"

The judge said, "Because you are not being convicted for writing your own name."

See also AMERICA GONIF!

Go talk to the wall

Firmly and flavorsomely entrenched in Yinglish. From Yiddish: *Red tsu der vant* [*vand*] or *Gai red tsum vant.*

1. You can't get him [her] to listen.
2. You can't persuade him [her] to change his [her] mind.
3. It won't do a bit of good to try to get through to him [her, them].
4. Don't waste your time!

The Reverend Raymond Whittlesey was visiting the Holy Land. He was especially moved by the Wailing Wall, before which, in a long line, men draped in prayer shawls were swaying back and forth, murmuring their ancient prayers.

Then the Reverend Whittlesey noticed a man far from all the praying ones, standing alone before the wall. He had no prayer shawl, no prayer book, and he was not swaying back and forth; indeed, he was not praying at all. He stood erect and made gestures . . .

The Reverend Whittlesey walked over: "*Shalom*, friend. I don't mean to be intruding . . . Do you come here often?"

The figure turned, "Avery day! For toity-vun years awready!"

"Thirty-one *years*? And how long do you pray?"

"Pray?" the Jew echoed. "I'm not praying. I *talk*—to God, blessed be His name. I esk His edvice."

The Reverend Whittlesey hesitated. "What type of advice?"

"All types. Vhat should Israel do about Jordan? Who should I vote for? How can I convince my vife ve should move?"

"My! . . . And what does the good Lord tell you?"

"Ha!" the Jew snorted. "*Nothing*! In toity-vun years! . . . Mister, I tell you, it's like talking to a wall!"

Gott
Gottenyu!

> Yiddish. From Middle and Old English, Gothic *Guth*, Icelandic *gooh*; cognate with Dutch *God* and German *Gott*.
>
> God. The Supreme Being, conceived to be perfect, infinite, Almighty, omniscient, the sole Maker and Ruler of the entire universe. (In Hebrew: *Adonai, q.v.*)

The Hebrew aspects of God are explored under the entries *Adonai* and *Adoshem*. Here I wish to address a different topic.

The story is told of the great pianist Leopold Godowski, who was having a formal, swallow-tailed suit made for a national tour. The tailor came to Godowski's apartment in New York for fittings, twice a week.

Driven to desperation by the endless delays of the tailor, Godowski finally cried, "Tailor, in the name of heaven! It has already taken you six *weeks*."

"So?"

"So?" fumed Godowski. "Six weeks for a pair of pants? It took God only six *days* to create the universe."

"*Nu*," sighed the tailor, "look at it."

———

Alex Turtzer came back from his trip abroad to announce, "Mama, Papa, I'm engaged! Look. Isn't she *wonderful*?" Proudly he showed his parents a snapshot.

They studied the snapshot without pleasure.

"Alex," asked his mother, "is she that—uh—fat?"

"N-no. She isn't *thin* . . ."

"And is she that tall?" asked Alex's father.

"Well, she's a *little* on the tall side, Papa, but—"

"Is she Jewish?"

"N-no, Mama."

"Migod, Alex," moaned his father, "doesn't she have *one* good feature?!"

Alex cried, "Certainly! I left this for the last—a real surprise. Her name is Katherine von Hochenfeld—and she—is—a—real *baroness*!"

Mama let out a nerve-wracking groan and sank to the sofa. "*Oy, Gottenyu!* She can't even have children!"

———

One of the most surprising and (to me) endearing aspects of the attitude of Jews to God is the candor of their complaints about Him: grievances phrased with such tact, felicity, irony or wit that they manage to stop just this side of the sacrilegious.

To be both pious and critical, loving and sardonic, fearful and unafraid, respectful and indignant—these are most delicate and sophisticated feats.

The Jewish complaints against the Lord are managed without guilt, which is the most remarkable aspect of all.

———

Here are some surprising, irreverent Jewish sayings:

If God lived on earth, people would knock out all His windows.

Dear God, You help *strangers*, so why don't you help me?

"Thou hast chosen us from among all the nations"— but why did you have to pick on the Jews?

God will provide—but why doesn't He provide *until* He provides?

Don't question God, for He may reply: "If you're so anxious for answers, come up here."

Oh God: please glance down from Heaven and take a good look at Your world!

Dear Lord: Just help me get up; I can fall down by myself.

Man thinks—and God laughs.

Lord, if you don't help me, I'll ask my uncle in America.

Sign on the Temple Bulletin Board:

ON FRIDAY, RABBI JACOB WALDBAUM WILL GIVE A SPECIAL LECTURE AFTER THE SERVICE:

Does God Forgive Agnostics?

COME EARLY IF YOU WANT TO BE SURE OF GETTING A SEAT IN THE BACK.

goy
goyish   (adjective)
goyim   (plural)

What Yinglishman does not know, use and enjoy *goy*? Forms rhyme respectively with "boy," "boyish," "doyen." The plural is pronounced GOY-*im*. The adjective is *goyish* (neuter), *goyisher* (masculine), or *goyisheh* (feminine). From the Hebrew: *goy*: "nation." Biblical texts called the Hebrews a *goy kadosh*: "a holy nation."

A gentile, *i.e.*, anyone who is not a Jew. A male gentile is a *shaygets*; the female, a *shiksa*.

1. It is important to note that the idea of respect for others, and the values of a pluralistic society, form an old, integral part of Judaism and Jewish tradition. The rabbis taught that all men are equal in the eyes of God—if they do the will of God: the Talmud says, "Whether Jew or gentile, man or woman, rich or poor—according to a man's *deeds* does God's presence rest on him."

2. Mormons call any non-Mormon a gentile; Jews are therefore gentiles to Mormons. (I have never met a

Jew who quite knows how to adjust to this startling idea.) I once spent three happy days in Utah, without observing any noticeable change in my disposition. Incidentally, the first non-Mormon to become governor of Utah was Simon Bamberger.

3. Just as some gentiles use "Jew" as a contemptuous synonym for driving too shrewd and sly a bargain ("He tried to Jew the price down," is about as odious an idiom as I know), so some Jews use *goy* in a pejorative sense. Relentless persecution of Jews, century after century, in nation after nation, left a legacy of bitter sayings: "*Dos ken nor a goy*" ("That, only a *goy* is capable of doing"); "*A goy bleibt a goy*" ("A gentile remains a gentile" or, less literally, "What did you expect? Once an anti-Semite, always an anti-Semite"). Experience made many Jews feel that gentiles are not gentle.

4. The plural, *goyim*, was frequently used in ellipses— a shortened reference with words omitted: "[other] nations [than we are]," therefore, non-Jews. In time, and by the well-known linguistic process of extension, a Jew who was not a practicing, religious Jew was called a *goy*.

Goy is generally used to mean "Christian," but the name long precedes Christianity: the Hebrews considered heathens, pagans, Egyptians, Assyrians, Greeks, Romans— all, *goyim*.

I must stress the fact that *goy* is not an invidious appellation. *Goy* means gentile—no more, no less. The fact that some Jews pronounce *goy* with distaste is comparable to the way some gentiles pronounce *Jew*.

The Talmud contains important references to the righteous *goyim* who will have their share of "the world to come," and enjoins Jews to treat such people the way they treat Jews. One Talmudic reference instructs Jews that where both a Jew and a gentile are in peril, it is the moral obligation of a Jew to rescue the gentile first.

Never let it be forgotten that the Talmud commands Jews to help the gentile, no less than the Jew; to succor the poor *goy*; to visit the gentile sick; to bury their dead.

God says: "Both the Gentiles and the Israelites are My
handiwork: Can I let the former perish on account of
the latter?"   —TALMUD: *Sanhedrin*, 98b

The rabbis long tried to moderate the bitterness of their
flock: "A gentile who observes the Torah is as good as a
High Priest," wrote a fourth-century sage.

The *Sefer Hasidim*, "Book of the Pious," a thirteenth-
century work, says: "If a Jew attempts to kill a non-Jew,
help the non-Jew."

The immortal Rashi, eleventh-century French rabbi and
scholar, reminded Jews that gentiles "of the present age
are not heathens."

And in the Talmud (*Baba Kamma*) it is solemnly noted
that to cheat a non-Jew is more heinous than to cheat a
Jew—because such swindling "involves the desecration of
the Name."

In Jerusalem today, an official garden contains the names
of many *goyim* who helped or sheltered or saved Jews
during the Holocaust. These brave and sainted souls are
identified as "righteous gentiles" ("*hasidei umot ha-
olam*").

A London Jew became so prosperous that he changed
his name from Nate Greenberg to Noël Greenhill, bought
a fine home on Park Lane and proceeded to acquire various
objets d'art, including a beautiful painting by Rubens.

The following year, his affluence having increased, he
exchanged the Rubens—for a Goya . . .

The actor Marvyn Lawton (né Manny Levy) turned his
profile toward his friend, Byron, and said, "So what do
you think?"

"That nose-job is amazing!" exclaimed Byron.

"You think it will help my career?"

"Help your car*eer*? Why, Manny, you had a hook-nose
must have cost you two dozen parts. Now—you look like
a thing of beauty and a *goy* forever."

The Joseph Levitoffs had moved to the suburbs. Their
next-door neighbors were the O'Connors.

One day Tim O'Connor, age six, was playing in the brook with little Rebecca Levitoff, age five. When they had splashed water all over their clothes, they took them off . . .

Little Rebecca's mother observed all this from her kitchen. And when her daughter came in, her mother said, "Dear, did you like playing with the new boy?"

"Yes, Mother."

"What—games did you play?"

"Oh, we didn't play any games . . . We just cleaned up the brook and splashed around—and we got wet, so we took off our clothes and played naked."

The mother hesitated. "Well, dear, is there *any*thing you'd like to tell me?"

Rebecca reflected. "Yes—one thing: I didn't know there was *that* much difference between gentiles and Jews!"

See also SHAYGETS, SHIKSA.

greeneh   (female)
greener   (male)
greenhorn

> *Greener* or *greeneh* were the Yinglish abbreviations of the familiar American western appellation "greenhorn." Pronounced in Yinglish: GREEN-*air*.

1. Newcomer to America.
2. One unversed in the ways, customs, and language of the New World.

Poor people had to help finance their rent by taking in a roomer—a boarder who usually ate with the family. Greenhorns could not afford a flat of their own. Furthermore, except for immigrants from the British Isles, the language problem was staggering; hence the wisdom of living for a while amidst *landsleit* (people from your old country) whom you could understand, who understood you and whose longer residence in the golden land made it possible for you to pick up the basic words, phrases, practices and mores of the bustling new world.

The *kind* of English that immigrants of, say, six months' standing confidently passed on to newer greenhorns created a rich argot all its own: Yinglish.

I trust that readers of this book are finding the argot as colorful, delightful, descriptive, functional, picturesque, imaginative and vigorous as I do.

The *greener* ran down the slip at the Staten Island ferry and flung himself into space, across the patch of water, landing on the ferryboat with a terrific crash. He picked himself up, breathing hard, and said in Yiddish, "I made it!"

"So what was your hurry?" remarked a passenger. "We're coming *in*!"

Here is how Hortense Dressler, age eighteen, filled out her first job application:

Name: Dressler, Hortense
Address: 70 Wayne Ave., Brooklyn
Sex: Not yet.

BOY: And everything in the South changed, Papa, when Eli Whitney invented the cotton gin.
FATHER: The what?
BOY: The cotton gin.
FATHER: *Gevalt!* In the South they drink *cotton*?

Within two weeks after Itzhak Gersh had landed in New York, he had begun a long, successful career. How did he begin? He opened a shoe-shine stand (an empty orange crate) on lower Broadway. The sign on the box, printed by his "American-born" nephew, read:

FREE! FREE!
ONE SHOE SHINED ABSOLUTELY FREE OF CHARGE!

Four years later, Itzhak Gersh opened a cafeteria. The sign *this* time read:

ITZHAK'S 100% CLEAN CAFETERIA
SWIFT, COURTEOUS SELF-SERVICE.

And after a string of these cafeterias proved successful, Itzhak opened a dance hall. His marquée blazed out these words:

> GOOD CLEAN DANCING
> EVERY NIGHT
> EXCEPT FRIDAY

And on the windows of his *next* store, Mr. Gersh proudly painted:

> WEDDING GOWNS
> FOR
> ALL OCCASIONS

Back in 1927, Yasha Weisbrod, not long ago arrived in New York from a little *shtetl*, beheld a double-decker bus. How he had longed to take a ride! And see New York from the open top deck!

"How much costs to ride?" he asked a bearded Jew.

"A nickel," the Jew replied.

So Yasha tripped up the circular steps that led to the open top deck of the bus. He sat down. Then his eyes popped. He ran down the stairs and cried to the conductor, "Mister! Mister! We can all be *killed! There's no one driving up there*!"

gunsel
gunzel
gendzl

> Yinglish: not Yiddish, not English—but Yinglish. Slang. Favored by underworld types, and popular in detective stories. Pronounced GUN-z'l or GON-z'l. Origin: fascinating, but not proved: possibly from a Jewish play on the word *gun* or from the Yiddish: *gendzl*: "gosling."

In American slang and underworld cant, *gunsel* was originally used to characterize an inexperienced young man. It has been drastically transformed to designate:

1. A drifter, a hobo.
2. A homosexual's love object. In 1915 or so, this meaning for *gonzil* or *gunsel* came into use among prisoners (and bums).
3. A young hoodlum. The first time I encountered *this* usage was in a piece in *The New Yorker* by S. J. Perelman: "Scores of hoodlums, gunsels, informers, shysters . . ."

4. A young gunman—not in the old West, but in urban criminal circles.
5. A bodyguard. You may remember this usage in the movie *The Maltese Falcon: gunsel* was what Humphrey Bogart tauntingly called Wilmer (Elisha Cook, Jr.), who was the bodyguard employed by Gutman (Sydney Greenstreet).

Gut Shabbes

Used in Yinglish to reinforce sentiment or authenticity. Pronounced *goot*-SHOB-*bes*, to rhyme with "could novice." From German *gut* and Hebrew *Shabbat*: "the Sabbath."

1. The customary greeting on Friday evening and Saturday; both a salutation and the expression of a hope to the one greeted. If you want to hear a fusillade of *Gut Shabbes!*'s, just stand at the entrance to any synagogue or temple on Friday night or Saturday. The greetings are delivered both on entering and leaving.
2. Sarcastic affirmation.
3. The climactic comment in an anecdote or joke.
4. Expression of irony or astonishment. An amusing adaptation of the traditional salutation occurs in many stories, to mean "Can you beat that?!" or "Would you *believe* it?"

The mayor of a certain town was a notorious anti-Semite. It astonished bystanders, therefore, when the mayor's auto caught fire and old man Tolovich ran over with a bucket, emptied the bucket, ran back into a store, filled the bucket, came out, emptied it again, started to run back, panting and sweating . . .

A woman tapped Tolovich on the shoulder. "Slow down. You'll get a heart attack. Anyway, a couple of pails of water can't do much good!"

Said Tolovich: "Who said it's water? It's kerosene. *Gut Shabbes.*"

Said the judge, "This case hinges on your testimony, madame, and you have described what you saw on a dark night a whole block away. So I must ask you: How old are you?''

"I," said Mrs. Olinsky, "am fifty-four—plus a few months.''

"Mmh . . . how many months?''

Mrs. Olinsky pondered. "A hundred and two.''

The judge, looking skeptical, murmured, "*Gut Shabbes*!''

H

Habdala
Havdala

Pronounced, in Yiddish, *hahv*-DOL-*lah*, to rhyme with "Bob lolla." Hebrew: "separation."

The ceremony that signalizes the ending of the Sabbath.
The sweet-sad rite that says farewell to "Queen Sabbath" is performed by the head of the family when he comes home from the evening service (*mairev*) in the synagogue.

He lights a braided candle and a saucer of alcohol, by which he warms his hands, and, his family around him, over a wine glass recites this benediction: "Blessed art Thou, O Lord our God, King of the Universe, who makes a distinction between holy and profane, between light and darkness, between Israel and the nations, between the seventh day and the six days of work."

A melody is sung in either Hebrew or Yiddish words, asking God's grace for the week ahead. Then an ornamental box, in which spices are kept, is raised, and its sweet aroma sniffed—to revive spirits saddened by Sabbath's end.

The Hasidim sometimes celebrate the *Habdala* with rhapsodic dances—in a moving circle of hasids. Cabalistic meanings were assigned to this occasion. Some Hasidim still regard the rite as a mystical event.

hachem (noun)
haham
chaucham
hachamim, chachamim (plural)

> Pronounced KWAW-*khem*, with two guttural *kh*'s.
> Rhymes with "Law men." Plural, *hachamim*, is pro-
> nounced *kha*-KHUM-*im*, to rhyme with "illumine." He-
> brew: "wise."
> An expert, sagacious, experienced or ingenious man
> or woman

A *hachem* need not be an intellectual nor a rabbi nor a
philosopher. Usually a *hachem* is a brilliant mind, rich with
learning, but *respected* for wisdom (*hachma*), judgment,
expertise.

The early sages of Israel were cobblers, vendors, barbers, butchers. What is of critical importance is that the
scholar stood atop the Jewish pyramid of respect—the
scholar, please note, not the conqueror, the prince,
the ruler, the rich man, or even the rabbi. Wealth, power,
honors—none was as respected as learning, and that meant
learning in the Torah and the Talmud.

One of my favorite childhood memories involves a men's
clothing store in our neighborhood on Roosevelt Road in
Chicago, which was owned by a pair of partners, *hachamim*, who, rumor had it, sent eight children through
college simply by—pretending to be deaf.

The ingenious haberdashers' caper is unmatched, I
think, for simplicity, duplicity and proper punishment of
the greedy. Here is how it worked:

One partner would wait on a customer, extolling the
excellence of the wool or the styling of this or that suit.
The customer would, naturally, ask, "How much is it?"

"What?" asked the "salesman," cupping his ear.

"How—much—does—it—cost?" the customer repeated more loudly.

"Hanh?"

"*How much is the suit*?" the customer would shout.

"Ah, the *price*! . . . I'll ask the boss." Whereupon the

"clerk" would turn and shout toward the back of the store: "*How much is the beautiful navy-blue, double-breasted suit?*"

The "boss" would shout back, "*Forty dollars!*"

The "deaf" clerk would tell the customer, "The boss says 'Twenty dollars.' "

Need I describe how swiftly many men, young and old, plunked down their twenty dollars and hastened out of the store, chortling?

Hadassah

> Pronounced *ha*-DAH-*sah*, to rhyme with "*la casa.*" Hebrew: "myrtle." *Hadassah* is the Hebrew and Yiddish form of the biblical Esther.
>
> 1. Esther.
> 2. The Women's Zionist Organization of America.

Founded in 1912, by the remarkable Henrietta Szold, the *Hadassah* organization today has over 385,000 members in twelve hundred chapters. It was originally organized to raise the standards of health, hygiene, and public medicine in Palestine, which was woefully ridden by diseases, and to widen the awareness, among Jews in America, of Jewish traditions and ideals.

In Israel, *Hadassah*'s hospitals and services have made striking contributions to medicine.

Haggada
Agada

> Pronounced *ha*-GOD-*da*, to rhyme with the way an Englishman pronounces "Nevada." Hebrew: "tale" or "telling."
>
> 1. The enormous repository of Jewish allegorical material, historical episodes, theology, folklore, fable, prayers, parables, witticisms, anecdotes, ruminations, sermons, etc., etc. that are to be found in the Talmud.

The *Haggadah* appealed to the common people, for it contains a wealth of enchanting stories—about scholars and saints and martyrs. Four qualities distinguish it, says Judah Goldin: charm, extraordinary piety, ethical fervor and God's love for the children of Israel.

2. The narrative that is read aloud at the Passover *Seder*, piecing together, from many sources, the story of Israel's bondage in, and flight from, Egypt.

The *Haggadah*, which draws material from Exodus and from the Talmud, contains psalms, prayers, hymns—even amusing jingles to hold the interest of the children, who must sit through a very long ceremony and feast.

When the youngest child asks "the Four Questions" on Passover, the father responds from the *Haggadah*: "Slaves were we unto Pharaoh in Egypt."

The *Haggadah* has grown over the centuries. Some of its contents trace back to ancient liturgy, but most of it is the creation of laymen throughout the years. The basic form seems to have been set in the second century; the first *Haggadah*, as a separate collection of prayers, appeared around the thirteenth century.

Do not confuse *Haggadah* with *Agada*, which comprises all of the Talmud's allegorical material: fables, folklore, parables, anecdotes. The legal and theological portions of the Talmud constitute *Halakha* (*q.v.*).

See also AGADAH, HALAKHA.

haimish
haimisher (masculine)
haimisheh (feminine)

Yinglish. Often encountered in Jewish writers' Englishing. Pronounced HAME-*ish*, to rhyme with "*Jame-ish*." From German and Yiddish: *Heim*: "home."

1. Cozy, warm.
2. Having the friendly characteristics that exist inside a happy home.
3. Without "side," unpretentious; putting on no airs.

President Lincoln was ever so *haimish*. No one in his right mind would call General MacArthur *haimish*. A "*hai-*

misher mensh" is someone with whom you can take your shoes off or let your hair down.

––––––––––

The offices of three optometrists were on the same block in Miami Beach. And here were the *haimisheh* signs in their windows:

DR. ELI SCHONBERG
EYES EXAMINED WHILE YOU WAIT!

––––

JOEL F. OPPELHEIM, D.O.
IF YOU DON'T SEE WHAT YOU WANT, WALK RIGHT IN.

––––

BERNARD SPAETH, OPTOMETRIST
OH, SAY, CAN YOU SEE?

––––––

The Burt Handels were having their apartment painted.
Bella Handel, a *haimisheh* woman, coming out of the shower, slipping into a bathrobe, suddenly noticed a large handprint on a freshly painted wall of the bedroom. "Painter!" she called down the stairs. "Painter! Would you please come up here?"
The painter came up the stairs.
"You won't *believe* this!" said Bella. "Would you like to see where my husband put his hand in the dark last night?"
The *haimisher* painter cleared his throat. "I sure would, lady. But first I've got to finish the downstairs closet."

hak a chainik

See HOCK A TCHYNIK.

Halakha
Halakheh

Pronounced *ha*-LOKH-*a*, with the guttural *kh* sound of Loch Lomond. Hebrew: "law."

1. Accumulated Jewish law, including all the decisions of the great rabbis and sages and commentators on the Talmud—but without biblical citations, notes and

references. The *Halakha* simply states the laws, as in a legal code.
2. The Oral Law of the Talmud, as distinguished from the Written Law (the Torah plus all legalisms from Scriptures).

"The Rabbinic Halakha," writes Judah Goldin, "protected legislation from inflexibility and society from fundamentalism."

The rabbis did not "create" Halakha; they codified and clarified Judaism's legal teachings and adapted them to the changing conditions of the post-Mosaic world. For example, the Torah forbids "all manner of work on the Sabbath." But two large tractates in the Talmud (*Shabbat* and *Eyruvin*) extensively examine and illuminate the possible meanings of "work."

Jews were originally forbidden to recite (or "read from memory") the Written Law *or* even to fix Oral Law by writing it down! The danger this presented, *i.e.*, the loss or misconstruction of passages—was magnified by repeated persecutions, which interfered with the considerable time required for the massive amount of memorization.

Rabbi Judah ha-Nasi (c. A.D. 135–220 , "the Prince," so revered in rabbinical literature that he is called simply "Rabbi," or "Our Teacher") decided to codify the oral tradition in the third century. That codification, in six "orders," is the *Mishnah*, the first part of an entry in the Talmud—which consists of *Halakha* and *Agandas* (anecdotes, folklore, fables).

See also MISHNAH, TALMUD.

Hallelujah
Allelujah   (Aramaic form)
Halleluyah

From Hebrew: "Praise ye Yah."
The *yah* is probably an abbreviation of JHVH or YHVH, from which comes (incorrectly) Jehovah (*q.v.*). *J* was a medieval variant of *i*, used to begin a Hebrew word. Both *j* and *i* were pronounced as *y* (when preceding a vowel). *Hallelujah* is pronounced with a *y* for the *j*.
        In the King James translation of the Bible (1611), the "Alleluia" of the Latin Vulgate version is used.

(The Vulgate, used for a thousand years in England and Germany, is still used in France, Spain and Italy.)

1. The joyous refrain used at the opening and/or closing of certain psalms.
2. The response of the congregation at the end of a hymn.
3. The joyous exclamation used spontaneously when sharing very good, surprising news.

> "They have agreed to the settlement? Hallelujah!"
> "After seventeen years, they're getting married? Hallelujah!"
> "The fire damage was negligible? Hallelujah!"

The *Hallel* (Psalms 113–118), also called the Egyptian *Hallel*, treated in Talmud as one entity, was regarded with such reverence that the rabbis declared it a commandment, and ordained it as the blessing to open and end hymns. The *Hallel* is recited in the synagogue on Passover eve (in some Judaic rites), during the *seder* (*q.v.*) and in the morning services of the first two days of Passover—and also on Chanukah, Pentecost and Tabernacles. Psalm 136 is called "the great *Hallel*."

Mitch Klopnitz was wild about the race track. His wife nagged him and nagged him about this reprehensible vice.

"Maybe if you get off my back about the horses, Minnie, I'll—I'll come to *shul* with you every Friday night!"

"To *shul*?! You? Oh, Mitch, I'll be the happiest woman in Queens! Okay. No more nagging! And on Friday nights—"

"I'll—come—to—*shul*," said Mitch.

And he did. He sat through the whole service. He even joined in the Hebrew prayers he had learned in *heder* years ago. He responded with enthusiasm, along with the congregation, to the rabbi's eloquent sermon. And when he and his wife left the synagogue, Mitch grinned. "*Nu*? Surprised? I did good, huh?"

"You did fine, Mitch—except for one thing you're going to have to learn to correct!"

"What's that, Minnie?"

"When the congregation chimes in to the rabbi, in his sermon, the word is *Hallelujah*—*not* 'Hialeah'!"

halutz

See CHALUTZ.

hamantash
homentash

During Purim, Jewish bakers and restaurants feature this word. Pronounced HAW-*men-tosh*, to rhyme with "Jaw men bosh." Presumably named after Haman (see below); *Tasch* is German for "pocket."

A special cake: a triangular "pocket" of dough filled with poppy seed or prune jelly. The plural is *hamantashen*, and children love them.

Hamantashen are the triangular little cakes that are special treats during the Feast of Purim, a happy day that celebrates the foiling of the plot of Haman, first minister to King Ahasuerus, who wanted to destroy all of the Jews in Persia.

See also PURIM.

Hanuka
Hanukkah

See CHANUKAH.

Ha-Shem
Hashem

Pronounced *ha*-SHEM, to rhyme with "bosh hem." Hebrew: "the Name."

See also ADOSHEM.

Hasid
Hasidic   (adjective)
Hasidim   (plural)
Chasid

Pronounced KHA-*sid*; rattle the *kh* as if clearing a bread-crumb out of your throat. Hebrew: "pious one."

1. A follower of the Hasidic sect. The men are always fully bearded, with *payess* (*q.v.*), usually wear a broad-brimmed black hat (with a *yarmulke* showing beneath it), a spotless white shirt but no necktie, and a long black coat. Hasidic wives and women dress with great simplicity, eschew cosmetics, and seek no career save that of woman, wife, mother.
2. A revered, often self-ordained, charismatic leader, treated by his disciples as a saint and a prophet.

The Hasidic movement is not an ancient (or even an old) sector of Judaism. It has been opposed by many rabbis and Jewish laymen, both in Israel and America, as being far too fundamentalist, mystical, reactionary.

This extraordinary religious group was founded by Israel ben Eliezer (c. 1700–1760) in the mid-eighteenth century. Eliezer, known to his followers as the *Baal Shem*, opposed the rabbinical emphasis on formal learning, and derogated the Talmudic casuistry and logic-splitting of the wise men.

Israel ben Eliezer sang the praises of simple faith, joyous worship and everyday pleasures. God can be worshiped anywhere, said the *Baal Shem*, directly and simply: God requires no synagogues, except "in the heart." Prayers should be spontaneous, personal, happy—not the formalized, automatic rote of the *shul*.

The Hasidim prefer gay songs and spontaneous dancing to magisterial invocations. They laugh and clap hands while singing out the Lord's praises; they invite group expressions of religious rapture.

The Hasidic celebration of God offered poor Jews a new kind of communion: warm, intimate, personal. The Hasidim preached their gospel with homely stories and parables, charming anecdotes and folk sayings that anyone could understand. Their ecstatic songs and dances offended many of Jewry's most august figures. Nonetheless, the Hasidic movement spread through eastern Europe with gusto.

A Hasid "*Rebbe*" is treated by his followers with greater awe than Jews customarily give a rabbi. Disciples repeated a Hasid's every phrase and sometimes imitated his every gesture. Hasidism's leaders became known as *tzaddikim*—seers, near-saints, prophets believed to possess supernatural powers. The title *tzaddik* even became hereditary.

Hasidism has passionate adherents in enclaves in and near New York.

See *The Hasidic Anthology*, edited by Louis Newman, and Elie Wiesel's vivid and moving *Souls on Fire*. I warmly recommend Martin Buber's *Tales of the Hasidim* and Meyer Levin's *Hasidic Tales*.

Hasidic piety often turns into bloody fanaticism. In the Williamsburg section of Brooklyn, riots periodically break out when hundreds of Hasidim hurl eggs, bottles and rocks at a rival Hasidic group.

Five or six hundred(!) loyal Satmars have attacked equally orthodox Belzers; the former are passionately anti-Zionist; the Belzers are just as vehemently Zionist.

A police officer later said: "It's like the Hatfields and the McCoys."

A departing Satmar said, "We're going to drive them out [of Brooklyn]!"

A departing Belzer said, "These are terrible people! They terrorize everyone!" (See *New York Times*, March 2, 1981.)

It is estimated that there are twenty thousand followers of "the Lubavitcher *Rebbe*," Menachem Schneerson, in Brooklyn, and tens of thousands more in the United States, Israel and other countries. These Hasidim seek the "*Rebbe*'s" advice on every conceivable religious, social or personal question: What profession to study for, whom to marry, how large a family to raise. Followers have more than once petitioned the *Rebbe* to intercede with God—to please speed up the coming of the Messiah. (*New York Times*, September 5, 1988)

Haskala
Haskalah

Pronounced *has*-KOL-*la*, to rhyme with "*La Scala*."
Hebrew: "education," "knowledge."

The movement of enlightenment, intellectual emancipation and secular education among Jews, akin to the European Enlightenment of the eighteenth century.

Haskala was bitterly denounced by many rabbis, Orthodox Jews, fundamentalists—all of whom recognized the threat that secular education and Western rationalism posed to traditional faith and orthodoxy.

Those who followed and furthered the *Haskala* called themselves "enlightened ones" or *Maskilim* (singular: *Maskil*).

The founder of the *Haskala* was the philosopher Moses Mendelssohn (1729–1786), the model for Lessing's *Nathan the Wise*, who was determined to end the superstition, the conformity, the poverty and social backwardness of ghetto and *shtetl* life. He attracted collaborators and students from all over Europe.

Mendelssohn inveighed against Judaism's "narrow labyrinth of ritual—theological casuistry." He opened the first school for Jews that included courses in German, French, geography, mathematics.

Mendelssohn's disciples published a Hebrew magazine (*Ha-Me'assef*) that served as a channel to Jewry of the whole ferment of ideas, literature, and political liberalism that swept Europe after the French Revolution. The *Haskala* transformed Hebrew itself into a living, changing language.

Haskala laid the groundwork for the strong social-democratic movement that captured the imagination of young Jews; it served to encourage the entry of Jews into politics; it spurred interest in agriculture and manual labor. It also aroused strong nationalism among some Jews, just as the Napoleonic era galvanized nationalist feelings among Germans, Italians, Poles.

The *Haskala* was the forerunner of Reform Judaism in religion and Zionism in politics.

Hatikvah
Hatikva

> Pronounced *ha*-TICK-*vuh*, to rhyme with "a kick huh."
> Hebrew: "the Hope."
> The national anthem of Israel.

The song "Hatikvah" was written in 1878 by Naftali Herz Imber, and set to music by Samuel Cohen. It was adopted as the Jewish national anthem at the first Zionist Congress in Basel, 1897.

When the state of Israel was established in 1948, "Hatik-vah," with a slight change in wording, became the national anthem.

hazzen

See CANTOR.

healthnik

One hundred percent Yinglish—the word exists in nei-ther Yiddish nor English.

1. A fanatic about health.
2. A monomaniac about staying healthy.
3. Someone obsessed by the fear of getting ill.
4. The opposite of a *sicknik.*

SCENE: **Doctor's Office: Park Avenue, New York City**

"Mr. Esner," said Dr. Pokrass as he completed his phys-ical examination, "You're in *terrible* shape! You simply must start taking exercise!"

"I hate exercise."

"You must begin—jogging!"

"Jogging?" wailed Esner.

"Slow, sensible jogging. Your first week, jog five blocks a day. The next week, jog ten. The week after that, fifteen . . . and so on. And after you've reached the point where you can run two to three miles every day, you'll be a new man! . . . Call me in a month."

The days passed. The weeks passed. Then Dr. Pokrass' phone rang. "Hello?"

A voice puffed, "Heh . . . heh . . . Doc . . . this—is— Mr. Yankel Esner . . ."

"How's the jogging, Mr. Esner?"

"Doc—you're talking to a dead man! Arches? No more . . . Spine? Like a needle! . . . Head? Like a boiler! Every *inch* of my whole body is on fire—"

"Mr. Esner, don't panic," said Dr. Pokrass soothingly. "Just jump in a cab and come over."

"Cab?" echoed Mr. Esner. "I'm in *Albany!*"

See also ALRIGHTNIK, COMPUTERNIK, HOLDUPNIK, JOKE-NIK, -NIK, REFUSENIK, SICKNIK.

Hebe

Yinglish slang: a disagreeable abbreviation of "Hebrew."

Jew (offensive).

Hebe is nasty, condescending, and pejorative. It is less offensive (if only slightly) than *kike*. Perhaps the soft *h* that begins *Hebe* is psychologically less abrasive (and offensive) than the percussive double *k* of *kike*.

I give you a jingle I heard at the University of London:

Roses are reddish,
Violets, bluish:
If it wasn't for Christmas,
We'd all be Jewish.

Said Albert Einstein when his astounding theory had not yet been confirmed: "If my theory is proved, Germany will claim me as a German and France will declare me a citizen of the world. But if my theory is proved wrong, the French will say I am a German, and the Germans will insist that I am a Jew."

Hebrew

Hebrew, from *ha-Ivri:* "he who crossed over [the Euphrates River]," about four thousand years ago, to reach the promised land, Canaan.

1. The name of an ancient people, later called Jews.
2. The name of a language. Hebrew and Yiddish are wholly, entirely, profoundly and eternally different languages.

What language did the ancient Israelites speak? The Old Testament says "the lip of Canaan" or "Judaic." The word "Hebrew" does not appear in any known text until A.D. 133—in a Greek translation of *Ecclesiasticus* (*Book of Proverbs*) by the grandson of Jesus (or Jeshua) ben Sirach.

Hebrew is wholly unrelated to the many tongues in the Indo-European family: Greek, Latin, German, Balto-Slavic, Iranian, etc. Millions of American immigrants swiftly learned that, say, *house, book, nose* are English analogues of the German *Haus, Buch, Nase*. Or that *seven* is related to the Dutch *zeven*. Or that *round* resembles the Italian *rotondo* and the Swedish *rund*. But such cognates were impossible to find for Hebrew, where *house* is *bayit*, *book* is *sefer*, and *nose* is *af*.

We must also remember that Hebrew texts originally contained *no vowels*: scribes added diacritical marks (in the margins of a text) above or below a consonant, to signal its pronunciation. These vowel signs followed different patterns, so different rabbis resolved the resulting ambiguities in different ways. (A uniform system was not adopted until the fifth or sixth century of the Christian era.)

Further complexities abound: In Hebrew, as in certain other languages (Native American Hopi, for example), tenses, as we know them in English, do not exist. Instead, there are "aspects of tense": one for processes, one for endings. In Hebrew, masculine and feminine gender change blithely. The singular is freely used to represent the collective.

Nor is that all. Hebrew employs many connectives, but especially uses the letter *vov*, added as a conjunction; the combination is often translated as "and," but it can *also* mean "however," "but," "when," "because," "despite," "accordingly," "yet," "thereupon," etc.

Hebrew sentences that contain *vov* were often given a syntactical content in English that is not justified by the Hebrew:

"He went into the garden and wept."

CAN ALSO MEAN

"He went into the garden because he was weeping."

OR

"He went into the garden after he wept."

OR

"He went into the garden and, because of that, wept."

OR

"Even though he went into the garden, he wept."

"Original texts" sounds impressive, but they often turn out to woefully deficient—in accuracy or completeness. Benzion Halper, who edited *Post-Biblical Hebrew Literature*, cautions us to remember that the old scribes often used abbreviations, dropped occasional letters at the end of words, and that individual words are not clearly divided, one from another, in old Hebrew manuscripts. "In a vast number of cases . . . the texts are hopelessly corrupt."

For a recent history of Hebrew, see William Chomsky's *Hebrew: The Eternal Language*.

See also YIDDISH.

heder
cheder

Pronounced KHAY-*der*, with a throat-clearing *kh*. Rhymes with "raider." Hebrew for "room." Plural: *chedarim*, pronounced *cheh-*DAW-*rim* in Yiddish.

A room or school where Hebrew is taught.

Jews held that the Jewish community must provide an education to every boy, no matter how poor. Virtually universal education (for males) existed among the Jews to a degree unknown, I think, among other people. Rabbinical authority even forbade any Jew to settle in any place that had no Hebrew teacher for the young!

At a time when the overwhelming majority of humankind was illiterate, there was hardly a Jewish male over the age of five who could not read and write. The enormous impact of this is for historians and sociologists to appraise.

Jewish boys would begin studying Hebrew as early as the age of three. They would study six to ten hours *a day*, six days a week. Many received their early Hebrew education in a room in the home of a *melamed* (teacher). In the larger Talmud Torah schools, there were several rooms and more than one teacher. These schools were supported by the synagogue, and charged no tuition.

The Torah (the Five Books of Moses) was the only *heder* text. Students would recite *en masse*, in a singsong, swaying back and forth in traditional rhythm, the tempo set by the teacher, the pace hastened or slowed by his appraisal of the students' comprehension of the passage they were droning out.

In the old country, before a boy entered a *heder* for the first time he was carried into the synagogue by his father (or the *melamed*) and placed in front of the *bema* (pulpit) to face the entire congregation; then the scroll of the Torah was unrolled, and the Ten Commandments were read aloud, addressed to the little boy directly, reenacting the scene on Mount Sinai.

On his first day in a *heder*, the boy's mother and father would stand over him as the teacher pointed to the letters of the alphabet. The lad repeated the names of the Hebrew letters *aleph . . . bayz . . . gimel . . . daled . . .*

And for each name, his mother would give him a little cookie, shaped in the form of that letter, or would put honey on his tongue, to show how sweet learning is.

At the end of this first lesson, the mother would enfold the boy and pray that her son fulfill his life with years of Torah study, marriage and good deeds.

A student of Abelard wrote that "Christians educate their sons . . . for gain. . . . A Jew, however poor, had he ten sons would put them all to letters, not for gain . . . but to the understanding of God's laws; and not only his sons, but his daughters."

The Jews are so often referred to as "the children of Israel" that a *heder* boy once asked. "Didn't the *grownups* ever do anything?"

hock (noun and verb)
hok

From Yiddish/German: "to hit," "to knock." Rhymes with "mock."

1. To yak-yak-yak.
2. To nag.
3. A blow.
4. To hit, to strike.

The most potent retort to anyone *hocking* you is the celebrated Yiddish saying, *Hock mir nit kayn tchynik*

("Don't knock me a teapot"). This robust congé has been shortened to the verb alone:

"I'll go, I'll go: don't *hock* me anymore."
"Stop your *hocking*! I'll think it over."

"I hear your season was disappointing," said Lang.
"It was a disaster!" said Kwitz.
"They say you were ready to sell out and move to Arizona."
"Right."
"But then Korngold came to you with a fantastic offer—"
"Wait a minute, Lang! You seem to know the whole story!"
"That's true."
"—So why are you *hocking* me?"
Said Lang, "This is my first chance to get all the details."

See also HOCK A TCHYNIK.

hock a tchynik
hok a tchynik
hak a chainik

Yiddish—but its English metaphrase would add a delightful, colorful phrase to our tongue. Pronounced TCHY-*nik*, to rhyme with "Guy Nick" (with the *tch* as in *church*). *Hock* is "strike"; *tchynik* is "teapot" or "tea kettle." From the Slavic: *tchay*, "tea."

I would not dream of urging the Yinglish deployment of *hock a tchynik*, "knock a kettle," or "beat a teakettle," if that's all it meant. To "knock a teapot" means:

1. To talk a great deal: to yammer, to yak.
2. To talk nonsense.
3. To utter meaningless sounds/syllables.

This is a widely used phrase in the coversational badminton of Jews. "Please, *hock nit kayn tchynik*! ("Please, stop talking so much!" or "Stop spouting all that nonsense!" or "Stop talking my ear off.")

The expression probably came from the meaningless rattling of a cover of a boiling pot or from the noisy whistling of steam in a kettle.

Or it may have come from the improvised toys of children at play. Since toys were a true rarity among the poor Jews in the *shtetl*, children made use of ordinary discarded objects. To simulate a drummer or a band, it was easy enough to bang away on a pot or a kettle.

In any case, "knocking a teapot" has become a most picturesque phrase for describing chatter.

Asher Norberg was an easy-going, likable sort. One day the chairman of the Entertainment Committee at Norberg's club asked him to give a speech to the members.

"Sure," said Asher. "On what subject?"

"Any subject you're comfortable with."

"What I'm most comfortable with is sex," laughed Asher, and thought no more of it.

Several days later Joanne, his wife, said, "Sophie Lessman tells me her husband told her you're giving a lecture to your club on—*sex*!"

Asher blushed and mumbled the first excuse that came to his mind. "Now, Joanie, that's a joke. I'm talking to the club on—on *sailing*!"

The following week a friend phoned Joanne to say how much *her* husband had enjoyed Asher's speech. "He said it was marvelous."

Joanne said, "*Don't hock me a tchynik!* There are only three times, since we were married, that Asher tried it. Once, he got so sick he threw up. The second time, he couldn't wait to get off and into a hot tub. And the third time, his hat blew off!"

holdupnik

Yinglish, obviously. Rhymes with "Hole *up*, Dick."

1. Anyone who robs people.
2. Anyone who *enjoys* holding up people.
3. Anyone who can't *help* robbing people, the way a kleptomaniac can't help stealing baubles.

Mr. Garfinkel got off the train and started for the lonely parking lot where he had left his car, as usual, that morning.

"Hends op!" called a voice.

Mr. Garfinkel froze in his tracks.

Out of the shadows stepped a middle-aged man, not badly dressed, neat and respectable in appearance. "Mister, I haven't had a decent mill in four days. I owe three mont's' rent. I sold my best overcoat. In fect, Mister, all I got to my name is the pistol that I'm holding in my hend . . ."

See also ALRIGHTNIK, COMPUTERNIK, HEALTHNIK, JOKE-NIK, -NIK, REFUSENIK, SICKNIK.

hole in the head

Pure Yinglish, accepted from Alaska to the Hebrides, a metaphrase from the Yiddish: *loch in kop* (pronounced LAUKH-*in-kup*): "hole in the head."

"I need it like a hole in the head."

This vivid and compelling phrase is widely heard in the United States and the United Kingdom. It frequently appears in newspapers, movies, television shows.

It was propelled into our vernacular by the play *A Hole in the Head*, by Arnold Schulman, and more forcibly impressed upon mass consciousness by the Frank Sinatra movie ("Movie," by the way, is a word so American it does not appear in the great thirteen-volume *Oxford Dictionary of the English Language*.)

"Hole in the head" was used with vigor, in Yiddish/English for a century B.S. (Before Sinatra).

Avrum Epstein, coming to America, shared a table in the ship's third-class dining room with a Frenchman. Mr. Epstein could speak neither French nor English; the Frenchman could speak neither Russian nor Yiddish.

The first day out, the Frenchman approached the table, smiled, bowed and said, "*Bon appetit!*"

Mr. Epstein, puzzled for a moment, bowed back and replied, "Epstein."

Every day, at every meal, the same routine occurred.

On the fifth day, another passenger took Epstein aside, and in Yiddish explained. "Listen, do you have a hole in your head? That Frenchman isn't telling you his *name*! He's saying 'Good appetite.' That's all *'Bon appetit!'* means.''

At the next meal, Mr. Epstein, beaming, bowed to the Frenchman and said, *"Bon appetit!"*

And the Frenchman, beaming back, replied, "Epstein!"

homentash

See HAMANTASH.

hoo-ha!
hoo-ha

Recommended for much wider use in Yinglish. Pronounce it with force: WHO HAH! Rhymes with the "Doo-dah" in "Camptown Races." Do not confuse with "Aha!" or "Ai-ai-ai," which are wholly different exclamations.

An immensely popular exclamatory flourish in Yiddish, with a rich repertory of meaning in Yinglish as well. The meanings may vary with the degree of emphasis—curt, long, trite, eloquent—accorded the syllables:

1. Surprise: "Did he murder me in gin rummy! Hoo-ha!"
2. Admiration: "That was the same book. Hoo-ha."
3. Envy: "Did she marry a marvelous man. Hoo-*ha*!"
4. Doubt: "He says he'll make you a fortune? Mneyh. Hoo-ha."
5. Outrage: "Six dollars for a sandwich? Hoo-ha!"
6. Scorn: "She wants to be a hostess? Hoo-ha."
7. Confusion, complexity, a tummel: "Hoo-*ha*, it was wild!"

Various and differing connotations are conveyed by varying facial expressions and vocal arabesques:

1. "That'll be the day!" ("He expects *me* to apologize? Hoo-ha!")

2. "Wow!" ("What a speech! Hoo-*ha!*")
3. "Like hell!" ("They want me to head the fund drive? Hoo-ha!")
4. "Can you believe it?" ("He shot his girl?! Hoo-ha.")
5. "You can't be serious!" ("Finkel is running for alderman? Hoo-ha.")
6. "Who do you think you're kidding?" ("You're going to fire Elmer? Hoo-ha.")
7. "Imagine that!" ("Danny and Judy are getting a divorce? Hoo-ha.")
8. "Don't be silly." ("Forty thousand dollars? Hoo-ha.")
9. "I'm absolutely speechless!" ("They've doubled their offer? Hoo-ha!")
10. "Everyone was running around crazy!" ("It was such a crazy *hoo-ha!*")

See also AHA!, AI-AI-AI, FEH!, MNYEH, OY, PSSSSH!

Hora

Rhymes with "Dora."
The most popular of folk dances in Israel, now known throughout the world as a "Jewish" dance.

The *Hora* is a Balkan dance, but it became popular in Palestine after 1920. It is danced in a circle with the dancers' arms on the shoulders of those adjacent to them. Israeli composers by the score have created music in the distinctive rhythm of the *Hora*.

This is as good a place as any to tell you that among very Orthodox Jews, men and women, even husbands and wives, do not dance together. Instead, at festive occasions (weddings, celebrations, anniversaries) the partners hold the ends of a handkerchief at arm's length to keep a distance between them as they dance.

how come?

A favorite with Yinglishmen everywhere: a metaphrase from Yiddish: *Vi kumt es* . . . ? "How comes [is] it . . . that you . . . ?"

Yinglish reduces "is it that" to one word: "come," the exact translation for *kumt*.

"How come Henry never showed up?"
"You never made your contribution. How come?"

The steady way in which alien words and phrases cross linguistic frontiers to infiltrate a language, all the while behaving as if they were citizens from way back, is nicely illustrated by this phrase. It sounds like perfectly acceptable, albeit colloquial, English.

———————

Saul Harbash met Yissel Fleisher on Essex Street. "*Sholem aleichem.*"

"*Gey in drerd*!" replied Fleisher.

"Hanh? Are you *crazy*?! How come—to my polite *Sholem aleichem*—you answer: 'Drop dead'?!"

Saul Harbash shrugged. "I'll explain. Suppose I answer '*Aleichem sholem.*' You naturally ask where I am going. I say I'm going to the *shul* on Avenue A. You say the *shul* on Avenue B is nicer. I say I never liked the *shul* on Avenue B. You holler, 'Any man who prefers the *shul* on Avenue A to the *shul* on Avenue B is nuts!' So I holler, 'Insults? From *you* yet? *Gey in drerd*!' . . . Fleisher, instead of going through such a long *hoo-ha*, I answer right away, 'Drop dead!' That stops the discussion . . . Now I say, '*Aleichem sholem.*' " And off he went.

how's by you?

Yinglish, ungrammatical, undesirable and unattractive. From Yiddish: *Vos iz mit dir*? ("What's wrong with you?" "Are you angry?") or *Vi geyts bei dir*? ("How goes it with [by] you?").

1. "How are you?"
2. "What's new with you?"
3. "How are things going?"

I think the phrase an outright, egregious solecism—except when deliberately used for humorous purposes, or by an immigrant or someone familiar with Yiddish.

The late Allan Sherman created a memorable Yinglish parody of the French nursery song *Frère Jacques*. It began:

> *Sarah Jackman, Sarah Jackman,*
> *How's by you, how's by you?*

hutspa

See CHUTZPA.

I

icky

Long a familiar adjective in American slang, especially among children and teenagers, this descriptive designation of the odious comes, possibly (I think, probably) from the Yiddish *eklen* or *iklen*: "to make nauseated," or from *ekedig*: "disgusting."

1. Unpleasant.
2. Nauseating.
3. Odious.

No one seems to know where *icky* came from: some believe it a clone of the *yeccch!* made so trendy by *Mad* magazine.

Jewish children picked *yekh!* up from their parents' frequent use of the uvular fricative *kh*. From *that* to the arresting unvoiced stop consonant *ck* is a breeze: indeed, it is easier said than proved. So sue me.

You want an icky story? *Here* is an icky story:

Mr. Abel Slutsker, age seventy-eight, was taking his first trip by air. He was given a seat next to a swarthy Arab wearing the traditional *kaffiyeh* (headdress) and *djellaba* (robe). The Arab stared at the old Jew, buckled his seatbelt, and deliberately spat on Mr. Slutsker's shoes . . .

The plane took off, leveled off . . . The Arab put his head back and dozed off . . .

Soon the aircraft ran into a storm: tremendous bouncings up and around, and fierce, sudden rains. Poor Mr. Slutsker grabbed for the airsickness bag stuffed in the pocket ahead—but alas, it was too late. Mr. Slutsker threw up all over the sleeping Arab's white robe.

The old Jew fearfully closed his eyes and made this prayer to the Lord, "Help me, Your pious servant. Give me an *idea*. When this crazy man awakens and sees his robe, he'll pull out that dagger and stab me in the heart! O *Adoshem*, *never* did I need Your help so badly!"

And when the Arab yawned and opened his eyes, Mr. Slutsker, hearing a divine whisper in his ears, leaned over and politely smiled, "So, Mister—are you feeling better now?"

I could bust from aggravation [anger, envy]

Yinglish, direct analogue of Yiddish: *Men ken plotsn*: "One can burst."

1. An expression used to convey supreme aggravation.
2. The expression used to describe the final, ultimate point of patience or tolerance.
3. The excuse given for whatever action followed the passing of the point described above.

"Bust" is, of course, English slang for *burst*. But "bust" is a better English word for *plots*, which is Yiddish. And in voicing "I could bust from . . ." the voiced emphasis is always on "bust."

The idea of someone actually exploding from emotional pressures is Yiddish to the core, and the core is precisely where such explosions originate.

See also FROM THAT, YOU COULD FAINT.

Mr. and Mrs. Ortov had been waiting for word from their son Joseph, away at summer camp for the first time. At last, a precious postcard arrived!

"From Joey! From Joey!" cried Mrs. Ortov. Her eyes

raced across the written words. Then she passed the card to her husband, moaning. "From this, a person could *bust*!"

Here is the message Mr. Ortov read:

DEAR MAMA AND PAPA,
 They are making everyone write home.

JOEY

_____

Another camp story in the same "You could *bust*" genre:

Mr. and Mrs. Frankheim received the following postcard from their son, Donny, in Camp Geduldik:

DEAR FOLKS:
 Just finished long hike in woods.
 Please send my other sneaker.

DONNY

_____

And still another heartburn inducer:

DEAR MA AND PA:
 The food here is okay—and they don't make you eat it.

LOVE,
SOPHIE

If my bubble had wheels, she would be a wagon [a trolley car, a bus]

Direct translation from the Yiddish, and often encountered, in one or another form, in Yinglish.

These fanciful hypotheses are used in Yinglish whenever an annihilating *reductio ad absurdum* is appropriate, or whenever someone lingers over an "iffy" conjecture or clings to a preposterous hope.

"Wheels" or transportation is easily replaced by other components of sarcasm:

"If your daughter had balls she would be part of the *minyan*."
"And if your *bubbe* had a beard, she would be your *zayde*."
"And if her grandpa had a trunk he would be an elephant!"

I'm telling you [that] . . .

Stuart Berg Flexner, co-author of *The Dictionary of American Slang*, attributes this expression to the influence of American Jews (*I Hear America Talking*). I agree with him.

Please distinguish between "I tell you . . ." and "*I'm* telling you . . ." The former is, of course, straightforward English; it is, indeed, elegant, when used in the hortatory mode; it is the phrase that takes on majesty in the numberless admonitions of the New Testament. In contrast, "*I'm* telling you . . ." is quintessential (translated) Yiddish: it uses the present participle dear to Jewish hearts; it calls attention beforehand to the fact that the speaker, and no lesser authority, is the source of the information to be revealed, and it places the self of the annunciator in the very center of the substance to be communicated.

I'm telling you: the best blurb I ever read was the one Groucho Marx wrote for one of my books:

"From the moment I picked this book up until the moment I put it down, I could not stop laughing. Someday I hope to read it."

indignation intensified by echoing a question without altering a syllable, to express resentment over being confronted by such an insensitive insinuation

Yinglish at its finest. The critical point in this ploy lies in echoing the exact words of the question asked—but without the interrogatory upbeat; *i.e.*, simply repeat the question as a declarative sentence, accompanied by whatever ironic, accusatory, even embittered intonations you can deploy, using facial expressions or gestures to magnify the refutation.

The repertoire of aggrievement (or repudiation) available in this tactical *tour de force* is more easily illustrated than defined:

1

Q: Have you talked to Dora?

A: (steely): Have I talked to Dora. (Meaning, "Am I made of stone *not* to telephone a friend who just had her leg amputated?!")

2

Q: Have you visited Mendelson?
A: (narrowing eyelids): Have I visited Mendelson. (Meaning: "How dare you imply I would not visit my best friend who just lost his wife?!")

3

Q: Did you return the pressure cooker Sally lent you?
A: (shocked): Did I return the pressure cooker Sally lent me. (Meaning: "What do you think I am—a *shnorrer* who doesn't return things of value lent to her by a trusting friend?")

4

Q: Did you send in a good recommendation for Mildred's son?
A: (pained): Did I send in a good recommendation for Mildred's son. (Meaning: "Do you think me a hypocrite, having heard me often praise Mildred's son to the skies?")

5

Q: Are you coming to the going-away party they're throwing for the Kassenmeiers?
A: (astounded): Am I coming to the going-away party they're throwing for the Kassenmeiers. (Meaning: "How could anyone even suggest that I would not go to the going-away party people are throwing for the parents of my sister's daughter-in-law?")

in good health

Yinglish, because introduced into conversational English by Jews familiar with the exact Yiddish analogue (from German): *gezunderhayt.*

This invocation is common among the children and grandchildren of Jewish immigrants, who often uttered obligatory phrases such as:

Wear it in good health.
Use it in good health.
Travel in good health.
Go in good health.

Note that *gezunderhayt* does not only mean "in good health." The expression is also employed to register the favorable feelings of the speaker: "Borrow it *gezunderhayt*" does not mean "Borrow it in good health," but "I'm glad to lend it to you."

"Your job application, Miss Kramer, looks quite good, but you say your reason for leaving your last job was—sickness. Was the sickness serious?"

The girl thought for a moment. "I never asked him."

"Him?"

"My boss. He said he just got good and sick of me."

SCENE: "Happy" Siegel's Fur Emporium

WOMAN: It's beautiful. I'll take it.

MR. SIEGEL: Thank you. Wear it in good health!

WOMAN: I just hope it won't be damaged if I wear it in the rain!

MR. SIEGEL: Lady, did you ever hear of a mink carrying an umbrella?

in the bath

Yinglish, from the Yiddish, as in *Khob'm in bod* ("I have him in the bath"), *Khob ir in bod* ("I have her in the bath") or *Khob zey in bod!* ("I have them in the bath").

A curse, not unlike "To hell with him!" or "To hell with that!" "I have you [him, her, them] in the bath!"

Please note: In this usage "bath" does *not* mean a tub, nor any form of ablution. "Bath" is symbolic, used in rather coarse response to any statement or allegation one wishes to dismiss out of hand—and with particular eloquence.

"You owe me an apology!"

"Khob dir in bod!" ("I have you in the bath.")

The interesting question is how or why this colorful idiom took this colorful form. After extensive research, I offer you the tantalizing explanation to be found under the entry "TAKING A BATH."

———

Here are some familiar uses of this malediction:

"I couldn't believe my two eyes! I walked into the bedroom and there was Manny Gross—in bed with my wife!"

"Oh, migod! What did you do?"

"Without a word, I went into the kitchen and made myself a big glass tea!"

"B-but, what about—Manny Gross?!"

"*Khob'm in bod!* Let him make his own tea!"

———

Old Mr. Fabricant was riding home on the train from New York to Hartford.

A pleasant young man sat down opposite him and in a moment said, "Excuse me, sir. What time is it? I don't have a watch."

Mr. Fabricant studied him. "You Jewish?"

"Yes, I am."

"Understand Yiddish?"

"Yes."

"So, *khob dir in bod*!" exclaimed Mr. Fabricant.

The young man reddened. "What a *nasty* thing to say! I just asked you a polite question—"

Fabricant raised a hand. "Don't jump to conclusions. Your question *was* polite, but if I give you a polite answer, you would go on with 'Nice day!' and 'What time do we arrive?' and 'Do you take this train often?' And soon it's what business *I'm* in, and then what do *you* do, and after we talk I invite you to my house. And there you meet my wife and my daughter, Sylvia. A *beautiful* girl, believe me, also very smart, a wonderful cook, a big reader—and you make a date, naturally. And you are positively *sure* to fall in love with her! . . . So you come to me, pop-eye, saying, 'Please Mr. Fabricant, I want your blessing. I want to marry your Sylvia!' Young man, how can I break your heart? Could I let my Sylvia marry a young man *who don't even own a watch*?! That's why I stop the whole business before it can even start! '*Khob dir in bod*!' "

See also TAKING A BATH.

I [you, he, she, they] should live so long!

Note the Yinglish *so* that replaces the conventional English *that*.

The declamatory "You should live so long!" (or "You should only live so long!") is far from a petitionary benediction. It is an ironic invocation in which the irony accentuates the absurdity of believing the behest.

1. May I only live as long as that will take!
2. He will take so long in delivering on that promise that I only wish I live long enough to see it—which I doubt.
3. Don't believe it!
4. (Current equivalent) *That*'ll be the day!

"Did you hear? Engelman pledged five thousand dollars to the Red Cross!?"

"I should only live so long." (Engelman will *never* cough up five thousand dollars.)

"She said she'll sign the petition!"

"She should live so long!" (Who can believe her?)

"I hear that your wife . . . ran away with another man."

"I should only live so long!" (Who could ask for anything more?)

I should worry . . .

Yinglish: origin uncertain. Several of my panelists think it related to *mayn bubbe's dayge*: "my grandma's worry [concern, problem]."

1. I won't worry about that.
2. I would be a fool to worry about that.

If you question whether this locution is Yinglish, or if you believe it to be demotic English, you must ask yourself whether Americans ever used the phrase for inverse meaning before it appeared in the Jewish sectors of New York. The answer, to my mind, is No.

The Yiddish equivalent, *mayn bubbe's dayge*, was used to mean, "Let my grandmother worry about that; I don't."

The phrase is uttered with a shrug, for (as noted) it is ironic, and its meaning is emphatically the opposite of its wording.

When I was young, the girls would chant in chorus, often while skipping rope, or playing jacks:

> *I should worry,*
> *I should care,*
> *I should marry a millionaire.*
>
> *He should die,*
> *I should cry*
> *I should marry another guy.*

In this doggerel, the meaning is:

> *I don't worry,*
> *I don't care.*
> *I hope to marry a millionaire.*
>
> *Should he die,*
> *I may cry,*
> *But I'll marry another guy.*

Israel

Hebrew: "Champion of God."

1. Popular first name for Jewish males.
2. Jewry.
3. The name of the sovereign state created on May 14, 1948.
4. The name once used for the people of the ancient northern kingdom in Palestine, where the Ten Tribes of Israel dwelled. (The southern kingdom was known as Judah.)

Ancient Palestine was divided into the northern and southern kingdoms in 933 B.C., after the death of King Solomon.

Ancient northern Israel is called, by "hardliners," Samaria, after the establishment of its capital (c. 890 B.C.).

The political influence and wealth of Israel was much greater than that of Judah: Israel had access to the Mediterranean and sat athwart important trade routes. Correspondingly, the domestic history of the kingdom was exceptionally unstable, characterized by constant strife and violent changes. During a history of 210 years, the unhappy land suffered constant revolutions: no fewer than nine different dynasties—and nineteen different kings. Of these, ten were slain, and seven ruled for two years or less.

In 1949, Herman Kaplowitz was invited by his Israeli cousin, Simeon, to the historic ceremonies dedicating the Tomb of the Unknown Soldier.

Speeches were made by the president of Israel, the minister of defense, the commanding general of the army. And at last the tarpaulin that covered the monument was pulled aside—to reveal a simple tomb. On the front was engraved:

SAM TENDLER
BORN: WARSAW, 1914
DIED: SINAI, 1948

All rose as the military band played Israel's national anthem. Soldiers saluted. Civilians placed their right hands over their hearts.

Then Prime Minister Ben-Gurion stepped to the lectern to address the throng.

Herman Kaplowitz whispered to his cousin: "Simeon . . . isn't this supposed to be the Tomb of the Unknown Soldier?"

Simeon nodded.

"But—'*Unknown*'? Why, there, plainly inscribed, is the man's *name*, his birthplace, his—"

"Ssh," hushed Simeon. "You don't understand: as a *soldier*, Sam Tendler was unknown; but as a fiddle player—!"

Is the bride too beautiful? What's wrong? Is the bride too beautiful?

Yinglish. The acme of caustic contempt; from the Yiddish: *Di kale iz tsu shayn*? ("Is the bride too beautiful?")

This lucid, forthright inquiry is not at all concerned with the bride—or any bride. It is an astringent challenge, meant to convey one's disgust with petty criticism, misguided reservations, or inane objections.

1. "What's wrong [with my offer]? Is the bride too beautiful?" (Is my offer too good?)
2. "Is the bride too beautiful?" (Are you carping about petty details in an arrangement so advantageous to you?)
3. "So you think the bride is too beautiful?" (Are you unhappy because you can't find anything to object to?)

The taunted challenge derives its counterpoint of force from the fact that a much-quoted and much-loved saying, based on a passage in Talmud (Kethubot, 17a), runs: "All brides are beautiful."

––––––––––

There is a heuristic explanation for this admirable apothegm: in a dozen places in Scripture, in the writings of the prophets, in the Talmud, Jews are severely instructed never to utter a falsehood. Fine. But what can kind Jews then say to a bride or her groom or her *parents* when the bride is, alas, homely, unattractive, emphatically unbeautiful?

This profound and perplexing dilemma was pondered and debated by rabbis and scholars and philosophers—who, thank the Lord, arrived at a superb solution: they solemnly decreed that *every* bride is beautiful! (At least, in the eyes of the groom or in the eyes of her mother or in her own inner vision.)

Is the whole world crazy?

From the Yiddish cry of indignation: *Iz der gantzer velt meshuggeh*?

1. A *denial* that the whole world must be crazy—hence, I [you] can't be wrong.
2. A desperate appeal to good sense: "Look at the *facts*!"
3. The whole *world* [except you, her, him, they] can't be crazy—i.e., *you* can't be the only person in the world who is sane!

4. Come to your senses: reconsider!
5. Sarcastic, embittered rebuke.

F. Goldstein
1121 Broadway
New York

Los Angeles jury just announced verdict in our case. Justice has prevailed!!

Benny

B. Feldscher
Hotel Symonds
Los Angeles, Calif.

Is the whole world crazy? Appeal at once!!

Freddy

———

When the foreman of the jury stood up and read their decision, "Not guilty," Judge Kesselman almost had a fit. The defendant was a well-known racketeer, had been convicted in three other crimes—and no fewer than six reputable witnesses had seen him commit prolonged assault and battery on his victim.

"Did you say '*Not Guilty*'?!" exclaimed the Judge.

"That's right, your honor."

"W-what possible evidence," seethed the Judge, "could have persuaded you to acquit the defendant?"

"We felt it was due to—insanity!" said the foreman.

"'Insanity'?" bleated Judge Kesselman. "All *twelve* of you?"

It can't [couldn't, won't, wouldn't] hurt!

Yinglish to a fare-thee-well. A pure metaphrase of the Yiddish *Es ken nisht [nit] shatn*. Emphasize the word *hurt*—pronounced by immigrant, Lower East Side or Bronxian Jews as "hoit."

Used for comic or satiric effect.

The most memorable (deservedly) use of this philosophical idiom occurred (unless it was fictitious, which in no way alters my enthusiasm) during a dramatic performance in the 1920s of *King Lear*, in Yiddish, in a theater on Second Avenue—when a leading actor, at the climax of his biggest scene, collapsed in a heap, right on the stage.

"Doctor!" cried another actor.

"Get a doctor!" shouted a stagehand.

"Is there a doctor in the house?!"

In the second row, a man rose. "I'm a doctor!" He hurried up the stairs to the stage, bent over the prostrate actor, pried open an eyelid, felt the recumbent's pulse . . .

From the balcony, an old lady rose to her feet, cupped her mouth with her hands, and shouted, "Give—him—an—*en*ema!"

The doctor leaned over and placed his ear against the fallen one's breast. Not a heartbeat was to be heard.

"Give—him—an—*en*ema!" trumpeted the old lady in the gallery.

The doctor straightened up, crying, "Lady, this man is *dead*! An enema can't help!"

"It vouldn't *hoit*!" snapped the old lady.

It shouldn't happen to a dog!

What makes this Yinglish, albeit the words and syntax are perfectly proper English, is the frequency and force with which this heartfelt invocation is heard in conversations among Jews, whether in Yiddish or English. I have heard this colorful supplication, uttered as an incantation, in a gorgeous repertoire of accents and intonations: grave, angry, quiet, agitated.

"It shouldn't happen to a *hoont* [dog]!"

"It shouldn't happen to a *dug*!"

"It shouldn't happen to a *duck*!"

"It shouldn't even happen to a *dawg*!"

"I wouldn't wish such a terrible thing on a *dog*!"

Whatever changes were rung on the theme, the central meaning was indisputable.

It should be emphasized that throughout their history, Jews have never hunted—for sport or pleasure, nor patronized cruel sports.

Rest on the Sabbath applies to animals no less than to humans, and the Torah is full of instances of God's displeasure with any who are unkind to dumb beasts (Deuteronomy 22:4).

What I find most admirable are the rabbinical injunctions to Jews that they must feed an animal before feeding themselves, that an animal may not be gelded, that any beast that falls under the weight of its burden must be helped up.

"It shouldn't happen to a dog!" carries overtones not apparent to those unfamiliar with Jewish traditions.

Dogs, incidentally, were rare in Jewish neighborhoods (they take feeding).

"Man, oh, man," sighed Al Motsner, "I had everything any man could want: the love of a gorgeous woman, a beautiful home, plenty of money, fine clothes—"

"What happened?" cried his friend.

"What happened—it shouldn't happen to a dog!—is, out of the blue, without any hint or warning—my wife walked in!"

Cecile Enteman, suffering from extreme hay fever, leaving for a posh dinner party, decided she might need two handkerchiefs for the evening—and stuck an extra one into her bodice.

At dinner, having used up one handkerchief, Cecile reached into her bosom for the fresh one. She rummaged around without success—and suddenly became aware that the conversation had stopped; all the guests were watching her.

"Excuse me!" Cecile exclaimed. "But I *know* I had two when I arrived."

(It shouldn't happen to a *hintele*.)

Joel Glickman met Weissman at a cafeteria near Union Square. No sooner did they sit down at a table than Glickman exclaimed, "I had a year, Phil, it shouldn't happen to a dog! In June, business was so bad I thought I'd go bankrupt. In July, I had to get a loan from the bank. In August, I wished it was still July. In September—"

"Stop!" cried Weissman. "Why are you ruining my lunch? You want problems? *I'll* give you problems! Last year, my wife ran away with my partner. Then a fire burned my apartment to a crisp. On New Year's, my daughter told me she had to have an abortion. Could anything have been worse?"

Glickman moaned. "November."

$\mathcal{J}$

J.A.P.
Jap

Yinglish, emphatically: neither English nor Yiddish.
And of recent origin. Pronounced "Jap." Acronym for
"Jewish American Princess."

An "in" word used to describe a rich, spoiled, nubile
Jew girl or woman.

Zelda Feibush, aspiring pianist and heiress, wrote to the
celebrated Leopold Mankovski: "You are my idol. It will
mean everything for me to hear your honest opinion of my
talent."

The impresario, famed for his kindness, invited Zelda to
his studio. There she played for him. She played Beethoven, Debussy, Chopin . . . Mankovski sat silent, his eyes
closed.

Finally, Zelda blurted, "Maestro, please—what should
I do now?"

The maestro opened one eye. "Get married."

Q: What do J.A.P.'s most often make for dinner?
A: Reservations.

BERNIE: Mr. Batzel, I—I want to marry your daughter.
MR. BATZEL: My! And have you seen my wife yet?
BERNIE: Oh, yes. But I prefer your daughter.

Scene: **Restaurant**

J.A.P.: Waiter! Waiter!
WAITER: Yes, miss?
J.A.P.: This steak. Do you call this *meat*? It's a disgrace.
WAITER: Miss, what's wrong with it?
J.A.P.: What's *wrong* with it? It—tastes—funny!
WAITER (shrugging): So, laugh.

Jehovah

This is not, believe it or not, a Hebrew word, much less
a Yiddish one. It is a Latin *mis*translation of Y H V H,
the Tetragrammaton, the Holy and Ineffable Name of
God.

The Judaic and Christian name for God, the Lord:
King and creator of all the universe.

It is one of history's more ironic truths that the sacrosanct title for the Almighty in the English language is incorrect, wrong, a flat mistake in translation. "Jehovah" is not
and was not ever the name of, or for, the Almighty. The
erroneous appellation first appeared in an English text in
1530.

The story of the historic error is fascinating. *Yahveh* is
the name formed by adding vowel sounds to the sacred four
Hebrew letters representing the unutterable name of the
Lord. (The English equivalents of these four letters are Y
H V H: *yud, hay, vov, hay.*)

The Masoretes (from *Masorah*, Hebrew for "exact
meaning is uncertain"), who preserved the "correct" interpretation and spelling and meaning of the ancient Hebrew
texts, added diacritical marks for the vowel sounds to Y H
V H—as a signal to readers to say *Adonai*, instead of trying
to pronounce the Name. Now, it was the *combination* of
Y H V H and its diacritical marks (for the vowels) that
was translated into Latin—incorrectly—as JeHoVa(ha) or
Je*hova*—used in this way for the first time in 1516.

How did this mistranslation occur? The answer is clear.
Four centuries ago, an unknown papal scribe, a German
(who probably would have rendered Y H V H orally as
"Yahveh" and written the *Y* as a *J*), attached the diacritical
marks meant for *Elohim* to the sacred four letters; thus,
JHVH became JeHoVaH.

The original pronunciation of Y H V H may have been "Yahveh" or "Yahiveh." This was replaced, after several thousand years, by "Jehovah," the version of the divine Name used in virtually all Protestant Bibles. (The sound of *ya* in Hallelujah is thought to be a short version of Y H V H.)

The meticulous editors of the Standard Edition of the New English Bible (Oxford and Cambridge Presses) retained "this incorrect but customary form," offering the following footnote of correction each time "Jehovah" appears in their text: "The Hebrew consonants are Y H V H, probably pronounced *Yahiveh*, but traditionally read *Jehovah*."

There is a tantalizing aspect to all this: The Holy Name was pronounced only in the ancient Temple in Jerusalem. But whenever that super-sacrosanct secret (which the Hebrew priests never confided to laypersons) was enunciated, the musical part of the service was designed to swell up so loud as to drown it out!

See also ADONAI, ADOSHEM, YAHVEH, Y H V H.

Jew

Jew, in Hebrew, is *Yehudi* (named after Judah, the son of Jacob); in Aramaic, *Jew* is *Yehudai*; in Greek, *Ioudais*; in Latin, *Judaeus*; in German, *Jude* (pronounced YOU-*deh*); in French, *Juif*; in Spanish, *Judio*; in Italian, *Guideo*; in Portuguese, *Judeu*. (I must tell you that the Japanese *judo* has nothing to do with Jews; *judo* means "soft art," more or less.) In Anglo-French, the word for *Jew* was *Iew* or *Geu*. Chaucer referred to Jewry as *Iewerie*.

1. A believer in Judaism.
2. One descended from Hebrew/Jewish parents.
3. Anyone who identifies himself or herself as Jewish.
4. The child of a Jewish mother.
5. One who observes the religious protocols of Judaism.

The English word *Jew*, says Max Weinreich (*History of the Yiddish Language*), is the Old French *Giu*; like the German *Jude*, the name comes from Latin, *Judaeus*, which was the Romans' way of translating the Hebrew *Yehudah*, the name of the Jewish commonwealth during the time of the Second Temple. *Yehudah*, in English, is "Judah." (Judah's descendants, of course, made up one of the tribes of Israel; they settled in Canaan and westward, from Jericho to the Mediterranean.)

Who are the Jews and what do they believe? A refreshing lucidity distinguishes the following passage from Dr. Morris Adler:

> Jews do not constitute a church but a people. One of the reasons the modern Jew finds it difficult to define his identity is that the English language offers no term to suggest the complex of ethnic, national, cultural and religious elements that constitute the collective life of the Jew. The irreligious Jew is not read out of the community. Affiliation . . . is not a matter of creed.
>
> The religion of the Jew embraces areas that modern man would call secular. There is no instance, in the Western world, of an ethnic group whose religion emerged out of its own history . . . The word church does not fit the Jewish situation.
>
> —*The World of the Talmud*, p. 124

The two main branches of Jewry are the Sephardim (from the Hebrew name for Spain) and the Ashkenazim (from the Hebrew name for Germany). The vast majority of Jews are Ashkenazim: a ratio of about twenty to one. The two divisions are distinguished from each other considerably: in their liturgy, ceremonials, food, customs.

There are about five million nine hundred thousand Jews in the United States—representing around 2.5 percent of the population, according to the Data Bank of the City University of New York.

Surveys of Jews in urban areas reveal that about one-third identify themselves as Conservative, about thirty percent as Reform, around nine percent as Orthodox; the remainder, twenty-eight percent, offer no formal religious affiliation. The greatest concentration of Orthodox Jews, outside of Israel, is in the southwestern part of Brooklyn.

By far the most authoritative and comprehensive compendium of Judaism, Jewish history, Jewish life, Jewish notables, Jewish religious practices, etc., is the ten-volumed *Encyclopedia Judaica*, edited by Cecil Roth. Prager

and Telushken's *The Questions People Ask About Judaism*
and Alfred J. Kolatch's several volumes called *The Jewish
Book of Why* offer simple answers for those with questions
about Judaism.

The past hundred years of Jewish emigration to the western hemisphere, where over half of world Jewry live, have
been dramatically recounted by Ronald Sanders, in his recent, huge *Shores of Refuge*. The intricacies of religious
affiliation and ideology are analyzed in Arnold Eisen's *The
Chosen People in America* and Leonard Fein's *Where We
Are*.

Mrs. Chauncey Ashley III telephoned the headquarters
of the infantry base near Great Oaks, her ancestral home.
"This is Mrs. Chauncey Ashley the Third, and with
Thanksgiving coming up, I would like ten of your fine enlisted men to share our family feast."

"That's very kind of you, Mrs. Ashley."

"There's only one thing—I'm sure you understand: my
husband and I prefer not to have any Jews . . ."

"Madam, I *quite* understand."

When her front door bell rang on Thanksgiving Day,
Mrs. Ashley hurried to the door herself. She flung it open.
"*Wel*come to Great—" She stopped, aghast, pale as a nap-
kin.

Under the great portico stood ten smiling black soldiers.

"Omigod," gasped Mrs. Ashley. "There has been a terrible mistake!"

The black sergeant grinned, "Oh, no, ma'am. Captain
Finkelstein *never* makes a mistake."

You are of course familiar with the witty and condescending quatrain created by (I believe) W. N. Ewer, although credited to Hilaire Belloc, who made no secret of
his anti-Semitism:

How odd
Of God
To choose
The Jews.

The jingle was answered by some unknown wag:

Not news
Not odd,
The Jews
Chose God.

To which some droll Jew responded:

Not odd
Of God:
Goyim
Annoy 'im.

———

Three rabbis, at a convention, were exchanging remarks. "My congregation is so modern," said Rabbi Gelfond, "that after services we adjourn for a buffet—and ham sandwiches are our most popular item!"

"My flock," said Rabbi Krantz, "is so emancipated that over sixty percent of the children married gentiles!"

The third rabbi cleared his throat. "*My* temple is closed on Jewish holidays."

———

A reporter, interviewing Rabbi Seligman after a bolt of lightning had struck the synagogue's roof and sent it crashing down into ruins, asked, "Rabbi, what was your reaction when you saw this terrible devastation?"

"My first reaction?" The rabbi chuckled. "I thought, thank goodness we took out insurance against acts of God."

———

What was their crime? Only that they were born. . . .
That is why the Portuguese burnt them.
                    —Voltaire, *Sermons du Rabbi Akib*
The study of the history of Europe teaches [this]
    lesson: the nations which dealt fairly with the Jew
    have prospered; the nations that tortured and
    oppressed him wrote out their own curse.
                    —Olive Schreiner
The Jews are not hated because they have evil
    qualities; evil qualities are searched for in them,
    because they are hated.
                    —Max Nordau
Dear God, if you really loved the Jews why did you
    make them the chosen people?

The happiness of Jews is never entirely free from fear.

See also ASHKENAZI, SEPHARDI.

jokenik

Yinglish, tacking the colorful, versatile particle -*nik* onto the English *joke* to designate:

1. A compulsive, unstoppable teller of jokes.
2. Someone addicted to the collection and telling of jokes, however old or unfunny.
3. One who acts in a jocular, insensitive fashion during an inappropriate time or occasion.

At the Hillcrest Country Club, in West Los Angeles, one large round table is a special preserve for comedians. Around this board I have seen, at one time or another, the likes of Milton Berle, George Burns, Groucho Marx, George Jessel, Danny Kaye, Henny Youngman, Phil Silvers, etc.

The jokes cascade here; the repartee is swift; the anecdotes never run out. But comedians usually listen to someone else with but one ear, preoccupied with thinking up or remembering japeries with which to "top" a rival.

At one luncheon, a famous jokenik sat down. He looked haggard.

"What's wrong?" someone asked.

"What's *not* wrong? Last month, my brother died. Last week, they put my wife's leg in a cast. Yesterday, my son went skiing and broke his nose. And just this morning, driving over here, I accidentally hit an old jalopy, driven by a lady must be eighty years old, who's going to sue me for a million dollars! . . ."

From across the table came: "You think *that's* funny? Let me tell you about the Arab and the Irishman. One day . . ."

See also -NIK.

Judah

1. Popular first name for Jewish males.
2. The kingdom, south of Israel, in ancient Palestine,

which was divided in 933 B.C., after the death of King Solomon.
3. The son of Jacob, from whose name comes the Hebrew *Yehuda*.

The Ten Tribes occupied the ancient Kingdom of Israel, the northern area, after Palestine was divided. Judah contained the tribes of Judah, Benjamin and (apparently) Simeon, in the extreme south.

Judah, only one-third the size of Israel, was nowhere as prosperous or influential, because it presided over no important trade route and had no access to the Mediterranean, as Israel did. But Judah contained Jerusalem and the Holy Temple! And its geographical position gave it insulation from the rivalries, international pressures and political agitations of Israel.

The Assyrians overran Israel, then invaded Judah, in 701 B.C. They were stopped before the very walls of Jerusalem.

But Judah and Jerusalem fell to the Babylonians, in 586 B.C., who enslaved and deported a vast number of Judeans.

Judah preserved the monotheism of Moses in a simpler, purer form than was true in Israel, and the intellectual life of the southern kingdom was remarkably vigorous and fertile. Most of the prophets worked in Judah, and vast portions of the Torah, or Pentateuch, were created there.

Judesmo

See LADINO.

𝒦

Kabala
Kabbala

See CABALA.

Kaddish

Increasingly well known in Yinglish. Pronounced KOD-*dish*, to rhyme with "codfish." Aramaic: *kadosh*: "holy."

1. The prayer, glorifying God's name, recited at the close of synagogue prayers; this is the most solemn and one of the most ancient of all Jewish prayers.
2. The Mourner's Prayer.
3. A son is sometimes called, affectionately, "*Kaddishel*," or "*My Kaddish*."

The *Kaddish* is *not* a prayer for the dead. It was originally recited after completing a reading from the Bible, or a religious discourse, or a lesson. It is a doxology that glorifies God's name, affirms faith in the establishment of His kingdom and expresses hope for peace within Israel.

The language of the prayer is not Hebrew but Aramaic, which was the vernacular spoken by the Jews in their Babylonian exile and during the days of the Second Temple, or Commonwealth.

In time, a belief arose among Jews that the praising of

God in the *Kaddish* would help the souls of the dead find lasting peace—and the prayer then became known as the Mourner's Prayer, even though it contained not one reference to death *or* resurrection.

The *Kaddish* begins "Magnified and glorified is His great name," and ends "May He who makes peace in His high places make peace for us and for all Israel, and say ye, Amen."

In the *Kaddish*, the mourner affirms his faith in God's goodness and life's being worthwhile. Some sages called the *Kaddish* "an echo of the Book of Job," for it was Job who said, "Though He slay me, yet will I trust in Him."

Traditionally, only a son was duty-bound to say *Kaddish* for his parents; today, among many Reform/Conservative Jews, daughters recite the hallowed mourning prayer for a parent.

The *Kaddish* is recited by the children of the deceased at the grave, for eleven months after a death and each year after that on *Yortzeit*, the anniversary of the death.

The fact that the mourner, even in the darkest depth of his suffering, glorifies God is thought to be the highest affirmation of God's righteousness—and the strongest statement of the mourner's resignation to His will. (But the Berditshever Rabbi wrote a poem in which he refuses to say *Kaddish* when he gets to Heaven, because of the Holocaust.)

Couples who had no son would sometimes adopt an orphan (a relative, if possible) and raise him as their own. He was called their *Kaddish*, and guaranteed that there would be someone to recite the hallowed prayer for them after their death.

Judaic law forbids any form of display or ostentation at a funeral. The rabbis of yore instituted simple burial rites; this served to enforce a "democracy in death" in which no family, however poor, would be shamed by the simplicity of the coffin or shroud.

May I give you my favorite prayer for the dead?

When you gaze upon the dead, remember this: You have been shown more than you can understand. Search not for what has been hidden from you. Seek not to understand what is so difficult to bear.

Mourn the dead, and hide not your grief; but fear not death, for we share it with all who ever lived and with all who ever will be. The good things in life last but limited days, but a good name will endure forever.

O God, forsake us not in the days of our desolation. . . . Now, help us to live on, for we have placed all our hope in Thee.

I adapted this moving invocation from *Ecclesiasticus*, written around 180 B.C., by Jeshua (or Jesus) ben Sirach.

———

With his particular and matchless humor, Sholem Aleichem described the prayer of mourning that he and his five brothers recited for their departed mother.

You should have heard us deliver that *Kaddish*! All our relatives beamed with pride, and strangers envied us. One of our relatives . . . exclaimed, "When a woman has six sons like that to say *Kaddish* after her, she will surely go straight to paradise. Either that or the world is coming to an end!"

———

"*Rebbe*," complained Mr. Flockman. "It's over a month my Joel has been going to your *heder*. And he doesn't know five words in Hebrew!"

"I know."

"So why are you teaching him the *Kaddish*? Do I look like a dying man?"

"No, no, Mr. Flockman," said the rabbi. "You should only live as long as it will take your boy to learn the *Kaddish*!"

See also YORTZEIT.

kaiser

The Yinglish, truncated form of "Kaiser roll."

A breakfast roll: high, fluffy, often sprinkled with poppy or sesame seeds.

The name "Kaiser rolls" seems to have been used in Chicago, not New York; when I first asked for the goody in New York, the counterman looked buffaloed. New Yorkers say "seeded roll."

These delicious rolls were named "Kaiser rolls" either because they were favored by some Austrian monarch (no mean distinction, considering the exalted art of Viennese baking) or because to poor Jews a light, airy, white-flour roll was thought to be fit for a kaiser (Caesar, in German).

kalyikeh (feminine)
kalyiker (masculine)

Strongly recommended for Yinglish. Pronounced KOLL-*yi-keh*. From Russian: cripple. The double *k* doubles the percussive power of the alveolar stops. (I hope you are impressed.)

1. A crippled person.
2. A clumsy or inept type.
3. A talentless performer.

"He has the social polish of a *kalyiker*."
"She walks like a queen, but she dances like a *kalyikeh*."

———

Shmuel Kipnis went to a cheap clothier on Twenty-fourth Street. A salesman took him in tow. "I have here a suit—*made* for you! Here. Just try it on!"

Shmuel got into the garment and surveyed himself in the mirror. "The right sleeve. It's too long!"

"So stick out your elbow," said the salesman. "See? That takes up the length."

"The collar is way up—"

"So raise your head! See? The collar goes *down*."

"But now the left shoulder is wider than the right!" cried Shmuel.

"So *bend*," said the salesman earnestly. "This way. Look how it evens out!"

Shmuel Kipnis left the store, right elbow stuck out, head back, left shoulder tilted . . .

A stranger accosted him. "Excuse me. I'm looking for a suit. Please tell me—who is your tailor?"

"My tailor?" groaned Shmuel. "Are you *meshugge*? Are you *crazy*?"

"No, *sir!*" the stranger retorted. "Any man who can fit a *kalyiker* like you must be a *genius!*"

See also KLUTZ.

kayn aynhoreh

See KINEAHORA.

khale

See CHALLA.

khutspa
khutspe

See CHUTZPA.

kibbitz

See KIBITZ.

kibbutz
kibbutzim   (plural)

> Often encountered in English. Pronounced *kib*-BUTZ, with the *u* as in *puts*, not *cuts*. Hebrew: "collective," "group." Plural: *kibbutzim* (*kib-butz*-IM).
>
> A cooperative settlement of farmers in Israel.
>
> Do not confuse *kibbutz* with *kibitz*, even though every *kibbutz* probably has a good many *kibitzers*. A fervent believer in *kibbutzim* is called (what else?) a *kibbutznik*.

The *kibbutzim* of Israel have won international respect for the courage, idealism and perseverance of their members: Jews from all parts of the world, who elect to live the extremely hard and dangerous life of settlers, under pioneer conditions. The *kibbutzim* play a central part in Israel's defenses; many were established near the frontiers of the surrounding Arab states.

Kibbutzim are farm collectives that vary greatly in size, degree of mechanization, details of authority, ownership, profit sharing. They have been intensively studied by economists, agronomists, social psychologists and educators from all over the world; their structure has been adopted in many of the underdeveloped countries of Africa and (less often) Asia. There is a Japanese Kibbutz Association, and some eighty Japanese students have worked on *kibbutzim* in Israel.

Kibbutzim are no longer increasing in number. There is an increasing desire on the part of young Israelis to leave the *kibbutzim* for cities, superior schools and broader opportunities.

"If you want to live forever," Fischel Farkis told a very rich cousin in Haifa, "come to live in our little *kibbutz*."

"Is it that beautiful?"

"Beautiful? It's the ugliest town you ever saw in your whole life!"

"Well, is the *climate* that good?" asked the cousin.

"The climate is without a doubt absolutely terrible. Maybe the worst in all of Israel!"

"Then why in God's name do you urge me to live there?!" the cousin sputtered.

"Look at the statistics!" exclaimed Farkis. "Not *once* has a rich man died there!"

kibitz
kibbitz

Yinglish, indeed! Pronounced KIB-*its*, to rhyme with "Tibbets." From German: *Kiebitz*: "lapwing," and "spectator at card game." (Do not confuse *kibbitz* with *kibbutz*.)

1. To comment while watching a game.
   "I was *kibitzing*, not playing." (I was watching, making comments.)
2. To joke, fool around, wisecrack; to socialize aimlessly.
   "We were just *kibitzing* around."
3. To tease, needle, gibe, second-guess.
   "Don't *kibitz*: he's sensitive." (Don't needle, tease, or "ride" him.)
4. To carry on a running commentary while someone else is working.

"He was *kibitzing* us all the way." (He was advising, second-guessing, criticizing.)

"He's not employed there, he just *kibitzes*."

It has been said that when you tell a joke to a German, he laughs. When you tell it to an Englishman, he laughs twice: when he hears it, and when he understands it. When you tell it to a Frenchman, he laughs three times: when you tell it, when he recalls it, and when he repeats it. But when you tell a joke to a Jew, he interrupts to say he's heard it before—then he tells it to you, in an "improved" version (*i.e.*, his).

In this sense Jews like to *kibitz*.

———

Mr. Kovalski started to mount the ladder, to hang up this new sign:

FRESH FISH

SOLD HERE

DAILY

Kovalski's neighbor, Finestein, sang out, "Hey, Julie. You nuts, puttin' up a sign like that?"

"What's wrong with it?"

"Why do you say '*Fresh* Fish'? You want your customers to think you ever sold them *stale* fish?"

"You're right." Kovalski took his brush and painted out "FRESH." He started up the ladder.

"Hold it," kibitzed Finestein. "Why 'Sold'? Could anyone think you gave fish away *free*?"

Kovalski expunged "SOLD."

"And why 'Here'? Obviously, you don't sell fish over *there* . . ."

"You're right." Kovalski painted out "HERE."

"That leaves 'Daily,' " said Finestein. "Is *that* smart? If fish are fresh, they *must* be caught and sold daily. Right?"

"Absolutely!" Kovalski crossed out "DAILY." The sign now read:

FISH

As Kovalski started up the ladder again, along came Isadore Gross, a *real* kibitzer. "Why are you putting up that *ridi*culous sign?"

"What's wrong with it?" bridled Kovalski.

"You don't have to put up a sign, Kovalski. Anyone can smell your fish a mile away!"

See also KIBITZER.

kibitzer

Firmly and widely established in Yinglish—as much as Yiddish words such as *chutzpa* or *gonif*. Pronounced KIB-*itz-er*, to rhyme with "Sid Hitzer."

Webster's *Third New International Dictionary* enters a second "acceptable" pronunciation: *ki*-BIT-*zer*. Not only have I never heard the word so pronounced; I would develop severe spasms if I did.

From the German name for a bird, the *Kiebitz* (Latin name: *vanellus*), a lapwing or peewit, reputed to be especially noisy and inquisitive, and called, colloquially, *Kibitzer*. Staunch Yiddishists seem to forget that in German *kiebitzen* (note the spelling) means to look over the shoulder of a card player!

One who *kibitzes*, that is:

1. Comments from the sidelines.
2. Offers unasked-for advice.
3. Wisecracks, needles.
4. Fools around, wastes time.
5. Second-guesses.
6. Distracts through irritating patter.
7. Sticks his nose into the business of others.
8. Humors others along.

Kibitzers are rarely knowledgeable or respected; if they were, they would be advisers, not *kibitzers*.

"What are you—a *kibitzer?*" (a wiseguy who doesn't participate but offers easy advice)

"As a poker player, he's a good *kibitzer*." (He second-guesses better than he plays; he's better as a cocky bystander than as a player.)

"As a worker, he's a fine *kibitzer*." (He talks more than he works; he puts on airs.)

"I'm afraid it's a slipped disk, and that *kibitzer* told me one good cha-cha will get me back in shape!"

"Oh, stop your *kibitzing*!" (He has carried flattery beyond credibility.)

I should think that by now no one needs to have *kibitzer* illustrated. *The Kibitzer*, a play by Jo Swerling (1920), made the word an overnight byword in English/Yinglish.

The sign on the doctors' door imparted this information:

DR. ROBERT LEWIN, BRAIN SURGERY
DR. J. O. BANKMAN, PSYCHIATRY
DR. CHARLES GOLUB, PROCTOLOGY

Under this imposing troika, some sardonic *kibitzer* scrawled:

WE SPECIALIZE IN
ODDS AND ENDS.

The four regular cardplayers at Kolinsky's Spa were cursed by a kibitzer, one Jesse Yager, of such persistence that they met secretly to try to figure out how to put an end to his ceaseless commentary.

"Let's tell him, once and for all, to shut up while we're playing!"

"I've tried that a dozen times."

"Wait! Let's *invent* a game! A game so cockamamy that Yager won't be able to figure out what's going on!"

The others applauded.

The next day, the four men appeared in the game room as usual; and, as usual, Jesse Yager pulled up a chair.

"Today—let's play *Jiffel and Kreitz*," suggested Mr. Garfinkel.

"Great!"

"How about a penny a point?"

"And double for a *plotch*!"

During all this nonsense, the kibitzer sat, frowning, silent.

Mr. Kruger riffled the deck of cards, dealt, picked up his portion, and tossed a card before Mr. Danenberg. "I bid one *jiffel*."

"Double—with a *schmeitz*!" exclaimed Mr. Danenberg.

"I have a *knotch*!" cried Garfinkel. "So I raise you—in spades!"

"Oh, boy!" chortled Mr. Schreiber. "*I* have a *schmatzer*! So I call you both and raise—"

"*Psst*!" hissed the kibitzer. "Schreiber, don't be a fool!"

"What do you mean?"

"A schmatzer can't beat a jiffel—especially when there's a knotch raise—in *spades*!"

Kiddush
Kiddish

Pronounced KID-*ish*, to rhyme with "Yiddish." From Hebrew: "sanctification." As used, *Kiddush* means "sanctification of the wine." (Please, *please* do not confuse *Kiddush* with *Kaddish, q.v.*)

The prayer and ceremony that sanctify the Sabbath and Jewish holy days.

The ceremony known as the *Kiddush* was practiced by Jews long before the Christian Consecration of bread and wine in Holy Communion and the Eucharist (from the Greek for "thanksgiving" or "gratitude").

The first Christians were Jews, of course, and the ancient sect among them called the Essenes, mystics of extreme piety, followed a ritual of Communion ("love feast"). The Essenes (perhaps from the Hebrew *tsenuim*: "pious ones") date from the second century B.C. to the second century of our era. They were close to the Pharisees, but practiced different customs. They were mostly farmers, opposed slavery, lived abstemious lives. Before eating, they would immerse themselves completely in water. They preached celibacy(!) but were sensible enough to noodge some of their congregants into marriage simply because they felt that God wanted humankind to be perpetuated.

The *Kiddush* recited in a Jewish home on Friday nights, before dinner, and also on the eve of various holidays is not the same as the *Kiddush* that follows the regular Sabbath and holiday services held in the synagogue.

1. At home, the father recites the *Kiddush* before the Friday-night Sabbath dinner begins, over a goblet or cup of wine. He begins with a recitation of Genesis

2:1–3, which tells how God rested on the seventh day of Creation and made it holy.

Two *broches* (blessings) follow; the first praising God for having created wine; the second thanking the Lord for having created the holy Sabbath "as an inheritance, a memorial of the Creation": and "in remembrance of the departure from Egypt."

All those at the table share in the *Kiddush* wine, as active participants in the ceremony.

Some Jews recite the *Kiddush* without wine, using *challa* (Sabbath bread) instead—for the rabbis long ago realized that thousands of Jews were too poor to afford wine, even a sip each Friday.

2. In the synagogue, by tradition, following the services on holidays or each Saturday morning, the worshipers gather to sample the *challa* loaf or taste the wine, engage in pleasant and festive conversation and then, after a while, go home for the noon meal.

See also KIDDUSH HASHEM.

Kiddush Hashem
Kiddush ha-Shem
Kiddish Hashem

Pronounced KID-*dish ha*-SHEM, to rhyme with "Yiddish posh hen." Hebrew: "sanctification of God's name."

The concept that God needs mortal men to hallow His name and that men become sanctified by following God's commandments.

The Book of Leviticus (22:32) has God say: "I will be hallowed among the children of Israel; I am the Lord which hallows you."

It is important to note that *Kiddush Hashem* involves any generous, noble, altruistic or considerate deed *that honors all Jews*. This comes from the old idea that the Jews are a kingdom of priests, and that each Jew therefore bears perpetual responsibility to act to all other men in such a way as to honor all Jewry. The Talmud cites as a case of true *Kiddush Hashem* a Jew's returning to an Arab, from whom he had purchased a camel, a jewel that he had found around the camel's neck: "I bought a camel, not a precious gem.'' The Arab cried, ''Blessed be [your] God; blessed be the God of Israel.''

The opposite of *Kiddush Hashem* is *Chillul Hashem*, or ''the profaning of God's name.''

kike

> Vulgarism; pronounced to rhyme with ''like.'' Yinglish. From Yiddish: *kikel*: ''circle.'' Note the Yiddish idiom: *Ikh kikel zikh fun gelechter*: ''I roll myself around with laughter.''

1. A thoroughly offensive, obnoxious way of referring to a Jew.
2. (As used by Jews) A cheap, vulgar, greedy Jew.

Kike was used in New York as early as 1914, and is included in H. L. Mencken's *American Language* (1919) as a common term of disparagement, akin to ''sheeny,'' or to ''dago'' or ''Wop'' for an Italian.

Why, in the United States, was *kike* coined as an epithet for ''Jew''? Assimilated German Jews, in the later decades of the nineteenth century, referred to the poorer, ''pushy'' immigrants from eastern Europe as ''kikey'' or ''kikes.'' One reason today advanced for this is that many Ashkenazic names ended in *-sky* or *-ski*; presumably the taunt ''ki-kis'' led to ''kikes.'' I find this quite unconvincing: the letters *ski* or *sky* were always pronounced ''skee'' never ''sky,'' and repetition-play would surely have given the neologisms ''kee-kees'' or ''keeks,'' but never *kikes*.

My research led me to the following conclusions. The word *kike* was born on Ellis Island, when Jewish immigrants who were illiterate (or could not use Roman-English letters), when asked to sign the entry-forms with the customary *X*, refused—and instead made a circle. The Yiddish word for ''circle'' is *kikel* (pronounced KY-*kel*), and for ''little circle,'' *kikeleh*. Before long the immigration inspectors were calling anyone who signed with an *O* instead of an *X* a *kikel* or *kikeleh* or *kikee* or, finally and succinctly, *kike*.

In time, the inspectors learned to call to each other: ''Don't put a cross on his card; put a circle,'' or ''Use a *kikel*,'' and, in time, ''Make it a *kike*,'' or ''He's a *kike*.''

I add another significant item: Jewish storekeepers and peddlers conducted much of their trade on credit. Many of these early merchants could not write English. They checked off a payment from a customer, in their own or the customer's account book, with a little circle ("I'll make you a *kikeleh*"). They never used a cross, as far as I know.

Why did Jews make an *O*, never an *X*? Because of the profound fear, not to say revulsion, felt for the symbol of the cross, which to them represented the very sign under which they had been persecuted, and their ancestors brutalized and slaughtered.

And so those who drew *kikelehs*, whether on Ellis Island or Avenue B, in Ohio or Kansas or wherever the hardy peddlers traveled into the Mid-and far West, came to be known as "*kike* men" or "*kikes*." Dr. Shlomo Noble told me that the miners of northeastern Pennsylvania would say, "I bought it from the *kike* man," or "The *kike* man will be coming around soon."

These early, or original, uses were purely descriptive, not pejorative.

Some irate *mavens* (or *meyvinim*) have written me triumphantly that the Yiddish word for "circle" is *krayz* (ring) or *tsirkl* (rod). True. But that does not mean that *kikel* is not! Alexander Harkavy's *English–Yiddish Dictionary* lies before me; he defines "circle" as *kikel*. The date of publication: 1910.

———————

Meyer Levinsky entered a certain tony restaurant in a certain persnickety suburb. As he started for a table, the maitre d' glared. "Wait! We don't serve kikes!"

"That's all right," said Levinsky. "I don't eat them."

See also YID.

kineahora
kayn aynhoreh
kine-ahora

To use this magical invocation is to show you are a true *maven*.

Pronounced *kyne-a-*HAW-*reh* or *kyne-ine-*HAW-*reh*.

Rhyme respectively with "lame Dame Dora" and "fine line Laura." Also pronounced, by the inexact, as *kin-a-*HUR-*a*. From German: *kein*: "not one"; and Hebrew: *ayin ha-rah*: "the evil eye." (The *kein* and *ayin* have blended into one Yiddish syncope, *kein* or *kayn*.)

1. The magical phrase uttered to ward off the evil eye: a reflex of mumbo-jumbo employed to protect a child or loved one.
2. The phrase uttered to show that one's praises are genuine and not contaminated by envy—*i.e.*, "I cast no evil eye . . ."
3. The Yiddish equivalent of "knock on wood."
4. A gnomic formula used in the hope of continuing a desirable state. ("He should only keep growing, *kineahora*.")

Our ancestors, Jew and *goy* alike, were constantly fearful of tempting the gods to anger: humankind's *hubris*, his boastings, his very successes, ran the risk of offending some god—and boomeranging into disaster. An envious, jealous mortal could cast an evil spell on another's luck— or health. *Kayn aynhoreh* (or more commonly *kineahora*) was articulated to thwart such demons.

Jewish women, especially, employed the rubric in contexts like these:

"My child? In perfect health, *kayn aynhoreh*." (Thank God!)
"We should only live, *kineahora*, to see that day."
"My son? First in his class, *kayn aynhoreh*."

Virtually all people and all religions hold uneasy ideas about the cacodemons who operate through the Evil Eye. Demonic spirits, diabolic ghouls, evil sprites abound everywhere—and are thought to "come out" through the eyes. So mothers would drop a little salt and a crumb into a child's pocket, to protect it—presumably to feed any goblins who came along. Little girls sometimes wore beads, as a necklace or bracelet, to ward off evil spirits.

Not all evil eyers were malevolent, incidentally; some were believed to be virtuous mortals to whom the powers of the supernatural had been given. Simeon bar Yochai was believed to have the awesome power of reducing evil people to bone with one mordant look. Other learned men were credited with incendiary ("blazing") eyesight.

A Jewish patriarch was on the witness stand.

"How old are you?" asked the district attorney.

"I am, *kayn aynhoreh*, eighty-one."

"What was that?"

"I said, 'I am, *kayn aynhoreh*, eighty-one.' "

"Just answer the question!" said the D.A. sharply. "Nothing else. Now, how old are you?"

"*Kayn aynhoreh*, eighty-one," said the old man.

Now the judge said, "The witness will answer the question and *only* the question, without additional comment, or be held in contempt of court."

Up rose the counsel for the defense. "Your Honor, may I ask the question? . . ." He turned to the old man, "*Kineahora*, how old are you?"

Said the old man, "Eighty-one."

kishka
kishkas
kishke

Yinglish, because *kishka* is a favorite word of Jewish comics and is on the menu of almost every Jewish restaurant or fancy deli. Pronounced KISH-*keh*. Russian: "intestines," "entrails."

1. Intestines.
2. Sausage made with pungent spices, stuffed into an intestine (as casing) and baked.
3. Plural: *kishkas*—even though the same intestine is being described. To hit someone "in the *kishkas*" means to hit him in the stomach or, in indelicate parlance, in the guts.

Kishka is a feature of Jewish cuisine (which, to tell the truth, is not noted for range). Aside from food, the words *kishka* and *kishkas* are used to mean intestine, innards, belly.

"His accusation hit me right in the *kishka*."

"I laughed until my *kishkas* were sore."

Dr. Peter Arkady, a psychiatrist of considerable repute, was hit in the *kishkas* (you might say) by a postcard he received from a patient who was vacationing in La Jolla:

HAVING WONDERFUL
TIME. WHY? *why?*
Sue Sorkin

klap

See KLOP.

klezmer
klezmorim   (plural)

This word is becoming familiar in English, for more and more *klezmorim* groups are giving recitals, or performing at weddings, in cities with large Jewish populations. Pronounced KLEZ-*mer* or KLETS-*mer* to rhyme with "Mesmer" or "gets her." Plural: *klezmorim* (*kletz*-MOR-*im*), to rhyme with "Let's bore 'em." From the Hebrew: *klei-zemer*: "musical instruments."

An informal group of musicians; many were itinerants who went from village to village in eastern Europe, playing traditional music, folk songs, folk dances, solemn hymns before prayer, at weddings.

These musicians rarely knew how to read music—what Jews could afford music lessons, and who in the *shtetl* would teach them? They passed their skill down from father to son. They earned very little. They had to keep moving, seeking out fairs, synagogue dedications, Purim festivities, etc.

The shabby *klezmorim* were familiar figures to all Ashkenazic Jews; they were regarded as drifters, odd types, itinerant minstrels. They are a recurrent theme in the paintings of Marc Chagall.

Klezmer music was played on trumpets, bugles, flutes, clarinets, fifes, violins, cellos, drums. A typical group would contain three to six members.

Klezmer music was like the music of modern jazz combos, in that it grew out of improvisation, ingenious harmonizations, and solo innovations. Hebraic themes were embroidered with motifs from the folk music of Russians, Poles, Czechs, Germans, Hungarians, Romanians, Slovenes, Greeks.

In many places, Jewish musicians played at Christian religious ceremonies! They were, indeed, often preferred to other minstrels because of their reputation for "modesty and sobriety." Once they came into demand, punitive taxes were imposed, of course, to discourage gentiles from hiring them.

klop   (noun and verb)
klap

> Yiddish, creeping into Yinglish because of its use by Jewish writers—and its mimetic appeal. Rhyme it with "crop." German: "blow," "hit."
>
> 1. A blow.
>   "Did he give me a *klop* on the head!"
> 2. To hit.
>   "She gave the boy a *klop*!"
> 3. More colorfully, to *klop* is "to talk someone's ears off," to blab, to yak and yammer without regard to the sensitivity of others.
>   "She *klopped* on and on 'til everyone left!"
>   "All day long, he *klops* about his troubles."

To klop der kop in der vant means "to beat your head against the wall."

See also HOCK A TCHYNIK, TALK TO THE WALL.

klutz

> Vivid Yinglish: blunt, direct, definitive. Rhyme it with "cuts." German: "a log," "a clumsy person," "a strong but stupid man."
>
> 1. A blockhead.
> 2. Anyone graceless, heavy-handed, all-thumbs.
> 3. An insensitive clod.

The klutziest *klutz* on earth was Feibel Glotz, who hurried to the hospital to announce: "Mr. Gerstein, I come with the best wishes for your recovery from the trustees of our synagogue! And that's not just a wish, Mr. Gerstein. It's an official resolution. Passed by a vote of thirteen to nine!"

_____

The girl who can't dance says the orchestra can't keep time.

_____

A *klutz* is easily seduced.
          —Folk saying

knaydl
knaydel
knaydlach (plural)

Yinglish: found on menus in Jewish restaurants. Pronounced *k*-NAY-*dl*, to rhyme with "ladle." The plural, *knaydlach*, is pronounced *k*-NAY-*dlokh*. From German.

A dumpling—usually made of matzo meal, usually served in chicken soup, usually on Friday night, generally at the Passover *Seder*.

Knaydl is used affectionately for a child, as we say in English, "my little dumpling."

_____

Sir Roland DeVere went into a Jewish restaurant in Philadelphia.

Observing a plate of soup at the next table, with two round yellow objects in it, he asked the waitress, "What sort of soup is that? I mean, with those two round spheres?"

"Them's matzo balls."

"Ah, I shall try them."

The waitress brought him the dish.

The Englishman ate it with relish. "Excellent!" he exclaimed. "Tell me, what other part of the matzo do you people cook?"

knish
knishes (plural)

Yinglish, seen on many menus of Jewish restaurants or delicatessens, and in recipes in English newspapers and magazines. Pronounce the *k* as well as the *n*. From Ukranian.

1. Little dumplings filled with groats, grated potatoes, onions, chopped liver, or cheese.
2. When you say you hit someone "with a *knish*" you mean you reward, instead of punish, him. (Don't ask me why.)
3. A crease. (As a verb, *to knish* means to crease.)
4. (Vulgar) Vagina.

The *knish* has become an American *nosh* through the efforts of celebrated *knish* makers on the Lower East Side. A famed *knish* bakery was established on Houston Street in 1910. It has flourished ever since.

You will find *knishes*, ready for rebaking, in many Jewish bakeries, delis, and gourmet food shops.

k'nocker
k'nyaker

Recommended with fervor for the enrichment of Yinglish. A unique word. Pronounced *not* "nocker," but *k'*NOCK-*er*, with the *k* a separate sound, as in "Canute." (I make the apostrophe part of the spelling to make sure you pronounce both the *k* and the *n*.) From German: *knacken*: "to crack or snap." For sarcastic prolongation, *k'nocker* is pronounced *k'nyocker*.

1. A "somebody"—a big shot.
2. A big shot—who knows it and acts that way.
3. A boastful, cocky, self-advertising fellow; a "show-off."

The use of the mocking Slavic gloss, *k'nyaker*, is not limited to Yinglish: American southerners are fond of the playful, palatal *y*: "My Aunt K'yate," "C'yaptain Cook . . ." "Pres'dent C'yarter." Mark Twain described this verbal play in *Life on the Mississippi*.

The braggadocio aspect is important: a successful but modest man is not called a *k'nocker*.

A *k'nocker* is someone who works crossword puzzles with *a pen* (especially if someone is watching).

Deep in the night, Irv Belzer shook his wife. "Mindy . . . Mindy."

Mindy mumbled, "Mmh . . . what?"

"Darling, I got you two aspirins and a glass water."

Mindy sat up. "What's with you, Irving?"

"For your headache, Mindy."

"*Who* knows from a headache?"

"You don't have a headache?"

"No."

"Great! So let's make love."

———

Litsky and Toybel, two Jewish *k'nockers*, approaching Honolulu, got into an argument about the correct pronunciation of Hawaii. Litsky was sure it was "Ha*w*aii." Toybel was positive it was "Ha*v*aii." They made a bet.

When they got off the plane, they hurried over to the first native they saw and said, "Aloha! How do you pronounce the name of this island: Ha*w*aii or Ha*v*aii?"

"Ha*v*aii," said the native.

"Thank you," laughed Toybel.

"You've *v*elcome," said the native.

know from

Bronxian Yinglish. From the Yiddish: *Vos vays ikh fun . . .*

Ungrammatical substitution of *from* for *about* or *of.*

"What does she know from Latin?"

"What do I know from investments?"

"What do they know from our *tsuris*?"

This phrase is not only ungrammatical; it is undesirable. Use it only for caricature or parody.

———

On a street in the Bronx, two hardware stores, directly across the street from each other, sprouted huge, two-story-high banners. One announced:

J. J. TSIPIN

bankruptcy sale!

GOING OUT OF BUSINESS!

EVERYTHING MUST GO! 50–75 PERCENT OFF!!

The banner across the street read:

> *lost lease! must move!*
> TREMENDOUS SALE!
> BARGAINS—BARGAINS—BARGAINS!
> MARGOLIS BROTHERS
> FOUNDED 1938

A passerby saw an old man, in shirt-sleeves and suspenders, standing in front of Margolis Brothers. A plastic name-tag on his shirt pocket read, "B. J. Margolis."

"Mr. Margolis," said the pedestrian, "you must be having quite a problem."

"What problem?"

"With your going-out-of-business sale. Your competitor, right across the street, is going out of business, too."

Margolis snorted. "That J. J. Tsipin? A Johnny-come-lately! What does he know from bankruptcy? He'll be out of business inside a week. But me and my brothers? We have built up a *reputation* for going out of business! People know they can *rely* on us. *We*—we'll be here another forty years!"

See also KNOW FROM NOTHING, WHO KNOWS?

know from nothing

Yinglish, from Bronxian English, which is an analogue for the Yiddish: *fun gornisht [gornit]*: "from nothing."

In Yiddish, double negatives are common, *epg., Zie hot nit keyn mon*: "She has not no man." One can even use a *triple* negative: *Keyner hot nit keyn vort gezugt*: "No one had not no word uttered"—which in English would be "No one uttered a word."

"He knows from nothin'!" has become quite familiar in English slang.

"He don't know from nothing" emphasizes meaning by mocking English grammar triply: (1) in using *don't* instead of *doesn't*; (2) in adding the unnecessary *from*; (3) in doubling the negatives.

Si Gordas was on the *Metsiye*, the yacht of his wholesaler, Charley Jacober. Off Montauk Point, the sea got very rough. Charley tripped, fell on the deck, and broke both legs. "Si!" he gasped. "The radio! The Coast Guard! They have to bring us in!"

Into the radio phone, Si Gordas called, "Coast Guard! Coast Guard! Here is the yacht *Metsiye*. The owner just broke both his legs! Help! Help! I know from nothing about boats!"

The speaker crackled; the Coast Guard came in: "We read you, *Metsiye*. What is your position?"

"Partner in Royal Carpets!" cried Si. "But is this a time for small talk?"

See also WHO KNOWS?

k'nyaker

See K'NOCKER.

kochleffl
kochleffel

Recommended for Yinglish, because of its sonic appeal and special meaning. Pronounced KOKH-*lef-fl*, with a Glaswegian *kh*, as in "loch." From German: *kochen*: "to cook"; *Leffl*: "spoon."

1. A cooking spoon. (The *kochleffl* was the long wooden spoon used for stirring a pot.)
2. A busybody. What word is better than *kochleffl* to describe someone who butts into everyone else's business?
3. A live wire, go-getter, organizer, activist, promoter; someone who stirs things up.
4. A troublemaker, an energetic gossip.
5. A bright, inquisitive, energetic toddler. "That little girl—a regular *kochleffl*!"

After Lenny Falk's wife delivered a boy, she received this telegram from her husband, a *kochleffl*, indeed:

LAURA FALK
LENOX HOSPITAL
MILWAUKEE, WIS.
   EVERYONE TELLS ME YOU HAD A BOY IN YOUR ROOM AT 3 A.M.

                      LENNY

Scene: A Cocktail Party in Houston

VISITOR: You say you've lived in Houston all your life?
  You must own a lot of cattle.
MR. TAUB: Nope.
VISITOR: You own oil wells . . .
MR. TAUB: Nope. I'm in land.
VISITOR: Ah, you must own a lot of land . . .
MR. TAUB: No. Six acres.
VISITOR: That's all? Six acres isn't very much for a Texan
  . . . What do you call your "spread"?
MR. TAUB: Downtown.

(Taub was a modest *kochleffl*.)

Mr. Fleishman asked the plumber, "So how much is
your bill for fixing my sink?"

"Seventy-five dollars."

"Seventy-five dollars? For *fifteen*-minutes work?" cried
Mr. Fleishman. "Why *I* only pay my doctor fifty dollars
for a complete checkup that lasts a full *hour*!"

"I know," grinned the plumber, who was a *kochleffl*.
"That's what I used to charge when I was a doctor."

See also SHTARKER, TUMMLER, YENTA.

Kohen
Cohen
Kohanim (plural)

Pronounced CO-*en*, to rhyme with "go when," or CANE,
to rhyme with "Dane." Hebrew: *kohen*: "priest." Plural: *kohanim*, pronounced ko-HA-*nim*.

1. Priest—*i.e.*, a Hebrew priest of yore.
2. A common Jewish surname.

Many Jewish family-names, such as Cohen, Cohn, Cahn,
Kahn, Kagen, Cahana, and even Echt and Katz (formed
from the initials of *kohen tzedek*, "a priest of justice"),
claim descent from the priests of ancient Israel—as do
some Germans named Kohne, Schiff (a pun on *Kahn*:
"boat") and even Bloch.

Aaron, brother of Moses, was the first high priest, the ancestor of all Hebrew priests, the *kohanim*, who conducted sacrifices and services in the desert sanctuary and, later, in the great Temple in Jerusalem.

After the Jews went into exile, the title of *kohen* was passed down, even though the priestly prerogatives and responsibilities no longer existed.

Many proscriptive laws circumscribed the actions of a *kohen*:

A *kohen* may not marry a divorcee.

A *kohen* may enter a cemetery only for the funeral of a member of his immediate family.

A *kohen* is the first one called to the Torah reading in the synagogue.

I know of no sound historical evidence that links the Cohanes of Ireland to the Cohens of Tel Aviv.

There is no evidence for the rumor that when Robert Briscoe, a Jew, was elected lord mayor of Dublin, the Irish began to see leprecohens.

The firm of Farnsworth, Sullivan and Cohen was one of the largest and finest in the city. A friend of Cohen's asked, "Why is your name *last*? Everyone knows that Farnsworth spends all of his time in the country and Sullivan most of it at the race track. Your name should be first!"

"You forget," smiled Cohen, "*my* clients read from right to left."

Kol Nidre

Yinglish. Used often in English newspapers and on television each year. Pronounced *cawl*-NID-*reh*, to rhyme with "Paul Sidra." Hebrew: "All vows."

The moving, awesome prayer that ushers in Yom Kippur.

The words, incidentally, are not Hebrew, but Aramaic. The confession of sins in *Kol Nidre* is collective, *not* individual. In synagogues and temples all around the globe, the cantor chants the *Kol Nidre* just before sunset on the eve of Yom Kippur, the last of the ten days of atonement (or penitence) that constitute Rosh Hashanah.

The cantor sings *Kol Nidre* three times: first, softly; then louder; then *fortissimo*. The congregation responds antiphonally, reciting the prayer as a recitative. Throughout all this, the Torah scrolls are solemnly held aloft by three worshipers.

The *Kol Nidre* is chanted very solemnly, with more anguish than any other prayer, for it seems to recapitulate, in each worshiper's memory, the long history of violence and humiliation to which Jews have been subjected. The melody, as sung by the cantor in the falling twilight, is immensely moving. Beethoven included a piece of it in his *Quartet in C sharp Minor*. Tolstoy said it "echoes the story of the martyrdom of a grief-stricken nation."

What is surprising, in this emotional context, is that the actual text of the *Kol Nidre* is that of a legal document, not a paean to God!

> *Kol Nidre* (all vows), obligations, oaths, anathemas . . . which we may vow or swear or pledge . . . from this Day of Atonement until the next . . . we do repent.
> May they be deemed to be forgiven, absolved, annulled or void—and made of no effect. They shall not bind us nor have power over us [and] the vows shall not be considered vows, nor the obligations obligatory, nor the oaths oaths.

Please note that *Kol Nidre* was originally *opposed* by the rabbis, because it suggested that human vows could be taken not too seriously, since they could be negated on Yom Kippur. But the chant/prayer became popular nevertheless, I think, for three important reasons:

1. Jewish law demands that every vow be fulfilled, even if the fulfillment entails severe sacrifices.
2. Charlemagne forbade Jews in a court to swear by their own religious oath; instead, Jews were forced to use the repellent *More Judaico*. Oaths were "administered" to Jews in brutal ways: a Jewish witness had to kneel or was forced to don a wreath of thorns or was made to stand in water (since he had declined baptism) or on a pigskin(!). He was instructed to repeat the oath while teetering on a low stool from which one leg had been removed . . . It is no wonder to

me that Jews asked God to exempt them from the performance of vows undertaken under such contemptible circumstances.

3. During the Inquisition, not to say during many local flare-ups, many Jews were forcibly converted. One can understand why these hapless "renegades" to their faith would want God to absolve them from guilt in having taken the vows they were compelled, by torture, to take, and to remit in advance any sin occasioned by vows they might have to take in the year *ahead*!

The rabbis taught that the dispensation allowed in *Kol Nidre* applies only to those vows that involve the vower alone—not any that entailed the interests of another. So a man might be absolved of responsibility for a vow of conscience to God—but not of a promise made to another man: *that* one *had* to be fulfilled.

———

Not until the eighth century was the *Kol Nidre* formally introduced in the liturgy (in a synagogue). The sage who had the temerity to oppose so many rabbis who disapproved of the "prayer" was Yehudai the Gaon (head of a Talmudic academy) of Babylonia.

kosher

Yinglish—now included in most English dictionaries. Pronounced KO-*sher*, to rhyme with "no sir." From the Hebrew: *kasher*: "fit," "proper," "permissible."

Ritually fit (approved) to eat by orthodox or observing Jews.

Kosher is probably the Hebrew word most widely encountered in English. (Its meanings in American slang, or as a form of Yinglish, are explored below.)

As a Hebrew/Yiddish word, *kosher* generally means only one thing: ritually clean, according to specific and numerous dietary laws.

Many a meat store in a Jewish neighborhood carries two Hebrew words on the window; they look alike but are not. They read, from right to left: *basar kasher* (pronounced, in Yiddish, BAW-*ser* KO-*sher*). *Basar* means "meat."

A *kosher* meat store or restaurant serves no un-*kosher* meats.

Eating and drinking, to the ancient Jews, involved grave religious obligations, and strongly reinforced the idea of the Jews as a people "set apart," chosen by the Lord as "Mine," "holy unto Me" (Leviticus).

The strict observance of dietary rules was believed to strengthen the dedication of a Jew to his role as one of God's instruments for the redemption of mankind. (Some scholars think *kosher* practices were designed as acts of moral self-discipline—to resist the influence of the Greeks and Romans, who were given to prodigious self-indulgence and sensuality.)

The strict observance of *kosher* laws has declined drastically among Western Jews.

In Yiddish and Yinglish, *kosher* is used to describe anything

1. Pertaining to Orthodox Jewry. ("He is a *kosher* Jew" means he observes the dietary laws.)
2. Pious, devout. ("He is a *kosherer* Jew" means he is very pious; a female would be "a *koshereh* Jew.")
3. Sympathetic. ("He is a *kosher* kind of man": he is kind, understanding.)
4. Dear, sweet, lovable. ("She has a *koshereh* soul.")

In American slang, *kosher* comes in a gorgeous array of flavors:

1. Authentic. "That's *kosher*" can mean fourteen-karat gold, sterling silver, genuine antique.
2. "The real McCoy," trustworthy, reliable. "Is he *kosher*?" which once meant "Is he Jewish?" is now taken to mean "Can I trust him?" or "Is he part of the group?" or (as I heard it used in the Pentagon) "Has he been cleared for classified information?"
3. Legitimate, legal, lawful. "Is this deal *kosher*?" means "Is this deal on the up-and-up?" "Everything is *kosher*" means "Everything is proper."
4. Approved by a higher source; bearing the stamp of approval. "It's *kosher*," when uttered by a company V.P., can mean that his president has approved.

5. Fair, fair and square, ethical. Eric Partridge says this usage came into English from London's East End around 1860.

All in all, *kosher* may be the most resourceful Yiddish word in the English language.

Kosher: Basic Dietary Data (in brief)

Meat and milk may not be eaten simultaneously. (Orthodox Jews allow six hours to pass between a meat and a dairy meal, but less time if vice versa.)

Separate cooking utensils and vessels for the service and storage of foods are used for dairy and meat products—*viz.*, Moses' thrice-uttered warning (Exodus, Deuteronomy) not to seethe a kid in its mother's milk.

"Clean" and "unclean" animals are listed in Leviticus (11) and Deuteronomy (14). Precisely forty-two animals are named as taboo.

Only those four-footed animals that chew their cud *and* possess a cloven hoof are *kosher*. (This includes goat, gazelle, pygarg and antelope, though I have yet to hear of a Jew going that far.) An animal that chews its cud but is not cloven-hoofed is *trayf* (non-*kosher*), *e.g.*, the camel, the rabbit. (It grieves me to inform the pious reader, however, that the camel, Bible notwithstanding, is cloven-hoofed.)

Creatures that crawl, like lizards and snakes, are forbidden. So is the mouse. So is the weasel.

Only fish having both scales and fins are *kosher*. Shellfish are taboo.

Birds of prey (vultures, owls, hawks, eagles) are taboo, as are nearly all wild fowl.

Any animal that has not been slaughtered according to ritual—even a chicken or cow—is unclean and *verboten*.

The *shochet*, a religious slaughterer, must examine each individual animal for signs of infection, disease or abnormality: he must dispatch an animal by slashing the throat with one stroke. If the knife binds or sticks, even for the tiniest instant, the animal is no longer *kosher*.

Kosher meat must be stamped or sealed by a *mashgiach* (supervisor).

A lucid account of all kosher provisions will be found in Seymour Siegel's *Jewish Dietary Laws*, or Samuel Dresner's book of the same name.

The jokes that Jews tell about matters *kosher* are endless. Here is one of my favorites:

Very late one rainy night, Rabbi Moses Aspin, seeing no customers inside, walked into an elegant but not *kosher* delicatessen. With elaborate insouciance, he asked (for the first time in his life), "By the way, how much costs that—uh—bacon?"

At once a terrific flash of lightning and a roaring clap of thunder shook the skies—and the shop.

Rabbi Aspin looked up to the heavens, protesting, "I was only *asking*."

See also GLATT KOSHER, PAREVEH, SHOCHET.

krechtz (verb and noun)

An incomparable word: It will do wonders for Yinglish. Pronounced KREKHTZ, to rhyme with "Brecht's." Rattle the uvular fricative *kh*. German: *krachzen*: "croak," "craw."

1. To grunt, groan, croak, moan or wheeze.
2. To fuss or complain—with audible sound effects.
3. To make cranky, gasping, ambiguous noises.
4. A sound of complaint, discontent or minor sadness.

Krechtzing is reserved for secondary discontents or minor ailments. You would never *krechtz* for real pain or genuine tragedy.

A *krechtz* is not a scream, which is a *kvitch*; nor is it a full-throated cry, which is a *geshrei*. Moreover, *krechtz* is neither a deep-throated moan nor a subtle sigh, which is *zifts*. You moan a bit and sigh quite often while *krechtzing*.

People who are hypochondriacs *krechtz* a good deal. So do middle-aged women in the menopause—and Jewish men losing at pinochle. So do chronic gripers. Old people *krechtz* a good deal, especially when their children are around.

Note: *krechtz* describes the sounds one makes, not the cause thereof. You *krechtz* about something, never *at* someone. And it is much more common to use *krechtz* about someone else than about one's self.

"Are you in pain? You've been *krechtzing* for an hour."
"Why are you *krechtzing* so much? Is the market down?"

The savor of *krechtzing* can be enhanced by liberal doses of "*Oy!*" In fact, "*Oy!*" is itself a *krechtz*.

Two men met on the street. Said the first: "How's business?"
Krechtzed the second, "Oy! Mnyeh!"
"You know," blurted the first man, "for this time of year, that's not bad!"

See also KVETCH.

kreplach
kreplech

Becoming Yinglish, because of the frequency with which *kreplach* appears on the menus of Jewish restaurants or in recipes on the food pages of English newspapers and magazines. Pronounced KREP-*lokh* or KREP-*lekh*, as a German would render the *kh* sound. From German: *kreppel*; note, too, the French *crêpes*.
A triangular or square dumpling, not unlike Italian ravioli, that contains chopped meat or cheese, etc. Usually served in soup.

Kreplach is both singular and plural. They are traditionally eaten on Purim and Rosh Hashanah, and the day before Yom Kippur.
I have never met anyone who does not enjoy *kreplach*.

In Feinshmeker's Kosher Restaurant, Mr. Waletsky sat down and, to the waiter, sighed: "I don't need a menu. I want chicken soup with *kreplach*."

"Okay," said the waiter.

"I'm from St. Louis," said Mr. Waletsky. "My first trip to New York. I've been walking all day. My feet are *killing* me. And people here are so *rude*! . . . So, Waiter, please, with the soup and *kreplach*, all I want is a nice smile—and a kind word."

"Okay," said the waiter.

In a few minutes the waiter returned, placed a bowl of soup before Mr. Waletsky, smiled, "Enjoy!" and started to leave.

"Wait!" said Mr. Waletsky, "You forgot the kind word."

The waiter bent over and whispered, "Don't eat the *kreplach*."

kvell

Strongly recommended for Yinglish. There is no English word quite like this. Pronounced exactly as it's spelled. From German: *quellen*: "to gush," "to swell."

1. To chortle and beam with immense pride and plea-sure, most commonly over an achievement of a child or grandchild; to be so proudly happy "your buttons can bust"; doting—with conspicuous pride, uncon-tainable delight.

   "Watch her *kvell* when she reads his report card!"

   "Let me *kvell* with you over such an honor!"

Jewish parents are most energetic in *kvell*ing over their children's endowments (real or illusory), achievements (ma-jor or minor) or praise from others (sincere or obligatory).

One authority I consulted put it this way: "Only from your children can anyone *shep* [derive] such *naches* [pride-ful pleasure] as makes you *kvell*—know what I mean?"

2. To enjoy, gloat or crow over someone's defeat or humiliation.

   "All right, be charitable, don't *kvell* over his mistake."

   "Every decent man will *kvell* when that sadist goes to jail."

The ladies met on the Grand Concourse, Mrs. Sonn car-rying her groceries, Mrs. Komer pushing a pram with two little boys in it.

"Good morning," said Mrs. Sonn. "Such darling little boys! So how old are they?"

"The doctor," kvelled Mrs. Komer, "is three, and the lawyer is two."

kvetch (verb and noun)
kvetsh
kvetcher (masculine)
kvetcherkeh (feminine)

Yinglish. Pronounced KVETCH, to rhyme with "fetch"; KVETCH-*er*, to rhyme with "stretcher"; KVETCH-*er-keh*, to rhyme with "fetch 'er a." (Do not confuse *kvetch* with *kvitch, q.v.*) From German: *quetschen*: "to squeeze," "to press."

Kvetch, a marvelously mimetic word, is a verb and a noun. (Compare with *krechtz, q.v.*)

As a verb
1. To squeeze, pinch, eke out.
   "Don't *kvetch* the peaches."
   "He manages to *kvetch* out a living."
   "No one knows how someone else's shoe *kvetches*."
2. To fuss around, to be ineffectual.
   "She *kvetches* all day long."
3. To fret, complain, nag, gripe, grunt, sigh.
   "What's she *kvetching* about now?"
   An excellent companion to *kvetch*, in this usage, is *krechtz*:
   "All she does is *kvetch* and *krechtz*!"
   This can hardly be improved upon for descriptive precision and power.
4. To delay, stall, show reluctance.
   "He's still *kvetching* around."
5. To shrug.
   "He *kvetches* his shoulders."

As a reflexive verb
Kvetchen zich: To exert or push oneself. This can be used to describe a soprano straining to hit a high note, or a woman in labor trying to hasten birth by squeezing, grunting, forcing.

As a noun

1. Anyone, male or female, who complains, gripes, fribbles, niggles, magnifies minor aches and pains. A chronic complainer.

   "What a congenital *kvetcher*!"

   To be strictly grammatical, a female *kvetcher* should certainly be called a *kvetcherkeh*, which, through the lilt of euphony, enhances the characterization.

2. One who works slowly, inefficiently or pedantically.

   "It will take forever, he's such a *kvetch*."

3. One who constantly alibis for poor or lazy performance.

   "That *kvetch* comes up with a different complaint every morning."

4. A "wet blanket," one who diminishes the pleasures of others.

   "Don't invite him to the party; he's a *kvetch*."

A lapel button I saw at NYU read:

> FRANZ KAFKA
> IS A
> KVETCH

I could say the same about Proust.

The head of a dress-manufacturing firm in New York received the following telegram from his best on-the-road salesman:

REUBEN SHULOVITZ
273 WEST 48TH STREET
NEW YORK, NEW YORK
   BLIZZARD HAS HIT THIS AREA. COMPLETELY SNOWED IN. ALL FLIGHTS CANCELED. ADVISE.

> JEFF ROGOVSKY
> HOTEL MASON
> PIERRE, SOUTH DAKOTA

Reuben Shulovitz did not waste a minute before replying:

J. ROGOVSKY
HOTEL MASON
PIERRE, SOUTH DAKOTA
   STOP KVETCHING. START VACATION AT ONCE.

> R. SHULOVITZ

kvitch

Rhymes with "snitch." From German: *quietschen*: "to squeal."

Do not confuse *kvitch* with *kvetch*. Do not confuse *kvitch* with *krechtz*. *Kvitch*, *kvetch* and *krechtz* work beautifully in tandem but are not synonymous.

As a verb

To scream—but not a scream of real terror. It is, rather, a yelp. A woman will *kvitch* or "give a *kvitch*" on sighting a mouse, singeing a finger, or meeting a long-lost friend.

As a noun

A scream—but a special, not-to-be-taken-too-seriously exclamation. A *kvitch* is not a *geshrei* (shriek); nor is it a substitute for "*Gevalt*." A *kvitch* is midway between a squeal and a scream—a small, unpretentious, often obligatory exclamation of dismay, surprise, or not-excessive alarm.

Standard forms of *kvitching*:

Surprise: "When I walked in, she gave a *kvitch* you could hear in Canarsie."
Distaste: "When she saw the wound, she let out a *kvitch*."
Pleasure: "When they called her to the platform, she gave out with a *kvitch*."
Minor pain: "She stubbed her toe and gave a *kvitch*."
Discombobulation: "Everyone was running around; the *kvitching* could drive you crazy."
Dismay: "Please, no more *kvitching* or you'll disturb the neighbors."
Disapproval: "She took one look at her son's girl and let out a *kvitch*. No one could blame her."

Distinguish *kvitch* from *kvetch* from *krechtz*. You can *kvitch* sedately, out of happiness, but to *kvetch* is always negative, bilious, complaining, and to *krechtz* is to utter grating noises of physical discomfort or spiritual woe.

Kvitching may be hard on the ears, but *kvetching* is hard on the nerves. As for *krechtzing*, it should be reserved for a hospital room.

———————

To the widow, who was shrieking and wailing over her dear departed's body, a friend said, "Please, restrain yourself. Enough *kvitching*."

To which the widow retorted, "This you call 'enough'? Wait until we get to the cemetery. *Then* you'll hear *kvitching*!"

———————

ACT I

REZNIK (on phone): Hello, Mr. Kaskel? I think you ought to buy a thousand shares of Weinrib Computers. That stock is going to go up to the sky!

KASKEL: What's it selling at?

REZNIK: Three point five.

KASKEL: Buy me a thousand shares.

ACT II

REZNIK: Hello, Mr. Kaskel. Weinrib Computers is up to seven dollars a share! Maybe you should sell . . .

KASKEL: No, sir! Buy me two thousand more shares.

REZNIK: Okay.

ACT III

KASKEL: Hello, Reznik! I just saw that Weinrib Computers is down six dollars a share! Sell! *Sell all my shares*!

REZNIK (after a *kvitch*): To who?

L

Ladino

Pronounced *lah*-DEE-*no*, to rhyme with "casino." Spanish: "familiar with several languages." The special vernacular used by Sephardic ("Spanioli") Jews in Spain, Portugal, Turkey, the Balkans and Morocco, and by Spanish- and Portuguese-speaking Jews in Central and South America. It is also called *Judesmo* or *Dzhudesmo* or *Judaeo-Spanish*.

A dialect form of fifteenth-century Castilian Spanish, profusely sprinkled with Talmudic expressions and Hebrew words, and some Arabic.

In Ladino, Spanish words are often given Hebrew prefixes or suffixes, and Hebrew words are "Spaniolized" by using them as roots, then creating Spanish verb-conjugations.

Some Spaniolized Hebrew words have become part of modern Spanish and Portuguese: *malsin*, for example, meaning "slanderer" or "informer" (from Hebrew *malshin*), which dates back to the Inquisition.

Ladino is often called by Spaniards *idioma castellano*, or *lingua vulgar*.

Wry Ashkenazim call Ladino "the Sephardic substitute for Yiddish."

See also ASHKENAZI, SEPHARDI.

L' Chaim
L' Chayim

Yinglishmen love to offer this charming toast. Hebrew: *Cha'yim*: "life." Pronounced in two syllables, accenting the first: KHY-*em*. Use the German *kh* sound, never the English plosive *ch* of "church." *Chaim* rhymes with "Brian."

In Yinglish *chaim* is often heard as the climaxing sound of the toast *L'Chaim*: "to life."

The opening toast at Jewish ceremonies, meetings, celebrations, anniversaries, is often "*L'Chaim!*"—and often joined with "*Mazel Tov!*" (Good luck!). *L'Chaim* is neither frivolous nor ironic—as *mazel tov* often is.

Once, when a Jewish child was gravely ill, the parents would suddenly give the name Chaim to the afflicted one, hoping in this way that health would be restored and life continued. Sometimes, among the very Orthodox, "*Chaim*" was added to the sick one's true name, at the very front, as a magical means of deceiving the Angel of Death (*moloch ha-Movess*).

The first man to exclaim "*L'Chaim!*" (according to the Talmud) was the great Rabbi Akiba (or Akiva).

Some innocents confuse *L'Chaim!* with *mazel tov!*—using one when only the other would be appropriate. There is no reason to err: *L'Chaim* is used whenever one would say in English "Your health," or "Cheers!" or (I shudder to say) "Here's mud in your eye." *Mazel tov!* is used as "Congratulations."

See MAZEL TOV for a surprising number of variations on this theme. See also CHAIM.

like

Used as Yinglish, the word is ungrammatical and unnecessary. Its use, alas, is growing among teenagers and on television, especially in talk shows or interviews. Please do not join that ilk.

1. Pretend, imitate, simulate.
   "I made like a detective and sat down."

"She made like a dancer, and walked through the stage door."

2. (Used before an adjective, instead of "rather") Sort of; in the manner of.

"He laughed it up like crazy."

"It's like freezing outside."

These usages have exact analogues in Yiddish: *Er makht zikh vi meshugge*: "He makes [himself] like crazy."

A third use in Yinglish does not have a Yiddish analogue, but is a distinctive (and regrettable) Jewish/Bronx/Brooklyn contribution to linguistics:

3. To finish a sentence.

"He was so skinny, he was a skeleton, like." [I detest this use, like.]

The recent vogue of "like" in teenage jive and the counterculture (to say nothing of drug-takers) should not mislead you into thinking that *like* is a recent slang innovation. It appeared in Yinglish decades ago. (See Wentworth and Flexner, *The Dictionary of American Slang*, page 319.)

CUSTOMER: Waiter! Waiter!

WAITER: Yeah? What do you want?

CUSTOMER: The service here is like terrible!!

WAITER: How do you know? You haven't had any.

See also LIKEWISE.

likewise

Yinglish, unfortunately. From Yiddish: *mir oykh*: "to me, also." Distinguish from "in a like wise." (See below.)

This genteelism, akin to crooking the little finger whilst drinking tea, is absurd—a dogged Bronxian response to a Bronxian introduction.

1. How do you do?

FREDA: Joe, meet Hilda.

HILDA: Glad to meet you.

JOE: Likewise.

In this usage, *likewise* is a "classy" rubric, exceeded in undesirability only by "My pleasure," or "The feeling is mutual." Ugh.

2. Me, too.
   DORIS: If I don't get something to eat, I'll *faint*!
   JENNY: Likewise.
3. I feel the same way.
   ISADORE: The way I feel, those punks ought to be arrested and sent to jail!
   JACOB: Likewise.

These locutions, strictly speaking, are acceptable, but as style they are deplorable. Good taste, whether in language or luggage, is difficult to describe though easy to label.

Take my word for it: *likewise* grates on the ear. Even worse is:

4. Likewise, I'm sure.

I'm sure this is gruesome. The *Oxford Dictionary of the English Language* asserts that *likewise* goes back to 1449, meaning "in a like wise," or "in the same way." But this is not the usage I cite. The Catskills meaning is different and distinctive: "I feel the same way," or "Me, too."

I would like to exile *likewise*, speechwise.

See also LIKE.

Listen

> Yinglish, undeniably—and regrettably.
> An interjection (not a verb) to gain attention or stress a point.

I do not mean to suggest that "Listen" is not English; but speakers of Yinglish use "Listen" at the beginning of a sentence with much greater frequency than do conventional speakers of conventional English—and with prolonged intonation: "Lis-sun."

In Yiddish, *Hayer* or *Herr* ("hear") or *Herr zikh tsu* ("Listen to what I am going to say") are very common as introduction signals. Hence, the transition into Yinglish.

"Did you see that TV special?"
"Listen, I wouldn't watch a piece of junk like that!"

"She said you *hate* her!"
"*Lis*ten, she wasn't exaggerating!"

"Did you hear that Congress is going to cut taxes?"
"Listen, it's about time."

"Listen" is often preceded by "Say" or "So," depending on the speaker's enslavement to his/her early environment.

One of the most literate men I know, a speaker of perfect English prose, will often toss a mocking "*Lis*-sun" or "Say *lis*ten," or "So listen awreddy" into his speech, mimicking the intonation of the Bedford-Stuyvesant (New York City) area in which he was raised.

"I hear you're going to Florida?"
"So listen, it's about time. I need the rest."

"Did you go to CCNY?"
"Say, listen, who could afford Harvard?"

Mrs. Nobloch and Mrs. Preiser sat rocking on the porch of the Villa Lipshitz, a Catskill resort. A young man approached.

"*Gottenyu!*" exclaimed Mrs. Nobloch. "*Look* at that boy! Did you ever see such a big nose? Such silly eyes? Such a crooked mouth?"

In a freezing voice, Mrs. Preiser replied, "It so happens, you are talking about my son!"

"Lis-ten," said Mrs. Nobloch, "on *him*, it's becoming!"

The two women were sharing confidences over their tea. "I don't know what to do about my husband anymore," said Louise. "Do you know that he never comes home until long, long past midnight?"

"My husband used to be like that—but no more. Never!"

"What changed him?"

Her friend smiled. "Listen. What changed him is that every time he stealthily opened the door, at one or two or three in the morning, I would call out, 'Is that you, Everett?' "

"That was all there was to it?"

"Uh-huh."

"But why would *that* stop him?"

"Because his name is Herbie."

Litvak

Yiddish. "A Lithuanian Jew." Pronounced LIT-*vok*, to rhyme with "bit lock."

1. A Jew from Lithuania, or neighboring regions.
2. Any erudite but pedantic type—thin, dry (so say Polish Jews).
3. A humorless Jew (so say the Galitzianers).
4. A learned but skeptical sort.
5. A shrewd, clever fellow.
6. (Derogatorily, by Galitzianer Jews) A sharp trader, a corner-cutting type—and one whose piety is shallow.

In some circles, *Litvak* is used not only to describe but to deride.

"What can you expect from a *Litvak*?"

"He's as sharp as a *Litvak*."

Sholem Aleichem once said, "A Litvak is so clever that he repents *before* he sins."

The Litvaks are famous for their peculiar inability to pronounce *sh*, converting it into *s* (*shiksa* becomes *siksa*, *shaygets* is rendered as *saygets*, and so on.) You will of course be reminded of the stratagem used by the Hebrews in using *shibboleth* ("stream") as a password for anyone wanting to cross the Jordan. The Hebrews were fighting the Ephraimites, who could never pronounce the Hebrew sound *sh*, but instead said *s*. The sibilant betrayed the Ephraimites.

Uri Sacks, age twenty-four, said to a rabbi, "I must tell you, *Rebbe*: I am an atheist!"

The rabbi frowned. "Do you know Talmud?"

"N-not really."

"Not even the *Pirke Abot* [Wisdom of the Fathers]?"

"I never had time for it."

The rabbi stared at Sacks in disgust. "I have news for you, *boychik*. You are not an atheist: you are an ignoramus."

(The rabbi was a Litvak.)

In a certain law office, above the water cooler, clearly visible to all the clerks and secretaries, hangs a large clock. Under the clock one of the partners, a dyed-in-the-wool Litvak, tired of the clock-watchers, placed this sign:

IT'S EARLIER THAN YOU THINK!

Nurse Sullivan picked up the ringing phone in the nurses' bay. "Can I help you?"

"Noisse," came a man's voice. "I'm calling about one of your patients. Could you please tell me how he's coming along?"

"I'll be glad to. What's the patient's name?"

"Kornfeld. Isadore Kornfeld."

The nurse ran through the records-rack. "Well, sir, Mr. Kornfeld seems to be doing very well. His condition is listed as stable. In fact, his doctor just this morning wrote down, 'Can be discharged Tuesday.'"

"Oh, that's good, *good* news, Noisse!"

"Who shall I tell Mr. Kornfeld called?"

"You don't have to tell *any*body, Noisse. *I'm* Isadore Kornfeld—and I was getting sick and tired of that doctor not telling me one damn *thing* about my condition!"

See also GALITZIANER.

Live a little!

Yinglish to the hilt.

1. Don't be stingy.
2. Don't skimp on your pleasures.
3. Don't be a Puritan, sad sack or wet blanket.

Ziff Ellenbogen, a seventy-four-year-old widower, told his family, "I want to live a little! So I'm going to get married. To a fine young lady, a good cook, cultured—"

"Young?" echoed his daughter. "How old is 'young'?"

"Nineteen."

Furor. Outrage. Astonishment.

"*Gottenyu!*" exclaimed his son. "Papa, you are seventy-four! Aren't you *ashamed*?"

"Why should I be ashamed?" blinked Ellenbogen. "When I married your mother, she was only *eighteen*!"

Look who's talking

Yinglish, a deflating phrase, an analogue of the Yiddish *Kuk nor ver s'ret*! ("Just take a look at who's talking!")

This sarcastic vocative is not intended to make you direct your eyes to the speaker. It is intended to announce to the world that the speaker is

1. Utterly unqualified.
2. Incompetent, even if qualified.
3. Shamelessly biased in the matter.
4. A well-known liar, not to be trusted in *any* matter.
5. Off his or her rocker.
6. The very person who loused everything up in the first place.
7. The pot calling the kettle black.

DOLLY PARTON: Look at the *bust* on that girl!
ANYONE: Look who's talking.

The Weizmann Institute perfected a Miracle Robot that could answer questions never before programmed into electronic devices.

At the first demonstration of this marvel, lines four blocks long formed. Scientists, tourists, journalists, laymen poured questions at the atonishing I-Can-Answer-Any-Question Robot.

The most memorable exchange of all, in my judgment, was this:

SCHNECKER: Where, at this very moment, is my father?

ROBOT: Your father is sunning . . . with a beautiful blonde . . . on the beach . . . in Tel Aviv.

SCHNECKER: Wrong! Wrong! (laughing) My father is Harry O. Schnecker, and I just spoke to him on the phone! He's with my mother in their apartment in Haifa! What do you say to that? Look who's talking!!

ROBOT: Harry O. Schnecker *is* . . . with your mother . . . in their apartment in Haifa. But your *father* is on the beach . . . with a beautiful blonde . . . in Tel Aviv.

See also ACCENTUATING SCORN OR DISDAIN . . . , FROM THAT YOU COULD FAINT, I SHOULD LIVE SO LONG!, THANKS A LOT.

low-life

Yinglish, with panache.

1. Someone who lacks character.
2. A vulgar, coarse person.
3. An untrustworthy, unreliable person.
4. One who lives and acts in a low-class manner.
5. A gambler, sharpie, dissembler, petty racketeer.
6. A no-goodnik, plain and simple.

You may think that *low-life* is so obvious a compound noun that it must have been used in English long, long before an immigrant Jew landed in London or New York. Yet the magisterial *Oxford English Dictionary* does not to this day contain "low-life" or "low life" as an entry. "Low-lived" is there, as an adjective, *e.g.*, a "low-lived man" (that means a mortal with a low life expectancy).

Like *a nothing, a low-life* is distinct and distinctive Yinglish.

Mike Pivnick was a Don Juan. Not a week passed without his bedding a girl, then sneaking home to his wife with explanations that were masterpieces of invention: He had been cajoled into a poker game with important salesmen; he had gotten a terrible toothache and the dentist gave him so much Novocain that he fell asleep for six hours; he had taken an injured child to a hospital.

Finally, his long-suffering wife Celia declaimed, "I'm sick and tired of this! Once more, Mike, and I leave you!"

"Never again!" vowed Mike. "I promise."

He meant it. But of what avail are intentions when a man is a low-life like Mike Pivnick? Came one afternoon when he met a particularly appetizing female morsel . . .

Not until three A.M. did Pivnick come to his senses.

In the girl's apartment, he dressed as fast as a fireman—then held his head in his hands. What—oh *what*—could he tell Celia? . . . Inventiveness did not fail him.

He picked up the phone and dialed his home. His wife answered.

Mike panted. "C-C-Celia . . . They'll c-call you any m-m-minute!"

"They?"

"They'll ask you for t-ten—thousand—dollars—*ransom*!"

"Mike! Migod! What hap—"

"Don't pay them a *penny*, Celia! I just escaped! . . . Be home in fifteen minutes."

See also BUMMER.

lox

Yinglish. Recognizable throughout the English-speaking world. From Scandinavian, via German.

Smoked salmon.

Lox has become the *sine qua non* of delicacies for Sunday brunches from Park Avenue to Nob Hill. When placed on a split bagel that has been toasted and lathered with butter and cream cheese, lox attains the gastronomic status of crêpes Suzette.

Contrary to popular belief, lox was *not* a feature of Ashkenazi cuisine. Lox was unknown in eastern Europe (except for kings and barons). Lox became a luxurious staple on the Lower East Side.

———

In 1967, when the troops of Israel reached the Suez Canal, the first thing they did was confiscate all the lox.

———

A Jewish bum runs away from home—lox, stock and bagel.

See also BAGEL, NOVA.

L'shone Toyve

Yiddish. Pronounced *l'*SHAW-*neh* TOY-*veh*, to rhyme
with "l'sauna Goya." Hebrew: "A happy New Year!"
The traditional happy salutation for Rosh Hashanah.

The entire greeting is *Leshana tova tikosevu*: "May you
be inscribed for a good year."
Inscribed where? In the fateful Book of Good Deeds, by
which your fate will be determined in the world to come.

See also ROSH HASHANAH.

luftmensh

An excellent Yinglish word. Its persistent use by Jews
made it familiar in English. Rhymes with "put bench."
German: *Luftmensch*: literally, "air man," meaning
"one who lives up in the air."

1. Someone with his head in the clouds.
2. An impractical fellow, incorrigibly optimistic.
3. A dreamy, sensitive, poetic type.
4. Someone without any occupation, who lives or works
   ad libitum.

So harsh were the limits placed by Czarist authorities on
Jewish residence, travel and occupations that a great many
bright, ambitious Jews were condemned to try to live as
luftmenshen.
Perhaps the best-known *luftmensh* in Yiddish literature
is Sholem Aleichem's "Menachem Mendel," a luckless
dreamer, a meek *shlimazl*, fate's perpetual patsy.

———

Leone da Modena, a sixteenth-century Venetian Jew,
listed his skills and cited no fewer than twenty-six professions! His talents ranged from preaching to composing epi-
taphs. Why would so accomplished a man be classified as
a *luftmensh*? Because out of all twenty-six professions (plus
assiduous alchemy on the side), he barely made a living.

———

Israel Zangwill wrote an amusing story, *The Luftmensch*,
about a gentleman whose business cards read, "Dentist
and Restaurateur."

The *luftmensh* forever searches for yesterday.

God protects a *luftmensh*; no one else can.

Whenever a *luftmensh* enters a shop, the merchants
smile.

—Folk sayings

Sholem Aleichem put it with an irony that electrifies
truth: "The *luftmensh* lives on hope—and hope is a liar."

Avrum Kolach, whose wife loved to ply a little straw fan
as she rocked on the porch in hot weather, was examining
the fans on a pushcart. "Eh . . . why are some fans a
quarter and some a dollar?"

The *baleboss* said, "With a dollar fan, you make like
this—" he waved a fan before his brow and cheeks. "But
with a quarter fan—" he picked up another—"you make
like this." He held the fan still, then vigorously waved his
head.

Kolach sighed. "I wonder if she'll think it's worth it."

(He was *eppes* a *luftmensh*.)

See also NAYFISH, NEBECH, SHLEMIEL, SHLIMAZEL, YE-
SHIVA BUCHER.

M

Ma-and-Pa store
Mom-and-Pop store

Yinglish, with bells on.

A small retail store owned and run by a man and his wife.

The traditional "corner stores" on the Lower East Side sold candy, cigarettes, newspapers, notions.

Ma-and-Pa store picturesquely conveys the central point about size, scale and ownership. Many a fortune started in one of these modest stores, in which Jewish parents worked long, long hours—and so *hard*.

The Hadassah truck stopped in front of Gittleson's corner store. The driver hopped out, singing, "Anything to contribute? Kitchenware, furniture? All proceeds go to charity. Old clothes—"

"Old clothes, I have—" said Mr. Gittleson.

"Fine!"

"—but I can't give them to you."

"Why not? What will you *do* with them?"

"What I'll do with them," said Gittleson, "is every night I'll hang them up and every morning I'll put them on."

maarev
maariv

See MAIREV.

macher
makher

I fervently urge that this unique word gain wider usage in Yinglish. Pronounced MOKH-*er*; be sure to use the German *kh*, as in "Ach!" German and Yiddish: *Macher*: "maker," "do-er."

1. Someone who arranges, fixes, has connections; a big wheel; an "operator."
2. A *k'nocker* (*q.v.*).
3. Someone who is active in an organization, like the zealous president of the Sisterhood or the PTA; on campus, a B.M.O.C.

The man who could miraculously produce a visa or provide immigration papers or get an exit permit for a Jew or arrange a loan or an important interview, etc., etc.—was known as a *macher*.

A *gontser macher* means a real operator, a real big shot.

Machers can be *k'nockers*, if they boast about their exploits (real *machers* don't).

Many a *k'nocker* is a tenth-rate *macher*.

———————————

During a convention in Miami, two female delegates, real *machers*, met in the lobby. Sadelle fell upon Shirley's neck and they embraced and chattered away.

"Darling, you look wonderful," said Sadelle. "A regular new woman! Tell me, what do you do to look so good?"

"Ssh. I'll tell you a secret. I'm having an affair!"

"Really? That's *mar*velous! Who's catering?"

See also ALRIGHTNIK, K'NOCKER, KOCHLEFFL, TUMMLER.

machetayneste
machetuneste
mekheteneste

From Hebrew: *machutenet*: "a female relative by marriage." Pronounced *ma-khe-*TAY*-ne-steh* (be sure to rattle the *kh*). The female form of *machuten*.

Female relative through marriage—more particularly:

1. Mother-in-law of your son or daughter.
2. Future mother-in-law-to-be of a daughter or son.

See also MACHETUNIM, MACHUTEN.

machetunim

Should certainly become Yinglish—because there just is no English word like (or close to) it. Pronounced *mokh-eh-*TU*-nim*, with a crumb-expelling *kh*. Rhyme it with "Bach attune him." Yiddish transformation of Hebrew *mechutan*: "relative by marriage."

1. The members of one's wife's extended family.
2. The members of one's husband's extended family.
   "His wife comes from a large family: she must have fifty *machetunim*."
   "I like her husband, but not all her *machetunim*."

The definitive explication of *machetunim* is to be found in this sardonic conundrum:

Q: Why did Adam and Eve live so long?
A: Because their lives were not shortened by *machetunim*.

machuten
machutin

Recommended for Yinglish. Pronounced *m'*KHOOT*-n*, to rhyme with "m'tootin." Note the Germanic *kh*. Derives from the Hebrew: *hatan*: "bridegroom." The masculine form of *machetayneste*.

> Your relationship to the father-in-law of your son or daughter.
> There is no English word for this relationship, and such a word is mighty useful.

I have a friend who regales me with the malapropisms of his *machuten*:

He escaped by the skin off his teeth.
If his mother was alive, she would be turning over in her grave.
Those three sure are a pair—if there ever was one!

Arnie's *machuten* was glum at lunch. "My new secretary
. . . After I was sure *this* one would be a godsend . . ."
"What happened?"
"This morning she came in after ten o'clock. I said,
'Mildred, you should have been here at nine-thirty!' And do
you know what she answered: 'Why? What happened?' "

mairev
maarev
maariv

> Pronounced MY-*rev*, to rhyme with "tire of." Hebrew:
> *maariv*: "the evening prayer."
>   The daily evening religious service.

The first Jewish astronaut returned from a hundred-orbit
voyage around the earth.
    When reporters asked him how he felt, he said, "Ex-
hausted! Do you know how many times I had to say
shachris, mincha, and *mairev*?"

See also DAVEN.

malech
malach
molech
malachem   (plural)
maluchem   (plural)

> Occasionally encountered in books/articles by Jewish
> writers. Pronounced MA-*lekh*, with a Caledonian *kh*, not
> the frontal *ch* of "chickadee." From Hebrew: "messen-
> ger."
>   Angel.

There is no point in asking angels for help by addressing
them in English: angels understand only Hebrew (*Shabbat*,
12b). But Ashkenazic Jews never question that the heavenly fold is perfectly at home with Yiddish.
    Cabalists of the fourteenth century held that there are
exactly 301,655,722 angels. They arrived at this number
through *gematria*. I have not checked it.

Followers of Martin Luther, in an odd work called *Theatrum Diabolorum*, raised the number of angels to 2,500,000,000—and later, four times that. As Origen solemnly concluded: "Angels multiply like flies."

Two angels accompany every mortal (*Ta'anith*, 11a). They are, of course, invisible.

Angels possess staggering powers: Michael tore up entire mountains; an angel lifted all of Jerusalem during Nebuchadnezzar's siege!

Johannes Kepler, a giant of science, stated that it is angels who push the planets around.

When Spinoza held *maluchem* to be no more than hallucinations, he was cast out of the Sephardic community of Amsterdam.

I recommend to you the learned, mischievous work by Gustav Davidson: *A Dictionary of Angels*.

Once upon a time angels walked the earth; today, they are not found even in heaven.

—Folk saying

When the governments of France and Great Britain opened the bidding for the digging of the great tunnel under the English Channel (cleverly dubbed "the chunnel"), engineering firms all over the world were invited to place sealed bids for the huge contract.

The lowest bid of all came from the firm of Weintraub and Weiler.

Their friends hurried to congratulate the lucky partners. "How do you plan to build this great tunnel?"

"It's easy," said Mr. Weintraub. "I'll start digging on the English side and my partner will start on the French side. And we'll dig and dig—until we meet."

"But Weintraub," an engineer protested, "don't you realize that one of the hardest problems in all of engineering—one that has stumped our finest scientists—is the problem of getting two tunnels to meet!"

"What do you mean 'meet'?" asked Mr. Weiler.

"I mean that the tunnel *you* start in France, and the tunnel your partner starts in England—they start miles and miles apart, and they must come together *exactly*! . . . What if they don't?"

Mr. Weintraub shrugged. "So, through the help of *maluchem*, my clients will get two tunnels for the price of one."

mad on . . . (instead of "mad at . . .")

Yinglish, Bronxian division. Analogue of Yiddish *broygez oyf*.

As a verb
To be angry with. ("I am mad on her.")

As a noun
  1. A grievance. ("Until he apologizes, I still have a mad on him.")
  2. A complaint. ("I have a mad on her.")

I emphatically disapprove of both of these barbarisms; but my task is to record, not acclaim.

———————

After his wife's cousin Tillie had spent five weeks in their spare bedroom, Mr. Goldbaum got a mad on her.

He went out, bought a sign, and hung it over Tillie's bed. The sign read:

> BE IT EVER SO HUMBLE,
> THERE'S NO PLACE LIKE HOME, HOME, HOME!!

make like a . . .

Yinglish, without a doubt. From Yiddish, *makh vi . . .*
   Act like.

The Yinglish aspect lies in the deplorable fact that *make* has replaced the perfectly proper *act, behave, imitate*, or *pretend to be*.

"Stop clowning; make like a gentleman."
"He's only a sergeant, but he makes like a general."

The breezy patois of television's talk shows has given this locution an immense audience and, perforce, an extremely fertile propagating *milieu*.

———————

The family was in the lawyer's office as he read the will of the late, rich Dov Hess. "To my beloved wife . . . To my daughter, Bernice . . . To my niece, Shirley . . . To our faithful cook . . ." On and on the lawyer droned. "Finally, to my nephew, Howard Kramer—"

The young man in the last row sat up.

"—who made like a son to me, and was always so curious to know if I would mention him in my will . . ."

The young man held his breath.

"Hello, Howie."

See also MAKE WITH . . .

make with . . .

Yinglish, widely used. Analogue for the Yiddish: *mach mit* . . .

I do not recommend the use of this Bronxian phrase except for purposes of parody, or for humorous effect.

1. Make.
2. Provide.

"Liven up the party: make with some jokes."

"You sing? So make with the voice."

"It's getting late: make with some food."

"Mr. Weintraub, how far away," smirked the lawyer, "was my client standing when he allegedly threw the rock?"

"Nine feet six-and-a-half inches away," said Mr. Weintraub.

"My, my . . ." smiled the lawyer. "How can you *possibly* be that precise?"

"Because I knew some smarty-pants lawyer would make with that question," said Mr. Weintraub. "So I measured the distance down to the half-inch."

makher

See MACHER.

maledictions, instantly canceled —as moral expediency or possible insurance against divine wrath

Yiddish is exceptionally rich (and fertile) in this ploy.

"Every bone in his body should *kholile* (God forbid) break the minute he gets here!"

"May both eyes drop out of his head, God forbid."
"Such a woman deserves the sweetest death: to be
run over by a truckload of sugar."

The following may be called a reverse malediction:

A tipsy tourist once placed his arm around Groucho
Marx's shoulders and cackled, "Groucho, you son-of-a-
gun! I bet you don't remember me!"

Marx fixed the oaf with a baleful eye. "I never forget a
face—but in your case I'll be glad to make an exception."

See also ANGER CONVERTED . . .

mama-loshn (noun)
mama-loshen

Often encountered in English writings by Jewish authors. Pronounced *ma-meh* LAW-*shen*, to rhyme with
"Mama Caution." Hebrew: *loshn*: "tongue."

1. "Mother language," or "mother's tongue."
2. Yiddish itself, sentimentally.
3. The "turkey" in "Let's talk turkey."

"Can I talk *mama-loshn*?" means "Will you understand
if I speak Yiddish?"

To say "Let's talk *mama-loshn*" means "Let's cut out
the double talk. Lay it on the line."

"Mama's language" has an interesting background: Hebrew was "the holy tongue" (*loshn kadosh*), therefore the
father's language, since the holy books were in Hebrew,
and usually only Jewish males were taught to read. (The
daughters of wealthy Jews often had Hebrew tutors, however.) Yiddish became known as "the mother's tongue,"
the language of the home.

To the Ashkenazim, Yiddish was and is the *mama-loshn*.
Sephardic Jews cannot even understand it. (Nor could the
Ashkenazim understand Ladino, the Sephardic equivalent
of Yiddish.)

One of the anomalies, rarely noticed, is that whereas
the sacred texts of the Jews are in Hebrew/Aramaic, the
discussions thereof, in the *heder*, the *shul*, the *yeshivas* of
eastern Europe, were conducted in Yiddish. Before Yid-

dish existed, Jews discussed their holy texts in whatever their regional vernacular was.

Philologists (as distinguished from psychologists) believe that the first syllables uttered by a baby are the whimpering or gurgling *em-em, mem-memm, ma-ma.* (Jewish mothers answer this with admiring clucks: "So young—and already it knows I'm the mother!") *Baba, papa, dada, tata, mama* develop later.

Are you aware of the number of languages in which the word for "mother" begins with an *m*? Swiftly: English, Yiddish, French, German, Russian, Polish, Spanish, Italian, Portuguese, Swedish, Danish, Norwegian, Polish, Dutch, Czech, Serbian, Croatian, Greek, Swahili . . . In Hebrew, mother is *em.*

In an extraordinary paper, "About the Sound *Mmh* . . . ," psychoanalyst Ralph Greenson remarked:

> . . . the sound "mmh . . ." . . . is the only sound one can make and still keep something safely within the mouth. Apparently it is the sound produced with the nipple in the mouth, or with the pleasant memory of expectation. . . . The word "Mama" which consists of a repetition of this sound [doubles] the pleasurable labial sensations associated with the act of nursing.
>
> —*Explorations in Psychoanalysis*

God could not be everywhere—so he made mothers.
The best fork is Mother's hand.
A child without a mother is like a door without a knob.
A mother has glass eyes (she cannot see her children's faults.)
Mothers understand what children do not say.

> —Folk sayings

Hearing the approaching step of his mother, Rab Joseph would rise. "I must stand, for the *Shekhinah* [Holy Spirit] enters."

> —TALMUD: *Kiddushin*, 31:2

Marrano

Pronounced *m'*-RAH-*no* to rhyme with "Milano." Spanish: "pig." Plural: *Marranos.* (Derivations other than Spanish are sometimes suggested.)

The contemptuous name used by Spanish and Portuguese Catholics, five hundred years ago, for converted Jews (such conversions being by force and *en masse*) who remained "secret Jews"—*i.e.*, who continued to practice their faith.

Conversions of the Jews were effected, in the name of a gentle Savior, on the rack, in the pyre, on a torture wheel, via hot lead poured into bodily orifices, branding irons, blinding rods; during a process of de-tonguing, de-nailing, skin-stripping, limb-separation through literal horsepower.

At least three popes (Clement VI, Boniface IX, Nicholas V) were scandalized by conversion-via-horror, threats of death, the expropriation of worldly possessions and the seizing of Jewish children as hostages. But the ecclesiasts in Spain and Portugal persisted in their un-Holy Inquisition.

Query: Did Iberia ever recover?

In Spain, before the expulsion of the Jews, many *Marrano* families, probably known to be *pro forma* converts, rose to positions of great influence and enjoyed high status. Many *Marranos* merged into the most rarefied ranks of Spanish aristocracy. "It was not long before the majority [!] of distinguished Spanish families married into newly converted Christian families," writes Poul Borchsenius.

When Torquemada, the Chief Inquisitor, persuaded Isabella and Ferdinand to expel all Jews in 1492, between one hundred fifty thousand and five hundred thousand human beings, including men at the heart of Spanish life and culture, were driven out. About one hundred thousand found their first sanctuary in Portugal (whence they were soon expelled). A few thousand went to Italy, a like number to North African cities, and some went as far as Poland and Turkey. *Marrano* Jews founded the modern Jewish communities in Amsterdam and London.

See Cecil Roth, *History of the Marranos*, and Poul Borchsenius, *History of the Jews*.

Would you believe that as the flames were consuming the innocent victims, the Inquisitors . . . were chanting our prayers? These pitiless monsters invoked the God of mercy and kindness and pardon while committing the most atrocious, barbarous crime, acting in a way which demons in their rage would not use against brother demons.

—Voltaire, *Sermons du Rabbin Akib*

matzo
matzoh

Yinglish. Comprehensible wherever English is spoken (probably). Pronounced MOTT-*seh* (not MOTT-*so*) to rhyme with "lotsa." Hebrew: The plural in Hebrew is *matzoth*, pronounced MOTT-*sez*, in Yiddish.

Unleavened bread (it comes in thin, flat, ridgy oblongs, and is semi-perforated to facilitate neat breaking).

During Passover, no bread, no yeast or leavened products are eaten. *Matzos* commemorate the kind of unleavened bread the Hebrews, fleeing from Egypt in the thirteenth century B.C., ate because they could not pause in their perilous flight long enough to wait for the dough to rise. Exodus 12:15: "Seven days shall ye eat unleavened bread. . . ."

Today, *matzos* are enjoyed all year round, and are served in many restaurants. Matzo ball dumplings are a feature of Jewish cuisine.

———

This may be the place to bring you the startling news that the Hebrews never crossed the Red Sea. They crossed "the sea of *reeds*," marshes, a hundred miles north of the Red Sea, quite near the Mediterranean. "*Red* Sea" is a boner (*boo-boo*) in translating Hebrew.

———

Mrs. Handelsman huffed into Kroloff's Grocery and banged a box of matzos on the counter. "This you call matzos? They're so hard I need already an *ax* to break them!"

"Just a minute!" retorted Mr. Kroloff. "If our ancestors, crossing that terrible desert in Egypt, had matzos like these they would be damn grateful!"

"Sure they would," sneered Mrs. Handelsman. "When they were crossing that desert these matzos were fresh!"

See also KNAYDL.

maven
mavin
mavens   (Yinglish, plural)
meyvenim   (Yiddish, plural)

Yinglish, beyond dispute.
One of the most well known and most widely used

Yiddish words in English. Pronounced MAY-*vin*, to rhyme with "raven." From Hebrew: "understanding."

1. An expert; a really knowledgeable person; a good judge of quality.
2. A connoisseur.

"He's a *maven* on Mozart."

"Don't buy it until you get the advice of a *maven*."

Maven has been given considerable publicity in a series of newspaper advertisements for herring tidbits. "The Herring *Maven* Strikes Again!" proclaimed the caption. The picture showed an empty jar.

American and English newspapers and magazines use *maven* so often, and so unerringly, that the word has become an integral part of English. In fact, *maven* is now in the *Oxford American Dictionary*.

———

The government of Israel, concerned over the growing division of support among American Jews, hired a hotshot public relations firm in New York. For three months, the PR *mavens* conducted polls, interviewed Jewish leaders, discussed the political parameters (tsk, tsk!) in Washington.

The final report, 168 pages long, contained graphs, charts, tables, statistics. And the last chapter, entitled *Recommendations*, began:

1. Change "Israel" to "Irving."

———

Dr. Poliakoff examined the new patient's teeth carefully, then took several x-rays and examined them, and said, "Mrs. Olitsny, tell me something: when was the last time you saw a dentist?"

"Oh, maybe a year-and-a-half or two. Then I consulted my pharmacist . . ."

"Your *phar*macist . . . ?" echoed Mr. Poliakoff, "What kind of sense does that make? You went to a *druggist*."

"Yes."

"And what advice," asked Dr. Poliakoff sarcastically, "did that *maven* give you?"

Mrs. Olitsny sighed, "He told me I should positively, without wasting another day, see you."

During the Passover party, the conversation sparkled. At one point, Mr. Sheineman asked Mrs. Glantz, "Someone told me you're an expert on Omar Khayyam."

"Who's a *maven*?" she asked. "I only know what I like."

"So? What's your feeling about the Rubaiyat?"

Mrs. Glantz shrugged. "Not bad, not great. But speaking personally, *I* prefer Chianti."

When the Glantzes left the party, Mr. Glantz said, "Mildred, why do you always have to show off? Why do you have to pretend you know it all? The Rubaiyat isn't a *wine!*"

"Omigod," moaned Mrs. Glantz.

"It's a cheese."

maybe

What makes *maybe* Yinglish is the places and contexts in which the word is not used—except by Jews. *Maybe* is a calque of the Yiddish *efsher*.

1. Perhaps. ("You are maybe joking?")
2. I don't believe it. ("He said he'll endow a chair in his late wife's name . . . maybe.")
3. Wouldn't that be nice? ("They maybe won't show up!")

Maybe is often used for its derisive overtones. This was the case often in the famous, long-running *Molly Goldberg Show*, or the *Fred Allen Show*. Both played a significant part in disseminating Yinglishisms.

ALLEN: Hello? Mrs. Nussbaum?

MRS. NUSSBAUM: You expected maybe the Queen of England?

MOLLY GOLDBERG: Yoo-hoo, Mr. Kipnis.

KIPNIS: Is that Mrs. Goldboig?

MOLLY: You expected maybe Elizabeth Taylor?

See also COULD BE.

mazel

Pronounced MOZ-*z'l*, to rhyme with "nozzle." Hebrew: "luck." *Mazel tov* is now accepted as English (you will find it in the *Oxford American Dictionary* and the *American Heritage Dictionary*), and *mazel* should soon be so, too.

Luck; good luck.

A buxom dowager wore, at a fine charity ball, an enormous diamond. In the powder room of the Waldorf, she explained to a circle of admiring women, "This happens to be the third most famous diamond in the whole world." She boasted, "The first is the Hope diamond, then comes the Kohinoor, and then comes this one, the Lipshitz."

"What a diamond!"

"How lucky you are!"

"Wait, wait, nothing is all *mazel*," said the diamonded dame. "Unfortunately, with this famous Lipshitz diamond you must take the famous Lipshitz curse."

The ladies buzzed and tsk'd. "And what's the Lipshitz curse?"

"Lipshitz," sighed the lady.

Many Jewish folk sayings revolve around luck. Here are a few:

Should luck come in—quick! Give him a seat.
Coins are round: if you're lucky, they roll toward you;
     if you're unlucky, they roll away.
From luck to misfortune is only an inch; from
     misfortune to luck is a hundred miles.
If you're lucky, you don't have to be smart.
Too good is bad.
Weep for the man who does not realize how lucky he is.

See also MAZEL TOV!

mazel tov!

Used so widely in English, *mazel tov* is now unchallenged Yinglish. The phrase is in the *American Heritage* and *Oxford American* dictionaries. Pronounced MOZ-z'l, to rhyme with "schnozzle"; tov is pronounced TUV, TUFF, or TAWF. Hebrew: *mazel*: "luck"; *tov*: "good."

1. "Congratulations!" or "Thank God!" rather than its literal meaning: "Good luck." (The distinction is important.)
2. Thank God!

3. At last!
4. What a surprise!

At all Jewish celebrations—a *bris*, wedding, graduation, *Bar Mitzva*—you will hear *mazel tov!*'s resounding like buckshot on a tin shed.
Some invaluable guidelines:

1. Don't *mazel tov!* anyone going into a hospital. Say "*Mazel tov!*" when he or she comes out.
2. Do not say "*Mazel tov!*" to a fighter entering a ring (it suggests you are congratulating him for having made it to the arena).
3. Say "*Mazel tov!*" to an Israeli ship captain when he first takes command: this congratulates him on his promotion; don't say "*Mazel tov!*" when the ship reaches port: this suggests you're surprised he got there.
4. Never say "*Mazel tov!*" where it might be taken to mean "And about time!"

   "I'm going to leave now."
   "*Mazel tov!*"

5. Don't say "*Mazel tov!*" to a surgeon, dentist, plumber or general about to plunge into action: the one thing these *mavens* are presumed to have is expertise; only amateurs need good luck.
6. Say "*Mazel tov!*" to a surgeon, dentist, etc., *after* the successful completion of a difficult operation. This congratulates him on his skill in performing what you now admit you knew was a risky business.
7. Say "*Mazel tov!*" to a man who comes out of prison. It means "At last."
8. Don't say "*Mazel tov!*" to a man about to go to prison. It means "So, at last, they caught you!"
9. "We're going to have a baby."
   "*Mazel tov!*" (Purists would say, "May it be in a fortunate hour.")
10. Say "*Mazel tov!*" where you would say "Thank God!" in English.

    "They found the lost boy!"
    "*Mazel tov!*"

In the Bible, *mazel* referred to a constellation of the zodiac, and the word was invoked when fate was involved. Later, Talmudic sages warned the Jews to eschew sooth-saying and diviners. (Poor believing Jews had a hard time knowing *what* to think: the Bible, after all, talks of the "signs of heaven"—in Jeremiah and Isaiah. But the *Midrash* teaches: "The Holy One forbade astrology in Israel;" and it is said that God made Abraham "a prophet, not an astrologer." The great Maimonides called astrology "a disease, not a science.")

Jews continued to utter "*Mazel tov!*" Soon the supernatural or divinational aspects were forgotten (just as "God be with you" became "good-bye"); *mazel* became simply "luck," and "*Mazel tov!*" became "Congratulations."

Mournfully, Mr. Joseph entered the offices of his burial society. "I've come to make the funeral arrangements for my dear wife."

"Your wife?" asked the astonished secretary. "But we buried her last year!"

"That was my *first* wife," sighed Mr. Joseph. "I'm talking about my second."

"Second? I didn't know you remarried. *Mazel tov!*"

"You ask how am I doing?" the writer answered his friend. "You have no idea how popular my writing has become. Why, since I last saw you, my readers have doubled!"

"Well, *mazel tov!* I didn't know you got married."

See also AGREEMENT DEPLOYED . . . , AMERICA GONIF!, ASSENT ENTHUSIASTICALLY ENLARGED . . . , CONTEMPT BY NOMINAL CONCURRENCE, GUT SHABBES, SARCASM AMPLIFIED . . . , THANKS A LOT.

mazuma
mezuma

Pronounced *m'*-ZOOM-*a*, to rhyme with "bazooka." From the Hebrew, originally meaning "prepared" or "ready."

(Slang) Money, particularly ready cash.

I always heard *mazuma* used to mean money (*gelt*), when a lingering, amusing effect was desired. Just as we say, "Man, is he loaded!" (to mean rich, not drunk), some say, "Has he got *ma-zuma*!"

It's not that money makes everything good; it's that no money makes everything bad.

—Folk saying

See also BREAD, GELT.

megilla
megillah

Yinglish, well-established in English and widely used. Pronounced *meh*-GILL-*eh*, to rhyme with "guerrilla." Hebrew: "scroll."

1. *Megilla* usually describes the Book of Esther, which is read in the synagogue during the Purim holiday; also the Book of Ruth. (There are five *megillas* in all.)
2. Anything very long, prolix, a rigmarole.
   The Book of Esther wanders through a crushing concatenation of detail, and the devout sit through the long, long reading after a day of fasting.
3. In popular parlance: anything complicated, boring, overly extended, fouled up.
   "He'll put you to sleep with that *megillah*."
   "Don't give me a *megilla*" means "Spare me all the dull details."

The origin of *megilla* is worth noting: the Book of Esther is a colorful tale, with a miraculous denouement: the saving of the Jews of Persia by Queen Esther, who succeeded Queen Vashti. Why is this tale considered a bore? Because the book is read aloud in the synagogue after the fast and the evening prayer on Purim. This reading is interrupted and prolonged by the permitted racket of youngsters every time the name of Haman (the would-be destroyer of the Hebrews) is uttered.

Now, since no food may be consumed before hearing the *megilla*, and since by convention a special Purim feast has been prepared and waits at home, Jews are on *shpilkes* for the services to end. Moreover, the reading is in Hebrew—which is not understood by many in the congregation, and by no more than a handful in Reform temples.

In the entertainment world, and in police circles, *megilla* has become a much-favored word. I have heard it on many a television program: the *Tonight Show*'s chit-chat; dramas where shady characters employ their special argot, not criminal but certainly *infra dig*; scenes between lawyers; in comedy routines, by Jewish and non-Jewish entertainers alike, used instead of "all that jazz," or "all that malarkey." Thus:

"Cut the *megilla*."
"He gave me a real *megilla*."
"Who needs a *megillah* like that?"

Nightclub habitués and jet-set jokers, in Hollywood, New York and Miami, use *megilla* as matter-of-factly as if they were in the synagogue during Purim—just as many Italians say "*una Iliade*" who have never read the *Iliad*.

A *gontzeh megilla*, meaning "a whole *megilla*," is a common phrase; it simply adds a note of dismissal via emphasis.

Two men sat opposite each other in the train. After a while, the first man said, "Uh—where are you from?"

"Newark," said the second, "and I'm going to Philadelphia. My business is insurance. My name is Boris Mishkin. I have a son at Rutgers and a daughter who's married. My wife's maiden name was Kowalsky. I don't fish or play golf. I spend my summers in the Catskills and go to Miami every December. I go to a Reform temple and I don't have a brother of the same name because I don't have a brother. My sister you couldn't have known because she died thirty years ago. Now, if I've forgotten anything in this *megilla*, please ask me right now, because I want to take a nap until we reach Philadelphia!"

I know I've told this story elsewhere. Choose the version you prefer.

One day Mrs. Hoff went to see her rabbi. "My health is so bad, *Rebbe*, I'm absolutely beside myself. My back is killing me—a back like that you wish on your worst enemy. Eyes? My eyes are so weak, I can barely hold them open. And I have to *see*, after all, because my *ears* are so bad that any day now I'll be deaf! . . ." On and on and on she yakked until, after fifteen uninterrupted minutes of this *megilla*, she paused to exclaim, "You know something, *Rebbe*? I came in with the most terrible headache of my whole life—and it just disappeared!"

The rabbi sighed. "No, no. Your headache didn't disappear. *I* have it!"

See also MISH-MOSH, SHTUSS, TSIMMES.

mekheteneste

See MACHETAYNESTE.

melamed
melamdim   (plural)

> Pronounced *m'*-LAH-*med*, to rhyme with "Muhammad." Plural: *melamdim*, pronounced *m'*-LAHM-*dim*. Hebrew: "teacher."

1. A teacher of elementary Hebrew. Hebrew teachers were not rabbis or sages, but an unworldly, impecunious lot whose social status was respectable but not enviable. The *melamed*'s work was teaching by rote. (My father used to say, "If they were smarter, they'd be rabbis.")
2. An incompetent. To call someone a *melamed* who does not earn his living as a *melamed* is to speak with condescension.
3. An unworldly, unsophisticated, impractical type. There is a saying: "A *melamed* remains a *melamed*." It means "He'll never get anywhere" or "What did you expect?"

It always puzzled me that the Jews, who so revere learning, should speak patronizingly of a teacher. The reason, I suppose, is that the *melamed* is the teacher of elementary Hebrew to young boys—teaching by sheer repetition. A Jew who had no way of making a living or who had failed in what he had undertaken could become a *melamed* as a last resort.

mench

See MENSH.

menorah

A familiar word in English-language newspapers and magazines. Pronounced *men-AW-ra*, to rhyme with "aurora." Hebrew: "candelabrum."

The *menorah* most commonly referred to is the eight-branched candelabrum lighted on the eight festive evenings of *Chanukah*.

The word first occurs in Exodus 37, where you can find a detailed description of the seven-branched gold candelabrum made by Bezalel, the artisan, for the Tabernacle in the wilderness. The *Menorah* was later placed in the Temple in Jerusalem. The original *menorah* had seven lamps; the Chanukah ("Feast of Lights") *menorah* has eight, plus the high center candle from which the others are lighted. The tallest candle is called the *shamus* (*q.v.*).

Originally, the menorah was an oil lamp that was lighted on Sabbath eve, with a flax wick soaked in eight or nine separate spouts arranged in a line or a circle. Oil lamps gave way to brass or silver candlesticks in the eighteenth century.

When candles replaced oil lamps, the charming custom arose of lighting one candle for each child in the family. In lighting these, the mother would close her eyes and pass her hands quickly across the candle flame, toward herself, as if to inhale divine spirit. "The soul," says Proverbs, "is the Lord's candle."

See also CHANUKAH.

mensh   (noun)
mench
mentch
mentsh

An absolutely unique word. Quintessential Yinglish. Widely used and understood in English. Rhymes with "bench." From German: *Mensch*: "person." Plural: *menschen*. I prefer the *mensh* spelling because in Yiddish one letter (*shin*) renders the *sh* sound, without the *c* used in German.

The word *mensh* is being heard and read more and more in American speech, newspapers, journals, books. The word is today to be found in many English dictionaries: *The American Heritage Dictionary*, *Webster's Ninth Collegiate Dictionary*, *The Random House Dictionary*, among others.

Mensh (also printed *mensch* and even *mentch*, both of which I regard as absurd) is descended from the German word meaning "person." As used in Yiddish and now in Yinglish *mensh* means:

1. Someone of admirable character. ("There is a *mensh*!")
2. Someone who is upright, honorable, trustworthy. ("Only a *mensh* would refuse an offer like that!")
3. Someone deserving of great respect. ("Okay, he lost the election by a hundred thousand votes, but his campaign showed he was a real *mensh*.")
4. Someone of surpassing decency—or tact. ("He opened the door to the bathroom—and there completely naked, stood a beautiful woman! He gulped, cleared his throat, then backing out said, 'Excuse *me*, sir . . .' ")
5. A human being. ("Act like a *mensh*—not like an animal!")

The most withering criticism one can make of someone else's conduct or character, manners or taste is to say, "He's not a *mensh*" or "She did not act like a *mensh*."

To be a *mensh* has nothing at all to do with success or wealth or social status. A king can be a *bulvon* (oaf). A millionaire can be a *momzer* (bastard). A doctor can be a *zhlub* (jerk). A professor can be a *gornisht* (nothing).

The key to being "a *mensh*" is nothing less than *character*, rectitude, dignity, a sense of what is *right* or ethically imperative. Many a poor man, even an ignoramus, conducts himself in the luminous manner of a *mensh*.

meshiach (noun)
mashiach

Pronounced *m'*-SHEE-*ach*, with a rattling *kh* sound at the end; rhyme it with "Marie, *ach!*" From Hebrew: *ha-mashiah*: "the anointed." The Hebrew *mashiah* became, in Greek, *messias*, or, in translation, *christos*; hence, *messias* = messiah; *christos* = Christ—and both denote "the anointed one."

Messiah.

1. Originally, in the Old Testament, *meshiach* was the title for kings ("God's anointed") and priests (who were given sacercdotal status by being anointed with sacred oil).
2. Later, *meshiach* meant a prophet, or anyone with a special mission from God.
3. Then, *meshiach* came to mean the awaited Deliverer of the Jews from their bondage and oppression, who will restore the kingdom of Israel.
4. Finally, *meshiach* means the Savior who will make the world acknowledge God's sovereignty, thus ushering in the Day of Judgment.

The Old Testament uses *mashiah* for Saul, David, Zedekiah and Cyrus of Persia (no Jew!). David, "the anointed of Yahweh," established the dynastic principle among the Jews.

Jews distinguished the earthly Messiah from a heavenly Messiah: the earthly Messiah was to be a man born of the line of David; but the heavenly Messiah lives in heaven "under the wings of the Lord" (Enoch, 39).

The doctrine of the Messiah has been one of the most powerful elements in the history of Judaism and Christianity. Whenever epidemics, starvation, pogroms, wars, expulsions or any of the thousand torments visited upon the Jews seemed unendurable, the faithful and desperate looked once more into their holy books for some hidden sign, some new revelation, some miraculous harbinger of hope: *when* would the Messiah arrive?

The elders of Chelm decided to give Muttel the Lame a face-saving job. "We will pay you two zlotys a day. Just sit on the hill outside our village every day from dawn to sunset. You will be our watchman—for the approach of the Messiah. And when you see him, run back to the *shtetl* as fast as you can, shouting, 'The Messiah! The *Meshiach*! He is coming!' "

Muttel's face lighted up just thinking of the glory . . .

Every morning he greeted the dawn from the hill outside Chelm. And not until sunset every day, did proud Muttel leave his treasured post.

A year went by, and a traveler, approaching the village, noticed the figure sitting on a hill, "*Sholem*," called the traveler. "What are you doing here?"

"I am waiting for the *Meshiach*! It's my job."

The traveler suppressed a smile. "Confidentially, how do you like this job?"

"Sssssh!" Muttel looked about. "Frankly, it doesn't pay much—but I think it's *steady*!"

meshpoche

See MISHPOCHE.

meshugge
meshuge
mishugeh

Yinglish, by any standard. I spell the word with a double *g*, to circumvent the two-syllable version, *meshug*, I heard in Connecticut. Pronounced *m'*-SHU-*geh*, to rhyme with "Paducah." Hebrew: "crazy."

1. Insane.
2. Bizarre.
3. Obsessed.
4. Phobic.

Is there anyone who does not know that *meshugge* means crazy? Crazy, nuts, wildly extravagant, absurd.

The potent *sh* and muscular *ug* unite to give *meshugge* a ripe combination of sounds that may account for the word's increasing popularity in English.

A crazy man is a *meshuggener*.

A crazy woman is a *meshuggeneh*.

Note: "That's *meshugge*," but "that's a *meshuggeneh* idea."

Perhaps the soundest insight into human behavior is this folk saying: "Every man has his own *mishegoss*."

Old Mr. Slabinsky could not sleep. His children had given the old man pills, syrups, tranquilizers—all to no avail.

The frantic children finally decided to call in a hypnotist. The children introduced him to the old man. "Papa, a man who works miracles, a *specialist* who makes people sleep!"

The hypnotist said, "Mr. Slabinsky, if you'll have just a little faith in me, you'll fall asleep like a child." He held up a watch and said, "Keep your eyes here. That's right . . . Good." The hypnotist swung the watch back and forth, intoning: "Left . . . right . . . Your eyes are getting tired . . . tired . . . Your eyelids are heavy . . . heavy . . . sleep . . . sleep . . . sleep."

The old man's head sank low, his eyes were shut, his breathing was as rhythmic as a babe's. The hypnotist placed his finger on his lips, cautioning the children to remain silent, and stole out.

When the door closed, the old man opened one eye. "That *meshuggener*! Has he gone already?"

Mr. Koppel returned from the hospital where he had visited an uncle in the psychiatric ward. "Poor Uncle," he sighed to his wife. "He raves nothing but *mishegoss*."

"How terrible. Couldn't you even *talk* to him?"

"I tried. I talked about his children, his old business, the fifty dollars he owes us—"

"Aha! And did he remember?"

Mr. Koppel snorted. "That *meshugge* he's not."

See also MISHEGOSS, TSEDOODELT.

mezuma

See MAZUMA.

mezuzah
mezuza
mezzuza

Often appears in English. Pronounced *meh-ZU-zah*, with a short "*u*" as in "put." Rhyme it with "kazoo's a." In Hebrew, *mezuzah* means "doorpost," but don't use it that way—unless you're in Israel.

The little oblong container (about the size of two cigarettes) that is affixed to the right of the front door-jamb of his home, in a slanting position, by a Jew who believes in putting up a *mezuzah*. Inside the *mezuzah* is a tiny, rolled-up paper or parchment on which are printed the verses from Deuteronomy 6:4–9 and 11:13–21.

An Orthodox Jew touches his finger to his lips, then to the *mezuzah*, each time he enters or leaves his home. The first sentence in the parchment's text is Israel's great watchword: "Hear, O Israel, the Lord our God is one."

The inscribed passages contain the command to "love the Lord your God and serve Him with all your heart and with all your soul"; they end with an inscription reminding the faithful that God's laws are to be observed away from, as well as at, home, and that children must have respect for God's laws instilled in them. (The enclosed material also includes the injunction to inscribe these words "upon the door posts of thine house.")

The *mezuzah* consecrates the home, which to Jews is a temple. (In Hebrew, a *migdash mehad*.)

midrash
midrashim (plural)

> Pronounced MID-*rosh*, to rhyme with "kid nosh." Hebrew: "commentary," "interpretation." From the root verb meaning "to study," "to investigate."
>
> The very highly developed analysis, exposition, and exegesis of the Holy Scriptures.

The ancient scholars of the period of the Second Temple (fifth century B.C. to A.D. 70), were convinced that the words of the Bible lent themselves to many interpretations and could be applied to all ages, to varied social conditions, and to all types of men. They initiated complex "midrashic" interpretations of the Bible. These savants read involved ideas into simple verses; they found esoteric meanings in every jot and tittle of the holy texts.

After the dispersion of the Jews, their leaders carried on the hermeneutic tradition; their sermons, based on biblical texts, included a great deal of homiletic material—parables, allegories, illustrative stories, inspirational interpretations—that spoke directly to the common people. And beginning in the fourth century, many of these curious sermons were written down and collected. There are over one hundred books of *midrashim* extant. (Soncino Press publishes an English translation of the *Midrash Rabbah* in ten volumes. It is crammed with folklore, anecdotes, parables, popular sayings and folk wisdom.)

What is the difference between a *midrash* and any other analysis of, say, a verse? The *midrash* purports to penetrate the "spirit" of the verse and derive an interpretation that is not obvious. (It is often also not persuasive.)

In the *midrash* there is total amnesty, I think, for learned but untenable *non sequiturs* and poetic license, which, greatly inflated, becomes philosophy or, at least, theology. Judah Goldin's *Studies in Midrash* is indispensable.

See also TALMUD.

mikva
mikvah
mikveh

> Pronounced MICK-*vuh*, to rhyme with "pick the." Hebrew: "a pool of water."
>
> The ritual bath a pious Jewish bride takes before her wedding and religious Jewish women take (a) at the end of their menstrual period, (b) after bearing a child.

Under rabbinical law, a husband and wife are not permitted to cohabit throughout the time of her menstruation—or for seven days afterward. On the seventh day, the wife is required to take a bath in running water.

A community of Jews was obligated to build and maintain a community *mikva*. The rules and regulations governing the *mikva* are quite detailed: in fact, a whole section of the *Mishnah* (*q.v.*) explores this recondite subject. The woman recites a benediction while in the water.

Today, only very religious Jewish women observe the *mikva* custom—or attend a bathhouse for *mikvas*, such as were found in Europe and on the Lower East Side.

Gentiles sometimes remarked on the unusual emphasis Jews placed upon cleanliness and hygiene; some said this amounted to a veritable "cult of purity." Thomas Sowell's *Ethnic America* comments on the strikingly lower rate of diseases and mortality among Jews on New York's Lower East Side, compared to that among their neighbors. bathing frequently must also have created and intensified a sense of self-respect. This seems all the more significant if one observes the differences in hygiene and sanitation, even today, between Jewish and Arab families/communities throughout North Africa and the Middle East.

mincha
minhah

Pronounced MIN-*kha*, with a Caledonian *kh*. Hebrew: "an offering."
The daily late-afternoon religious service.

By tradition, pious Jews pray thrice a day: *shachris*, in the morning; *mincha*, in the afternoon; *mairev* in the evening. The vast majority of Jews today do not.

See also DAVEN.

minyan (noun)
minyon

Becoming part of Yinglish—and slang. Pronounced MIN-*yon*; rhyme it with "Binyon." Hebrew: "number," or "counting."

1. Quorum.
2. The ten male Jews required for religious services. No congregational prayers or rites can begin until "we have a *minyan*."

To have ten men is to have a "synagogue." (Children do not count; they are not mature enough to understand the prayers.) Since one cannot always find ten adult male Jews, exceptions to the *minyan* are permitted for a wedding, for instance, or a circumcision. A *minyan* possesses special merit to the observant, who hold that when ten male Jews assemble, God's Presence (*Shechinah*) dwells among them.

3. *Minyan* is often used in a jocular way for secular occasions, to mean, "Do we have a quorum (or a majority)?" or "Have most of those we expected arrived?"

Consider the number of times the magical number ten appears in Judaic law, lore, and history:

1. The Ten Commandments.
2. The ten plagues visited on Pharoah.

3. The ten days of penitence.
4. The ten generations cited in the Bible from Adam to Noah and from Noah to Abraham.
5. The ten tests of faith God gave Abraham.
6. The unit of ten, in the clan structure, established by Moses (Exodus 18:25).

Nine wise men don't make a *minyan*, but ten cobblers do.
Nine saints do not make a *minyan*, but one ordinary man can—by joining them.

—Folk sayings

See also DAVEN.

mischling

See MISHLING.

mishegoss
mishegaas

Yinglish/Yiddish. Pronounced *mish-eh-*GOSS, to rhyme with "dish o' Joss." Hebrew: *meshuga:* "insane."

Literally: insanity, madness. But *mishegoss* is more often used in a lighter vein to describe not mental disease, but:

1. An absurd belief; nonsense; hallucinations.
   "Did you ever hear such a piece of *mishegoss?*"
2. A state of affairs so silly or unreal that it defies explanation.
   "No one can figure it out; it's plain *mishegoss*."
   "How can you cope with such *mishegoss?*"
3. A piece of tomfoolery, clowning, "horsing around."
   "He's the life of the party with his jokes and *mishegoss*."
   "Please, cut out the *mishegoss*."
4. A fixation, an *idée fixe*.
   "She has a new *mishegoss*—that the neighbors are trying to ruin her."

Note that *meshugge* can be used both seriously ("The psychiatrists declare him *meshugge*") and playfully ("Oh, he's hilarious when he acts *meshugge*"); but *mishegoss* is nearly always used in an amused, indulgent way.

———

Samuel Goldwyn once remarked, during an argument about psychiatry: "Anyone who goes to a psychiatrist ought to have his head examined." (Yes, I know I have used this elsewhere.)

———

The office of three psychoanalysts is alleged to carry this shingle:

S. M. SPERO, M.D.
J. MELNICK, M.D.
R. GABRILOWITZ, M.D.
6 couches—no waiting.

———

And since we're on the subject, you may be interested in this definition: "A psychoanalyst is a Jewish doctor who hates the sight of blood."

———

Harvey Krausse and Leonard Mishstein, two Hollywood writers, were going to the same psychoanalyst, Dr. Pforzheim. "Nothing ever *throws* him," remarked Krausse. "Have you ever seen or heard him act surprised?"

"Never," said Mishstein.

They bemoaned their healer's inhuman unflappability.

"I have an idea," said Harvey. "Let's make up a dream! A really fantastic, hair-raising dream. I'll report it at my hour—nine to ten—and—"

"And I'll report precisely the same dream at my hour: five to six!" laughed Mishstein.

With many a laugh and gloat of anticipation, the two writers concocted a dream: "A naked boy in a green gondola is drifting under a Gothic archway—and suddenly a bearded warrior, with a hissing serpent in one hand and a club in the other, jumps into the gondola—at which point a woman in white cries, 'Rape! Snake! . . .' The dream breaks off . . ."

"What a beaut of a dream!" Krausse chortled.

"Wait until Pforzheim hears *that* twice in one day!" gloated Mishstein.

And so, the next morning, at around 9:05, in Couch Canyon (as Roxbury Drive is called), Leonard Mishstein reported the bizarre dream to Dr. Pforzheim.

And at 5:05, Harvey Krausse reported the identical phantasmagoria—

"That dream . . ." Dr. Pforzheim cleared his throat. "Strange . . . very strange. That's the *third* time I've heard it today!"

See also MESHUGGE.

mishling
mischling

> Recommended with zest for Yinglish. Pronounced MISH-*ling*. From the German: "hybrid," "crossbreed."
> Someone of mixed ethnic or religious parentage.

As used in my circles, *mishling* refers to someone with one Jewish and one non-Jewish parent. History bursts with the names of important *mishlings*—in science, philosophy, art, politics.

Although many anthropologists use *mishling*, I have not found it in a single dictionary of English, including the great *Oxford*. *Mishling* is much nicer than "half-Jewish" or "half-gentile" or "half-breed" or half-anything.

———

Groucho Marx, married to a *shiksa*, asked a friend, "How do I go about joining that posh beach club in Santa Monica?"

"Don't try to get into that club," said the friend, uneasily. "They're—well, anti-Semitic."

Groucho reflected. "My son is only half-Jewish. Do you think they'd let him go into the water up to his knees?"

See also SHAYGETS, SHIKSA.

mish-mosh
mish-mash

> Quintessential and irreplaceable Yinglish. Pronounce it MISH-MOSH, please, to rhyme with "pish-posh"—and not with "dish-dash." I prefer to spell this delicious word *mish-mosh*, as it is pronounced, but the thirteen-

volume *Oxford English Dictionary* spells it *mish-mash*, and traces it to the German *mischmasch* and the Danish (!) *misk-mask*. Still, the total acceptance of mish-mosh/ mash in current English is surely a consequence of the vigorous and incessant use of the word, in conversation and in newspapers and books, by Jews.

1. A mixup, a mess, a hodgepodge, a fouled-up state of things.
2. Confusion galore.
   "What a *mish-mosh!*"
   "You never heard such a *mish-mosh* of ideas."

No Jew pronounces this "mish-m*a*sh."
I consider *mish-mosh* a triumph of onomatopoeia—and a word unlike any I know to suggest flagrant disorder.

———

Regarding the Danish provenance (*misk-mask*): In the United States, where little Danish is heard or spoken, it was Jews on the lower East Side who latched onto the vivid German compound noun (with two *sh*'s) to enrich their Yinglish. Remember that the *sh* sibilant was and is conspicuous in Yiddish mocking appellations: *shlemiel, shlep, shlimazel, shloomp, shmendrick, shmuck*. . . .

See also MEGILLA, SHTUSS, TARARAM, TSIMMES.

Mishnah

Often appears in learned articles in English. Pronounced MISH-*nah*, to rhyme with "Krishna." Hebrew: literally, "to repeat or review one's learning."
    One of the two basic parts of the Talmud. (The other, much later, part is the Gemara.)

The Mishnah is the codified core of the Oral Law, that vast body of technical analysis and philosophical interpretations that was originally not written down, for fear of affecting the sanctity of the Torah. It was written in Hebrew. (The Gemara was written in Aramaic.) The Mishnah is divided into six *sedarim* (orders), which, in turn, comprise sixty-three tractates. (Only half of these have a *gemara* appended.) Each tractate is divided into *perakim* (chapters), which are organized by paragraphs.
The Mishnah's six "orders" are:

1. *Seeds*: discusses agricultural problems, rituals, and laws.
2. *Festivals*: sets forth the *halakha* (law) for fast days, festivals, the Sabbath.
3. *Women*: covers relations between men and women, betrothals, nuptials—and divorce.
4. *Damages*: a detailed code of civil and criminal law.
5. *Sacred things*: rituals, sacrifices, services.
6. *Purities*, or *Purifications*: matters of personal hygiene, clean and unclean foods, etc.

———

After the Jews returned to Judea from their Babylonian exile (537 B.C.) the scholars of the Great Assembly, the Jews' religious and legislative body, established the basic rules for the interpretation of Jewish law.

The Great Assembly produced a group of scribes (*soferim*) who became the official copyists and teachers of the Bible. They were followed by the *tannaim*, sages who continued to interpret biblical laws and apply them to changing historical circumstances. Their discussions, ordinances and interpretations were transmitted orally, lest they diminish the sanctity of the Bible, *i.e.*, the Written Law!

Hillel (c. 30 B.C.–A.D. 20), the greatest Pharisee, a tower of wisdom and humility (Jesus was clearly influenced by Hillel's teachings), made one of the earliest attempts to codify the vast, tangled body of oral teachings. Alas, no one knows what happened to his effort.

The illustrious Rabbi Akiba initiated the pioneer work of collecting and classifying the oral traditions, legal decisions and precedents into a *mishnah* (review). Akiba's work was continued by Judah ha-Nasi, "the Prince," known simply as "Rabbi." He was head of the Sanhedrin, the high court that compiled and edited the accumulated body of oral law, and around A.D. 200 declared the canonical labor closed. Soon after Rabbi Judah completed the Mishnah, collections of additional material appeared: the *Tosefta* (supplement), *Baraitas* (excluded traditions), and material pertaining to the Pentateuch.

But Judah's Mishnah has remained the central authority.

See TALMUD.

mishpoche (noun)
meshpoche
mishpokhe

I urge the instant recruitment of this excellent word into Yinglish: there is no English word like it. Pronounce it *mish*-PAWKH-*eh*, with the palatal *kh* rattle. Hebrew: "family."

1. A family, including the most remote kin: cousins, cousins' cousins, third cousins once removed, nephews of nephews, *et alia*.
2. Ancestors, lineage, "clan."

Anthropologists are careful to study the "extended family" (*mishpokhe*) of any tribe they examine.

3. Sometimes used as an "in" word among Jews to mean "Is he/she one of us?"

For reasons I cannot fathom, Brockhaus' *German–English English–German Dictionary* identifies *mishpokhe* as "vulgar" and defines it as "rabble." To me, this illustrates the fact that lexicographers need not have an ounce of sense.

Many Jews are not familiar with the Yiddish names for members of a family. Perhaps I should offer them (and you) the entire *megilla* (*q.v.*) at no extra charge:

father	*tateh* or *tata* (TAH-*teh*)
mother	*mameh* or *mama* (MAH-*meh*)
husband	*mann* (MON)
wife	*veib; froy* (VIBE; FROY or FRO)
son	*zun* (ZUHN) or *zian* (ZEEN)
daughter	*tochter* (TAWKH-*ter*)
brother	*bruder* (BROO-*der* or BREE-*der*)
sister	*shvester* (SHVES-*ter*)
uncle	*fetter* (FEH-*ter*)
	onkel (AWN-*kel*)
aunt	*tante; mummeh*
	(TAHN-*teh*; MOO-*meh* or ME-*mah*)
nephew	*plemenik* (*pleh*-MEN-*ik*)
niece	*plemenitza* (*pleh*-MEN-*it-zeh*)

cousin	*kuzin* (m.) (koo-ZIN)
	kuzineh (f.) (koo-ZEE-neh)
	shvesterkind (SHVES-ter-kind)
grandchild	*aynekel* (ANE-ek-el)
grandchildren	*ayneklach* (ANE-ek-lekh)
grandfather	*zayde* (ZAY-deh)
grandmother	*bubbe* (BAW-beh or BUB-beh)
great-grandfather	*elter zayde* (EHL-ter ZAY-deh)
great-grandmother	*elter bubbe* (EHL-ter BAW-beh)
great-grandchild	*ur-aynekel* (oor-ANE-ek-el)
great-grandchildren	*ur-ayneklach* (oor-ANE-ek-lekh)

The Family-by-Marriage

father-in-law	*shver* (SHVAYR)
mother-in-law	*shviger* (SHVI-ger)
brother-in-law	*shvoger* (SHVAW-ger)
sister-in-law	*shvegerin* (SHVEH-geh-rin)
son-in-law	*aidem* (AID-'m)
daughter-in-law	*shnur* (SHNOOR or SHNEE-air)

For relationships via marriage, *machuten, machetayne-ste* and *machetunim* (q.v.) offer excellent words for which there are no English equivalents.

Chase Manhattan Bank's memorable advertising campaign is built around the slogan "You have a friend at Chase Manhattan."

'Tis said that a sign in the window of a bank next to a Chase Manhattan branch read:

"—BUT HERE YOU HAVE MISHPOCHE!"

mitzva
mitzve
mitzvah
mitzvas   (plural)
mitzvoth   (plural, Hebrew)

A most important word in Yiddish. Pronounced MITZ-*veh*, to rhyme with "fits a"; the plural, *mitzvoth*, is pronounced MITZ-*vas*. Hebrew: "commandment."

1. Commandment; divine commandment.
2. A meritorious act, one that expresses God's will.

3. A "good work," a truly kind, considerate, ethical deed.

Mitzva is second only to Torah in the vocabulary of Judaism. The Talmud elaborates the concept in many places.

Mitzvas are of various kinds: those of positive performance (caring for the widow and orphan) and those of negative resolve (not accepting a bribe); those between man and God (fasting on Yom Kippur), and those between man and man (paying a servant promptly); those that specify the duties required of rabbis, and those that state the special sympathy for suffering required of any Jew. *Mitzvas* are regarded as profound obligations, as inescapable burdens—yet must be performed not from a sense of duty but with "a joyous heart."

The rabbis often used the phrase *simcha shel mitzva* (the joy of fulfilling a pious act, or commandment) to hammer home the notion that good deeds that are performed out of a sense of duty are not as meaningful as those performed out of desire. One sage said that God prefers the joy to the *mitzva*. (How the wise man found this out, I do not know.)

It has been said that the basic principle of Jewish ethics lies in the idea of mandatory *mitzvas*. Israel Zangwill called *mitzvoth* the Jews' "sacred sociology."

If you do something honorable, especially kind or considerate, a Jew may beam, "Oh, that was a *mitzva!*" or "You performed a real *mitzva!*"

One *mitzva* leads to another.
The reward of a *mitzva*? Another *mitzva*.
   —Folk sayings

At the end of a pier in Tel Aviv, a man was about to jump into the sea. A policeman came running up to him. "No, no!" he cried. "How can you, in the very prime of life, think of jumping into the water?"

"Because I can't stand it any more! I don't want to live!"

"But listen, mister, *please*," pleaded the policeman. "If you jump in the water, I'll have to jump in after you, to try to save you. Right? Well, *I can't swim!* Do you know what that means? I have a wife and four children. And in the line of duty, I would drown! Would you want to have such a terrible thing on your conscience? . . . No, I'm sure. So be a good Jew, and do a real *mitzva*. Go home. And in the privacy and comfort of your own home, *hang* yourself.''

———

Ari Lovitz stood before the Admitting Angel anxiously. And the Admitting Angel exclaimed, "But this is fantastic! This is unprecedented. In your entire lifetime did you not commit *one* little sin?"

"I tried to live in virtue," faltered Mr. Lovitz. "As a God-fearing man . . ."

"But not one—little—sin? In an entire lifetime?" sputtered the Admitting Angel. "We *can't* let you into Heaven. No, no. You must be *human*, subjected to temptation . . . at least once. So, I am going to send you back to Earth for twenty-four hours. During that time, you must commit at least *one little sin*, Mr. Lovitz . . . It is now seven A.M.!"

The bewildered innocent found himself back on Earth, determined to take one step from the path of righteousness. An hour passed, then two, then three; poor Mr. Lovitz simply could find no opportunity to commit a sin.

Then a buxom woman winked at him. . . . Mr. Lovitz responded with alacrity. The lady was neither young nor beautiful—but she *was* willing. And when she blushingly hinted that he might spend the night with her, Mr. Lovitz was in sixth heaven.

At last, in bed, having truly sinned, in the wee hours— Mr. Lovitz looked at his watch: only one more hour before the Angel would whisk him back to heaven . . . only half an hour . . .

And as Mr. Lovitz put on his clothes, preparing for his return to the celestial region, his blood turned to ice—for the old maid in bed sighed, "Oh, Lovitz, Lovitz—what a *mitzva* you performed this night!"

See also BAR MITZVA, BAS MITZVA, DAVEN.

mizrach
mizrachi

Pronounced MIZZ-*rokh*, with the Germanic *kh* sound as in "*Ach!*" Hebrew: *mizrach*: "east," "sunrise." (For *Mizrachi*, see below.)

A framed picture that hangs on the wall of every House of Study (or *Bes Midrash*) and in front of the synagogue lectern from which the Torah readings are delivered.

The *mizrach*, which is beautifully embroidered, is intended simply to show the congregation in which direction to face while praying—the direction always being where Jerusalem is. Thus, Jews in Persia or China or India turn to the west when praying.

Fifty years ago, a *mizrach* adorned many a Jewish home; not so today.

————

Mizrach is the name of an organization of Orthodox Jews, staunch Zionists, who conduct much fund-raising for Israel. The *Mizrachi* were important in Hebrew education in America, and *very* important in working for the creation of an independent Jewish state in Palestine.

mnyeh
m'nye

This euphonic quasi-expletive would simply *flourish* in Yinglish. Pronounced *m'n*-YEH. A sonic marvel.

1. Maybe—maybe not.
2. Who knows?
3. What difference does it make?
4. N-no.
5. I should live so long.
6. You should live so long.
7. Don't you be*lieve* it!
8. Nonsense! . . .
9. That's what *you* say!
10. Well, what can you expect?

The range, subtleties and dialectical force of *mnyeh* are rivaled only by such Yinglish All-American winners as *oy, nu, feh* and *aiai-ai*!

A master of intonation, such as my father was, can make *mnyeh* jump through hoops of deft sarcasm, polite dubiety, heartless deflation, ironic dismissal or icy derision.

Just match the definitions above to the illustrations below:

1. "Aren't you anxious to go to the lecture?"
   "Mnyeh."
2. "Are they going to get married? What's your opinion?"
   "Mnyeh."
3. "Who do you think will be the new chairman?"
   "Mnyeh."
4. "Are you coming to Julie's?"
   "Mnyeh."
5. "I hear you're going to buy a Lincoln."
   "Mnyeh."
6. "I am going to win the lottery, I'm *sure!*"
   "Mnyeh."
7. "They say your son is in trouble . . ."
   "Mnyeh."
8. "I hear you've won a lot at gin rummy."
   "Mnyeh."
9. "Casper is a cinch for Treasurer."
   "Mnyeh."
10. "Wasn't it terrible about Ira and Mildred?"
    "Mnyeh."

Mr. Offits said to Mr. Plotkin, a prominent lawyer, "I want to retain you on an important case, *if* you are positive I'll win!"

"Let's hear the facts," said Mr. Plotkin.

Mr. Offits gave a careful account of the case, which involved a written agreement and his partner's duplicity. "So—can I sue and get back all my money?"

"Absolutely!" said Mr. Plotkin. "I've *rarely* heard such an open-and-shut case!"

Offits made a sour face. *"Mnyeh."* He stood up to leave.

"What's the matter?"

Offits sighed. "I told you *his* side of the story!"

mockery through repetition

Yinglish.

A very popular form of ridicule in television's sitcoms. Actors love it because the ploy permits expressions not called for by a simple "yes" or "I do."

No sarcasm is more devastating than that which answers a question simply by repeating it to the questioner:

Q: Do you like cheesecake?
A: Do I like cheesecake?

What the answerer means, put bluntly, is: "What sort of *idiot* goes around asking people if they like cheesecake?" Or if you prefer: "What kind of dope does *not* like cheesecake?"

The question-repeated is a double-edged sword, for it also cuts in reverse, namely, "What kind of person do you think I am? Some creep who *doesn't* like cheesecake?"

At this point some readers may cavil: "But surely this is English? Why classify it as Yinglish?"

Well, the words are English; the syntax is English; but the force and function are Yinglish. The intonation, inflection and expressions accompanying the seemingly straight-forward echo surround the answer with accusatory ridicule: "Surely you can't mean what you've just asked: just listen to the words . . ." And *that* brand of fraudulent literalness is a feature of Jewish parlance.

Another way of making my point: Was it not the persistent deployment of this ploy by Jewish writers/comedians that rooted and nourished it in the soil of English?

See also ACCENTUATING DISAGREEMENT . . . , ACCUSING SOMEONE OF IDIOCY . . . , CASTING DOUBT . . .

mockery via bland, "innocent"
interrogation

"For that she wants to be *paid*?"

"Would a hundred thousand dollars soothe his hurt feelings?"

———

"These young barbarians!" exclaimed Walter. "Dope, booze, no *morals*!"

"Terrible," agreed Norman. "They hop into bed with any bum!"

"*I* didn't sleep with my wife until we were married! . . ." said Walter. "How about you?"

Norm thought for a moment, then looked at Walter. "I can't remember . . . What was her maiden name?"

See also CONCURRENCE AS A VEHICLE FOR SARCASM, EX-
PRESSING CONTEMPT . . . , UNDERLINING THE ABSURDITY
OF A QUESTION . . .

mockie
mockey

A well-established (unfortunately) Yinglish vulgarism.
Origin unknown.

A nasty synonym for *Jew*.

Don't confuse *mockie* with *moxey*, which you will find
elsewhere in this lexicon.

No one seems to know where *mockie* comes from. I
never heard *mockie* until I came to New York: In my innocence, I thought it meant courage or guts. (I was confusing
mockie with *moxey*, *q.v.*)

The list of derogatory appellations for a descendant of
Abraham is long: *Abie, Ikey, Izzy, Jake, kike, motzer,
sheeny, shonacker, shnozzle, shnozzola, Yid, Yiddisher*.

But before you conclude that the Chosen People are
chosen for special opprobrium, consult section #385 in
Berrey and van den Bark's monumental *American Thesaurus of Slang*. The list of offensive names for everyone from
an Australian to a Zionist would fill five of these pages.

See also HEBE, KIKE, MOXEY, YID.

Mogen David
Mogen Dovid

Often appears in English print and conversations. Pronounced MAW-*ghen* DU-*vid* or DAW-*vid*. Hebrew:
"Shield of David."

1. The six-pointed Star of David.
2. The symbol of the nation of Israel.
3. The shield of King David.

No one is sure when the Star of David came into use as
a symbol of Jewry. No reference to the *Mogen David* is
found in rabbinical writings until the thirteenth century; the
first Jewish association did not occur until the seventeenth.
(Sorry.)

The double triangle, making a six-pointed star, seems to

have been first used in amulets, on a shield, to protect the wearer from evil forces from all six directions. "*Six* directions?" you ask, grinning? Certainly: north, south, east, west—up and down.

In time the symbol was used to decorate sacred objects: a *talis*, the *tefillen* cover, the wrapping around the scrolls of the Torah. During the Middle Ages, the *Mogen David* won popularity as a talisman for warriors, and as a family escutcheon.

mohel

See MOYL.

mole

See MOYL.

molech

See MALECH.

momzer
mamzarim   (plural)

A quintessential Yiddish word, now invading Yinglish. Pronounced MOM-*zer*; rhymes with "bombs her." Hebrew: "bastard." Plural pronounced *mom-*ZAY-*rim*.

1. A bastard, illegitimate.
   "She left home and gave birth to a *momzer*."
2. An untrustworthy person.
   "I wouldn't trust that *momzer*."
3. A stubborn, difficult, dislikable man.
   "How can you get anywhere with such a stubborn *momzer*?"

But Jews also use *momzer* in a rather affectionate way:

4. A clever, quick, skillful fellow.
   (Admiringly) "Oh, is he a *momzer*!"
5. An impudent sort.
   "Imagine such nerve: what a *momzer*!"
6. An irreverent (but not offensive) character; a scalawag.
   "That *momzer* brings life to any party."

Momzer is often used to describe a very bright child, a clever or ingenious person, a resourceful gets-things-done, corner-cutting type.

"Most bastards are bright," observed Abba Saul. In many other cultures, bastards are believed to be exceptionally clever.

A proud grandfather may beam, "My grandson, *smart*? He's a regular *momzer*!"

Mothers are less likely to employ the word—at least about their own—and consider *momzer* a vulgar word, not to be used in "mixed company" or without blushing. (Perhaps they remember the caustic adage: "When a mother calls her child a *momzer*, you can believe her.")

CAUTION: Don't call anyone a *momzer* to his face unless you are on friendly terms, and don't call a child a *momzer* unless you're sure Papa or Mamma will not be offended.

The Jews' reverence for learning is seen in the *Mishnah*'s judgment: "A learned bastard stands higher than an ignorant high priest" (*Horayot*, 3, 8).

Julie kept trying to persuade Ethel to come to his apartment—and she kept refusing.

"Why *not*?" he persisted.

The girl blushed. "Well, I just know I'd—hate myself in the morning."

"So sleep *late*," suggested Julie.

(He was a *momzer*.)

A *momzer* I know likes to discombobulate barbers who annoy him by talking too much. When they finish their ministrations and hold the mirror behind his head for approval, he studies the reflected image, then says, "N-no. A little longer in back, please."

The woman on the phone sounded hysterical: "Doctor, doctor, my baby just swallowed *six aspirins*!"

"Oh, is she flushed?"

"No, but—"

"Did she throw up?"

"No, no, but—"

"Is she drowsy or sleeping?"

"No. But, *Doc*tor, *six aspirins*! What should I do?"

Said the doctor: "Try to give her a headache."

———

A lovely but lonely, miserable girl, walking along the East River, suddenly decided to end it all.

She was poised to jump from the pier when a sailor shouted, "No! No! Miss! *Don't!*" He ran up to her and pulled her to safety. "How can you even *think* of doing such a terrible thing?"

Weeping, the girl told him of her plight. "I want to go home . . . to Puerto Rico."

The sailor thought for a moment. "My boat is a freighter. We make many stops, but San Juan is our final port . . . I can hide you in one of the lifeboats. I'll bring you food and water . . ."

In the pitch of the moonless darkness that night, the sailor smuggled the girl aboard and hid her under the tarpaulin of a lifeboat. And soon he brought her food. And after that he began to share his meals with her.

And after four nights, the sailor and his stowaway made love . . . For three weeks, they made love.

One morning, the captain of the vessel discovered the girl in the lifeboat. She told him her story. "Puerto Rico?" frowned the captain. "What low-down sailor—what *momzer*—"

"How can you *talk* that way?" cried the girl. "He is kind and good and—"

"And you," said the captain, "are on the Staten Island Ferry!"

See also A.M., BUMMER, LOW-LIFE.

moxey
moxie

A staple of Yinglish among Jews in the Bronx and on the Lower East Side. Rhymes with "Coxey." Derivation: completely baffling. Do not confuse *moxey* with *mockie* (*q.v.*)

1. Nerve, brass, know-how, *chutzpah*.
2. Courage, guts.

3. "Street-smart," shrewd.
4. Resourceful.
5. A very popular soft drink in New York (no longer).

Moxey is used a good deal in sports circles. It was used by Dashiell Hammett to describe the brashness of a young prizefighter.

"So—eh—Mr. Shumacher," asked Mrs. Krementz coquettishly, "how old do you think I *am*?"

"Mrs. Krementz," replied Mr. Shumacher, "you certainly don't look it!"

Solly Ziegel was a compulsive gambler and a constant loser. His wife warned him that if he gambled once more she would leave him.

Business took Solly to Florida for three days. And for three nights he participated in poker games. He lost everything but his return ticket.

On the plane back to New York, Solly pondered long and hard how to keep his wife from learning the truth . . .

When he got off the plane, he went to a men's shop, bought a red handkerchief and took a taxi home. At the door, he tied the red handkerchief around his face—then rang the bell.

His wife opened the door. "Solly! Oh, my God! What *happened*?"

"I was mugged! By three men. They put a knife to my throat. Said unless I gave them every penny, *they would cut off my nose!*"

Mrs. Ziegel fell to the floor in a faint.

Solly got some ice. The red handkerchief he kept on.

When his wife came to, she gasped. "Oh, God. Without a nose! . . . Solly, Solly—why didn't you give them all your money?!"

Solly removed the kerchief, grinning, "I did."

(You wanted an example of *moxey*? That's an example of *moxey*.)

Old Mr. Karpas stared at the waiter who was placing the soup before him. "Are you the same vaiter who took mine order?"

"Yeah."

"Are you *sure*?"

"Sure I'm sure," huffed the waiter. "Why do you ask such a question?"

"Because by now, I expected a much older man . . ."

(Now *there* is moxey.)

————

Jack Freeman was late returning from lunch.

His boss, Mr. Oskin, snapped, "You're over an hour late!"

"That's true," said Freeman.

"Would you mind giving me a hint *why*?" asked Mr. Oskin sarcastically.

"I was having my hair cut."

"Your *hair* cut? Do you think you ought to do that on company time?"

"Why not?" said Freeman. "The hair *grew* on company time."

Mr. Oskin's eyes narrowed: "That hair didn't *all* grow on company time!"

"T-true," said Freeman. "That's why I didn't have it all cut off."

————

Hilda Gans, a pretty model, skipped up the stairs to the studio of Shelley Kleinfeld, for whom she was posing in the nude. She entered the studio with a bright "Good morning."

"Hilda," sighed Kleinfeld, "don't undress. I'm not feeling right. I don't feel like working. . . . Let's have some coffee. We'll get back to the painting tomorrow."

They were having coffee, chatting, when Shelley suddenly froze: Footsteps were heard coming up the stairs.

The painter listened, put down his cup, and said, with superlative *moxey*, "My wife! Hilda, quick, take off your clothes!"

See also AMERICA GONIF!, BOYCHIK, BUMMER, CHUTZPA.

moyl (as pronounced)
mohel (as properly spelled)
mole (absurdly spelled)

Must become Yinglish, because English lacks an exact analogue. Rhymes with "Boyle" (and if you ever hear of a *moyl* named Boyle, phone me). Unwary souls who know no Yiddish sometimes pronounce it *mole*. Hebrew: *circumcizer*.

The professional who circumcises a male baby born of a Jewish mother on the eighth day after his birth. The ritual is called *Brith Milah*: "the circumcision covenant" (Genesis 17:7–12).

Oriental Jews perform this ceremony in a synagogue. In the West, the *brith* (or *bris, q.v.*) takes place at home or in the hospital.

———————

No story I ever heard struck me as so triumphant as the classic about the Englishman in New York who stopped at a window in the middle of which stood—a clock.

The Englishman went inside. "Hel-lo!" he sang out.

From behind a curtain stepped a bearded man in a skull-cap.

"Would you please inspect this watch?" The Englishman worked at the strap. "Tell me whether it needs—"

"Why are you asking me?" asked the bearded one. "I don't fix watches. I'm a *moyl*."

"A what?"

"A *moyl*. I make circumcisions."

"Good Lord!" exclaimed the Englishman. "But why do you have a *clock* in your window?"

"Mister," sighed the *moyl*, "what would *you* put in the window?"

———————

The *mohel* holds no hallowed spot in the Jewish hierarchy of respect. He is regarded as a technician. (God *forbid* he should perform any other type of surgery!)

Like cantors, *mohels* are often the butt of Jewish jokes.

See also BRIS.

N

naches (noun)
nakhes

A Yiddish word much needed in English—rich, large and varied though our language is. Pronounced NOKH-*ess*, to rhyme with "Loch Ness"—with the *kh* sound a Scot would use in pronouncing *loch*. Hebrew: *nachat*: "contentment."

1. Proud pleasure; special joy—particularly from the achievements of a child.

Jews use *naches* to describe the glow of pleasure-plus-pride that only a child can give its parents.

"I have such *naches*: My son is chief of his play group."
"Are you *shepping* [getting] *naches* from your daughter's career?"

2. Psychological reward or gratification.
(I am getting *naches* from writing this book, since a new book is indeed a brainchild.)

"Tell me," asked Mrs. Gershik, "what ever happened to your son?"

"My son—what a misfortune!" wailed Mrs. Tanzer. "He married—a disaster! She doesn't lift a *finger* around the house! She can't cook, she can't sew a button on a shirt; all she does is sleep late. My poor boy even brings her breakfast in bed! And all day long she stays there, loafing . . ."

"How terrible," said Mrs. Gershik. "And what about your daughter?"

"Ah, my daughter!" beamed Mrs. Tanzer. "She married a man—an *angel*! He won't let her set *foot* in the kitchen! He gives her a full-time maid, a cook, and every morning *he* brings her breakfast in bed! And he makes her stay in bed all day . . ."

Mrs. Herman and Mrs. Gerges were exchanging *naches* about their children. "My son?" said Mrs. Herman. "Who could ask for a better boy? Every Friday, he eats dinner at my house. Every summer, he makes me spend a month with him in the country. Every winter, he sends me to a hotel in Florida."

To which Mrs. Gerges replied, "*I* have a son, an angel. For a whole year, he's been going to the most expensive psychiatrist in New York. Every day, month in and out, he goes there. And he talks—each day—for an hour. And do you know what he talks about, paying *fifty dollars an hour*?! . . . Me!"

See also KVELL.

---

nayfish (noun)
nafish
nefish

A percipient character description that pops up from time to time in fiction or essays written by Jewish authors. Pronounced NAY-*fish*, to rhyme with "crayfish." From Hebrew: "a being," "person," "soul."

1. An innocent.
2. A person of no consequence—weak, ineffectual, pathetic.
3. A contemptible or cowardly sort.

A *nayfish* is clearly a clone of a *shlemiel* (*q.v.*).

A *nayfish* handed the druggist a prescription. The druggist gave him three little bottles of pills.

"All these?" asked the *nayfish*. "What are they for?"

"The red ones calm your nerves; the white ones relieve your headache; the blue ones are for asthma."

"Amazing. Such little pills and each one knows exactly what to do!"

———

The *nayfish* demanded: "Mr. Schlaum, either you give me a twenty-dollar raise—or else!"

"Or else what?"

"Or else—I'll work at the same salary."

See also DOPPESS, FEYGELE, NEBECH, SHLEMIEL, SHLIMA-ZEL, SHMEGEGGE, SHMO, SHNOOK.

nebech (noun and interjection)
nebbech
nebbish
neb (abbreviation; an apocope)
nebochem (plural)
nebechel (diminutive)

A quintessential Yiddish word—and triumphant characterization. A stellar contribution to Yinglish. Pronounced NEB-*ekh* or NEB-*ikh*, with the *kh* as sounded by Scots or Germans, not the *ch* of "choo-choo." From Czech: *neboky*.

In recent years, no doubt to help the laryngeally unagile, the pronunciation NEB-*bish* (note the *sh*) has gained currency. The word is even spelled *nebbish*, notably in a collection of cartoons on cocktail napkins, matchbooks, ashtrays and, for all I know, Cape Cod lighters. My feeling is that *nebbish* should be used only by people unable to clear their throats.

Nebech has a provenance that stretches back to the fifteenth century. (See Max Weinreich, *History of the Yiddish Language*.)

As an interjection, *nebech* means:

1. Alas, too bad, unfortunately, "the poor thing."
   "He went to the doctor, *nebech*."

"She, *nebech*, didn't have a dime."

In this usage, *nebech* expresses:

a. Sympathy: "He lost his job, *nebech*."
b. Regret: "They asked me, *nebech*, to break the sad news."
c. Dismay: "He looked, *nebech*, like a ghost!"
d. Poor thing: "His wife, *nebech*, has to put up with him."

You never say *nebech* about something you welcome, enjoy, are happy to report or are glad about. Hence the irony of this: "What would make me the happiest man in the world? To be sitting on a park bench in the sun, saying to my best friend, "Look! There, *nebech*, goes Hitler."

As a noun, *nebech* is an expressive name for a kind of person found in any culture:

2. An innocuous, ineffectual, weak, helpless or hapless unfortunate.
3. A Sad Sack, a "loser." First cousin to a *shlemiel* (*q.v.*).
4. A namby-pamby.
5. A nonentity, "a nothing of a person."

To define a *nebech* simply as an unlucky man is to miss the many nuances, from pity to contempt, the word affords: "When a *nebech* leaves the room, you feel as if someone fascinating just came in!"

A *nebech* is sometimes defined as the kind of person who always picks up—what a *shlemiel* knocks over.

A *nebech* is more to be pitied than a *shlemiel*. You feel sorry for a *nebech*; you *can* dislike a *shlemiel*.

Stories, jokes, and wisecracks about the *nebech* are, by careful count, countless.

As the apothegm has it: "A man is, *nebech*, only a man."

My favorite definition of a *nebech* is this: "A *nebech* is the one in a group you always forget to introduce."

"Officer, Officer!" the driver called from his car on Thirty-eighth Street.

A policeman sauntered over. "Yeah?"

"Officer, is it okay for me to park here?"

"Absolutely not."

"But, Officer," the *nebech* protested. "How about all those other cars—parked up and down the whole street?!"

"They," said the cop, "didn't ask."

"Doctor Mertz," the *nebech* complained, "why doesn't anyone ever pay attention to me? My wife, my children, my friends—I might as well not even *be* here, the way they just don't listen to anything I say. Why, Doctor? Why?"

Dr. Mertz thought for a moment, stepped to his door, and loudly called into the waiting room, "Next!"

Yuri Smolenski, the last Jewish engineer in the Commissariat on Electrical Energy, had been ordered to move to a minor post in a faraway, godforsaken Siberian outpost.

His parents, in tears, were watching him pack.

"I'll write every day," said Yuri.

"But the censorship," wailed his mother. "They'll watch every word."

Yuri's father said, "I have an idea. Anything you write in black, we'll know is true. But anything you put in red ink, we'll know is nonsense!"

A month passed; then from Siberia came a long letter—all in black ink!

Dear Mama and Papa,

I can't tell you how happy I am here. It is a workers' paradise! We are treated like kings. I live in a fine apartment—and the local butcher has meat every single day! There are many concerts, theater, movies—all free. And there is not one tiny bit of anti-Semitism!

Your son,
Yuri

P.S. There is only one thing, *nebech*, you can't find here: red ink.

See also DOPPESS, NAYFISH, SHLEMIEL, SHLIMAZEL, SHMEGEGGE, SHMO, SHMUCK, SHNOOK.

nefish

See NAYFISH.

nexdoorekeh (feminine)
nexdooreker (masculine)

Exemplary Yinglish. Pronounced *neks*-DOR-*eh-keh*. Rhymes with "Sex Florida."

The female neighbor who lives next door: "My *nexdoorekeh* is very friendly."

The masculine form, for a male neighbor, is *nexdooreker*.

This is a good example of how deftly newly arrived Jews adopted and adapted English to their needs. *Nexdoorekeh* is a crisp, economic way of saying "the woman who lives next door to me," just as *donstairsiker* (*q.v.*) is a toothsome way of saying "the man who lives below me."

I once had a *nexdooreker* who told me this memorable story:

Two *shlemiels* were discussing the meaning of life and death. Finally, one sighed: "Considering how many heartaches and sorrows and pains life holds, death is really no misfortune. In fact, I think sometimes it's better for a man not to have been born at all!"

"True," the other nodded. "But how many people do you meet who were that lucky?"

Neturey Karta

Pronounced *ne*-TU (as in "put")-*rie* KAR-*ta*. Rhymes with "pet jury parka." Aramaic: guardians of the city.

A Jewish sect that refuses to recognize Israel as an independent state, and periodically attacks Zionism as "the enemy of the Jews."

Ultra-Orthodox Jews maintain that Israel, a holy sovereignty, can only be established by the (*meshiach*) Messiah—and the Messiah has surely not yet come.

In Israel, these Jews stone automobiles that move about on the Sabbath and curse male Jewish tourists who do not wear a hat or *yarmulke*. The hysterical mass demonstrations against Israel by the American *Neturey Karta* are familiar to New Yorkers. An advertisement of the group attacked Israel:

> The Jewish nation was not founded by Zionist politicians . . . but was determined on Mount Sinai. . . . The Jewish redemption will come with the coming of the Meshiach. The establishment of the Zionist state before that time is heretic and indeed blasphemous.
> —*New York Times*, May 15, 1981

-nik (suffix intensifier)
-nick

Hurrah for Yinglish, to whose bosom *-nik* is firmly clasped. Pronounced NICK. From Slavic languages. I prefer the *-nik* spelling.

A suffix particle that converts a verb, noun or adjective into an emphatic characterization of an ardent practitioner, believer, lover, cultist or devotee of something.

-nik lends itself to delightful *ad hoc* inventions. A *sicknik* would be one who fancies "sick" or "black" humor. A *Freudnik* would be an uncritical acolyte of the father of psychoanalysis. And homosexuals refer to heterosexuals, with some amusement, as straightniks. In Las Vegas, compulsive slot-machine helots are "slotniks."

NOTE: I prefer the *-nik* to the *-nick* spelling because in Yiddish the single letter *k* is more than adequate. Besides, there are no *ck*'s; in fact, there are no *c*'s in Yiddish, since *k* takes care of the unvoiced stop consonant.

———

PEACENIK: Why don't the leaders of the world realize that nations can solve all their problems if they just decide to live together like one big family?
CYNIC: God forbid.

no-good (noun)
no-goodnik

Firmly and viably established in Yinglish/English. Pronounced *no*-GOOD-*nik*, to rhyme with "so good, Nick."

This mutation borrows the phrase "no-good" and adds the stalwart Slavic suffix *-nik*.

1. Someone who is "no good": unethical, irresponsible, undependable. A man who does not keep his word or honor his obligations.
2. One who does not earn an honest living; a wastrel; a drifter.
3. A shady character; a bum; a low-life; a be-careful-you-shouldn't-get-involved-with-that-type type.
4. A petty lawbreaker; a trickster; a cheat.

"Remember Mrs. Schatz, she had three sons? *Nu*, the oldest became an *alrightnik*, he lives in Scarsdale; the second went to Columbia, he became a Ph.D.; but the *boychick*, who does who-knows-what-for-a-living, turned out a real *no-goodnik*! From him, be sure, Mrs. Schatz will never get *naches*."

KAHN: You are a no-good! You went back on your word!
TARSHER: I resent that! In my whole life, did you ever hear my honesty questioned?
KAHN: Questioned? I never even heard it *men*tioned!

It shook me up, recently, "more than somewhat" (to use Damon Runyon's dry coinage), to learn that there is a Russian word *negodnik* which means exactly what *no-goodnik* means. It may well have been, therefore, that Russian immigrants to New York would say that someone was a *negodnik*—and the non-Russian Jew would take it for granted that the greenhorn was saying "no-goodnik." After all, the two nouns ran on identical tracks to mean exactly the same kind of person. Never underestimate the element of surprise, or the bizarre Burbankism, of philology.

no one here to talk to
There's no one here to talk to!

I yearn to draft this into Yinglish. Hyperbole from Yiddish: *Nito tsu vemen tsu reydn*!—which deserves wider usage by Yinglishmen.

1. It's useless for me to talk to you: you refuse to listen.
2. You are not *capable* of understanding!
3. You are too stubborn; why waste my breath trying to reason with you?
4. You really don't *exist*: you're too stupid!

The words are English and the syntax ordinary: What then makes the content Yinglish? The rhetorical murder of everyone except the aggrieved speaker.

Dr. Soloway spent a full hour on his examination, then said, "You are in *excellent* shape. In fact, to me you look like a man who could live to be eighty!"

"That's nice," said the patient.

"Nice? Only 'nice'?! My God! Is there no one here to *talk* to? Do you know how few people who come to this office are as healthy as you?! By the way, how old *are* you?"

"Eighty-one."

"See?" cried Dr. Soloway. "What did I tell you?!"

See also GO TALK TO THE WALL, WHO KNOWS?

noo-noo . . .

See NU.

nosh (verb and noun)
nosher (noun)
noshen (verb)
nosherei (noun)
noshery (noun)

So firmly established in Yinglish is *nosh* that you will find the word in many English dictionaries—especially those with editions published since 1950. Rhyme, respectively, with "gosh," "josher," "joshin'." German: *naschen*, "to eat on the sly."

Nosh
1. A snack, a tidbit, a "bite," a small portion.
2. Anything eaten between meals and, presumably, in small quantity—fruit, a cookie, "a piece cake," a candy.

Jews loved to *nosh* long before they ever went to a cocktail party.

Nosher
1. One who eats between meals.
2. One who has a sweet tooth.
3. One who is weak-willed about food and dieting.

Noshen
To *nosh* is to "have a little bite to eat before dinner is ready," or to "have a little something between meals."

"I came in to find her *noshing*."
"He's used to *noshing* after midnight."

Noshery
An assortment or display of nosh delicacies.

Many delicatessen counters today display plates with small slices of salami or pieces of halvah, with a little flag affixed to a toothpick, reading, "Have a *nosh*."

"Noshery" is a neologism for places that sell comestibles to *nosh*. The first "*Noshery*" sign I ever saw was in (of all places!) London, c. 1960.

See also EAT A LITTLE SOMETHING.

Nova

Yinglish—flatly, firmly. Abbreviation for Nova Scotia salmon, a delicacy much prized by Jews—less salty (and much more expensive) than lox (*q.v.*).

Nova on a toasted bagel smeared with cream cheese is one of the masterpieces of Jewish cuisine, a feature of Sunday brunches from Easthampton to Santa Monica.

SCENE: **A Famous Deli**

CUSTOMER: Waiter. This salmon. Is it from a can?
WAITER: A *can*?! Mister, this salmon comes from Nova Scotia!
CUSTOMER: Uh, was it imported or *de*ported?

See also BAGEL, DELI, LOX.

Now—

Ironic prefactory remark, well established in Yinglish.

"He turned us down five times, so we went elsewhere and got the stock for less. *Now* he says he'll accept our offer!"

"Last December I wanted to take her to Palm Beach, when it was below zero in New York and eighty in Florida. Today, it's a beautiful day in New York and ninety-eight in Palm Beach. *Now* she wants to go!"

The nuclear complaint packed into that simple, one-syllable *now* is an example of Yinglish at its most acidulous.

Perhaps the most famous (and justified) deployment of the adverb followed the revelation that a soldier of the American army had undergone a change-of-sex operation in Denmark, to become Miss Christine Jorgenson.

In Jorgenson's old barracks, above the cot Jorgenson had recently occupied, this sign appeared:

NOW HE TELLS US!

nu
nu?
nu!
nu-nu?
noo-noo . . .

Rapidly winning favor among Yinglish *mavens*. The above variations are all pronounced NOO, to rhyme with "coo," but with various intonations and meanings. From Russian: *nu*: "well," "well now," etc. Cognates are common in Indo-European languages, but in none is the word put through such psychological acrobatics as in Yinglish.

A remarkably versatile and colorful exclamation, interjection, interrogation and expletive.

Nu is the word most frequently used (aside from *oy*) in spoken Yiddish. And with good reasons. *Nu* is the verbal equivalent of a sigh, a frown, a grin, a grunt, a sneer.

Nu is an expression of amusement or recognition or uncertainty or disapproval. It can be used fondly, acidly, tritely, belligerently.

Nu is a qualification, an emphasizer, an interrogation, a caster of doubt, an arrow of ire. It can convey pride or deliver scorn or demand response.

When used in tandem, as *nu-nu*, it carries another cargo of nuances.

Here are a score of shadings of this two-lettered miracle:

1. "*Nu?*" (Well?)
2. "I saw you come out of her apartment." "*Noo-oo?*" (So-so?)
3. "*Nu*, after such a plea, what could I do?" (Well, then.)
4. "*Nu?*" (How are things with you?)
5. "*Nu?*" (What's new?)
6. "I need the money . . . *Nu?*" (How about it?)
7. "—and he walked right out. *Nu?!*" (How do you like that?! Imagine!)
8. "I'm going to the dentist." "*Nu?*" (What's the hurry?)
9. "*Nu*, I guess that's all." (I'll be finishing or going along now.)
10. "—and you're supposed to be there by noon. *Nu?!*" (What are you waiting for?)
11. "—and I signed the contract. *Nu!*" (That's that!)
12. "*Nu-nu?*" (Come on, open up, tell me.)
13. "My wife was wondering what happened to the pot she lent you . . . *Nu?*" (I hate to mention it, but . . .)
14. "They doubled the rent! *Nu?*" (What can one do?)
15. "Did you or didn't you tell him. *Nu?!*" (I challenge you.)
16. "*Nu-nu*, my friend?" (One must resign oneself.)
17. "They all agreed with him. But I—*nu?*" (I, for one, am dubious.)
18. "They waited and waited. *Nu*, he finally showed up." (And so; in the course of time . . .)
19. "She accused him, he blamed her. *Nu*, it ended in court." (One thing led to another, and . . .)

Nu is so very Yiddish an interjection that it has become the one word that can identify a Jew. In fact, it is sometimes used just that way: instead of asking, "Are you Jewish?" one can say, "*Nu?*" (The answer is likely to be "*Nu-nu.*")

Sign over an ice machine in Miami Beach:

NOTICE
IF EVERYTHING ELSE YOU TRY DOESN'T WORK, *nu*— TRY READING THE DIRECTIONS.

Not until 11 A.M. did Al Kislin come to work—a bandage on his head, one arm in a sling.

The boss said, "You're two—hours—late!"

"Mr. Lipsky, I was trying to fix my screen—and I fell down three stories!"

"*Nu?* That takes *two hours?!*"

See also AI-AI-AI, MNEYH.

nudnik (noun)
nudnick

Often appears in Yinglish. Pronounced NOOD-*nick*, to rhyme with "could pick." *Nudnik* may come from the Russian *nudna*, but it has become as uniquely Yiddish a word as there is. It is sometimes pronounced as a palatalized NUD-*nyik* (just as *paskudnak* is often pronounced *poss-kood*-NYOK) by those who wish to add a vocal prolongation of distaste.

1. A pest, a nag, an annoyer.
2. A monumental bore.

A *nudnik* is not just a nuisance; to merit the status of *nudnik*, a nuisance must be a persistent, talkative, obnoxious and indefatigable nag.

I regard *nudnik* as a peerless word for the characterization of a universal type.

A mother often says to a child, "Stop bothering me. Don't be a *nudnik*!"

Sometimes *nudnik* is shortened to *nudzh*: one who bores, pesters, nags, annoys.

In the 1967 movie *You're a Big Boy Now*, the actress snaps at an adolescent who is stage-struck: "Don't be a *nudzh*!" The word is increasingly used in television sitcoms.

A derivative of *nudnik*, recently coined, covers the special category of pedantic or pedagogical bores: *phudnik*.
What is a *phudnik*? A *nudnik* with a Ph.D.

Mr. Polanski complained to his doctor, "Something terrible has happened to me. I try to stop it, but I can't . . . Morning, noon, and night—I keep talking to myself!"

"Now, now," the doctor crooned, "that isn't such a bad habit. Why, thousands of people do it."

"But, Doctor," protested Polanski, "do you know what a *nudnik* I am?!"

See also FIFER, FONFER, KIBITZER, KVETCH, NAYFISH, PLOSHER, SHLUMP, SHMEGEGGE.

nudzh (verb)
noodge

See NUDNICK.

nyotting

Recommended for special comic uses in Yinglish.
Pronounced *nee-*YOTT*-ing*. Fashioned by Jews from eastern Europe to accentuate meaning with playfulness.
Nothing.

A palatalized embellishment of "nothing": humorous embroidery, prolonging both utterance and enjoyment.

"Listen, Joe; are you having an affair with our new telephone operator?"

"You bet I am, Donald. I took her to a hotel last night—and I tell you, compared to her, my wife is *nyotting!*"

TWO WEEKS LATER

"Listen, Donald. Are *you* having an affair with our telephone operator?"

"*Am I!* And you were right, Joe: compared to her, your wife is *nyotting!*"

omeyn

See AMEN.

omission of preposition "of" or pronouns "who" or "that"

Yinglish. Ungrammatical, unaesthetic, undesirable.

Americans and Englishmen ask for a "cup of coffee" or "a glass of milk." Even in haste, they do not drop the preposition; they may resort to a slurred fusion: "cuppa" or "glassa."

But Yinglish speakers do not use the preposition at all, because in Yiddish it is impossible to say "a bowl *of* soup" or "a glass *of* milk." (*Many* languages have gotten rid of the parative genitive, you should excuse the expression.)

In American fiction and theater, the omission of *of* brands the speaker as (1) Jewish, (2) from New York, (3) not a college graduate, or (4) deliberately parodying the déclassé.

American journalism, to say nothing of oratory, is opening its arms wide to such barbarisms as "He is the type person. . . ." This type usage should positively be avoided: it is a type barbarism.

Nor is this all: misguided genteelism leads many a worthy innocent to favor such arch solecisms as:

"She's the type girl makes passes at your husband."
"Is he the kind fellow needs warning you're not the type allows liberties right off?"
"They're the style neighbors you wish on people want lots noise and excitement."

Oneg Shabbat

Hebrew: celebration of the Sabbath.

On the bulletin board of (and outside) many Conservative synagogues and Reform Temples an announcement of *Oneg Shabbat* weekly appears as a Saturday afternoon event. This cheerful assemblage is of recent origin: it was introduced by the great Hebrew poet Chaim Bialik (1873–1934).

See also SHABBES.

ongepotchket

Recommended for Yinglish. Pronounced AWN-*ge-potch-ket*, to rhyme with "Fonda Lodge Kit," or OON-ge-potch-kit. From Russian: *pachkat*: "to soil," "to sully."

1. Slapped together; assembled without form or sense.
2. Messed up; excessively and unesthetically decorated; overly baroque.
   "She wore her new diamond earrings, a necklace, bracelet, two rings and a brooch. *Oy*, was she *ongepotchket*!"

Gus Fleishman, a new art collector, bought a painting that was much admired by his friend Meyerson: the painting was one very large square of black, with a dot of white in the center.

A year later, Mr. Fleishman bought another painting by the same modernist genius: a large black square with *two* white dots.

Proudly, Fleishman hung the picture over his fireplace and telephoned his *maven* friend Meyerson to come right over.

Meyerson took one look at the picture and wrinkled his nose: "Frankly, Gus, I don't like it: too *ongepotchket*."

See also POTCH.

Only in America

Yinglish to a fare-thee-well, uttered with fervor and gratitude.

"Only in America!" is the immigrants' heartfelt affirmation of the opportunities, the freedom, the safety, the liberation from Old World prejudices and privileges that this sweet, blessed land has provided them. My boyhood rang with the sounds of this exclamatory tribute: upon hearing of some triumph of civil liberty; upon learning of a new, ingenious product (say, zippers); upon reading of some economic advance or technological miracle.

"*Galoshes?* Only in America!"
"A radio you can tune to hear the opera in New York? Only in America!"
"A Jew [Benny Leonard] lightweight boxing champion? Only in America!"

It is not at all surprising that the author of "God Bless America" was an East Side Jew, Irving Berlin (*né* Baline).

———————

Little Henry and Norman got into such a violent argument that little Norman cried out: "And, besides that—my *father can knock the kishkes out of your father!*"
Little Henry's jaw dropped. He looked stunned. He finally recovered long enough to sputter, "You crazy or somep'n? My father is also *your* father!!"
Only in Hollywood.

See also AMERICA GONIF!

out of this world

Very widely used—and emphatically Yinglish. From the Yiddish; possibly from the Yiddish: *an oysnam fun der velt*: "an exception from the world." A comparable Hebrew idiom states that something exceptionally pleasurable (sleep, sex) is a whiff of the "world to come"— *i.e.*, something "not of this world," hence "out of" it.

1. Beyond comparison.
   "What sort of singer is she?"
   "She's out of this *world*!"
2. Utterly unique.
   "How would you describe sex?" "It's just—out of this world."
3. Remarkable.
   "As a composer, he's out of this world."

Out of this world is exceptionally popular as a superlative.

———————

Here's a joke that is surely out of this world:

The great throng waited at the front of Mount Sinai. Moses had been gone for *hours*.

Suddenly his white robe was seen. Breathlessly, the Lawgiver stood before his flock: "People of Israel! I have been four hours with—*baruch ha-Shem*—the Lord! And I now come to you with—good news, and bad news . . . The good news is that I have managed to bring His Commandments down to—*ten!*"

A great cheer swept across the land.

"And O Moses, our Teacher," cried a patriarch, "what is the bad news?"

Moses fussed and clucked and cleared his throat. "The bad news? . . . Adultery is still in."

oy
oy-oy!
oy-oy-oy!

Yinglish of necessity. Perhaps the single most characteristic expletive/exclamation/declamation in all of Yiddish—and therefore Yinglish. Pronounced—well, how else *can* you pronounce it? The exclamation point is part of the spelling when *oy!* has a full head of steam.

The most expressive and ubiquitous exclamation/declamation in Yiddish.

Oy is not a word; it is a vocabulary. It is uttered in as many ways as the utterer's histrionic ability permits. It is a lament, a protest, a cry of dismay, a reflex of delight.

Oy is an expletive, an ejaculation, a threnody, a monologue. It may be employed to express anything from ecstasy to horror, depending on (a) the catharsis desired by the utterer, (b) the effect intended on the listener, (c) the protocol of affect that governs the intensity and duration of emotion required (by tradition) for the given occasion or crisis.

Oy is often used to lead off "*oy vay!*" which means, literally, "Oh, pain," but is used as an all-purpose ejaculation to express anything from trivial delight to abysmal woe. *Oy vay!* is the short form of "*Oy vay iz mir!*" (pronounced "*oy* VAY *iz meer*"), an omnibus phrase for everything from personal pain to empathetic condolence. (*Vay* comes from the German *Weh*, meaning "woe.")

Oy is also used in duet form, *oy-oy!*, or in a resourceful trio: *oy-oy-oy!* The individual *oy!*'s can play varying solo roles, to embellish subtleties of feeling: thus *OY!-oy-oy* or *oy, oy, OY! OY-oy!* can mean "And how!"

It is worth noting that *oy!* is not *ai!* and runs a decidedly different gamut of sensibilities. *Ai!* is also used in tandem ("*ai-ai!*)" and *à trois*, as the French (no novitiates in the *ai-ai-ai!* league) would put it.

As for the difference between *oy!* and *ah!*, there is (naturally) a saying to illustrate the distinction:

"When you jump into cold water you cry '*Oy!*' then, enjoying it, say 'a-aah.' When you commit a sin, you revel in the pleasure, 'a-aah'; then, realizing what you've done, you cry '*oy!*'"

Oy, accordingly, can be used to express:

1. Simple surprise. "When she saw me there, she said, '*Oy!* I didn't expect you!'"
2. Startledness. "She heard a noise and exclaimed, '*Oy!* Who's there?"
3. Small fear. "*Oy!* It could be a mouse!"
4. Minor sadness (sighed). "When I think of what you went through, all I can say is *oy-y*." (Note the *oy* prolonged, to indicate how sensitive one is to the troubles of others.)
5. Contentment. "*Oy*, was that a delicious dinner!"
6. Joy. "*Oy!* What a party!"
7. Euphoria. "Was I *happy? Oy!* I was dancing on air!"
8. Relief; reassurance. "*Oy*, now I can sleep."

9. Uncertainty. "What should I do? *Oy*, I wish I knew."
10. Apprehension. "Maybe he's sick? *Oy!*"
11. Awe. "He came back alive yet? *Oy!*"
12. Astonishment. "*Oy gevalt*, how he has changed!"
13. Indignation. "Take it away from me! *Oy!*"
14. Irritation. "*Oy*, is that some *metsieh* [bargain]!"
15. Irony. "*Oy*, have you got the wrong party!"
16. Pain (moderate). "*Oy*, it hurts."
17. Pain (serious). "*Oy, Gottenyu!*"
18. Revulsion. "*Feh!* Who could eat that? *Oy-y!*"
19. Anguish. "I beg you, *tell* me! *Oy!*"
20. Dismay. "*Oy*, I gained ten pounds!"
21. Despair. "It's hopeless, I tell you. *Oy!*"
22. Regret. "*Him* we have to invite? *Oy!*"
23. Lamentation. "*Oy*, we cried our eyes out."
24. Shock. "What? Her? Here? *Oy!*"
25. Outrage. "That man will never set foot in this house so long as I live! *Oy!*"
26. Horror. "—married a dwarf? *Oy gevalt!*"
27. Stupefaction. "My own partner . . . *oy-y-y*."
28. Flabbergastedness. "Who ever *heard* such a thing? *Oy!* I could *plotz!*"
29. At-the-end-of-one's-wittedness, or I-can't-stand-any-more. "Get out! Leave me alone! *O-O-Oy-y-y-y-y!*

There are certain similarities between *oy* and *gevalt!*—but the differences are greater. *Gevalt!* is rarely used for declamations of relief or pleasure, but is associated with "Help!" or "Oh, God!"

Distinguish *oy* from *ai* or even *ah!* (and *oy-oy* from *ay-yay-yay*).

Permit me to shed light: when you find a purse with $10,000 in bills, you shout "*Ay-yay-yay-yay-yay!*" When you find out they're counterfeit, you moan "*Oy-oy-oy-oy-y-y-y-y!*"

Mrs. Gittelman's phone rang.

"Hul-lo," a cultivated voice intoned, "I'm telephoning to ask if you and your husband can come to a tea for Lady Windermere—"

"*Oy*," Mrs. Gittelman cut in, "have *you* got the wrong number!"

SCENE: **A Restaurant in Hitler's Berlin**

Four Jews are in a coffee house, seated glumly before their *schlag*.

FIRST MAN: *Oy* . . .
SECOND MAN: *Oy, vay* . . .
THIRD MAN: *Vay iz mir* . . .
FOURTH MAN: If you three don't stop talking politics, I'll get out of here.

Old Hyman Sisselberg, crossing Fifth Avenue in front of St. Patrick's Cathedral, was knocked down by a hit-and-run driver.

He lay there; people crowded around him.

A priest pushed his way through the crowd, knelt beside Hyman Sisselberg, and quickly said, "My son, do you believe in God the Father, God the Son, and God the Holy Ghost?"

"Oy!" croaked Sisselberg. "I'm dying, and he asks me riddles!"

The television reporter asked Lewis Tykner, age eighty-four, "do you regret how you spent your life?"

"Oh, sure," said Mr. Tykner. "I spent a *lot* of money on fine wines, a lot at expensive restaurants, a lot on lovely women—and *oy!*—the rest I spent foolishly!"

See also AI-AI-AI, AMEN, GEVALT!, GOTT.

𝒫

pareveh

Often seen on food packages in kosher foods section of supermarkets. Pronounced PAAR-*eh-va*, to rhyme with "jar of a," or (more often) PAAR-*va*, to rhyme with "larva." From Russian: *parovoy*.

Neutral dietetically, therefore does not violate the *kosher* laws.

Pareveh foods include neither animal nor dairy products, and can therefore be eaten with either. (Jewish dietary laws dictate that meat and dairy foods may not be consumed at the same meal.) A *pareveh* cake can be made with fruit juice instead of milk and with vegetable fat substituted for butter.

Modern chemistry has expanded the roster of *pareveh* foods to include margarine made without milk solids or butter fat (often sold as "diet" margarine), as well as *pareveh* milk, cream and even ice cream, which is made with hydrogenated soy bean oil.

See also DAIRY, KOSHER.

paskudna   (adjective)
paskudnak   (masculine)
paskudnika   (feminine)
paskudnyak   (masculine and feminine)

I urge every Yinglishman to learn and use these extraordinary, peerless appellations. No word in English remotely approaches *paskudnak* for greasy contumely. Pronounce it *poss-kood-*NOOK, and with full fruitness: *poss-kood-*NYOK, slurring the *n* into the *Y* as in *canyon*, to rhyme with "Joss would nyok." From Polish/Ukrainian: "nasty," "dirty." Pronounced with the palatalized *Y* adds greatly to *paskudnak*'s nauseous distaste.

1. A man or woman who is *paskudna* (purists prefer to say *paskudnika* for the female of this species): coarse, disgusting, nasty, odious, low-class, contemptible, vulgar. (Whew!)
   "I wouldn't say 'Hello' to a *paskudnyak* like that!"
   "Did you ever hear of such a *paskudnyak*?"
2. An ungrateful person.
   "That *paskudnyak* never repaid a debt in his life."
3. A greedy con man or woman.
   "That *paskudnyak* would steal from a blind orphan."
4. A mean, unkind person.
   "She wouldn't let the boy borrow an umbrella."
5. A hypocrite.
   "You never know what *paskudna* lie he's working up to."
   "No one has a good word to say about that woman: she is a *paskudnyak* through and through."

This efflorescent epithet is one of the most greasily graphic in Yiddish. It offers the connoisseur of disgust three nice, long syllables, starting with a sibilant of loathing and ending with a nasality of abomination. It adds cadence to contempt.

———————

Mr. Tcherikov said to the rabbi: "It's too sad. Imagine, Rabbi: a poor widow, two darling little children, owes almost three hundred dollars in rent—and unless she pays before Saturday, she'll be evicted!"

"How terrible!" said the rabbi. "I'll make an appeal to the congregation. And here is fifty dollars of my own!"

"Thank you, Rabbi."

"You are a good man, Mr. Tcherikov. Are you related to the poor widow?"

"Oh, no."

"What got you so interested in her case?"

Mr. Tcherikov replied, "I'm the landlord." (Now, *there* is a *paskudnyak*!)

See also BUMMER, LOW-LIFE, SHLUMP, SHMEGEGGE.

Passover

See PESACH.

patchke

See POTCHKE.

payess

> Often encountered in English. Pronounced PAY-*ess*. From Hebrew: *pe'ah* (singular) and *pe'ot* (plural): "side earlocks," "curls."
>
> The unshorn ear-ringlet hair and sideburn-locks worn by Orthodox Jewish males, especially Hasidim.

The custom among Orthodox Jews of letting their ear curls grow long and wearing a full beard comes from an instruction in Leviticus 19:27: "Ye shall not round the corners of your heads, neither shalt thou mar the corners of thy beard." (*Payess* are regarded as symbolizing the uncut corners of a field at harvest time, which were by tradition left to be gleaned by the widow, the orphan, the stranger.)

In the Middle Ages, church and secular powers often *forbade* Jews to trim their beards in any way. Why? To be certain that a Jew could be identified. *Payess* were forbidden by law (for a time) in Czarist Russia.

To wear or to cut the *payess* became an important question among American Jews: to shave was an open, defiant departure from orthodoxy, a desire to become Americanized as soon as possible. Families were split asunder over *payess*.

In that section of Brooklyn which is an enclave of Hasidic Jews, the main street is sometimes called *Rue de la Payess* . . .

The slovenly, bearded young beatnik confronted his girl's father arrogantly: "Man, how come you treat me so nasty? *Your* old man always gives me the big Hello!"

"My 'old man,' " scowled the father, "thinks you're a student at the Yeshiva."

See also ASHKENAZI, HASID.

pekl (noun)
pekel
peckel
peklach (plural)

Pronounced PECK-*l* to rhyme with "freckle." From the Bavarian dialect of German: *Päckl*: "little package." Plural: *peklach*, pronounced PECK-*lakh* (rattle the *kh*).

1. A bundle or little package.
2. A knapsack or bundle carried on the back or shoulders (see below).
3. "To send a *pekl*" means to send food and gifts for a holiday or (with clothing) to relatives overseas.
4. "To have a *pekl*" means to be in trouble, to have a "passel" of problems.
5. "He left her a *pekl*" is an idiomatic expression for "He got her pregnant."
6. "He always carries his *pekl* with him" is a way of describing a hunchback.

Among immigrant Jews, or Jews whose grandparents came from the Old Country, the Yiddish *pekl* evokes special and warm responses. For it was from the little *peklach* of wares, containing needles, thread, pins, buttons, ribbons, hooks and eyes, laces, scissors, etc., that many Jews made their living, in Europe no less than in the New World to which they came. (The first peddlers in America, incidentally, were not Jews, but "Connecticut Yankees.")

The *pekl* of the Jewish peddler and itinerant merchant in time grew into a wagon of wares, then a little store, then an "emporium," then a department store, and in future generations a retail chain . . .

The adventures and adversities of the peddler who set off on foot, crossing strange new land and hills and even mountains, daring to venture into hostile Indian country, sometimes settling in the West and Far West (over thirty-eight states contain towns bearing the name of the Jew who founded them!) bringing his commodities to farmers' and miners' and trappers' wives; the dietary difficulties he endured; the prejudices and *popularity* he encountered (in New England and the South, Jews were welcomed by many as "people of the Book," "living witnesses" of the Word, authorities on Hebrew and the Old Testament)—all this forms one of the sagas of the aliens who made America what it is.

Interesting material about the Jewish peddlers will be found in Harry Golden's *Frontier Jews*.

(a) person

Yinglish, plain and simple, though certainly not elegant, recommended or desirable.

The genteelism used instead of "I," "one," or "someone."

This is the English analogue of the Yiddish *emetzer* (someone).

"A *per*son could think you're having an affair!"
"Listen, don't you share your happiness with a person?"

H. W. Fowler lividly excoriated such fustian, "which is foolishly thought by its users to be less vulgar, less improper, less apt to come unhandsomely betwixt the wind and our nobility."

The most famous deployment of this too-too genteel euphemism is, of course, the immortal threnody, "Adelaide's Lament," in Frank Loesser's *Guys and Dolls*: "A per-son could develop a cold . . ."

———————

Mrs. Issachar, lying on the couch, said, "My family physician insisted I should come to see you, doctor. God only knows what gave him such an idea! A person happily married, who loves her home, who hasn't been sick a *day* in her whole life—"

"Stop," exclaimed the psychoanalyst. "Madame, *how long has this been going on?*"

Pesach

Pronounced PAY-*sokh*, with a Scottish *kh*, to rhyme with "bays Bach." Hebrew: "to pass over," "to spare."

The Passover holiday and celebration, first observed 3,400 years ago.

This "festival of Freedom" is the most cherished of Jewish holidays, and one of the oldest still celebrated on our globe. It lasts seven days in Israel and eight days elsewhere. The first two and last two days are full holidays; the intermediate days are semi-holidays.

Pesach commemorates Israel's dramatic deliverance from enslavement in Egypt, as recounted in Exodus 12. The Revised Standard Version of the Bible recounts how the Lord told the Israelites to kill a lamb "and take some of the blood, and put it on the two doorposts and the lintel of [your] houses . . . [and] I will pass through the land of Egypt that night, and I will smite all the first-born [but] when I see the blood, I will pass over you. . . ."

On the evenings preceding the first and second nights of Passover (Israeli Jews and Reform Jews celebrate only the first), a great family *Seder* (SAY-*der*) is held. (*Seder* means order of procedure.)

On the table are symbolic foods commemorating events connected with Passover: the matzo, or unleavened bread, a reminder of the haste in which the Israelites left Egypt, without waiting for their bread to rise; bitter herbs, marking the bitterness of slavery; a roasted egg and bone, symbolic of the offerings brought to the Temple on this festival; *charoseth* (*kha*-RO-*ses*), a mixture of chopped nuts, apples, cinnamon, and wine, representing the clay from which the Israelites made bricks while in slavery. Each setting has a wine glass. The father half-reclines at the head of the table, propped up on pillows or on a sofa; this dramatizes freedom and ease (perhaps in imitation of Roman patricians at a banquet).

By custom, guests are sought for a family *Seder*: friends, friends of the children, a student away from home, a traveler, a neighbor, a soldier.

The grandfather or father or oldest son is the leader of the service. He opens the *Seder* with an Aramaic prayer. (Aramaic was the vernacular of the post-Exilic Jews from the sixth century B.C.) He raises a tray with three matzos on it, displays them to the company and intones the ancient litany:

This is the bread of affliction that our fathers ate in the land of Egypt. All who are hungry, let them come and eat—all who are needy, let them come and celebrate Passover with us. Now we are here: next year may we be in Israel. Now we are slaves; in the year ahead may we be free men.

A favorite moment of the *Seder* arrives when the youngest child at the table asks why this night is different from all other nights of the year and poses the Four Questions (the *Fier Kashehs*) to the father: Why do we eat unleavened bread? Why do we use bitter herbs? Why do we dip the herbs in the salt water? Why do we recline at the table?

The father replies with the phrase, "Slaves were we unto Pharaoh in Egypt," and continues retelling the ancient story of the Pharaoh's refusal to let the children of Israel go, the plagues God visited upon the Egyptians, the miraculous salvation at the Red Sea, and the arrival at Mount Sinai, where the Torah was given to the children of Israel. (The name of Moses occurs only once, oddly enough!)

When the *Haggadah*, the narrative read at the *Seder*, reaches the story of the Ten Plagues that afflicted the Egyptians, everyone at the table spills a little wine from his or her glass as each plague is named. Why? So that their cup of joy, even when celebrating deliverance, should not be full: The sages taught the Jews: "Rejoice not when thine enemy falleth" (Proverbs 24:17). (I must confess that *I* have always enjoyed any come-uppance suffered by the detestable, regardless of race, color or creed.)

Late in the *Seder* ritual, a large goblet of wine is poured for the Prophet Elijah, and the front door is opened, while all sing a hymn welcoming him in—Elijah being the herald of the Messiah.

Some hold that it was the terrible "Blood Accusation" against Jews, used both to terrorize and murder them (the charge that Jews drank Christian blood at Passover), that led the Jews to open their doors during the holiday feast—to allay any suspicion on the part of gentile neighbors that secret, heinous practices were being followed inside.

The repeated, fanatical slaughter of Jews during Passover finally led some rabbis to ban the use of red wine at the *Seder* entirely. Until a hundred years or so ago, white wine (raisin wine) was used sacramentally on Sabbaths and holidays alike.

Sholem Aleichem dryly remarks somewhere that even though *Pesach* comes only once a year, Jews insist on asking questions all year long.

A fully informative *Passover Anthology* has been deftly edited by Philip Goodman.

See also HAGGADA, SEDER.

pfui!
phooey!

English, Yiddish, Yinglish. From the German expletive, via Yiddish.
Phooey!

I would hesitate to offer Yiddish as the original provenance for this emphatic expletive (which has come into wide English usage since the 1920s) except for the confident attribution by Stuart Berg Flexner (*I Hear America Talking*).

Pfui is a clone of *feh!*—than which no phoneme is more expressive.

Jews are not the only people, of course, who enlist the labiodental fricative (*f* or *v*) for the utterance of sounds of disapproval or disgust. Rex Stout loved to put *pfui!* into the conversation of the master sleuth, Nero Wolfe.

Mrs. Horkheim marched her son into Dr. Shinkin's office. "Doctor," she demanded, "is a nine-year-old boy really qualified to perform an appendectomy?"

"What?!"

"I asked you: is a nine-year-old boy qualified to take out someone's appendix?"

"Certainly not!" exclaimed Dr. Shinkin. *"Pfui!"*

Mrs. Horkheim turned to her son. "Okay, Melvin. You heard the doctor . . . Go put it back!"

Nora Feit was in Las Vegas to get a divorce. There she met a pleasant woman, Cindy Gittel, who was in Las Vegas for the same reason. When they got to a roulette table,

Nora said, "I've never gambled. How do you choose a number?"

"I play different 'lucky' numbers," said Cindy. "Like my address, my graduation date, my phone—"

Nora said, "I don't have a lucky number . . ."

"Your age," said Cindy. "Why not put a chip on your age?"

Nora placed twenty dollars' worth of chips on number thirty-eight.

"Bets closed!" The croupier spun the wheel. The ball bounced and clacked and nestled into its cradle. "Number forty-four," intoned the croupier.

"Oh, *pfui*, dear!" said Cindy, turning to Nora.

Nora lay stretched out on the floor. She had fainted.

"A building development? *Pfui!* That's where they tear down all the trees, then name the streets after them."

See also AHA!, AI-AI-AI, FEH!

pilpul

A most desirable word for Yinglish. Pronounced PILL-*pull*, to rhyme with "fill full." Hebrew: "analytic debate," "dialectics."

1. A form of hyper-analysis and debate used in Talmudic discussions, *i.e.*, unproductive hair-splitting that is employed not so much to advance clarity or reveal meaning as to display one's own cleverness. There is a Yiddish folk saying I cherish: "Don't confuse 'For instance' with *proof*."
2. (Colloquially) Any hair-splitting or logic-chopping that leaves the main boulevard of a problem to bog down in the sterile side streets. Another Yiddish folk saying makes this point: "If you insist long enough that you're right, you'll be wrong."

Groucho Marx's letter of resignation from a club is pristine *pilpul*:

I do not care to belong to the kind of club that accepts people like me as members.

The logic of lunacy here mocks the lunacy of logic.

See also HACHEM, MIDRASH.

pisher (noun, masculine)
pisherkeh (diminutive)

> Strongly recommended for Yinglish. Vivid and colorful.
> Rhymes with "fisher." From German: *pissen*: "to uri-
> nate."
>   (Vulgarism)
>
> 1. A bed-wetter.
> 2. A young, inexperienced person; a "young squirt."
> 3. An insignificant or inconsequential person; a "no-
>   body."

Literally, a *pisher* is one who urinates, boy or girl; but
that is a far cry from popular usage. "He's a mere *pisher*"
means "He's very young" or "He's still wet behind the
ears." (Excuse the misleading metaphor.)

"You can't let her decide: she's only a *pisher*!" means
she's too young or inexperienced to be given such responsibility.

"He's just a *pisher*," means "He's a nobody"; he has
no influence.

A common saying (common in both senses) is "So call
me *pisher*" or "So let him call me a *pisher*," which means
"I don't care," "What does that matter?" or "Sticks and
stones may break my bones, but names can never harm
me."

In France, an elderly Jew, tired of hearing young Maurice
La Fontaine boast of his ancestry, finally grimaced, "Listen, La Fontaine: I knew your grandfather, who changed
his name to La Fontaine from Schpritzwasser [Squirt-
water]. And he told me that *his* father had changed his
name to Schpritzwasser from what everyone called him—
which was Moishe the *Pisher*! So don't put on airs, 'La
Fontaine.' To *me* you will always be Maury the *pisher*."

Rabbi Dov Laib, famed for the power of his analytic
reasoning, was said to be capable of answering any question
put to him. "Our beloved *rebbe* has a mind of unparalleled
clarity and power," a disciple remarked. "But what if he
is too *tired* to think hard? Maybe drowsy? Even a bit
tipsy? . . ."

This question so fascinated the acolytes that they decided to put it to the test. At the next Sabbath feast, they surreptitiously poured enough wine in the rabbi's glass to make him tipsy. Then, while he slept, the disciples carried him, reverently, to the cemetery.

There, they laid *Rebbe* Dov Laib on the grass and hid behind the tombstones, waiting to see what the great rabbi would say when he realized where he was . . .

The rabbi snored away for a time, then yawned, opened his eyes, looked about—and sat up. Stroking his beard, he then proceeded to speculate: "Nu? . . . *If* I am living, what am I doing here? . . . And if I am dead, why do I have to go *pishin'*?"

pishke

See PUSHKE.

plain and simple

Yinglish, popular among immigrants.

I do not know how widespread the English use of "plain and simple" was before, say, 1920. I call the phrase Yinglish because I heard it so often in the Jewish sections of Chicago, New York and Los Angeles, and so rarely in non-Jewish quarters or by non-Jews. I came to associate "plain and simple" with English-as-used-by-Jews:

"Plain and simple, I'm not going!"
"She said, plain and simple, she needs a vacation."
"Answer me, plain and simple: yes or no."

Q: Why is Sunday morning the best time to drive on a California freeway?
A: Plain and simple: because the Catholics are in church, the Protestants are still asleep, the Chinese are stuffing fortune cookies, the Jews are in Palm Springs and the Mexicans can't get their cars started.

Meyer Klantz was famed among his peers for his phenomenal success as a door-to-door salesman of kitchen appliances.

One day, George Maxon, who worked for the same firm,

said, "Meyer, how do you do it? You just racked up another first in sales! With me, I'm lucky if I can get into the kitchen of one out of three prospects. You must get into three out of four."

"That's right."

"Man, that's phenomenal! How do you do it?"

Meyer winked. "Plain and simple. Every time a woman answers the doorbell, I say, 'Good morning, ma'am—*you won't believe what I just saw in your neighbor's place*!' . . . Georgie, they can't wait to let me in!"

See also BOTTOM LINE, T.O.T.

pletsl

Often heard in Jewish bakeries. Pronounced PLETS-'*l*; rhymes with "Edsel."

A thin, flat, crisp roll, garnished with poppy seeds or onion. A staple in Jewish breadstuffs.

Try a pletsl. Some people prefer them to bagels; others prefer them to bialies. I like all three. So give them a try. They *are* unique.

See also BAGEL, BIALY, CHALLA.

plosher

I find this word for a character-type so expressive that I feel confident it will become part of Yinglish. Pronounced PLOE-*sh'r*, to rhyme with (what else?) "kosher." From German: *Plauschen* (to chat), via Yiddish, where it is energetically utilized.

1. A braggart, a blowhard.
2. An indiscreet gossip.
3. A blabbermouth, a chatterbox, a windbag.
4. One who exaggerates his or her own talents or resources.

Plosher is a synonym, in one or another subtle aspect, for *bluffer, fonfer, fifer, hoo-ha-nik, k'nocker, smarkatch, tummler, trombenik.* The plosive *plo* and the rushing *sh* create an aural image as admirable as it is accurate.

Have you heard of the Texan *plosher* who announced he did not need his glasses when driving his Rolls-Royce: "I had the *windshield* ground to my prescription."

PROUD MOTHER (to guests): My Sammy, only six weeks in school, and you should see how much he knows already! I'll show you. Sammy, tell us: if you take three apples and add three apples, how many apples do you have?
SAMMY (knitting brow): Five.
MOTHER (beaming): See! Only missed by one!!

In the plane headed for Arizona, two of Abraham's progeny were chatting.

"I can't wait to get to the hotel," said the first, "and change and *rush* out to the golf course! . . . Are you a golfer?"

The other replied, "Me? Golf is practically my whole life! I'd rather play than eat."

"Really? . . . Well, I play in the low seventies . . ."

"So do I," exclaimed the *plosher*. "But if it gets one degree colder I go right back to the hotel!"

The *nouveaux riches* Karlinskys had gone to Europe and visited Israel and were now home, boasting about their trip to their friends.

"And in Rome we had an audience with—the pope!" said Mrs. Karlinsky.

"With the *pope*?" echoed an astonished friend. "So how did you like him?"

"He was marvelous," said Mrs. Karlinsky. "*Her*, I didn't care for!"

(What a *plosher*.)

"Hey, Seymour!" cried Morty Pearl, a tireless *plosher*. "Did I hear a joke for you! A knockout. It's a new one about a rabbi and a hooker. Stop me if you've heard it."

"How?" sighed Seymour.

Governor Parnis, running for re-election (and a *plosher*), prided himself on having a phenomenal memory. He was pumping hands in the receiving line. A modest little man approached him, saying, "You don't remember me, but back in the seventies, I made your shirts—"

"Major Shurtz," the governor boomed, "I'd recognize you anywhere!"

See also BLUFFER, CHUTZPA, FIFER, FONFER, HOCK, K'NOCKER, PASKUDNA, TROMBENIK.

plotz
platz

Yinglish. An extremely echoic word with a percussive punch. Rhymes with "Watts." From the German: *Platz*: "place," *platzen*: "to burst." Runs rife in Yiddish.

1. A place, a seat.
   "Save my *plotz*."
   (But this is not why I include *plotz*, a word with an ambience all its own.)
2. To split, to burst, to explode.
   "From so much pleasure, one could *plotz*!"
   "What they went through would make a person *plotz*."
   "I can't laugh any more or I'll *plotz*!"
3. To be aggravated beyond bearing; to be infuriated; to be outraged.
   "His heart will *plotz* from such suffering."
   "He makes me so angry I could *plotz*."
   "I wish he would *plotz* from frustration!"

Plotst is the Yinglish past tense of *plotz*:

"He laughed so hard he practically *plotst*."
"Angry?! What did he do? He *plotst*!"
"Is he a comedian? Why, the whole theater *plotst*!"

Pincus and Bernstein were walking down a street in Berlin when they saw an SS cop approaching. Only Pincus had an identity card.

Bernstein said, "Quick, you run! He'll chase *you*, so I'll get away."

So Pincus broke into a run, and he ran and he ran until he thought his heart would *plotz*.

"Stop! Stop!" cried the policeman, who finally caught up. "Jew!" he roared. "Show me your papers."

The gasping Pincus produced his papers.

The Nazi examined them and saw they were in order. "But why did you run away?"

"Eh—my doctor told me to run half a mile after each meal!"

"But you *saw* me chasing after you and yelling!" snapped the policeman. "Why didn't you stop?"

"I—thought maybe you go to the same doctor!"

———

"Front desk?" Mr. Bristik shouted into the hotel phone at 2:30 A.M. "I'm ready to *plotz*! Nothing less! You ever heard of the straw that broke the camel's back?"

"Yes, sir."

"Well, I'm sleeping on it!"

See also I COULD BUST.

potch
patch

A fine mimetic word. It would enrich Yinglish. Rhymes with "botch." Both noun and verb. From German: *Patsch*: "a smack," "a blow."

1. A slap, a smack.
   "Man, did she give him a *potch*!"
   "Don't be fresh or I'll *potch* you."
2. An insult, a blow to one's pride.
   "To me, his words were a terrible *potch*."
   "When I read it, it was like a *potch*."
3. A reverse or setback to one's hopes.
   "Last season gave me a real *potch*."

There is a Yiddish saying: "*A potch fargeyt, a vort bash-teyt,*" "A slap passes, but a word [*i.e.*, an insult] remains."

———

Potch in tochis is the Yiddish for "spank." See TOCHIS.

potchke
patchke
potchkee

Yinglish. Much used by interior decorators and other aesthetes in a derogatory fashion. Pronounce it POTCH-*keh* and, for playful effect, POTCH-*kee*. Rhymes with "notch key." From Russian: *pochkat*: "to soil, to dirty," and German *patschen*: "to slap, to splash," via Yiddish, of course.

1. To fuss around or mess around.
 "I spent the weekend *potchkeeing* around the house."
2. To spend time aimlessly, to waste time.

Note *ongepotchket* (*q.v.*), which means overdecorated, ornate, "gussied up." It is the echoic attraction of *potchke* that recommends itself to Yinglish. Linguists may note how vivid are the unvoiced stopped consonants *p* and *k*. ("Unvoiced" does not mean silent, but without vibration of the vocal cords.)

———————

Said the mechanic, "Mr. Kroloff, your car needs a real overhaul. Three hundred dollars. But when I'm done, she'll purr like a cat!"

Kroloff gulped. "How much will it cost if you don't *potchke* around—and just make it meow like a pussy?"

psssssh!

I push this colorful, versatile interjection to the attention of Yinglish users as the very epitome of Yiddish and a triumph of onomatopoeia. And not in English dictionaries, alas.

1. How remarkable!
2. How astonishing!
3. Can you imagine that?!
4. Oh, my, my, my!

This all-purpose expression is one of the fondest recollections of my boyhood, perhaps because my father (who never lost his keenness of appreciation) cried "*Pssssh!*" so often. He greatly enjoyed sharing his astonishments. In the course of a day he might exclaim:

"You read in the paper what Roosevelt said? *Pssssh!*"

"So just take a look on this picture! *Pssssh!*"

"If I had that much money . . . *pssssh*, what would I do!"

"You *did*? . . . *Pssssh!*"

———————

Mr. Greenwald leaned back in his chair and sighed heavily. "Ah, Paris, Paris. I just came back from there. *Pssssh!*"

"*I*," said Mr. Fidelman, "don't think Paris is the same . . . Now, in the good old days—"

"You mean when Paris was *Paris*?"

"No," said Mr. Fidelman. "I mean when Fidelman was Fidelman."

———

The phone rang in Rabbi Liebman's study at the temple. The rabbi lifted the phone. "Hello. Rabbi Liebman."

"Rabbi, my name is Lawson, of the Internal Revenue Service. I am calling—quite confidentially—about a problem we've run into in the tax returns of a member of your congregation—Mr. Victor Gerzoff . . ."

"Y-yes," said the rabbi cautiously.

"Mr. Gerzoff has claimed a tax deduction of ten thousand dollars—for a contribution to your temple—which, he says, he made in *cash*. . . . In strict confidence, Rabbi, do you remember receiving such a sum from Mr. Gerzoff?"

A moment's silence. Then Rabbi Liebman said, "Uh— Mr. Lawson, please phone me tomorrow—the same time— and I *assure* you, the answer to your question will be 'Yes.' "

(Of Rabbi Liebman's astuteness, my father, *alavasholem*, would have exclaimed, "*Pssssh!*")

See also AHA!, AI-AI-AI.

pupik

Would make a superb addition to Yinglish. Pronounced PU (the *u* of *put*)-*pik*, to rhyme with "look it." Slavic. Navel.

Why should one use *pupik* for *navel*? Because it just *sounds* funnier. The combination of the bilabial *p* and the stop-consonant *k* is irresistibly effective.

"Pupik" is a sonic tonic. It can be used in a variety of colorful ways: ironic, maledictory, and ribald:

> *"A shaynim donk in pupik."* ("A pretty thanks in the navel": "Thanks for nothing.")
>
> *"Zoll vaksen tsibiliss in zein pupik!"* ("Onions should grow in his navel!")
>
> "What does he do? He sits around all day looking at his *pupik*."

Moishe Pupik is a generic name for dummies, oafs or the clumsy and inept.

The classic definition of an impractical mortal is this: "He [she] is the type who sits around wondering whether a flea has a *pupik*."

Other colorful uses of *pupik*:

> "That just goes into my *pupik*." ("It doesn't make a dent on me.")
>
> "Stick it in your *pupik*!"
>
> "I've had it right up to my *pupik*!" ("I'm fed to the teeth!")

Jay Crovitz had a fine, big toy store. Children loved to try out the hobby-horses, the rockers, the swings—but never seemed to want to get off. Whenever a parent or a salesman tried to coax a little one off a toy, the tot would throw a violent temper tantrum. The store often sounded like a madhouse.

One day there appeared before Mr. Crovitz a white-haired gentleman, who said: "I am Professor Howard Spiegelman, Ph.D., consultant on children's behavior. I have heard of your difficulties. I can solve them—for good. My fee is one hundred dollars." Professor Spiegelman smiled. "No obligation. If I fail to give full satisfaction, you don't pay a penny!"

Mr. Crovitz led the professor into the toy department. "Listen. Did you ever *hear* such craziness?"

On one tricycle, from which his frantic mother was trying to lift him, a little boy was screaming like a banshee. On a hobby-horse, a little girl was screeching at the salesman who was trying to coax her off. On a rocking horse, a child was caterwauling at her father.

The professor observed the howling scene but a moment, went over to the tricycle, patted the screaming lad on the head, leaned over and, smiling, whispered a few words into the boy's ear. At once, the lad leaped off the tricycle and leaped into his mother's arms.

The professor went to the little girl on the hobby-horse, leaned over, whispered something into her ear—and the tyke stopped screaming and jumped off the hobby-horse.

With the squalling tyke on the rocking horse, Professor Spiegelman plied his same swift magic: a pat, a smile, those mesmeric words—and instant obedience replaced delinquent obstinacy.

"I can't believe my eyes!" said Mr. Crovitz. "What in the world do you say to them?"

"My fee . . ."

"Fine! Here's my check . . . Now, what's the secret?"

"I pat their hair fondly," said the great psychologist, folding the check into his wallet, "then I put my mouth close to their little ears, and I whisper, 'Listen, darling. Get off this thing—at once—or I'll give you such a *potch in tochis* [kick in the ass] your *pupik* will hurt for a month!' "

Purim

Pronounced POOR-*im* (not PURE-*im*); rhymes with "tour 'em." Hebrew: *pur*: "lot."

The Feast of Lots, commemorating the rescue of the Jews of Persia from Haman's plot to exterminate every man, woman and child of them.

Lots had already been drawn (or cast) by Haman, first minister of King Ahasuerus (possibly Artaxerxes II), to determine the date on which all the Jews of Persia would be slaughtered. A miraculous deliverance was effected by the heroism of beautiful Queen Esther, his wife, who was Jewish, and the sagacity of Mordecai, her uncle and guardian. Haman ended up being executed on the gallows he had erected to dispatch Mordecai. The story is told in the Book of Esther. Are the events recounted true? (See below.) The time? Around 300 B.C.

Deliverances from other calamitous events have been celebrated (and called Purim) by Jewish communities in Saragossa, Frankfurt, Egypt and Tiberia. There is a saying, of rueful sagacity: "There are so many Hamans, but only one Purim."

In synagogues and temples, the *Megillah* (Scroll of Esther) is read on the eve and morning of Purim. Whenever the name of Haman is uttered, the children set up a racket of boos and jeers and spin ratchety noisemakers. In some communities, Haman's name is written upon the soles of one's shoes, so that his name may literally be wiped out!

Among the customs associated with Purim are the sending of gifts (food and money) to the poor, and the exchanging of gifts with friends. Feasts, dances and masquerades are held. Purim is the closest thing to the carnival in Jewish life; in Israel, it is celebrated with public processions, complete with floats and costumes, and in private masquerade parties.

The symbolic food of Purim is the *hamantash* (*q.v.*), a three-cornered sweet pastry filled with prunes or poppy seeds.

———

I think you should know that many scholars question the authenticity of the Esther–Mordecai–Haman story. Two thousand years ago, Jews challenged the validity of the Book of Esther (which was first written in Persian) and rejected its right to be included among the canonical works of the Bible. As for the feast of *Purim*, "little or nothing is known" about its origin (*Jewish Encyclopedia*, vol. 5).

The Purim festival may be a carryover from an old pagan carnival that used to take place on the Babylonian New Year—a festival that Persians and Jews alike loved because of its masks, dances and Mardi Gras shenanigans.

The celebration of Purim has been strictly forbidden to Jews in different times and places by hostile governments.

Yet Purim may be the most Jewish of holidays, in the sense that it is the most beloved; *i.e.*, thousands of celebrations, called "little Purims," are held in Jewish families around the world to commemorate a miraculous personal deliverance, escape or rescue. One authority told me he considers Purim *the* holiday *par excellence*, "more Jewish than Yom Kippur and Rosh Hashanah."

The Purim Anthology, edited by Philip Goodman, contains a vast cornucopia of information, costumes, Purim *spiels* (playlets) and historical data.

pushke
pishke

A symbol of nostalgia, used in English for its warm overtones. Pronounced PUSH-*keh*, PUSH-*key*, or PISH-*key*. From the Polish: *puszka*.

1. The little can or container kept in the home, often in the kitchen, in which money to be donated to charity is accumulated.

Each charitable organization would provide its own *pushke*. (Jewish housewives customarily put a few coins in the *pushke* every Friday night, before lighting the Sabbath candles.) Collectors for the various charities would come around at regular intervals, and the *baleboosteh* (housewife) would empty each one's particular *pushke*.

The *pushkes*, set out on a shelf or the kitchen windowsill, carried labels that read like a catalogue of human misery—and benevolence:

For Orphans
For Widows
For Victims of Persecution
For the Blind
For the Hebrew Home for the Aged
For Milk for Jewish Children in Hospitals in the Old Country
For Meetings to Protest Pogroms in the Ukraine
For the Training of Newly Arrived Immigrants
For Resettlement of Jewish Refugees from Turkey
For Farm Equipment to Be Sent to Jewish Farmers in Kansas
For the Jewish Chicken Raisers in Kankakee Recently Bankrupted by the Ravages of Red Tick among Rhode Island Roosters
To Send a Rabbi-Saint to the Holy Land before He Dies

I can't, offhand, remember *all* the titles.

NOTE: There is no Hebrew or Yiddish word for charity.

The word used for charity is *tzedaka*, which means "justice." Charity was, and is, considered a duty, an obligation, a necessity, a God-forbid-you-should-ever-forget-to-give-to-the-poor-and-orphaned-and-needy-or-any-other-worthy-cause. A *contribution* is called a *neduvah*.

2. The money saved up by a married woman, out of the household funds her husband gave her; a nest-egg (often known as a *knippl*.)

Women fiercely guarded as earnings the small amounts their careful management of the household made it possible for them to divert to personal, undisclosed causes.

The woman would spend her "little *pushke*" as she saw fit. Often the *pushke* was the family's only emergency fund for doctor bills, operations, etc.

Isaac Topolov was reading in his living room when the window-blind went awry. Topolov tried to fix the blind but it was hopelessly knotted. So he picked up his Classified telephone directory and called a repair service. The serviceman, one Julio Nunces, could not, of course, come right over. "I come Thursday. You be there?"

"What time?"

"Between one and four," said Nunces.

"No, I'll be in my office—but don't worry. My wife will be here."

Topolov entirely forgot to tell his wife. On Thursday, the repairman came to the Topolov's back door. He rang the bell.

Mrs. Topolov appeared. "Yeah?"

"I come for the venetian blind," said Nunces.

"One minute." Mrs. Topolov disappeared. Soon she came back. She handed him a dollar.

putz (noun and verb.)

A stalwart part of Yinglish, prized by *aficionados*. Rhymes with "nuts." From German: *Putz*: "ornament," "finery." Vulgar, taboo—but hugely popular.

As a noun

1. Literally: vulgar slang for *penis*. (But the vulgarism

is rarely used to designate the male member; the word *shmuck* does that.)

2. A fool, an ass.
3. A simpleton or yokel; an easy mark.
   CAUTION: *Putz* is not to be used lightly or when women or children are around. It is more offensive than *shmuck*; the latter may be used in a teasing and affectionate way, vulgar though it is, but *putz* has a pejorative ambience.
4. A *shmegegge*.

As a verb

5. To fool around and waste time (exactly like the English "*futz* around").
6. To be sexually promiscuous.

Some arbiters of usage hold that *putz* is slightly less vulgar than *shmuck*; others consider *putz* slightly more offensive—because it aims to be euphemistic.

Avoid both words. But for those who knowingly want to enlist the colorful punch of the colloquial: use *putz* only after you see who's present.

See also DUMKOP, FONFER, SHMEGEGGE, SHMUCK, YOLD, ZHLUB.

R

rabbi
rebbe (but not *Reb, q.v.*)

Rabbi is, of course, by now part of English; *rebbe* is
not—it is Yiddish. Pronounced RAB-*bye* and REB-*ba*,
respectively, to rhyme with "dab eye" and "jeb-a."
Hebrew: *rabi* (*rah*-BEE): "my teacher." In Yiddish, *rov*
(*rawv*).

1. An ordained clergyman in Judaism.
2. The spiritual leader of a Hasidic group or sect, not
   necessarily ordained (having inherited the office).

Rabbi does not have the same meaning as *priest* or *minister*. A rabbi is *not* an intermediary between God and man.
His position traditionally gives him no power or hierarchi-
cal status; this may be hard to believe, but it is so. The
authority of a rabbi rests on his learning, his personal qualities, his *character*. (Ordination has ancient roots, but it
did not become institutionalized until modern times.) In
Orthodox worship, the rabbi rarely leads the religious services; the *chazzen* (cantor) usually does—but any learned
layman may take the pulpit to lead the prayers.

What does a rabbi do? He performs the ceremonials that
attend birth, confirmation, marriage, death; interprets the
tenets of Judaism; is responsible for teaching and oversee-
ing religious instruction in the synagogue or temple school;
delivers sermons (not prayers); offers comfort and consola-

tion and counsels families; tries to "guide the perplexed."
. . . Rabbis are graduates of a *yeshiva*, or seminary. In
addition, Reform, Conservative and a growing number of
Orthodox rabbis hold higher degrees (often more than one)
from secular universities.

Rabbis used to earn their living *not* from a salary or
fee from their congregations, but in ordinary occupations:
Rashi was a vintner in France; Yochenan was a shoemaker;
other rabbis were carpenters, bookbinders, leather workers
. . . Not until the fifteenth century (!) were rabbis paid a
salary by their flock.

A Hasidic rabbi may never have been ordained. He may
have inherited his position from his father, or he may have
been invited to assume the leadership of a group of Hasidim
because of his personal qualities.

The Bible mentions great prophets who were women.
Conservative synagogues and Reform temples today ordain
women. The Orthodox branch of Judaism has strongly resisted such an astounding idea.

I never cease to marvel over the impudence of Yiddish
sayings about rabbis:

> It was hard for Satan alone to mislead the whole world,
> so he appointed prominent rabbis in different localities.
> —Attributed to Nahman of Bratzlav

> A rabbi whose congregation does not want to drive him
> out of town isn't a rabbi, and a rabbi they do drive
> out of town isn't a man.
>
> —Folk saying

A terrible hurricane hit the Florida coast. In one town,
a rowboat moved along the totally flooded streets. The
rescuer spied a strange figure on the roof of a bungalow: a
tall, bearded man, wearing a wide, flat black hat, his arms
crossed.

"Come down!" shouted the samaritan. "Get in the
boat!"

The tall figure gestured calmly. "Save others. Don't
worry about me. I am a rabbi. The *Lord* will save me!"

An hour later, another boat, with an outboard motor—

approached. "Hey! You up on the roof! Come down! The waters are still rising! You'll be drowned!"

The rabbi, standing cross-armed, despite water up to his waist, called out, "Save others! I am a rabbi. I have complete faith in my Lord!"

And an hour after *that* a helicopter hovered above the roof. The pilot lowered a ladder, his voice booming out of a bullhorn: "Grab that ladder, Rabbi! The water's up to your *chin*! This is your last chance!"

"Fear not!" sang the rabbi. "I am a man of God! And He—will—*glub, glub, kmpf . . .*"

Rabbi Gershon Rosenbloom, that good and faithful servant of the Lord, sank beneath the rising waters. Being a soul of the utmost virtue, within an instant after drowning he found himself among the Heavenly Throng—gazing at the radiance of God Himself. "Oh, Lord!" cried the rabbi. "How *could* You? I had absolute faith, and You let me drown! How *could* you?"

" 'Let you *drown*?' " bridled the Lord. "I sent two boats and a helicopter to take you off that roof, you idiot!"

See also HASID.

Reb

> From Hebrew: *rabi*: "master."
> Mister.

Many Jews think *Reb* is an affectionate abbreviation of *rebbe* (rabbi), but this is incorrect. *Rebbe* means "my spiritual master," "my teacher," whereas *Reb* is simply a term of address like "mister" or "sir."

Reb (unlike *rebbe* or rabbi) is never used by itself. *Reb* must be followed by a first name: Reb Norman, Reb Yankel, Reb Timothy. ("*Timothy*?" Yep, I know several Timothys whose parents are—or were born—Jews.)

Reb Yankel: A foolish Jew.

One recent census form contained the following crucial information:

Name: Yankel Kinsky
Address: 70 Oak St., Queens, N.Y.
Length of residence: 68 feet (including garage)

See also RABBI.

rebbe

See RABBI.

rebbitsin
rebbetsen

Pronounced REB-*bi-tzin*, to rhyme with "debits in."
The wife of a rabbi.

The *rebbitsin* played an important role in the Jewish community of yesteryear. She often served as mother-surrogate to her husband's students.

There is a saying (*naturally*, there's a saying): "Better close to the *rebbitsin* than to the rabbi."

The modern *rebbitsin* often teaches in the congregational school, lectures on Jewish customs to women's organizations, visits the sick, comforts the bereaved, serves as hostess for many occasions.

———

One day, a *rebbitsin* accused the maid of having stolen a candlestick. The poor maid wailed that she was innocent.

"Very well," said the *rebbitsin*, "let us go to the rabbinical court! Let them decide!"

The rabbi said, "I'll come along."

"You don't need to," said his wife. "I can plead the case against this wretched girl."

"I'm sure you can," said the rabbi. "But who will plead her defense?"

Red Sea

Mistaken translation from Hebrew: *Yom sof*, or *Yom suph*: "sea of reeds."

A mistranslation for the place the fleeing Israelites crossed during their deliverance from slavery in Egypt: the "Sea of Reeds"—marshlands, bulrushes.

Please believe me when I tell you that the Israelites never crossed the Red Sea. They entered Sinai about a hundred miles north of that (!), very near the Mediterranean, in a marshy sea of reeds or bulrushes.

refusenik

Neither Hebrew nor Yiddish, this highly evocative word entered the world as Yinglish (note the -*nik*).

Someone behind the Iron Curtain who is refused an exit visa, no matter how often he or she applies for one. Many refuseniks are Jews.

Refusenik was invented by the Committee of Concerned Scientists, which sponsors meetings of Soviet scientists who have been denied exit visas to Israel from the glorious Fatherland, and who lose their jobs or research posts as well.

———————

It is probably apocryphal, but good to believe, that a Jewish pharmacist in Moscow placed this sign in his window:

LAXATIVE

SOFT . . . PAINLESS . . . PROVEN . . .

TO

let my people go

———

Boris Zivek stood before the commissar of Passport Controls and with the utmost earnestness pleaded, "Comrade Commissar Kreznev, I am seventy years old, and it is now sixteen *years* since I began filing applications for permission to emigrate from the Soviet Union."

Commissar Kreznev nodded.

"All of my immigration papers from Israel have been approved and are in your files—"

Kreznev nodded.

"Comrade Commissar, please tell me—why, *why* will you not let me leave the Soviet Union?"

The commissar assumed his sternest expression. "Because in your brain, Zivek, you hold important secrets—*scientific* secrets! Those secrets—if we let you out of Soviet Union—you will give to Israelis, allies of capitalistic USA—"

"But that's impossible!" cried Zivek. "I no longer know a *single* scientific secret! Have you forgotten? I have been barred from my laboratory for over fifteen *years*! I have not been allowed to attend any scientific meetings. I have not been given a single classified document about a single weapon or experiment—"

"*Da, da*," nodded Kreznev.

"—and even when I *was* working on missiles fifteen years ago, we were so far behind the Americans—"

"*Dot*," thundered the commissar, "*is the secret!*"

See also -NIK.

regular

Do not be misled: this entirely English (in no way Yiddish) word is entered here because of its emphatic and unique Yinglish usage.

1. Actually, really.
2. Practically—though not actually.
3. Authentic.

Examples, in same numerical order:

1. "That Nat: a regular expert." (English usage would be "a real [or true] expert.")
2. "Sonya? She's a regular pharmacist." (But not a certified one.)
3. "What do you mean you don't believe Marvin? He's a regular lawyer!" (Marvin is not an amateur nor does he *pretend* to be a lawyer. He is a *bona fide* counselor-at-law, with a diploma and a J.D.)

Years ago a bearded Hasidic Jew from Boston, wearing a long caftan, visiting a relative in Alabama, was followed everywhere by a group of goggle-eyed Southern children.

Finally the old man addressed the magpies: "What's a mare, kiddies? You never before saw a regular Yenkee?"

See also EPPES, THAT'S FOR SURE.

relieving guilt by linking a malediction to instant, but pro forma, cancellation

> "May God give her *shingles*—God forbid!"
> "He should drop dead in front of my eyes—may God prevent that."
> "She should *chollileh* (God forbid) not have a miscarriage."

resentment vented by placing the grammatical object before the subject

> "The race? Sure he won. Last place, he won."
> "*Thanks* she expects for wrecking my car?"
> "*Two* arms he broke yet."

See also ACCENTUATING SCORN . . . , ADJECTIVE FRONTED . . .

ridicule via an apparently innocent question

Nothing is more characteristic of Yiddish humor (or Yinglish sarcasm) than the deployment of a simple question to:

1. Demolish whatever validity the substance of a question may have seemed to possess.
   "*Now* he wants to take a vacation?"
2. Expose the stupidity or tactlessness of anyone who made such a statement.
   "*Me* he asked to decide whether my son has more brains than his son-in-law?!"
3. Castigate the gall of anyone who did that which is questioned.
   "To my wife he complained about my *mother*?"

A variation of this ploy appears in the guise of the apparently innocent afterthought:

Arloff's success as a life-insurance agent was the talk of all his colleagues. One day a friend asked, "Herb, what's your secret?"

Arloff shrugged. "Whenever a prospect can't make up his mind, I say, 'Think it over. Don't rush. Sleep on it. Let me know tomorrow—if you get up.' "

See also ACCENTUATING SCORN . . . , ANGER CON-
VERTED . . .

Rosh Hashanah
Rosh Hashonah
Rosh Hashona
Rosh Hoshanah

> Not one in a hundred people, Jew or gentile, who read
> or hear the name of this holiday, knows what the name
> means. Pronounced *rawsh-ha-*SHAW*-neh* (rhyme with
> "cautious fauna"); or *rosh-ha-*SHO*-na* (rhyme with "cau-
> tious Mona"); or *rawsh-ha-*SHAH*-na* (rhyme with "cau-
> tious Donna"). Hebrew: "beginning [of the] year."
>
> Rosh Hashanah is the holy day that commemorates
> the birthday of—the world!

So said the rabbis, in the Talmud and Midrash, who held
that Rosh Hashanah is nothing less than the anniversary of
creation itself.

Orthodox and Conservative Jews observe two days of
Rosh Hashonah; Reform Jews celebrate only one. Rosh
Hashanah begins the Ten Days of Penitence (also known
as the Days of Awe), which period ends with the most
solemn of religious days in the Jewish calendar: Yom Kippur. During these days of penitence and prayer, all mankind
presumably passes before the Heavenly Throne, and there
God Himself looks into their deeds and hearts. Judgment
will be passed on Yom Kippur, the devout aver, but
"prayer, penitence, and charity may avert the evil decree."

The dominant and recurring theme throughout Rosh
Hashanah services is the sovereignty of Adonai. The *shofar*
(ram's horn) is blown several times, in a prescribed pattern
of notes: the first celebrates God's kingship, the second
stresses the role of the individual, the third reminds the
congregation of all the events associated with the blowing
of the ram's horn. (In ancient Judea, the ram's horn was
used to send signals from peak to peak. The ancient Hebrews used to sound the *shofar* to lead their armies into
battle, to welcome the new moon or to herald a king.)

Rosh Hashanah is a solemn yet very happy time: entire
families gather from everywhere for the holiday and the
feast. Bread or apple is dipped in honey to symbolize a

hoped-for sweetness in the year ahead. A blessing thanks the Lord for having "sustained us to this day."

Pickles (sour, half-sour and crunchy cucumbers—great favorites of Jewish cuisine) are never served at the festive Rosh Hashanah dinners. You know why? Because it is considered inappropriate to start a New Year with a sour taste.

The traditional Rosh Hashanah greeting is "*Leshana tova tikosevu*" (*le*-SHAH-*nah* TOE-*vah tee-kah*-SAY-*vu*): "May you be inscribed for a good year."

Rosh Hashanah, like all Jewish holidays, is determined by the lunar calendar, and falls in late September or early October. Rosh Hashanah may never fall on a Wednesday, Friday or Sunday, because the holiday symbolizes—a whole year.

See also YOM KIPPUR.

rov

See RABBI.

S

Sabbath

See SHABBES.

Sanhedrin

A word often encountered—and misunderstood in English. Pronounced *san*-HED-*rin*, to rhyme with "tan red bin." From Greek: *synedrion*: "assembly."

The seventy elders, plus a patriarch or president (*nasi*), who sat in Jerusalem until A.D. 70, as a combination of Supreme Court and College of Cardinals, ruling on theological, ethical, civil and political matters.

A deplorable amount of nonsense, and a lamentable flood of demagoguery, have made the name Sanhedrin appear far more malevolent and mysterious than it ever was. Bigots have exploited the myth of a supposed "international council," or "Elders of Zion," who secretly rule over all Jews and plot vicious deeds in "a worldwide conspiracy."

But the Sanhedrin was simply a court in ancient Jerusalem, composed of learned men and priests who interpreted Scripture and exercised ecclesiastical and civil authority in certain cases.

There were probably *two* Sanhedrins, one of twenty-three members, concerned with political and civil matters, and the Great Sanhedrin of seventy-one elders, that ruled on religious problems. Titus destroyed the Great Temple in 70 A.D. and the *Sanhedrin* lost all political powers—and moved to Tiberias, there to lay the foundation for rabbinical scholarship. Its legal functions were replaced by those of the *Beth Din* ("Court of law").

Many centuries later, Napoleon established a Sanhedrin of seventy-one members that included distinguished Jewish laymen as well as rabbis. It did not carve much of a niche in French (or European) history.

After Israel was founded (1948) there were requests for the revival of the Sanhedrin. This was not done because of legal and constitutional problems.

sarcasm amplified via innocuous words used ironically

"He knocked out only three of my teeth."
"I doubt that she ate more than fourteen sandwiches."
"Was that much to ask: a measly five million dollars?"

———

Here is a true tale:

"I don't like airplanes. I don't trust airplanes. I don't *need* airplanes!" said the great pianist, Leopold Godowsky.

"But Leopold, I have gone over the actual statistics! Do you realize you're safer in an airplane than in a bathtub? Or in an auto—"

"You can do anything with statistics."

The friend paused. "Perhaps you're right, Leopold. After all, deep down, we each feel that wherever we are—we go—when *God* calls us!"

"Sure," said Godowsky. "But why should I be twenty thousand feet up in the air when God calls the *pilot*?"

———

SCENE: Rabinow's Kosher Restaurant

"Waiter!" sang out Mr. Kressman. "*Wai*ter!"

A waiter ambled over. "You called?"

"No, you heard a *flute*," said Mr. Kressman bitterly.

"So what did the flute want?"

"What it wanted," said Mr. Kressman, "is to know the exact nature of my offense!"

The waiter rubbed his chin. "What offense? Who's talking about an offense?"

"That's what I want *you* to tell me, because since I came in here, a good half-hour ago, I've been living on nothing but bread and water!"

See also ACCENTUATING SCORN . . . , DEFLATION . . . , DESTROYING A PROUD CLAIM . . . , THANKS A LOT.

schlemiel

See SHLEMIEL.

schlock

See SHLOCK.

schmaltz

See SHMALTZ.

schmooze

See SHMOOZE.

schnaps

See SHNAPS.

schnorrer

See SHNORRER.

seder

Pronounced SAY-*d'r*. Rhymes with "labor." Hebrew: "order," or "order of the services."

The Passover feast and religious ritual, held in the home.

For the family *Seder*, these foods, in addition to those listed under PESACH, are required: a shank bone of roast lamb, to remind everyone of the paschal lamb that once was sacrificed; a hard-boiled egg (a *beitzah*), standing for life or immortality, even for Israel itself (the egg becomes harder the more you boil it); a piece of radish or horseradish (*maror*), to symbolize how bitter life was during the bondage in Egypt; a sprig of parsley (*karpas*), to remind Jews that this is a spring festival; salt water (into which the parsley is dipped), to recall the tears shed by mothers in Egypt whose babies were snatched from them—and the miracle of the Red Sea (*q.v.*); a little mound of crushed apples-raisins-almonds-nuts-cinnamon-wine (*haroset*), to represent the brick and mortar with which Jewish slaves built the palaces and monuments of their oppressors.

The opening of the door during the *Seder* has several interpretations. It invites Elijah to enter; that Prophet, being the Messiah's herald and messenger, may speed up God's appearance on Earth. On the other hand, some hold that it was the terrible "Blood Accusation" (the charge that Jews drank Christian blood at Passover), that led Jews to open their doors during the holiday feast: to allay any suspicion on the part of gentile neighbors.

The repeated, fanatical slaughter of Jews during Passover finally led some rabbis to ban the use of red wine at the *Seder*: until a hundred years or so ago, white wine was used sacramentally on Sabbaths and holidays alike.

See also PESACH.

seltzer water

The fizzy beverage made by charging water with carbon dioxide or adding a pellet of bicarbonate of soda.

This drink was a great favorite with East European immigrants. It was sometimes known as "for two cents plain"—that being the price, in happier times, for a glass of plain soda without syrup (chocolate, strawberry, etc.), believed to end heartburn, acidity, constipation, "nervous stomach," and so on and on.

"Seltzer" comes from the name of the town in Germany, Niederselters (near Wiesbaden), where a natural spring provided bubbly water believed to contain salubrious chemicals. "Soda" derives from the fact that bicarbonate of soda was added for an effervescent and supposedly restorative effect.

This drink has been replaced by the *chic* "club *soda*," since "seltzer" has become identified as a remedy for headaches, indigestion and hangovers.

The big Beckerman Seltzer Water delivery truck, fully loaded, ran into a fire hydrant and turned over on its side with a terrific crash. Bottles and siphons flew out in all directions and bubbling waters poured into the street. A crowd swiftly assembled.

"Oh, *oy!*" the driver was crying. "My boss will expect me to *pay* for all this!"

An elderly man turned to the crowd. "This is terrible! A hard-working Jew—ruined . . ." He took off his hat. "Let's take up a collection. Ladies, open your purses! Gentleman, dig into your pockets! This is a real *mitzve* we can perform!" Dollar bills and coins soon filled the hat.

The old man dumped the contents of the hat into the driver's spread apron and went off.

"My, my!" sang one onlooker. "There is a real Jewish heart!"

The driver made a grimace. "*That* was Mr. Beckerman."

See also FOR TWO CENTS PLAIN . . .

Sephardi
Sephardic (adjective)
Sephardim (plural)

> Well established in English. Pronounced *seh*-FAR-*dee*, to rhyme with "Bacardi." Hebrew: "Spanish." (Spain, in Hebrew, is *Sepharad*.)

1. Spanish and Portuguese Jews, and the descendants of the Jews of Spain and Portugal. (In modern Israel, Sephardim includes Jews of the Middle East.)
2. Those Hasidim, otherwise Ashkenazim, who follow part of the Sephardic liturgy.

Sephardic Judaism, which dominated Jewish culture from around A.D. 600 until the expulsion of the Jews from Spain at the end of the fifteenth century, was an exceptionally sophisticated blend of Talmudic thought, Greek philosophy, Aristotelianism, such science as then existed—and the ideas of Averroes, the great Islamic scholar (whom medieval Christians were not permitted to read because of Church prohibitions). Sephardic Jews were familiar with Latin, Spanish, French, geometry, algebra, astronomy, medicine, metaphysics, music, mechanics.

They rose to positions of great eminence in Spain, Portugal and kingdoms in North Africa—as physicians, philosophers, poets, financiers, advisers to kings and courts. Sephardic writers wrote mostly in Arabic (or Judeo-Arabic), even when writing about Torah and Talmud! They were aristocratic: their religious services, no less than their style of living, were invested with a splendor such as Ashkenazic (East European) Jews never knew.

The Sephardic Jews were expelled from the Iberian countries in 1492 and later, to Iberia's everlasting misfortune. The exiles suffered terrible disaster, drownings, enslavement by pirates and African tribes. The survivors settled along the coastline of the Mediterranean, throughout the friendly Ottoman Empire, and in Holland and England and their colonies.

Communities of Sephardic Jews are today found in Israel, Turkey, Greece, England, Holland, Latin America and, of course, the United States, where Sephardic Jews were the first Jewish immigrants.

Sephardic Jews differ from Ashkenazic Jews in many customs, in the order and text of their prayers, in the intonation of the chants used in their synagogues.

For more information, see *The Other Jews: The Sephardim Today*, by Daniel Elazar, and Herbert Dobrinsky's *A Treasury of Sephardic Laws and Customs*.

See also ASHKENAZI.

sh-
shm-
sch-
schm-

These particles are solidly entrenched in Yinglish as prefatory expressions of mockery, scorn or derogation.

IMPORTANT NOTE: I strongly disapprove of using *sch* or *schm* instead of *sh* for English transliterations of Yiddish words. *Sch* is German; *sh* is Yiddish—which, in fact, uses a single letter (*shin*) for the *sh* sound. There is no letter for *sch* in Yiddish. I use the *sh* and exile the *sch* wherever possible.*

*In some cases, to use *sch* is flatly wrong: *e.g.*, *borsht* is a Slavic word, not at all connected to German, as the commonly used English

1. To deride a word in Yinglish (as in Yiddish), the word is repeated—but with *sh-* or *shm-* prefixed to the repetition.

   The doctor says she has a serious virus?"

   "Virus-shmirus, as long as she's O.K."

   "The mayor? Mayor-shmayor, it's his wife who runs the show."

2. *sh-* or *shm-* is the signal for an astringent symphony of disesteem. A great many Yiddish (and Yinglish) words jeer, sneer and snicker via this simple sonic introduction:

shlemiel	shlump	shmo
shlepper	shmegegge	shmuck
shlimazel	shmendrick	shnook

   . . .in German the use of this mock-mechanism (*sh-, shm-*) has progressively declined since the Middle Ages; the cases recorded from modern German dialects seem to be *loans from Yiddish*. [My italics]
      —Max Weinreich, *History of the Yiddish Language*,
   p. 623

   ———————

Mrs. Weinberg confided to her neighbor that her son had gone through so miserable a phase that he was now seeing a psychoanalyst. "And the doctor says my Marvin is suffering from an Oedipus complex!"

"Oedipus-Schmoedipus," scoffed her neighbor, "so long as he loves his mother."

———————

"Doctor Leffman!" said Mrs. Menzel. "All of a sudden I have developed this ringing in my ear!"

"Which ear?" asked the doctor.

"*Both* ears. It's driving me crazy. Doctor, how can I stop this *ring*ing?"

———

borscht would make it seem. *Shlemiel*, for instance, comes from Hebrew/Yiddish and should no more be spelled with a *c* (*schlemiel*) than *Shabbes* be rendered as *Schabbes*. Moreover, to the Anglo-Saxon eye, the cluster *sch* signals a *sk* sound: *school, scholar, schooner*: why tempt non-Jews to pronounce *schlemiel* as "skemiel" or *schlep* as "sklep"?

"Ringing-shminging," shrugged Doctor Leffman. "Don't *answer!*"

See also ACCENTUATING DISAGREEMENT . . . , CONTEMPT VIA CONFIRMATION . . .

Shabbes

This name for the Sabbath adorns many Jewish novels and stories. Pronounced SHAH-*biss*. Hebrew: *shabbat*: "rest," "cessation of labor." *Shabbes* is often retained in translations of Yiddish writers.

1. Sabbath.
2. "Make *Shabbes*" means to celebrate something, to break into festivity, song, or dance.

The life of Jews was so very hard for so very long that the Sabbath became more than a weekly respite from servitude, from bone-wearying labor and anxiety, if not terror. *Shabbes* is called "the Queen of the week," or "the Bride."

In however bitter a time and place, the Sabbath was the miraculous time when even the lowliest, poorest, least consequential Jew could feel in communion with the Almighty, favored by God's special concern: "It is a sign between me and the children of Israel" (Exodus 13). *Shabbes* crowned the week with splendor and sanctity. Mystics believed that the *Shechinah*, or Divine Presence, descends each Friday when the sun sets.

The Fourth Commandment says: "Remember the Sabbath day to keep it holy." Note that the Commandment ordains the Sabbath for beasts of burden no less than for men. (Jews are allowed to break the Sabbath if that is necessary to save the life or relieve the pain of an animal.)

Down the generations, in every land, for *Shabbes* Jews have scrubbed every nook of their dwelling, bathed themselves with care, donned fresh garments, laid out their best linens, glasses, utensils. *Shabbes* brought—each week, throughout a lifetime—a sense of personal grandeur.

In the *shtetl, Shabbes* was redolent with intimations of divinity, the hint of angels and visions of heaven, with all the blessed seated on golden thrones under the sparkling stars.

It is a long-honored custom for Jews to invite a stranger—a traveler, a student or poor man—to the *Shabbes* meal. However poor a Jew might be, he sought to find someone to be his family's *oyrech*. It is hard to overestimate how this served to make Jews everywhere feel part of one universal fellowship.

Harry Golden, reminiscing about life on New York's Lower East Side:

> The Irish and Italian boys had Christmas once a year; we had exaltation every Friday. In the most populous neighborhood of the world, rent by the shouts of peddlers, the screams of children, and the myriad noises of the city, there was every Friday evening a wondrous stillness, an eloquent silence. So quiet was it that two blocks from the synagogue you could hear the muffled chant of the cantor and the murmured prayers of the congregation. Once the service was over, you came home to find your mother dressed in her wedding dress with a white silk scarf around her head. And your father told you all the sufferings throughout the centuries were dedicated for this moment, the celebration of the Sabbath.
> —In Hutchins Hapgood, *The Spirit of the Ghetto*, p. 26

Shabbes begins just before sunset on Friday. The wife and mother lights the *Shabbes* candles and offers a benediction, as a priestess. (Before lighting the candles, the *balebosteh* (*q.v.*), however poor, has set aside a sum for charity.) As she lights the *Shabbes* candles, she closes her eyes and passes her palms over the candles, toward herself ("The soul is the Lord's candle," it is said in the Talmud) and whispers, "Blessed art Thou, O Lord our God, King of the Universe, Who has sanctified us by Thy commandments, and has commanded us to kindle the Sabbath lights." Then, silently, she asks God to preserve her family: its health, its peace, its honor.

Traditionally, the pious father returns from synagogue services to bless his children; then he recites the *Kiddush* (*q.v.*) and sips the wine. The entire family joins in welcoming the Sabbath angels who (it is believed) accompanied the father from the synagogue, singing, "Welcome to you, O ministering angels, may your coming be in peace, may you bless us with peace, and may you depart in peace."

Jewish husbands often sing a tribute to their wives (*Eshes Chayil*, "A Woman of Valor"), on the eve of *Shabbes*, in the words of Proverbs 31:

> *Strength and honor are her clothing . . .*
> *She openeth her mouth with wisdom . . .*
> *Her children arise up, and call her blessed; her husband also, and he praiseth her.*

What did the Jews do with their *time* on *Shabbes?* They prayed—and they studied; they read; they discussed the Torah and the Talmud. Every Sabbath, a rabbi or elder would read the laws "and expounded them point by point, until the late afternoon, when [all would] depart, having gained expert knowledge . . . and an advance in piety." This still governs the conduct of Orthodox Jews.

At home, on the six Sabbaths between Passover and Shevuos, fathers and grandfathers would traditionally engage the children in discussions of the *Wisdom of the Fathers* (*Pirke Abot*) or portions of the *Mishnah* that discuss ethical problems.

I leave it to cultural historians to appraise the magnitude of the consequence of an entire people, young and old, spending one day a week, year after year, generation after generation, century after century, in a seminar on religion, morals, ethics, responsibility.

Shabbes ends at sundown, Saturday, with a home religious service called *Habdala*, which marks the "separation" of the Sabbath from the weekdays. A special braided candle is lighted, wine is poured, blessings are uttered and the aroma of spices is inhaled—in the symbolic hope that the coming week will be sweet.

Gut Shabbes is sometimes used as a litany of dismay or disapproval; cynically disguised as a *pro forma* blessing/incantation.

REZNIK: They're raising the city taxes.
MENDEL: No! . . . *Gut Shabbes*.

"After fifteen years of marriage," said Sadie, "he wants to go to a marriage counselor with me! What should I do?"

"Tell him *Gut Shabbes* and move out until he comes to his senses."

"Remember you told me not to trust Bertha?"
"Do *I* remember!"
"You were right. She's ruining my reputation."
"*Gut Shabbes*. So ruin hers!"

Sign on store window:

SHIMON PARSIK
HI-CLASS TAILOR
I WILL MEND FOR YOU.
I WILL PRESS FOR YOU.
I WILL EVEN DYE FOR YOU.

Gut Shabbes!

For more about *Shabbes*, see the anthology *Sabbath: The Day of Delight*, edited by Abraham E. Millgram; Rabbi Hayim Donin's *To Be a Jew*, with the Hebrew prayers and their translation; and the lovely book by Abram Joshua Heschel called *The Sabbath*.

See also GUT SHABBES, HABDALA, KIDDUSH, MISHNAH, ONEG SHABBAT.

Shabuot

See SHEVUOS.

shachris

Pronounced SHAKH-*ris*, to rhyme with "Bach kiss." Hebrew: "morning."
The daily morning prayer of religious Jews.

One of the Jews' three daily prayers. A small minority of Jews, in America *or* Israel, pray thrice a day.

See also MAIREV, MINCHA.

shadchen
shadchonim   (plural)

Destined to become a part of Yinglish. An indispensable word for a unique professional man. You will surely run into *shadchen* in translations of the great Yiddish writers of the past. Pronounced SHOD-*khen*, to rhyme with "bodkin"—if you pronounce the *k* as a hearty *kh*. Plural: *shadchonim*: *shod*-KHUN-*im*. From the Hebrew: *shidukh*: "marital match."

1. A professional matchmaker, one who works for a fee.
2. Anyone who brings together, introduces, or maneuvers a man and woman into a meeting in the hope of effecting a marriage.
3. (Humorously) The "go-between" in, say, a business deal or merger, or the meeting of a lawyer and a new client.

Historically, Jewish marriages were arranged by the heads of two families. Rabbis were sometimes *shadchonim*, for the task of arranging marriages was considered a sacred matter. God was considered the Great *Shadchen*.

The professional *shadchen* also performed a social function: gathering information about eligible mates, weighing family background, individual qualities and personality factors. As the Jewish communities in eastern Europe grew larger, the *shadchonim* became seedy Cupids, more venal in their concern, more cunning in their salesmanship, less exact in their representations. (See Bernard Malamud's *The Magic Barrel*.)

The fate of the *shadchen* was sealed when Jews broke away from the *shtetl*; when economic and social progress made dowries no longer imperative; with the decline in orthodoxy; with the rise of proletarian consciousness; in the rebellion of the young against parental authority and tradition; and with the dramatic change in the feelings of Jews who wanted to marry for love, not by parental fiat.

Muttel the marriage broker, having sung the praises of a female client, brought a potential *chaussen* to see her.

The prospect took one look at the damsel, paled, and signaled to Muttel.

"What's the matter?" asked the *shadchen*.

The young man whispered, "You said she was young? She's almost forty! You said she was attractive? She looks like a chicken! You said she was—"

"You don't need to whisper," Muttel chuckled. "She's also hard of hearing."

————

A wisecrack defines a *shadchen* as "a marriage broker who knows the perfect girl for you—and married the wrong girl himself."

————

The *shadchen* was impressing the young man with the boundless virtues of a female, and ended: "And to look at, she's a regular picture!"

The young man could not wait for his blind date. But when he accosted the *shadchen* the next day, his voice was frosty: "Her eyes are crossed, her nose is crooked, and when she smiles, one side of her mouth goes down—"

"Just a minute!" interrupted the *shadchen*. "Is it my fault you don't like Picasso?"

————

Willy Dorman, having patiently listened to the *shadchen*'s panegyric about Sophie Brechstein, interrupted: "Sure, sure, she's nice, a fine cook, keeps kosher—but why do you leave me out that one important detail—that explains why she still is single?!"

"What? Me?" retorted the *shadchen*. "What did I leave out?"

"That the poor girl," said Willy, slowly and deliberately, "*limps*!"

The *shadchen* did not take two seconds before protesting, "Only when she *walks*, Willy! Don't forget that. Only when she walks!"

shalom

See SHOLEM.

shamus
shammes
shammus

Unequivocal Yinglish. Very widely used in American detective or private-eye stories, mysteries and novels about crime. Pronounced SHAH-*mes*, to rhyme with "promise." Hebrew: *shamash*: "servant." (Sometimes mispronounced as SHAY-*mus*.)

1. The sexton or caretaker of the synagogue; the "servant" of a congregation of worshipers.

In the old country, and in the early decades of this century in America, a *shamus* had many duties beyond the janitorial. He was expected to keep the synagogue clean and warm; to repair minor damage; to see that prayer books and ceremonial objects were safely preserved.

In the *shtetl*, the *shamus* would go around waking up congregation members, calling them to prayer, announcing sunset and Sabbath times. He also acted as a bailiff to the religious court. He collected synagogue dues, made funeral arrangements, and rounded up a *minyan*. He would even fill in for a cantor with a sore throat.

2. (In American slang) A detective, policeman, guard.

Shamus, in this usage, enjoys wide popularity in detective fiction and among the Irish; *shamus* sounds more like Gaelic than Yiddish. Eric Partridge claims that since so many Irish immigrants became policemen, the name Seamus (pronounced SHAY-*mus*) grew to be associated with police personnel.

3. A "private eye."
4. A functionary on a low level; an unimportant menial. "A *shamus* in a pickle factory" is a Yiddish phrase for a low man on anyone's totem pole.
5. Sycophant; a hanger-on around someone. "Every movie producer has to have a *shamus*."
6. A "stool pigeon"; an informer.
7. The ninth candle of the Chanukah *menorah (q.v.)*, used to light the others.

Rabbi Walpert stopped in the middle of his sermon and beckoned the *shamus* to the *bema*. "Look, fourth row," whispered the rabbi. "That heavy-set man. Absolutely asleep!"

"So?" the *shamus* grunted.

"*So*?! Wake him up!"

"I don't think that's fair."

"Not *fair*? What does that mean?"

"*Rebbe*, it was you who put him to sleep. Why don't *you* wake him up?"

Shavuot

See SHEVUOS.

shaygets (masculine)
shkotzim (plural)

Often encountered in stories or essays written by Jewish writers. Pronounced SHAY-*gits*, to rhyme with "hay kits." Hebrew origin. Plural: *shkotzim*. Feminine: *shiksa* or *shikse*.

1. A gentile boy or young man.
2. A clever lad; a rascal; a handsome, mischievous, charming devil—Jewish or gentile.
   "Oh, is he a *shaygets* with the girls!"
3. An arrogant cock-of-the-walk.
   "He strutted in as boldly as a *shaygets*."

Mrs. Lakish was dreaming ecstatically—for into her dream had wandered a handsome *shaygets*, who began making love to her. She sighed and moaned, then cried, "Oh, God! Footsteps! *It's my husband!*"

Mr. Lakish jumped out the window.

See also GOY, SHIKSA.

Shechinah
Shekhinah

Pronounced sh'-KHEE-*neh*, to rhyme with "Salina." Use the Scottish *kh*. Hebrew: "Divine Presence."

1. The term used to symbolize God's spirit and omni-presence.
2. Another way of referring to God without using His Name.
3. The actual dazzling, radiant, shining Presence of the Lord Himself.

The *Shechinah* was said to have appeared to Moses in the burning bush. It also descended in the pillar of smoke that guided the Israelites through the desert. It rested on

Mount Sinai when the Ten Commandments were given to the children of Israel.

The Talmud declares that the *Shechinah* is everywhere. Observing Jews say that the *Shechinah* descends each Friday at sunset to transform each Jewish home during the Sabbath.

Emperor Hadrian once approached Rabbi Joshua ben Hananiah and said, "I desire to see your God."

Rabbi Joshua said, "Your Majesty, face the sun—and gaze upon it."

The Emperor did so for a moment, then said, "I cannot! It is too bright. It blinds my eyes!"

Said Rabbi Joshua, "If you are not able to look upon the sun, which is only a servant of God, how much less can you gaze upon the *Shechinah*?"

See also ADONAI, ADOSHEM.

sheeny

Long a part (unpleasant) of Yinglish. Vulgarism. Pronounced SHEE-*nee*, to rhyme with "gleamy." Origin: debatable.

1. A thoroughly offensive name, combining contempt and disparagement, for a Jew.

C. T. Onions' *Oxford Dictionary of English Etymology* says that *sheeny* appeared in the nineteenth century, origin unknown. Ernest Weekley (*Etymological Dictionary of Modern English*) suggests that *sheeny* is derived from the way Jews pronounced the German word *schön* ("pretty," "beautiful") in describing the merchandise they offered for sale.

British slang for
2. A pawnbroker.
3. A tramp.
4. (In the military) A frugal, economy-minded man.
5. Fraudulent.

In such company, it is small wonder that "sheeny" raises the hackles of Jews.

See also ESKIMO, KIKE, YID.

shekel

> Yinglish. Slang. Pronounced SHEH-*kl*, to rhyme with "heckle." Hebrew: "coin," "weight." Plural *shkolim*, pronounced "SHKO-*lim*."

> 1. A coin.
> 2. Money.

A *shekel* was the most important silver coin in biblical times. It is mentioned in Genesis (33:12–16) as the money used by Abraham when he purchased the Cave of Machpela as a burying ground.

Shekel or *shekels* is widely used, in American slang, to mean "coins" or "money."

> "Come on, lay out some *shekels*."
> "He has more *shekels* than you have hairs."

> Shakespeare uses the word in *Measure for Measure* (II, 2): "Not with fond shekels of tested gold. . . ."

Shema
Shma

> A word of immense importance to pious Jews. Pronounced *sheh*-MA. Rhymes with "aha." Hebrew: "hearken," "hear."

> The first word of the prayer that proclaims the Jews' faith: "Hear, O Israel, the Lord our God, the Lord is One. . . ."

See also SHEMA YISRAEL.

Shema Yisrael
Shma Yisrael

> Pronounced *sheh*-MA *yis-roe*-AIL. From Hebrew: *shema*: "hearken," "hear"; *Yisrael*: "Israel."

> 1. The most common of Hebrew prayers, recited three—or four—times a day by an Orthodox Jew.
> 2. The last prayer a pious Jew utters on his deathbed.

This lyrical declaration of faith reads:

> Hear, O Israel: The Lord our God, the Lord is One!—
> And thou shalt love the Lord thy God with all thy heart,
> and with all thy soul, and with all thy might. And these
> words, which I command thee this day, shall be upon
> thy heart, and thou shalt teach them diligently unto thy
> children, and thou shalt talk of them when thou sittest in
> thy house, and when thou walkest by the way, and when
> thou liest down, and when thou risest up. And thou shalt
> bind them for a sign upon thy hand, and they shall be for
> frontlets between thine eyes. And thou shalt write them
> upon the door-posts of thy house and upon thy gates.
> —Deuteronomy, 6:4–7

Jews who were being tortured, flogged, flayed, hanged,
torn apart, burned at the stake, boiled in oil, or otherwise
introduced to pious efforts to convert them, would try to
die with the prayer on their lips.

Unlearned observers came to think that *Shema Yisrael*
meant "Long live the Jews!"—but they were wrong.

See also MEZUZAH, TEFILLIN.

Shevuos
Shavuot
Shabuot

Name of important Jewish holiday. Pronounced *sheh-*
vu-*ess*, to rhyme with "the Lewis." Hebrew: "weeks."

1. The Festival of Weeks, or Pentecost. (It was called
   Pentecost by Greek Jews, meaning "the fiftieth," for
   Shevuos occurred fifty days after the second day of
   Passover.)
2. The anniversary of the covenant between God and
   Israel on Mount Sinai—called "the season of the
   giving to us of our Holy Torah."

This two-day holiday (one day in Israel, or among Reform Jews) falls seven weeks after the second day of Passover. It is also "the holiday of the first fruits." To
commemorate this aspect of the holiday, synagogues are
decorated with greens.

The section of Exodus dealing with Sinai and the Ten

Commandments is read on *Shevuos*, as is the Book of Ruth, which tells the story of the lovely Moabite who became converted to Judaism and accepted its laws: "Thy people shall be my people . . . and thy God my God."

It is customary to eat dairy dishes on this holiday, especially delicacies made of cheese: cheese *blintzes (q.v.)*, cheese *latkes*, cheesecakes. It is also a time to forget diets.

A useful reference work is *The Shavuot Anthology*, edited by Philip Goodman.

shikker   (noun and adjective)

Common in Yinglish. Pronounced SHICK-*er*, to rhyme with "stick her." Hebrew: *shikor*: "drunk."

1. A drunk. "He's a *shikker*."
2. Drunk. "She got a wee bit *shikker*."

Jewish drunkards are exceedingly rare. The souse is almost unknown in Jewish folklore. The goodness of wine is often mentioned in the Bible. The rabbis believed: "Wine is the greatest of all medicines," "Where wine is lacking, drugs are necessary." But the sages always stressed moderation, in drinking as in all else—except study.

> By three things a man gives himself away: by his tippling, his tipping and his temper.
>
> —TALMUD

DOCTOR: I'm afraid I can't do any more for your husband, Mrs. Weiss. Has he tried Alcoholics Anonymous?
MRS. WEISS: I suppose so. He'll drink *any*thing.

Solly's Saloon, on Delancey Street, sported this sign in its window:

IF YOU MUST DRIVE YOUR MAN TO DRINK,
drive him here!

Traditional Jewish pride in sobriety is expressed by Israel Zangwill in his classic *Children of the Ghetto* (1892):

> The Ghetto welcomed the Sabbath Bride with proud sound and humble feast. . . . All around, their neighbors sought distraction in the public-houses, and their tipsy

bellowings resounded through the streets. . . . Here and there the voice of a beaten woman rose on the air. But no Son of the Covenant was among the [drunken] revellers or the wife-beaters. The Jews remained a chosen race, a peculiar people, faulty enough, but redeemed at least from the grosser vices—a little human islet won from the waters of animalism by the genius of ancient engineers.

SCENE: A Cocktail Party at the Finkelhoffs

WIFE: Arthur! Don't you think you ought to stop drinking? Your face is already beginning to look fuzzy!

"Milly," Si whispered, "drinking brings out all your beauty!"
"But I haven't been drinking!"
"I know . . . *I* have."

shiksa
shikseh

Common in Yinglish. Pronounced SHIK-*seh*, to rhyme with "pick the." The feminine of *shaygets*. From Hebrew.

1. A non-Jewish woman, especially a young one.
2. (As used, on occasion, by Orthodox Jews) A Jewish woman who is not pious, does not keep a *kosher* household, etc.

Yiddish has borrowed so many words from German that it is nice to report that German has borrowed from Yiddish, too—but incorrectly: *e.g., shicksel*: "Jewish girl"(!). I cannot for the life of me explain this. (See Heath's *New German–English Dictionary*.) For another Teutonic boo-boo see *mishpoche*.

As the Polish servant girl carried bucket after bucket of water from the well to the house, the rabbi sat down to eat with his disciples. But he sprinkled a very few drops of water on his hands, before making the traditional *broche* (blessing).
A disciple asked why he was so stingy about water.
The rabbi replied: "It is pious to wash before each meal;

but one must not be pious at even a servant's—a *shiksa*'s—expense."

See also GOY, SHAYGETS.

shiva
shivah

> Pronounced SHIH-*vah*, to rhyme with a Southerner's pronunciation of "river." From the Hebrew: "seven."
>
> The seven solemn days of mourning for the dead, beginning immediately after the funeral, when Jews "sit *shiva*" in the home of the deceased.

The traditional practice requires members of the immediate family to remove their shoes, don cloth slippers, and sit on stools or low benches—customs derived from ancient mourning rituals.

Mirrors are covered. The mourners wear garments with a rip in the lapel—the age-old symbol of grief: the rending of the garments. (The tear is made just before the funeral, after the mourner has uttered the words "Blessed be the righteous Judge.")

During the *shiva* period, mourners remain in the house and do not work or even study the Torah (save for certain portions). A *minyan* of ten men comes to the house, morning and evening, to hold services and enable the mourners to recite the *Kaddish*, or mourner's prayer. Friends pay visits, but conversation is limited to praise of the dead. The mourners do not offer or acknowledge greetings, for they must be entirely preoccupied with their grief and the memory of the dead.

The Talmud prescribes the protocol and phrasing of grief: three days of weeping, followed by four days of eulogy.

The seven-day *shiva* period is followed by a thirty-day period (*sheloshim*) of lesser mourning, and an eleven-month period during which the mourner recites the *Kaddish* twice daily. Thereafter, the deceased is remembered each year on the anniversary of his death.

So sad is this entry, that a bit of mirth may be welcome. Here are startling portions of some obituaries I have collected down the years:

Born poor, entirely through his own efforts, he worked his way up to within a few cents of a fabulous fortune.

Those who knew him said that underneath his ragged trousers beat a heart of gold.

One half of his estate went to his wife, and the other half to each of his four children by a previous marriage.

See also YORTZEIT.

shlemiel
schlemiel

An absolutely priceless word for Yinglish. There is no precise English synonym. Pronounced *shleh*-MEAL, to rhyme with "reveal." (Note: *Shlemiel* is often spelled *schlemiel*, or even *schlemiehl*, but I sternly oppose such complications. In Hebrew and Yiddish, a single letter, *shin*, represents the *sh* sound. And in English, to begin a word with *sch* is to call for the *sk* sound, as in "school" or "scheme.") Origin: probably #7 below.

1. A foolish person; a simpleton.
2. A "fall guy"; a hard-luck type; a submissive and uncomplaining victim.
   "That poor *shlemiel* always gets the short end of the stick."
3. A clumsy, butterfingered, all-thumbs type.
   "Why does a *shlemiel* like that ever try to fix anything?"
4. A social misfit, congenitally maladjusted.
   "Don't invite that *shlemiel* to the party."
5. A pipsqueak, a Caspar Milquetoast.
   "No one pays attention to that *shlemiel*."
6. A naive, trusting, gullible customer.
7. Anyone who makes a foolish bargain or wagers a foolish bet. This usage is wide in Europe; it probably comes from Chamisso's tale, *Peter Schlemihl's Wunderbare Geschichte*, a fable in which the protagonist gives up his shadow in return for Fortunatas's purse.

It is important to observe that *shlemiel*, like *nebech* or *shlimazel*, carries a distinctive note of pity. In fact, a *shlemiel* is often the *nebech*'s twin and the *shlimazel*'s clone.

The classic attempt to discriminate between the types runs: "A *shlemiel* is always spilling hot soup—down the neck of a *shlimazel*." Or, to make a triple distinction: "When a *shlemiel* trips, he knocks down a *shlimazel*; and a *nebech* repairs the *shlimazel*'s glasses."

A *shlemiel* can make a fortune—through luck. A *shlimazel* can't: he loses a fortune, through bad luck. Can a brilliant man be a *shlemiel*? Of course he can; many a savant is: the absent-minded professor, the impractical genius, are paradigms of *shlemielkeit*.

Shlemiel is said to come from the name Shlumiel, the son of a leader of the tribe of Simeon (Numbers, 2). Whereas the other generals in Zion often triumphed on the field of war, poor Shlumiel was always losing . . . But men far more knowledgeable than I (or you) call this interpretation a *bubbe-myseh*.

As mentioned above, *shlemiels* are usually regarded with pity, not scorn: they cannot be blamed for the infirmities of their judgment, the folly of their choices, or the naivete that governs their hapless course through life. I know no better way to pinpoint the characterization than with these classic definitions:

> A *shlemiel* falls on his back and breaks his nose.
> A *shlemiel* takes a bath, and forgets to wash his face.
> A *shlemiel* is always knocking things off tables—and a *nebech* always picks them up.
> A *shlemiel* rushes to throw a drowning man a rope—both ends.
> When a *shlemiel* wants to hang himself, he grabs a knife.
> A *shlemiel* measures water with a sieve.
> A *shlemiel* doesn't know how to find a notch in a saw.

Do not confuse a *shlemiel* with a *shlimazel* or a *nebech* or a *shnook* or a *shmendrick* or a *shmuck*. Each of these human types has its own distinctive attributes, albeit several are so close to each other that the distinctions are extremely subtle—indeed, so subtle that they seem synonymous. Each of these typologies has its own entry in this lexicon.

Jack Benny was the grand master at portraying a *shlemiel*. (Woody Allen is his heir but may often be just as well characterized as portraying a *nebech* or a *shlimazel*.) Mr. Benny once, receiving a cherished national award, accepted the honor with these memorable words: "I don't really deserve this beautiful award. . . . But I have arthritis, and I don't deserve that either."

Eddie Plish, an indubitable *shlemiel*, came home early one afternoon to find his wife and his best friend in bed. "Omi*god*!" cried Eddie. "What are you two doing?"

His wife turned to her bed-partner: "See, didn't I tell you he was a dummy?!"

See also DOPPESS, KLUTZ, LUFTMENSH, NAYFISH, NEBECH, SHLIMAZEL, SHMEGEGGE, SHMENDRICK, SHMO, SHNOOK, YOLD.

shlep (noun and verb)
shlepper (noun)

Firmly rooted in Yinglish. Widely used by Yippies and Yuppies alike. Pronounced SHLEP, to rhyme with "hep," and SHLEP-*per*, to rhyme with "pepper." From the German: *schleppen*: "to drag."

As a verb
1. To drag, or pull, or lag behind.
   "Who wants to act with a *shlepper* [or *shlep*] like that?"
   "Ever since then, she acts like a *shlepper* [or *shlep*]."

As a noun
2. Someone unkempt, untidy.
   "Why doesn't she do her hair and stop looking like a *shlepper*?"
3. A beggar or petty thief.
   "How does he earn a living? He's a *shlepper*."

Shlep and *shlepper* have become part of movie and theater argot, just as have *shtick, cockamamy, bubeleh*.

Mrs. Aronstein, visiting London, went to the famous gourmet emporium, Fortnum and Mason. She bought jars of marmalade, biscuits, tins of cookies and candies to take back to her hotel.

"And where," asked the striped-trousered salesman, "shall we deliver these, madam?"

"Don't bother. I'll carry them."

"But madam, we'll be *happy* to deliver this order—"

"I know, but I don't mind, I'm from the Bronx."

"I understand that, madam," said the clerk, "but still— why *shlep*?"

See also NAYFISH, NEBECH, SHLEMIEL, SHMEGEGGE, SHNOOK.

shlimazel
shlemazel

Rhymes with "rim nozzle." From German: *shlimm*: "bad," and Hebrew: *mazel*: "luck," "fortune."

1. Someone for whom nothing goes right or turns out well.
2. A "born loser," a Calamity Jane.

Let me illustrate the parameters of *shlimazel* by combining four folk sayings: "When a *shlimazel* winds a clock, it stops; when he kills a chicken, it walks; when he sells umbrellas, the sun comes out; when he makes coffins, people stop dying."

Do not confuse a *shlimazel* with a *shlemiel*, a *nebech*, a *shlump*, a *shnook*, a *shmendrick*, a *shmuck*. Each of these is part of the same human family: the luckless, the losers, the suckers, the pigeons of fate, the hapless. (Study each of these entries in this volume.)

He is such a *shlimazel* that his junk mail arrives "Postage due."

"They say the poor have no *mazel*, which is true; for if the poor did have *mazel* would they be poor?"

"Only a *shlimazel* believes in *mazel*."

—————

A twelfth-century poet, Abraham ibn Ezra (Browning's Rabbi ben Ezra, may his tribe increase), acutely described the *shlimazel's* fate when he wrote:

If I sold lamps,
The sun,
In spite,
Would shine
At night.

———

If it rained soup, a *shlimazel* would be caught with only a fork.   —Folk saying

See also LUFTMENSH, NAYFISH, NEBECH, SHMEGEGGE, SHNOOK, YOLD.

shlock
schlock

Familiar to any Yinglishman. Rhymes with "clock." *Shlock* is both an adjective and a noun. From German: *Schlag*: a "blow"; perhaps the Yiddish means merchandise that has been "knocked around."

1. A shoddy, cheaply made article.
   "It's a piece of *shlock*."
   "Where did you buy that? In a *shlock-house*?"
2. A defective or fake article; an object one was cheated over.
   "That watch will never keep time. It's *shlock*."
3. A disagreeable, peevish person.
4. A shrew, a whining wife, a *yenta*—and a slob, to boot.
   "His beloved? There's a *shlock* of a girl."
5. The gawdy, gim-crack articles sold at circuses and carnivals or in fly-by-night stores.
6. Dope, narcotics. (*Shlock* means "junk" and "junk" has come to mean narcotics.)
7. (Television) *Shlock-meister* ("*shlock*-master") is the agent who provides free gifts (for free plugs) on television game programs. Manufacturers employ a *shlock-meister* to get their products displayed on TV. Never was such huge publicity gained at such low cost.

shlock-house

In New York, Chicago, Los Angeles and Miami Beach (at least) this is revised standard English—therefore Yinglish.

1. A store that sells cheap, defective, "fire sale" articles.
2. A gyp joint.

In the furniture business, *shlock-house* merchandise is called borax. No one has a satisfactory explanation.

For years, Mordecai Schmelkin's friends had been begging him to get a hearing aid. "I hear fine!" the old man objected. "People just don't talk loud enough!"

One day, he passed a discount store on whose window a large sign announced:

SELLING OUT!
FANTASTIC BARGAINS! EVERYTING MUST GO!
POCKET RADIOS—SUN GLASSES
HEARING AIDS

Mordecai Schmelkin hurried in. Within five minutes he had been fitted for a hearing aid that had been reduced to ten dollars. (What it had been reduced from, I do not know.)

The old man went into the street with a smile on his lips, prepared to savor the pleasures of an amplified world. Soon he saw Moey Glickstein. "Say, Moey—come here! Look!" He pointed to his ear. "I bought a hearing aid. You were all absolutely right. What a *dif*ference! I can hear like a twelve-year-old! What an instrument!"

"That's wonderful," said Moey. "What kind is it?"

Mordecai glanced at his wrist. "Half-past three."

See also A.K., BLUFFER.

shlub

See ZHLUB.

shlump (noun and verb)
shloomp

Gaining ground in Yinglish, particularly among the young. Pronounce the *u* as in "put." German: *Schlumpe*: a "slovenly female," a "slattern."

As a noun
1. A drip, a "drag," a wet blanket.
   "That *shlump* can depress anyone."

A *shlump* is a *shlep* with droopy shoulders, or a *shmo* who drags his feet.

As a verb
2. To drag about, to shuffle.
3. To perform in a *pro forma* way; to "kiss off" with nominal effort or enthusiasm.
   "She *shlumps* through a role." (*Time*)

I have heard *shlump* from two Radcliffe girls, neither of whom knew a word of Yiddish; they also tossed off *shtuss* and *noodge* (or *nudzh*) with ease. *Shlump* seems popular on Broadway, in college theatricals, and among young people.

See also SHLEMIEL, SHLEP, SHMO, SHMUCK.

Shma

See SHEMA.

Shma Yisrael

See SHEMA YISRAEL.

shmaltz   (noun, adjective, verb)
schmaltz
shmaltzy   (adjective)

A staunch, proud Yinglish noun, especially in the entertainment world, where it is simply invaluable. Pronounced SHMOLTS, to rhyme with "doll" plus *tz*. German: *Schmaltz*: "fat," "drippings."

As a noun
1. Cooking fat; melted or rendered fat—usually, chicken fat.

If you like chopped liver, be sure to have a little *shmaltz* over, or mixed into, it.

2. "Corn" (as in "corny"); pathos; mawkish substance; excessive sentimentality; overly emotional mush.

"Tone it down; it's as *shmaltzy* as organ music."
"The way he delivered that speech, you could cut
the *shmaltz* with a fork."

This usage is wide in theatrical circles, which are a haven
for the self-dramatizing.

3. Luxury, wealth, good luck.
"He fell into a tub of *shmaltz*, that's how lucky he
is."

As an adjective
4. *Shmaltzy*: Corny, mawkish, hackneyed emotional-
ism.
"*Hearts and Flowers* is about as *shmaltzy* a song as
I ever heard."

As a verb
5. To *shmaltz* ("to *shmaltz* it up"): to add "corn," pathos, mawkishness.
6. To exaggerate greatly.

This story has no *shmaltz* in it:

SCENE: **Lembaum's Framers**

"I want a frame," said Mrs. Caplan, "for a thirty-thou-
sand-dollar picture."

Mr. Lembaum gasped. "Thirty thousand dollars?!!
Lady, I never before had an order like that! Where is the
picture?"

"Here." She handed Mr. Lembaum her son's college
diploma.

See also FARPATSHKET, ZAFTIG.

shmatte
shmotte

Used as English by anyone in the fashion world or
women's-wear business. Pronounced SHMOT-*ta*, to
rhyme with "pot a." From Polish: *szmata*: a "rag,"
"piece of cloth."

1. A rag.
   "That you call a dress? It's a *shmatte*."
2. Cheap, shoddy, junk.
   "I wouldn't drive in a *shmatte* like that."
   "The movie? A *shmatte!*"
3. A person unworthy of respect; someone "you can wipe your feet on."
   "She changes her opinion to suit everyone, that *shmatte*."
   "Stand up for your rights; don't be a *shmatte*."
4. A woman of weak character or wicked ways; a slattern.
   "She has as much self-respect as the *shmatte* she is."
5. A fawner; a sycophant; a toady.
   "Praise drips from that *shmatte* for everyone."

Paris: A Boutique

MRS. PETTLER: How much is *cette chemise*?

PROPRIETRESS: *Cette chemise?* Four hundred francs.

MRS. PETTLER: Four hundred francs?! *Mais*, it is *un shmatte*!

PROPRIETRESS: *Un shmatte*, Madame? *Quelle chutzpa*!

shmeer   (verb and noun)

Widely used in Yinglish—especially in sports, news, police and shady circles. Pronounced as it is written; rhymes with "shear." From German: *Schmiere*: "grease," or "bribe."

1. To paint.
2. To smear.
3. To spread.
   "*Shmeer* it on the bread."
4. A spread or paste.
   "With drinks, a caviar *shmeer* on crackers goes well."
5. To bribe; a bribe. This is the most interesting usage and has long been part of American slang. It is related to "greasing the palm."
   "Do the officials expect to be *shmeered* there?"

There is a saying: "*Az men shmeert nit, fort men nit.*" ("If you don't bribe, you don't ride.")

6. To strike or beat.

"He landed me a *shmeer* between the eyes."

7. The whole package, "the entire deal."

This verb/noun thrives wherever Yinglish has penetrated or seduced English: in Hollywood, on Broadway, in Washington or London's West End. I have heard it used in the most matter-of-fact manner from San Francisco to Park Lane, and in between.

———————

"I think it will help, Miss Kleinfeld, if you took this simple test." The psychiatrist drew a large circle on the blackboard. "What does that bring to your mind?"

"A handsome, naked man—ready for you-know-what."

The psychiatrist drew a large square. "And this?"

Miss Kleinfeld narrowed her eyes. "A virile, naked boy—doing it."

The psychiatrist now *shmeered* a meaningless blob on the board. "And this?"

"That's a big, naked brute—advancing right toward me!"

The psychiatrist hesitated. "Miss Kleinfeld . . . your responses show an unusual obsession—with sex."

"*My* responses?" cried the girl. "*You* drew all those dirty pictures!"

shmegegge

Yinglish. Slang. Unique. Delightful. Pronounced, always with disdain, *shmeh-GEH-geh* or *shmeh-GEH-gy*, to rhyme with "the mega" or "the Peggy." Ameridish slang. Origin: unknown; probably a dazzling onomatopoetic child of the Lower East Side (or the Ukraine, some Jews say).

1. An unadmirable, petty person.
2. A maladroit, untalented type.
3. A sycophant, a *shlepper*, a whiner, a drip.
4. A clumsy person, a *klutz*, a jerk.

Also used to describe:

5. A lot of "hot air," "baloney," a *cockamamy* story. "Don't give me that *shmegegge!*" (This will be contested, but usage is usage.)

I think of a *shmegegge* as a cross between a *shlimazel* and a *shlemiel*—or even between a *nudnik* and a *nebech*. Sophia Loren used the word with considerable *brio* in an interview with a *New York Times* reporter.

The word owes much of its vitality to the sneering sibilant *shm-* followed by double-voiced aspirate *g*'s—a combination any French phoneticist would hail as *formidable!*

"Did you hear about Sig Oletsky?"
"What?"
"He made a *killing* in the market!"
"That *shmegegge* made a killing—?!"
"He shot his broker."

See also KLUTZ, PASKUDNA, SHMENDRICK, SHMO, SHNOOK, TROMBENIK.

shmendrick

Would make an excellent addition to the namby-pamby human types so generously described in Yinglish. Pronounced SHMEN-*drick*, to rhyme with "Hendrick." From the name of a character in an operetta by Abraham Goldfaden.

1. A Caspar Milquetoast; a kind of *shlemiel*—but weak and thin. A *shlemiel* can be big and strong, but not a *shmendrick*. A *shmendrick* is short, weak, thin, a young *nebech*, perhaps an apprentice *shlemiel*, a clone of a *shlep*.
2. A pipsqueak; a no-account.
   "That *shmendrick*, maybe he'll grow up to be a *mensh*."
3. A nobody; someone lacking in influence or importance or both.
4. A boy, or young man; someone "wet behind the ears."
   "That *shmendrick* can't be trusted with such responsibility."

5. (Affectionate) A child.
   "How's my little *shmendrick*?"
6. (Colloquial) Penis. (Rarely used by men. When used by a female, the intention is to deride by diminutizing.)

See also NAYFISH, NEBECH, SHLEMIEL, SHLEP, SHMO, SHNOOK.

shmo (noun)

Entirely Yinglish. Rhymes with "stow."

1. Euphemism for the taboo *shmuck*.
2. A boob; a hapless, clumsy, unlucky jerk.
3. A "butt"; a fall guy; the goat of a joke.

Al Capp, the fertile intelligence who took L'il Abner down several exuberant decades of hillbilly hi-jinks, adopted *shmoo* for the name of an egg-shaped creature that loves to be kicked and gives milk.

But *shmo* was in use long before that, as an abbreviation for the lusty, but offbounds, *shmuck*. Fred Allen, on a radio program in 1947, protested: "I've been standing here like a *shmo* for twenty minutes."

———————

Joe Retzig was going up the stoop of the building in which he and his wife lived. "Psst! Psst!" came a hiss from the janitor, who whispered, "I don't want you to have a heart attack. . . . In your bedroom, your wife is in bed—with your best friend!"

Retzig turned white, then rushed through the front door like a man insane.

The janitor shook his head sadly.

In a few minutes, the front door opened and Retzig came out. "Mr. Janitor," he said, "you're crazy. Didn't you tell me my wife is in bed with my best friend?"

The janitor nodded.

"That man my best friend?" scoffed Retzig. "I never laid eyes on him in my whole life!"

See also SHMUCK, ZHLUB.

shmooze (verb and noun)
shmoos
schmooze
shmues

Has become a widely used colloquialism in Yinglish. Rhymes with "loose"; most Yinglishmen pronounce it to rhyme with "ooze." Hebrew: *shmuos*: (originally) "things heard"; (in time) "rumors," "idle talk."

As a noun
1. A friendly, gossipy, casual conversation.
"They had a long *shmooze*."

As a verb
2. To have a warm, heart-to-heart talk with a friend.
"Call me back; I'd love to *shmooze* with you."
"They *shmoozed* for over an hour."

I have never encountered a word that conveys a warm, "heart-to-heart chit-chat" as vividly as does *shmooze*.

———

Gelett Burgess, who invented the word *blurb* and was the creator of the limerick about "the purple cow," once tried to smuggle "huzzlecoo," a word he coined, into English. "Huzzlecoo" never caught on; but it was a dead ringer for *shmooze*.

———

One reason for the great success of Saul Lipsky's Fashion Haircut Salon was this sign in the window.

FOUR BARBERS
CONSTANT SHMOOZING!

See also DOPPESS, TSITSER, YENTA.

shmotte

See SHMATTE.

shmuck (noun)
shmekel (diminutive)

Vulgar, obscene, *shmuck* has become a forceful and very popular epithet in Yinglish. I have heard gentile women (especially executives) use it as a snort of contempt or disdain. Rhymes with "stuck." From German, one way or another, where *Schmuck* is "an ornament," or "jewelry"; *shmuck* is "neat," "smart," and *schmucken* means "to decorate." In Yiddish, *shmock* means an "ornament."

1. (Obscene) Penis.

Never utter *shmuck* lightly or in the presence of women and children. Indeed, it was uneasiness about *shmuck* that led to the truncated euphemism *shmo*. Any *shmo* should know what *shmo* comes from.

Jews tend to be puritanical about public references to the pubic.

I never heard any Jewish elders use *shmuck*, which was regarded as so vulgar as to be taboo. But vulgarity has its *raison d'être*.

2. (Taboo) A dope, a jerk, a boob.
3. A clumsy bumbler.

In this sense, *shmuck*, like its English equivalent, is widely used by males, and with gusto; few impolite words express comparable contempt.

"What a *shmuck* I was to believe him!"

4. (Vulgar) A detestable fellow; a son of a bitch.
5. A trickster, hypocrite.
   "That low-down, hypocritical *shmuck*!"

Note the curious etymological anatomy of *shmuck*. The German word means an ornament or jewel. The word was not lewd in German nor obscene in Yiddish. How did the connotational leap take place from "jewel" to "penis"?

By mothers bathing or drying their baby sons. They would croon over them. What better word for the "member" than "little jewel" . . . "ornament" . . . "cute pendant."

In English, men josh about "the family jewels" (and they do not mean rubies). German or Hungarian nurses and governesses, I am reliably informed, used the euphemistic *shmuck*. Jewish mothers and sisters were puritanicalenough to refer to "that . . . place" or "that [his, her] . . . thing."

A scholarly literature has grown up about the etymology of *shmuck, putz* and *shlemiel*, guided by the researches of Dr. Gerald Cohen of the University of Missouri.

I have no doubt that among my readers are proper souls who would not disapprove of the custom in fifteenth-century France of slitting the lips of those who used profane language. For their edification I offer an immortal verse by some unknown genius:

> *O banish the use of those four-letter words*
> *Whose meaning is never obscure;*
> *The Romans and Britons, those bawdy old birds,*
> *Were vulgar, obscene and impure.*
> *You stubbornly use any weaseling phrase*
> *That never says just what you mean,*
> *You prefer to be known for your hypocrite ways*
> *Than be vulgar, impure or obscene.*
> *Let your morals be loose as a libertine's vest,*
> *But your language keep always obscure;*
> *It's the word, not the act, that's the absolute test*
> *Of what's vulgar, obscene or impure.*

Danger: Vulgarity

The following story is bound to become a classic, but you had better skip it if you are finicky about *shmuck*.

Mr. Zachary Pinchik—sixty-five, a widower—was having a lonely time in Miami Beach. He observed a man of his age who was never without a companion; people forever streamed around him, extending invitations, swapping jokes.

So Pinchik screwed up his courage and said to the popular paragon, "Mister, excuse me, I'm so lonesome. What should I do to—to make friends here?"

"Get—a camel," sneered the other.

"A camel?" gasped Pinchik.

"Sure. Ride it up and down Collins Avenue every day, and before you know it, everyone in Miami will be asking 'Who *is* that man?' You'll have to hire a secretary to handle all the invitations!"

So Zachary Pinchik bought a paper and looked through the ads, and by good fortune read of a circus, stranded in Miami, that needed capital. Mr. Pinchik telephoned the circus owner, and within half an hour he had rented a camel!

The next morning, Mr. Pinchik, wearing khaki shorts and a pith helmet, mounted his camel and set forth on Collins Avenue. Everywhere people stopped, buzzed, gawked, pointed.

Every day for a week, Mr. Pinchik rode his trusty steed. One morning, his telephone rang. "Mr. Pinchik! This is the parking lot! Your camel—it's gone! Stolen!"

At once, Mr. Pinchik phoned the police. A Sergeant O'Neill answered: "*What*? . . . It sounded as though you said someone had stolen your *camel*!"

"That's right."

"Er—I'll fill out a form . . . How tall was the animal?"

"From the sidewalk to his back, where I sat, a good six feet."

"What color was it?"

"What *color*?" echoed Pinchik. "*Camel* color!"

"Male or female?"

"*Hanh*?" gasped Mr. Pinchik.

"Was the animal male or female?"

"How am I supposed to know about the sex of a *camel*?" exclaimed Mr. Pinchik. "Wait! Aha! Yes, yes! It was a male!"

"Are you sure?"

"I'm *positive*, Officer, because I just remembered: Every place I was riding on that camel, I could hear the people hollering, 'Hey! Look! Look at the *shmuck* on that camel!' "

See also PUTZ, SHMEGEGGE, SHMENDRICK, SHMO, SHNOOK, ZHLUB.

shmues

See SHMOOZE.

shnaps (noun)
schnaps

An old part of the English vernacular. Rhymes with "tops." German: *Schnaps*: "intoxicating spirits."

1. Brandy.
2. Any intoxicating spirits.

Any holiday or happy event was (and still is) the occasion for a little toast with *shnaps*. The phrase used to introduce the toasting is *Lomir machn a shnaps* (LAW-*mir* MAKH-*en a* SHNOPS): "Let us 'make' a *shnaps*."

A drunkard smells of *shnaps*, but so does a saloon-keeper.
A tavern can't corrupt a good man, and a synagogue can't reform a bad one.
Wine helps open the heart to reason.
When *shnaps* goes in, secrets come out.
　　　　　　　　　　　　　　　—Folk sayings

The Talmud decrees that judges may not drink any spirits for twenty-four hours before deciding a case that involves a capital crime.　　　—*Sanhedrin*: V, 1–5

shnook
shnuk

Well known to Yinglishmen.

This clone of a *shlemiel* was so named in New York. It has no English or European analogues. Pronounced to rhyme with "crook." Derivation: unknown. Possibly from the German *Schnuck*, "a kind of small sheep," or from *Schnucki*, the German colloquialism for "pet," a pet dog, one's "darling," or wife—but I doubt it (see below).

1. A timid *shlemiel*; a meek patsy; a passive, unassert-ive, ineffectual type.
2. A "Sad Sack," more to be pitied than despised. A *shnook* is pathetic but likable; if not likable, he would probably be called a *shmuck* (you should excuse my frankness).

Shnook is almost certainly an American–Yiddish coin-age. None of my panel of experts had ever heard it in any East European tongue, nor in German, nor in European

Yiddish; and every person I questioned said he had first heard *shnook* in America. Max Weinreich's *History of the Yiddish Language* does not have a single mention of *shnook, shnuk* or *schnook*.

I know that there is a German word *Schnuck* ("a small sheep") and that *Schnucki* is used in German vernacular for "darling," "pet," "wife." But experts assure me there is no demonstrable connection between those two words and the Yinglish pejorative noun. Still, if *shnook* is an American–Jewish coinage: what *did* it come from?

On October 9, 1951, Jack Benny, in the midst of a comic imbroglio on his radio program, said, "All the other *shnooks* in the business thought—"

The word soon appeared in movies, in comic strips and (emphatically) in nightclub routines. In the movie *The Apartment*, Jack Lemmon is characterized as "a *shnook*."

Solomon Duvno was in the hospital after an operation. To see him came Ellis Twersky, secretary of their synagogue—and a *shnook*. "So," said Ellis, "I am bringing you the good vishes from our board—that you should get vell soon, comm back to the congregation, and live to be a hondred and tan years—at least!"

"Oh, that's nice," said Duvno. "Vary nice."

"*Nice*? Listen, Sol. That vasn't just a simple 'get-better' from the board. It was an official *rasolution*—"

"My!"

"Passed by a vote of fourtin to seven!"

(You say I have used this joke before? . . . So?)

See also NAYFISH, SHLEMIEL, SHLEP, SHLUMP, SHMEN-DRICK, SHMO, ZHLUB.

shnorrer (noun)
shnorer
schnorrer
shnor (verb)

Few words are as distinctive and as essential to an understanding of Jewish ethics and mores. Pronounced

SHNOR-*rer*, to rhyme with "scorer." German: *schnor-ren*: "to beg." Related to *schnarchen* ("to snore" or "to whine") by some philologists, who relate the whining of beggars to snoring. But Jewish beggars do not whine or snore—as you may read below.

As a noun
1. A professional beggar, a panhandler.
2. A cheapskate, a chiseler.
3. A compulsive bargainer.
4. An impudent indigent.

As a verb
5. *Shnorren*: to beg, to mooch, to "borrow."

Once upon a time, in any land, every Jewish community had at least one *shnorrer*—and often a platoon. The *shnorrer* was no run-of-the-mill mendicant. He was not apologetic; he did not fawn or whine. He regarded himself as a professional. He did not so much ask for alms as *claim* them.

For *shnorrers* considered they had a license from the Lord Himself: after all, they were *helping* Jews discharge solemn obligations to the poor and the unfortunate. Through contributions to the needy, a good Jew could accumulate *mitzvas! Shnorrers* seemed to know that they were both exploiting and assuaging one of the most powerful psychological forces in the psyche of Jews: guilt.

The *shnorrer* was no fool. He often had read a good deal, could quote from the Talmud, and was quick on the verbal draw. *Shnorrers* were "regulars" in the synagogue and, between prayers, took part in long discussions of theology with their benefactors.

In Chicago, "our *shnorrer*" (as my parents thought of him) would come up to my parents, extend his palm, receive his nickel or dime, and proceed to his next "clients." Not a word was exchanged: no greeting, no "*shalom*" or "*sholem aleichem*," merely a nod from the mendicant, a sigh from my father, a smile from my mother: a worthy transaction, one approved by the sages, had been concluded.

One Sunday, the *shnorrer* was nowhere to be seen. After we walked the length of his usual territory without encountering him, my mother said, "I wonder what's happened to our *shnorrer*? I hope he's not sick."

"Sick?" my father snorted. "He's as healthy as a horse!"

"Then why isn't he on the street?"

"He's probably in Florida," said my father, "taking his vacation."

———

I have explored the ethical assumptions and psychological rewards of both *shnorrer* and *shnorree* in "The Shnorrer: A Study in Piety and Paradox," in *Next Year in Jerusalem*, edited by Douglas Villiers.

Whenever genius is discussed, I think of the Jewish *shnorrer* who stood on a busy street in Berlin, during Hitler's reign, with a tin cup and this sign:

I DO NOT ACCEPT
MONEY FROM JEWS

The coins of the *Herrenvolk* dropped into that tin cup in a constant shower.

———

The *shnorrer* stopped the alrightnik and held out his palm.

"I," said the alrightnik, "don't hand out money on the street!"

"So what should I do," asked the *shnorrer*, "open an office?"

See also CHUTZPA, TROMBENICK.

shnoz
shnozzle

Well established in Yinglish.
Pronounced SHNOZ, to rhyme with "Pa's" and SHNOZ-*z'l*, to rhyme with "sozzle." From German: *Schnauze*, "snout."

1. (Slang) Nose.
2. A long, very large or unattractive nose.

shochet

Pronounced SHOW-*khet* or SHOY-*khet* (Yiddish); render the *kh* as a MacTavish would. Rhymes respectively with "show bet," and "joy net." Hebrew: "slaughterer."

The authorized slaughterer of animals, according to *kosher* ritual requirements.

The *shochet*'s credentials are certified by rabbis, and his work is supervised by them. A *shochet* has to be thoroughly conversant with the many rules governing *kosher* food in the *Shulchan Aruch*, the code adopted in the sixteenth century. He serves an apprenticeship before he can use his own initials in the branding iron used to signify approval of slaughtered animals.

On Maxwell Street in Chicago there was a butcher of such spotless reputation that his sign read:

strictly kosher!!
THE SHOCHET KILLS HIMSELF
EVERY MORNING!

See also KOSHER.

shofar

This word is widely read and heard in English, and in profusion, every Rosh Hashanah and Yom Kippur. Pronounced SHOW-*fer*, or SHOY-*fur* (Yiddish), to rhyme with "goiter," or SHAY-*fer* (another form of Yiddish), like the name of the beer. Hebrew for "trumpet," "horn," specifically a "ram's horn."

A ram's horn, ten to twelve inches long, that is blown in the synagogue during the high holidays of Rosh Hashanah and Yom Kippur.

Exodus reports that the ram's horn was heard on Mount Sinai, when God gave Moses the Ten Commandments. The curious curved bend in the *shofar* is supposed to represent how a human heart, in true repentance, bends before the Lord. Being a ram's horn, it serves to remind the pious how Abraham, offering his son Isaac in sacrifice, was reprieved when God decided that Abraham could sacrifice a ram instead. The *shofar* was used in the Temple as a musical instrument and in ceremonial processionals and as a trumpet of war.

In Israel, the *shofar* is blown on important occasions, for example, during the inauguration of a new president. It was blown when the Western Wall was liberated.

sholem (Yiddish)
sholom (Yiddish)
shalom (Hebrew)

> Widely used and understood by Yinglishmen. *Shalom* is Hebrew, pronounced *sha*-LOHM; *sholem* is Yiddish, pronounced SHO-*lem* or SHAW-*lem*. From the Hebrew root word meaning "whole," "entire": "peace."
>
> 1. Peace.
>
> *As a greeting or salutation*
> 2. Hello.
> 3. So long, good-bye.
> 4. *Au revoir.*
>
> Why is *sholem* used for both "hello" and "good-bye"? Israelis say: "Because we have so many problems that we don't know whether we're coming or going."

> On its maiden voyage, the S.S. *Shalom*, the first ocean liner of Israel, steamed into the harbor of New York to a truly tumultuous greeting. Even those who were not tumultuous said, "It doesn't *look* Jewish!"

sholem aleichem
sholom aleichem

> This phrase and name are becoming readily understood by Yinglishmen. Pronounced SHO-*lem* (or SHAW-*lem*) *a*-LAY-*khem*; deliver the *kh* as if clearing a bread crumb from the roof of your mouth. Hebrew: *shalom alekhem*: "peace unto you."
>
> 1. The traditional greeting or salutation of Jews; it is used for "Hello," "How do you do?" etc. The

response to this greeting reverses the words—thus:

2. *"Aleichem sholem"* ("And unto you, peace") is the traditional response to *"sholem aleichem"*; the exchange is uttered by Jews when parting, as well as when meeting.

3. (Ironically) "Finally we get to the heart of the matter!" "At long last!" "Hallelujah!" Thus:
"O.K., I owe you ten dollars."
"Sholem aleichem!"

4. The pen name of Sholem (Solomon) Rabinowitz (1859–1916), the immortal Jewish writer and humorist, a master of the monologue and the short story (he wrote over three hundred, and five novels), a brilliant wit, a fecund aphorist, the greatest chronicler of the life of the *shtetl*, author of the Tevye stories, on which the international hit *Fiddler on the Roof* was based.

It is said that when Mark Twain met Rabinowitz in New York, Rabinowitz said, "This is a great honor for me. People say I am the Jewish Mark Twain."

To which Sam Clemens replied, with typical grace and wit, "And people call *me* the American Sholem Aleichem!"

Underlying all of Sholem Aleichem's work is a running sense of the sad plight of his characters—and of Jews in general. Chilling irony often ends a funny tale.

When asked why he wrote about poverty, illness, stupidity, tragedy, with such humor, Rabinowitz said, "If I didn't laugh, I would weep."

Incidentally, Muslims use the same salutation ("*sholem aleichem*") and virtually the same phrasing—except that Muslims begin with an *s* instead of a *sh*, and use a *k* instead of a *kh*; thus: *salaam aleikum*. (This is acceptable Arabic, at no extra charge.)

"Hello, Skolnick! I haven't seen you in years. How are you, how's the wife, the children?"

"Everyone's fine. My wife is flourishing, my children are doing well, and I couldn't be happier. Well—*sholem aleichem*."

"Wait a minute, Skolnick! Are you going away just like that? Don't you even ask *me* one question? Can't you even ask an old friend how he's doing in his business?"

"Oh, I'm terribly sorry. Tell me: How's business?"

"Don't ask. *Aleichem sholem.*"

See also ALEICHEM SHOLEM.

should (for "may")
shouldn't (God forbid)

Yiddish is rich in invocational phrases such as this. Encountered in parody aspects of fiction or essays by Jewish writers.

1. May you [I, he, she] . . .
2. If only . . .
3. I hope that . . .

"You should [may you] live to a hundred and twenty!"

In English, such supplications are phrased "I wish that . . ." and (in earlier centuries) "Would that we [I, they] . . ."

"It shouldn't happen to a dog!" (*q.v.*) is an eloquent example of typical Yinglish petitions to fate.

shpritz (verb and noun)
shpritzer (noun)

Yinglish. From German/Yiddish: *spritzen*: "to sprinkle," "to spray," "to squirt."

1. To squirt soda into a tall glass of wine.
   "*Shpritz* an inch or two into the glass."
2. A *shpritzer* is a drink: wine to which soda/seltzer has been added.
   "Give me a *shpritzer*: Beaujolais."
3. A slight drizzle of rain. Weather forecasters on television, in the New York area, have used this expression: "We may have a *shpritz* of rain this afternoon." An actor who sprays saliva is a *shpritzer*.

See also FOR TWO CENTS PLAIN . . .

shtarker (masculine)
shtarkeh (feminine)

A word pregnant with connotations. Recommended without reservation for Yinglish. Pronounced SHTARK-er. From German: *stark*: strong.

1. A strong man or woman.
2. Someone brave or fearless.
3. A "big shot."
4. (Derisive) No hero.
5. Someone boastful, full of false bravado

That last usage is prized by connoisseurs of irony: "Don't rely on that *shtarker*."

"Listen, *shtarker*, if you have no choice, at least be brave."

Mrs. Zupman was on the beach with her little boy. The tot wandered into the water. A big wave came up.

"My boy! My boy!" screamed Mrs. Zupman.

On every side, people leaped to their feet—but stood transfixed as the wave sucked the lad out to sea.

And then a *shtarker* ripped off his shoes and pants, plunged into the surf and with powerful strokes swam out— and finally grabbed the lad and swam him back to shore.

Mrs. Zupman smothered the lad with kisses and hugged him hard and, with beams of gratitude, surveyed her miraculously saved child. Then she noticed something. She wheeled toward the *shtarker* and cried in indignation, "Mister! My boy was—wearing—a *hat*!"

A Jewish gambler, Label Trupin, lost all his money playing blackjack—and dropped dead.

His friends debated who should bring the sad, sad news to Trupin's widow.

They finally agreed that the best man for this delicate duty was Morty Samech, a *shtarker*.

So Morty took a taxi to the Trupin apartment house, walked up two flights of stairs and knocked on the door. A comely woman opened it.

"Do I have the privilege," asked Morty, "of addressing the *almoona* [widow] Trupin?"

"Absolutely *not*!" said Alma.

"I'll betcha," said Morty.

See also K'NOCKER, PLOSHER, TSITSER.

shtetl   (noun)
shtetlach   (plural)

A vast range of memoirs, the stories of Sholem Aleichem, novels, plays (*Fiddler on the Roof*) and the work of cultural anthropologists have rocketed *shtetl* into familiar Yinglish. Pronounced SHTEH-*t'l*, to rhyme with "kettle," or SHTAY-*t'l*, to rhyme with "fatal." From German: *Stadt*: "a little town." Plural: *shtetlach*.

Little city, small town, poor village—in particular, the little Jewish communities of eastern Europe, where the remarkable culture of the Ashkenazim flourished (before World War II) and where *Yiddishkeit* reached its apogee.

Shtetl is a term of special importance in the history of Ashkenazic culture—different, in so many profound ways, from that of Sephardim (*q.v.*).

The Jews of the *shtetl* were poor folk, fundamentalist in faith, earthy, superstitious. They considered their exile temporary and dreamed of the messianic miracle that would—any day now—return them (and their brethren around the world) to the shining glory of a restored Israel in the Holy Land.

Catherine II, in 1791, confined all Jews to the "Pale of Settlement," twenty-five provinces of the Russian empire. To live outside, a Jew needed special permission from the authorities. Skilled workers and clever businessmen did receive (or purchase via bribery) such permission. But the vast majority of Jews in the Czarist empire lived within a restricted area. They could not move without permission from the police. The list of prohibitions, ostracisms, restrictions and indignities inflicted upon the reviled and persecuted Jews was simply staggering: they were forbidden to own land; they were barred (with minor exceptions) from attending colleges or universities; they were excluded from the humblest government jobs; they were not allowed to practice certain crafts, skills and trades.

Fiddler on the Roof, that super-colossal hit, painted a highly romanticized picture of *shtetl* life. Let me be plain: life in those medieval enclaves was dreadful: hunger was endemic, sanitation disgusting, housing unspeakable. The muddy streets, open latrines and ubiquitous garbage offended the nostrils. Neither water nor light blessed the huts and hovels.

Safety was nowhere. Jews were spat upon, beaten, tormented. Their synagogues were frequently vandalized, their women raped, their children kidnapped to be forcibly converted or sent into the Czar's army, "robbed of their very souls."

Russian or Polish police officials shrugged off the repeated hooliganism of drunken thugs, the periodic bloodbaths of murderous Cossacks, the recurring pogroms instigated by fanatical priests.

Every morning of the year, in a *shtetl*, was heard the same loud summons: *Yiden, Yiden! Shtayt of l'avodat habora*! "Jews, Jews! Rise—and serve the Lord!" For in those desolate backwaters the only raft of hope was—faith. Faith—intense, impassioned, invulnerable—in a merciful God and His promise of the Messiah soon to come. Torah offered the miracle of deliverance, the inner light that healed pain, that sanctified poverty and despair and fear.

The world of the Jews in Germany, France, England, Holland, Italy, Austria was vastly different from the world of *shtetl* Jews in eastern Europe. *City* Jews in eastern (and western) Europe were caught up in political and libertarian movements; they became trade unionists, social democrats, socialists, revolutionaries. They slipped away from orthodoxy.

———

The *shtetl* exists no more. Hundreds of thousands of Jews left those muddy, dreary clusters for England, France, Holland, Brazil and—America, America! Those who did not leave were rounded up for the Nazis' "final solution."

It is not hard to write "six million Jews were slaughtered." But it is impossible—simply *impossible*—to grasp the enormity of the horror. Even the survivors cannot do that. (Read *Voices from the Holocaust*, edited by Sylvia Rothchild.) The simplicity and calmness of their recollections are a testimonial to human endurance in the face of monstrous *evil*.

Excellent data and insights into the *shtetl* will be found in *Life Is with People*, by Mark Zborowski and Ruth Herzog, *The World of Sholem Aleichem*, by Maurice Samuel, and *The Golden Tradition*, edited by Lucy Davidowicz.

shtik (noun)
shtikel (diminutive)
shtikl (diminutive)
shtikeleh (more diminutive)
shtiklech (plural)

Solidly Yinglish. *Shtik* is as much a part of English theatrical argot as "a take," "pratfall" or "upstage." Pronounced SHTIK, to rhyme with "quick"; SHTIK-'*l*, to rhyme with "pickle"; SHTIH-*k'l-leh*, to rhyme with "piccolo" (but with an "eh," not "oh," at the end); and SHTIK-*lekh*, which rhymes with "wick loch" or "wick ech!" (Just be sure to pronounce that final *kh* as a Scotsman would.) German: *Stuck*: "piece."

1. A piece.
   "Give him a *shtik* cake." (Never say a *shtik* "of" anything.)
2. A part, part of, bit of.
   "He is a *shtik narr* [fool]."
3. A prank, a piece of clowning.
   "He made us laugh with his *shtik*."
4. A piece of misconduct.
   "In company, one should not perpetrate a *shtik* like that."
5. A devious trick; a bit of cheating.
   "How did you ever fall for a *shtik* like that?"
6. A studied, contrived or characteristic piece of visual "business" employed by an actor or actress; overly used gestures, grimaces or devices to steal attention.
   "Watch him use his *shtik*."
   "Play it straight: no *shtik*."

Shtikl, the diminutive of *shtik*, means:

1. A small piece.
   "She is a *shtikl* crazy." ("She is slightly 'off.' ")
2. A bit of.
   "Oh, is he a *shtikl* cheap."
   Shtikeleh, a further diminutive for *shtikl*: A really *small* little piece.
   Shtiklech: Plural of all the meanings cited above.

A woman in Wolfowitz's delicatessen saw some small pickles on the counter, under a sign "*Nosh.*"

"How much costs today a pickle?" she asked.

"A pickle," said Mr. Wolfowitz, "is a nickel."

"A *nickel*? . . . So tell me: How much is this—eh—*shtikl?*"

"That *shtikl*—is a nickel."

"My God! . . . And this *pickeleh?*"

"That *pickeleh*," said steely Wolfowitz, "is a *nickeleh!*" (Yep, I've used this doozy before.)

shtup (noun and verb)
shtoop

Vulgar, even obscene, but enlivens the discourse of many Yinglishmen. Pronounced with the *u* of *put*, not the *u* of *cup*. From the German: *stupsen*: "to push."

1. To push, press. "Don't *shtup*," means "Don't push"—both literally and figuratively; *i.e.*, don't be aggressive.

Shtup, in vulgar vernacular, also means:

2. To fornicate. This usage is often heard in American slang.
   "Did he *shtup* her?"
   "Does she or doesn't she *shtup?*" has nothing to do with hair tinting.
3. The act of copulation.
   "He gave her a real *shtup*."
4. A female who fornicates.
   "That one is a hot *shtup* [or *shtupper*]."

"Listen, Goldie. Do you think a widower—a father of forty—ought to get married again?"

"Migod, *no*, Tillie. That's more than enough children for *any* man!"

See also SHMUCK, YENTZ.

shtuss (noun)

> Yinglish. Popular among the young, especially on college campuses. Rhymes with "puss," not with "cuss." Hebrew: "stupidity."

> 1. Nonsense.
>   "What he says is a lot of *shtuss*."
> 2. A commotion.
>   "Pipe down; don't make such a *shtuss*."
> 3. A *contretemps*, a disturbance, a "rhubarb" caused by a complaint or protest.
>   "She made such a *shtuss* that they had to go to court."
> 4. A disproportionate response, protest or objection.
>   "From the *shtuss* they're making, that toy was worth ten thousand dollars!"

See also KOCHLEFFL, TARARAM, TSIMMES.

shul

> Rhymes with "full." From the Greek *schola* via the German *Schule*. The Hebrew word for a house of prayer is *bet-ha-knesset*, a house of assembly. Similarly, the Greek word *synagogue* means "assembly," "congregation."
>   School—therefore, synagogue.

The *shul* was the very center of Jewish communal life. Day and night men sat, read, prayed, studied, debated—in the synagogues. Many never closed their doors.

The synagogue seems to date from 586 B.C., when Nebuchadnezzar drove the Jews into exile. In Babylonia they sought to replace the Great Temple of Jerusalem, which had been destroyed.

God Himself proceeds from synagogue to synagogue, says the Talmud, "and from *Bet Midrash* [House of Study] to *Bet Midrash* . . . [to] give His blessings to Israel."

In time it became a solemn obligation for Jews to build a *shul* as soon as a community contained a *minyan* (ten males). Synagogues were established, in time, all through Palestine, Babylonia, Arabia, Egypt, Persia, around the Crimea, Syria—in the cities of Greece, in Rome and eventually in every country where Jews were taken as slaves or allowed to reside. Philo, who was a rabbi and a Platonist at the time of Jesus of Nazareth, said it was the synagogue that made all Jews philosophers.

A valuable history of the synagogue is Azriel Eisenberg's *The Synagogue Through the Ages* (Bloch).

A visitor to a *shul* in a tiny village whose inhabitants believed their *tzaddik* possessed miraculous powers asked, "What miracle did your rabbi perform recently?"

"Well, there are miracles and miracles. For instance: would you think it a miracle if God did *exactly* what our rabbi asked of Him?"

"I certainly would!"

"Well, here we think it is a miracle when our rabbi does what God asks of *him*."

shvartz (adjective)
shvartzer (masculine noun and adjective)
shvartzeh (feminine noun and adjective)

These words are establishing a foothold in Yinglish usage. Pronounced to rhyme respectively with "darts," "Hart-zer," "parts a." From German: *schwarz*: "black."

1. Black.
2. Unfortunate, unhappy, ill-starred. (A common Yiddish curse goes: "*A shvartz yor oif ihm!*" "A black year may he have!")
3. Ominous, gloomy, boding, no good.
   "It looks pretty *shvartz* to me."
4. Contraband or "black market" goods.
   "*Shvartzeh s'khoyre* [merchandise] was his downfall."
5. A *shvartzer* or *shvartzeh* is a black man or woman, often a servant.

Shvartzer and *shvartzeh*, to mean a black man and woman, became "inside" words among Jews—cryptonyms for Negro servants or employees. Since the growth of the civil rights movement, these uses have declined. Many Jews would not, for instance, approve of the retelling now of the following true, well-known and (to me, at least) disarming story:

A Jewish matron dialed a number and asked, "Hello. Mrs. Weiss?"

"No, ma'am," came a melodious voice. "This is the *shvartzeh*."

———

The great pianist Gregor Arkovski was rehearsing for an important concert. While he was running off one brilliant arpeggio, the phone rang.

Swiftly, the black maid picked it up. "Arkovski residence."

"I *must* talk to the maestro!" said a woman's voice.

"He ain't here."

"But—I can hear him playing!"

"Uh . . . that ain't him playin'," said the *shvartzeh*. "That's me—jest dustin' the keys."

shviger

Pronounced SHVI-*ger*, to rhyme with "trigger." From German: *Schwiegermutter*: "mother-in-law."

Mother-in-law.

Jessie Schoenfeld had delivered triplets. Her *shviger* came to the hospital. "What a miracle! Triplets! Say, *no* one on our side of the family *ever* had triplets!"

The new mother said, "I'm not surprised. My doctor told me it happens only once in two million times!"

"My God, Jessie!" cried her *shviger*. "When did you have time to do the housework?"

See also MISHPOCHE.

sicknik

A recent and delightful Yinglish coinage.

1. One who is (or *maybe* is) sick most of the time.
2. A hypochondriac.
3. Someone who enjoys the curious usufructs of ill health.
4. One who enjoys the psychological experience of *fearing* he will be sick.

The connotational advantage of *sicknik* over, say, "hypochondriac" is that the latter describes a propensity, the former, a hang-up. Hypochondriacs cannot help themselves; sickniks choose not to. A hypochondriac pays the price of apprehension: anxiety, depression. But a sicknik, being as much a malingerer as an invalid, even enjoys the attention he gives himself.

I am especially fond of this triumphant definition: "She is such a sicknik she asked to be buried next to a doctor."

DOCTOR: What are you taking for that terrible cold?
PATIENT: Make me an offer.

See also HEALTHNIK, KALYIKEH.

Siddur

Appears in Yinglish because that one word takes six English words to express (see below). Pronounced SID-*der*, to rhyme with "kidder." Hebrew: "arrangement," "order." (Do not confuse with *seder*.)
The daily and Sabbath prayer book.

The *Siddur* contains the three daily services, the Sabbath prayers and (in some editions) the festival prayers, *Ethics of the Fathers* and special readings.

The first printed *Siddur* appeared in 1486—just thirty years after the Gutenberg Bible.

See also DAVEN, SHUL.

Simchath Torah
Simchas Torah
Simhat Torah

Pronounced SIM-*khess* TOY-*rah* (in Yiddish) and in Hebrew SIM-*khess* TOE-*rah*, or TOY-*rah*, with a MacGregorish *kh*. Hebrew: "the day of rejoicing in the law."
The festival, observed on the ninth and final day of Succoth (*q.v.*), honoring the Torah, the Five Books of Moses (the first five books in the Old Testament).

Simchath Torah celebrates the yearly end-and-new-beginning of the consecutive weekly readings of the Torah in

the synagogue. On this day, the last chapter of Deuteronomy is read—and instantly the entire congregation de-
claims with excitement, "*Chazak, chazak, venit chazak!*"
("Be strong, be strong, and let us gather new strength!")

And at once the cycle of reading and praying begins,
from the first word in Genesis, to signal the continuing
cycle of worship, and to show that the Torah has neither
beginning nor end.

The Holy Scrolls—adorned with their silver breastplates
and crowns—are removed from the synagogue's Ark on
the eve of Simchath Torah; each male in the congregation
takes a turn conveying them around. At least seven "turns"
are made around the synagogue, during which the congregation sings and the men honored by carrying the Torah
scrolls dance. Hasidic congregations rise to feverish exalta-
tion during this celebration.

On Simchath Torah, children join in the procession of
the scrolls and are rewarded with goodies. Children not yet
of *Bar Mitzva* age gather around the *bema* (pulpit); a prayer-
shawl is spread over their heads like a canopy; a passage
from the Torah is read, and the rabbi blesses them as Jacob
blessed Ephraim and Menasseh (Genesis 48).

On the eve of "the day of rejoicing in the Law," in
Antwerp, during the very first year of the Nazi occupation,
the bells of the Catholic Cathedral rang out the tune of
"Hatikvah" (*q.v.*), "The Hope," which became the national anthem of Israel. I have never forgotten this.

For more on Simchath Torah, see *The Sukkot/Simchat
Torah Anthology*, edited by Philip Goodman.

snuk

See SHNOOK.

so

The overuse of "So . . ." or "So?" (except in conscious
parody) is a telling revelation of years spent in immigrant
or Lower East Side, Bronx or Brooklyn neighborhoods.
Yinglish for the Yiddish *tsi* or *nu*.

The use of *so* to begin a question is characteristically
Jewish, from *tsi*, which often opens a question in Yiddish:

"So have you called your father?"
"So did he like the book?"
"So when can you get here?"

1. So?
2. So . . .
3. So!
4. So-o . . .
5. So what?

Each vocalization contains its own distinct message. Thus:

1. So? ("Well? What are you going to do about it?")
2. So . . . ("following that"; "in any event")
3. So! ("Let's get on with it!")
4. So-o . . . ("meanwhile"; "I think"; "perhaps")
5. So what? ("*Nu?*")

———————

Before the entire ship's complement, Israeli Commander Zvi Amrachi, a champion of morale, made this statement: "Officers, men, I want you all to realize how deeply I am committed to one simple principle: the S.S. *Menorah* is not '*my*' ship. It is not the *officers'* ship. It is not *your* ship . . . Gentlemen, the S.S. *Menorah* is *our* ship!"

Up went a hand.

"Yes?"

"So let's sell it."

———————

Two old friends were reminiscing. The first said, "So, listen—I can't drink anymore, I can't smoke a cigar, chasing a woman is altogether impossible—but still and all, last week I celebrated my ninetieth birthday!!"

The second man coughed. "How?"

See also NU.

So it shouldn't be wasted [a total loss, etc.]

Yinglish. From Yiddish: *Zol nit zayn aroysgevarfene verter*: "So my words should not be entirely thrown away . . ."

Our home rang with such declamatory invocations:

"So your visit shouldn't be a disappointment, take home a piece cake."

"So it shouldn't be a shock, I'm telling you now that I'm not talking to him!"

CUSTOMER: Coffee.
WAITRESS: With or without cream?
CUSTOMER: No cream.
(*Waitress goes away; returns*)
WAITRESS: I'm sorry; we're out of cream.
CUSTOMER: Do you have any milk?
WAITRESS: Sure.
CUSTOMER: So—it shouldn't be a waste of your time, I'll take my coffee without milk.

So—uh . . .

Yinglish—northeast American division.

1. Abrupt introductory signal for a delicate question.
2. Introduction to an unexpected statement.
3. The English equivalent of "*Nu* . . . ?"

The Yinglish "So—uh . . ." replaces the accepted "Well . . ." or "Well now . . ." of proper English. Those who dispute this simple assertion may resolve their doubts by asking one question: "Would one ever hear 'So-uh' at a dinner table or a club in London?"

"So—uh—Sam . . . how about you pay back part of the loan?"

"So—uh—Peter . . . are you cheating on your wife?"
Peter: "Who else?"

I have told you this story, in a different form . . . So enjoy!

Two men sat opposite each other in the Amtrak train. One was reading a newspaper. After a while, the other man said, "Uh—are you going to Philadelphia?"

The first man lowered his newspaper. "No," he said. "So listen. I'm going to Baltimore. My business is insurance. My name is Henry Slott. I live in Great Neck. I have a son at Swarthmore and a daughter who's married. My wife's maiden name was Portnow. I'm a Republican. I can't play golf. I do play bridge. In winter I spend two weeks every December in Pompano Beach. I go to a Reform temple, contribute to the UJA and the Community Chest. I don't have a brother and my sister died thirty years ago. So listen: if I've forgotten anything you're interested in, please ask me right now—because I want to take a nap until we get to Baltimore.''

some

This Yinglish usage serves two separate, albeit grotesque, functions:

1. Synonym for *very*. (''She is some smart!'')
2. Synonym for *truly . . . certainly.* (''You are some lucky!'')

Usage 1 drops the noun to which the adjective is usually attached:

''She is some smart [student, person]!''

Usage 2 both omits the final noun and substitutes *some* for any adverb of emphasis (*truly, certainly*) or singularity:

''You are some [really] lucky!''

This cockamamy Brooklyn–Bronx concoction (no other word can do it justice) is a distinctive (and deplorable) characteristic of certain clusters of Yinglishmen. I heard it first in Hollywood, used by screenwriters, with intentional amusement, who cherish their childhood.

––––––––––––

''Dora! Dora!'' cried Mr. Braun. ''I just won a thousand dollars! In the state lottery! One of my tickets won!''

''*Mazel tov!* You are some lucky!'' Mrs. Braun paused. ''But—what did you mean, '*one* of my tickets'?''

''I bought four, and one of them won.''

''Dummy! Why did you need the other three?''

something

Yinglish, well rooted and blooming. Direct analogue from Yiddish: *eppes*.

1. Remarkable.
2. Noteworthy.

I am not suggesting that the English use of *something* is (in most cases) anything but English. The Yinglish usage to which I refer, and the reason for this entry, is *something* employed in *non*conventional ways, such as:

"Man, that's something!" (Meaning, "That's something remarkable.")
"He's something!" ("He's someone of great consequence.")
"At a keyboard, he's really something!"

These usages have become familiar in the cant spoken by the young, the black, the aberrant and the addicted. I believe the Yinglish usage, by Jews, long preceded that.

So sue me

This vocative démarche has become a staple of Yinglish irony and sarcasm ever since *Guys and Dolls*—and the Damon Runyon stories from which they came.

1. Try and do something about it.
2. There's not a thing you can do about it.

These crisp, defiant ultimatums are scornful responses to an inquiry; or contemptuous retorts to a question; or confident "toppers" to a challenge.

"Sue me" is proper English, of course, but the prefixed "So" or "Go" or even "So go and . . ." bristle with the taunting aspect of Yiddish—and therefore Yinglish.

The line "Sue me, sue me! (What can you do me?)" was immortalized in Nathan Detroit's protestations of ardor in the cantata to Adelaide, "Sue Me," one of the many jewels in *Guys and Dolls*.

———————

Asher Abel, a fishing nut, was angling in a lovely lake in the Adirondacks.

A local watched him for a spell, then called, "Hi, stranger. Are you fishin'?"

"Nope," said Asher, who was a laconic wit.

"Then why're ya standin' there, with a fishin' pole, and a line danglin' in the water?!"

"So sue me," scowled Asher. "I just like to drown worms."

See also NU, SO WHAT?

So what?

"So what?" was straight English long before Jewish immigrants transformed the tongue in England/United States. But the particular laconic, derisive use of the phrase is authentic Yinglish. From Yiddish: *Iz vus*?: "Is what?"

1. So what?
   a. What's the point of telling me that?
      "I never answered her letter."
      "So what?"
   b. What difference does that make?
      "They're going to paint the hall."
      "So what?"
   c. Who *cares*?
      "She doesn't like you."
      "*So* what?"
   d. I can't do anything about that.
      "They're leaving New York?"
      "So what?"

Few idiomatic phrases are used as often and as pertly as the flippant, caustic "So what?" It is, indeed, a substitute for repartée—in circles not noted for originality of language or inventiveness of rejoinder.

"So what?" has become a popular improvement upon the brusque, defiant "Sez who?" that peppered the patois of the 1920s.

2. So what else is new?

This is a deceptive idiom. It serves a slightly different function than "So what?" It is not only a retort: it contains reproval—slightly mocking, somewhat crowing:

    a. Did you really think I didn't know that?
       "They're moving to Texas."
       "So what else is new?"
    b. Don't bore me with more of this.
       "People are buying bonds!"
       "So what else is new?"
    c. Do you know how many times I've heard that before?
       "She's going to buy a new car."
       "So what else is new?"
    d. But you've said that before—and didn't do it.
       "I'm going to contribute a thousand dollars!"
       "So what else is new?"
    e. That's hardly news to anyone.
       "She's been sleeping with that no-goodnik for years!"
       "So what else is new?"

Never place a comma after *so* ("So, what else is new?"); that converts "so" into "well," and separates "so" from "what"—which kills both the point and the pungency of this amusing intensifier.

stood (for "stayed")

    Slang, inelegant, but amusing.
    "You [I, he, we, they] should of stood in bed!"

The most celebrated instance of this inspired usage occurred when Mike Jacobs, the fight promoter, observing the small line at his ticket windows, moaned, "I should of stood in bed!"

Stood is the English calque for the Yiddish *geshtanen*, which can mean both "stood" and "remained."

Mr. Jacobs' use of *of* ("should of") simply followed the speech pattern of his childhood. He could have resorted to the solecism had he been Irish, Italian, Polish. But H. L. Mencken and other language-watchers credit the American–Yiddish influence—hence I call this amusing barbarism Yinglish.

**stressing a virtue by repeating the critical word
plus the seemingly derogatory prefix**

"Hard up—shmard up, he'd give you the shirt off his back
if you needed help!"

Succoth

Pronounced suk-*kess*, in Yiddish, to rhyme with "took
us." Hebrew: "booths."
The Festival of Tabernacles, or the Feast of Booths.

In Leviticus (23:43) God says: "I made the children of
Israel to dwell in booths, when I brought them out of the
land of Egypt." This holiday starts the fifth day after *Yom
Kippur* and is celebrated for eight days by the Orthodox,
seven in Israel and among Reform Jews.

Throughout the week, an observing family eats its meals
in a *succah* (booth) that is set up out of doors, roofed with
branches (the stars must be visible from the inside), and
decorated with flowers and fruit. Succoth is a thanksgiving
holiday, held at the time of the full moon, when the crops
had been harvested in ancient Palestine.

Hoshanah Rabbah, "the great Hosanna," is observed
on the seventh day of Succoth by a procession around the
synagogue; the men carry palm branches, and willow and
myrtle twigs, and the entire congregation chants praise of
God. The men beat their willow branches against the pulpit
or platform, some say as a symbol of penitence. (By tradition, the fate of a Jew is sealed on *Hoshanah Rabbah* in, I
suppose, a celestial Bureau of Records.)

Philo considered the *succah* an important institution because all Jews, rich or poor, were asked to dwell in a
primitive shelter. Democracy of this sort, he reckoned,
moved the concept out of theory into practice. See *The
Succoth Anthology* (Jewish Publication Society).

T

---

taking (took) a bath

This idiom has won a firm foothold in Yinglish/English—
especially among stockbrokers, real estate entrepre-
neurs, businessmen. In Yiddish, "He led me to the
bath" (*Er haut mikh gefirt in bod arayn*) means "He
tricked (deceived) me," "He led me up the garden
path."

Losing (lost) a great deal of money.

"I am taking a bath" does not (except when engaged in
personal hygiene) mean that the speaker is bathing—or
even showering. The Yinglish usage refers to monetary
losses.

"How did that deal turn out?"
"She took a *bath*!"
There is, of course, a marked resemblance between "I
took a bath" and the English "They cleaned me out,"
"They took me to the cleaners" or "I took a beating."
The etymology of the Yiddish usage is astonishing. In
the *shtetlach* of eastern Europe, strangers, or guests (in or
from a poorhouse) were urged, cajoled, pressured to take
a bath (go to the *shvitsbod*). While such persons were in
the baths, their clothes were disinfected by steam. Since
not all guests relished the prospect of being deloused, or
having their hair closely clipped, they were tricked, one

way or another, into the baths. Hence: *"M'firt im in bod arayn* ("They are tricking him into the bath") . . . All clothing was hung on hooks outside the steam (Turkish) baths—and knaves sometimes picked the pockets. Hence, "They took me to the baths" meant "They cleaned me out!": "They robbed me!"

APPLICATION FOR A DRIVER'S LICENSE
Name: Judah Flek.
Born: Absolutely.
Address: 18 Avenue B.
Business: Terrible. I'm taking a bath!

talk to the wall

Expressive Yinglish. From Yiddish: *Red tsu der vand*, or *Red tsum vand*.

1. It won't do a bit of good.
2. You can't get through to him (her).
3. Don't waste your time.

I know of few phrasings so steeped in despair and frustration as "Go talk to the wall."

The lamentation is often uttered without the imperative, especially by non-Jews, who may simply say, "It was like talking to the wall."

Mr. Solovay said to his wife: "The new doctor in our neighborhood charges twenty-five dollars for the first visit—but only ten dollars after that. Well, I'm going to outsmart him! I'll go in and say, 'Hello, Doc. Here I am *again*!' "

Off Mr. Solovay went to the doctor.

When he returned, his wife asked, "So what happened?"

With a gloomy sigh, Mr. Solovay said, "Go talk to the wall! I said 'Hello, Doc, here I am again!' So he examined me and said, 'Continue the same treatment I recommended before.' "

See also DISMISSING AN IDEA . . . , GO FIGHT CITY HALL, GO TALK TO THE WALL.

tallis   (Yiddish)
talith   (Hebrew)
tallit
talaysem   (plural)

Jews almost never use the English translation of *tallis*.
Pronounced TAHLL-*iss*, to rhyme with "Hollis" or "so-
lace." Hebrew: "prayer shawl." But the plural, *talaysem* (*ta*-LAY-*sem*), is Yiddish.

The prayer shawl used by Jewish men at prayer or
religious services.

The Good Book tells the Jewish male always to wear a
four-fringed garment to remind him of his bond and duty
to God. At one time, the *tallis* was a gown or cloak, but
because of public humiliations, the rabbis decreed it be
used in the synagogue—or at home, during prayer services.

An Orthodox bride gives her groom a *tallis*, just as a
boy's father gives him one on the occasion of his *Bar Mitzva*. Sometimes a *tallis* serves as a canopy during the marriage ceremony.

In America, most Jews fold the *tallis*, which is made of
silk and crossed with black or blue bands, and wear it rather
like a long scarf. But Orthodox Jews use a voluminous,
robelike *tallis* and during the most solemn portions of
prayer place part of the shawl over their heads—to shut
out anything that might diminish the intensity of their concentration.

See also DAVEN, TEFILLIN.

Talmud

If your English dictionary does not contain this magisterial word, get another. Pronounced TOL-*mud*, to rhyme
with "doll could." From Hebrew: *lamod*: "to study,"
or *lamade*: "to teach."

The Talmud. It is not the Bible. It is not the Old
Testament. It is not "a" book. It is not meant to be
read, but to be studied—and studied and studied.

The Talmud is a massive compendium of sixty-three
books: the learned debates, conclusions, commentaries,

commentaries upon commentaries, commentaries upon commentaries *upon* commentaries of all the scholars and jurists who for over a thousand *years* interpreted the Torah (the first five books in the Bible), and applied its teachings to new problems of law, ethics, traditions, economics, heaven, guilt, sex, children, the earth, the cosmos, angels, demons . . .

The Talmud embraces everything from theology to contracts, cosmology to cosmetics, criminal law to diet, delusions and drinking. It is crammed with anecdotes, aphorisms, thumbnail biographies, philosophical treatises and charming parables.

It is majestic—and pedantic; brilliant—and dreary; awesome—and maddeningly obscure. Sophistry runs rife; profundity often ends in mythology or astrology or numerology; wrestlings with the Devil and his demons, and revelations from angels and celestial messengers, end in mystical miasmas beyond measuring. Like Catholic scholastics, the Talmudists spent a good deal of time in dialectical taffy-pulls.

> . . . for generation after generation, the wits of the Jew were sharpened by continuous exercise from earliest youth upon the acute Talmudic dialectic. But the Talmud meant much more to him than this. It brought him another world, vivid, calm, and peaceful, after the continuous humiliation of ordinary existence. It provided him with a second life, so different from the sordid round of everyday. After each successive [pogrom] was stilled, and the shouting of the mob had died down, he crept back to the ruins of his home, and put away his Jewish badge of shame, and set himself to pore again over the yellowed pages. He was transported back into the Babylonian schools of a thousand years before, and there his troubled soul found rest.
>
> —Cecil Roth, *A History of the Jews*

I

The first division of the Talmud is the Mishnah, a collection of interpretations of the biblical laws as they were applied to social conditions in Palestine between the fifth century before, and the second century of, the Christian era. These laws, which included court decisions, opinions, ethical teachings, etc., were transmitted orally; the Mishnah is therefore known as the "Oral Law," as distinct from the "Written Law" of the Torah.

The Israelites were afraid that written judgments might limit or diminish the authority of the sacred Torah. But they knew that the Oral Laws would surely be changed unless *some* written document served as authority; so they secretly made abbreviated notations! (These notes also helped them in the stupendous task of memorizing the Mishnah.)

Little by little, the task of codifying the Mishnah was undertaken. It was completed in about 200 A.D. by the great Judah ha-Nasi (the Prince), the head of the Sanhedrin (*q.v.*).

II

The second division of the Talmud is the Gemara (from the Aramaic "to learn"), the vast compendium of commentaries upon the Mishnah. The language of the Gemara is Aramaic, but it contains a great deal of Hebrew.

III

The legal parts of the Talmud are called the Halakha. The elements that are poetic, allegorical, anecdotal are known as Haggadah.

IV

The continuing colloquium that resulted in the Gemara took place in the great academies of Palestine and Babylonia from the second to the fifth centuries, when the Talmud was assembled and edited.

V

The Palestinian and the Babylonian academies produced separate Talmuds: the Talmud Yerushalmi, which was redacted around the fifth century, and the Talmud Babli, about a century later.

When we speak of the Talmud today, we generally refer to the Babylonian Talmud, because it had a much greater influence on Jewish law and life. (Besides, the Jerusalem text was not preserved *in toto*.)

There is an excellent English translation of the Talmud: eighteen volumes, edited by Rabbi I. Epstein, and published by the Soncino Press. *Back to the Sources*, edited by Barry W. Holtz, is a modern interpretation of the Torah, Talmud, Midrash (and Cabala). These books may be obtained from the Jewish Publication Society of Philadelphia.

You would be surprised by the number of aphorisms, now widespread, that are to be found in the *Talmud*.

"Give every man the benefit of the doubt."
"Look at the contents, not at the bottle."
"One good deed leads to another."
"Don't threaten a child: Either punish or forgive him."
"Begin a lesson with a humorous illustration."
"All's well that ends well."

See also AGADAH, BES MIDRASH, CABALA, HALAKHA, MIDRASH, MISHNAH, MITZVA, PILPUL, TORAH.

Talmud Torah

Pronounced TOL-*m'd* TOY-*reh*, or TOE-*reh*, to rhyme with "doll mid Moira" or "doll mid Nora," or "doll mid Roma."
A Hebrew school (in America).

The Talmud Torah in the United States offered a two-hour Hebrew session after the public schools closed each day, and classes all Sunday morning. Many Jewish children thus spent ten to fifteen hours a week in schooling in addition to their public school attendance.

Talmud Torah schools have greatly declined in number, partly because many of their activities were absorbed into the educational departments of synagogue and temple.

See also HAGGADA, HALAKHA, MELAMED.

tararam (noun)
tarrarom

This vivid noun, for which English equivalents seem pale, is a lively candidate for Yinglish. Onomatopoetic. Rhymes with "bar a bomb."

1. A hullabaloo, a noisy ruckus.
2. A big fuss, an argument, a shtuss (*q.v.*).
3. Gallivanting confusion.

"Did you ever hear such a *tararam*?"
"Don't make such a *tararam*; it's only a game!"

At the crowded area around a pool in Miami Beach, a heated argument was heard above the lotioned bodies.

"Oh, God," moaned a sunbather. "What's all that *tararam* about?"

"It's the daily battle of wits."

"Wits? *Here*? Who are the wits?"

"Horovitz, Borowitz, Mankowitz, and Shmulewitz."

Only Hollywood could create a wacky fantasy such as this: When Moses reached the Red Sea he blew his ram's horn frantically and shouted, "Sid! Sid! Where are you?"

Up ran his publicity man. "Yes, Chief?"

"Okay, Sid. Launch the boats," snapped Moses.

"What?"

"The *boats*!" said Moses. "Launch the—"

"Oh, God," wailed Sid. "In all the *tararam*, I forgot!"

"You forgot to arrange for *boats*?" shouted Moses. "You fool—the Egyptians will be here in twenty minutes! What do you expect me to do—talk to *God*? Get Him to part the waters? Let us Hebrews across—and drown all the Egyptians?"

"Boss," cried Sid, "if you pull that off I'll get you two pages in the Old Testament."

See also FARTUMELT, SHTUSS, TSIMMES.

tchotchke (noun)
tsatske
tsatskeleh
tchotchkeleh (diminutive)

An expressive epithet deserving of wider usage in Yinglish. Pronounced CHOCH-*keh*, to rhyme with "botch a"; or TSAHTS-*keh*, to rhyme with "Tosca"; or TSAHTS-*keh-leh*, to rhyme with "Oscela"; or TCHOCH-*keh*, to rhyme with "botch a"; or TCHOCH-*keh-leh*, to rhyme with "notch a la." From the Slavic: *shalet*: "to play pranks." The pronunciation of this incomparable word depends on where your parents came from: Galician Jews say *tsatske*; Polish, *tchatchke*.

A *tchotchke*, or *tsatske*, is:

1. A toy, a small plaything.
   "I bought the child a *tchotchke*."
2. An inexpensive, unimportant thing: a gewgaw; a trinket.
   "He gave her some *tsatske* or other for her trouble."

But the usages I most relish are:

3. A cute female; a pretty little number; a "chick."
4. A sexy but brainless broad.
5. A kept woman; a mistress.

It was a smashing success of a cocktail party the Feinbergs threw, so much so that after an hour a *tchotchke* tugged at her date's sleeve and declared, "Harry, don't you think you ought to stop drinking? . . . Why, your whole face is beginning to look blurred!"

———

Lana Lipmann, age eight, soberly studied the goodies in the case at the candy store and said, "I want a chocolate Easter Bunny—a boy."

"A boy?" The owner laughed. "Why, darling, there isn't that—" (snapping his fingers) "—much difference between a boy bunny and a girl bunny."

The little *tchotchke* replied, "But there's *that*—" (snapping fingers) "—much more chocolate."

———

Onto Lastov's used car lot drove a fine Rolls Royce, out of which stepped a woman all in black.

Mr. Lastov hurried over to her. "Yes, ma'am?"

The woman said, "I want to sell this car."

Lastov got behind the wheel, glanced at the mileage counter (only 6,420 miles), turned on the ignition, listened to the motor . . . "Madam, how much do you want?"

"Fifty dollars."

Lastov's jaw almost hit his chest. "What is this, lady— some kind of joke?"

"No," said the elegantly dressed woman. "Just give me fifty dollars and a signed bill of sale."

"Lady, are you out of your mind?" exclaimed Lastov. "Don't you know that this Rolls is worth, secondhand, thirty or forty *thou*sand dollars? . . . Is this a *stolen* car?"

"Certainly not!"

"Is there a lien on it?"

"Absolutely not . . . Now look, do you or don't you want to buy—?"

"Certainly I want to buy it! But *fifty dollars*! There *must* be a trick! Why would *anyone* in her right mind—"

The woman arched an eyebrow. "I am entirely in my right mind. You see, my husband just died. And in his will, he carefully provided that Flora Delago, who was his secretary—and his goddam mistress—should get the full proceeds from the sale of his Rolls Royce! . . . *Nu*? So give me the fifty dollars."

———

The two full-bosomed, stunningly coiffured starlets were sitting side by side in the Marie Antoinette powder room of the Beverly Hilton Hotel. "By the way, Dolores," asked Lorraine, the first *tchotchke*, "whose date are you to-night?"

"My date is Waldo Kantroviz, the producer."

"Oh, wow!" said Lorraine. "I've gone out with him. He's a classy dresser!"

"I know," said Dolores. "And so *fast*."

See also BUMMERKEH, NO-GOOD, YENTA.

tefillin
t'fillin

Often appears in fiction by American Jewish writers. Pronounced *te*-FILL-*in*, to rhyme with "a 'willin'." Hebrew: *tefilla*: "prayer." From the Greek *phylakterion*: "protection," "fortress."

Phylacteries.

A charming old folk saying says, "God Himself wears *tefillin*."

Tefillin are two long, thin leather straps, with a two-or three-inch-square black leather box on each. The boxes contain tiny parchments on which are inscribed, in Hebrew, four passages from Exodus and Deuteronomy. *Tefillin* are worn during morning prayers by Orthodox and many Conservative men. Reform Jews do not wear *tefillin*.

The custom of donning *tefillin* is an ancient one, derived from the injunction in Exodus 13:9: "And it shall be for a sign unto thee upon thine hand, and for a memorial between thine eyes, that the Lord's law may be in thy mouth." There is a similar commandment in Deuteronomy 6:8.

The process of putting on *tefillin* is quite elaborate, and carefully prescribed. The *Shulchan Aruch* (sixteenth century) lists one hundred sixty laws governing *tefillin*, which are worn when the one who prays is standing . . . as a mark of reverence. The entire ritual has the effect of removing mundane preoccupations from the praying person's mind and focusing his attention entirely on his devotions. Maimonides argued that while *tefillin* are worn, a man devotes his entire mind "to truth and righteousness."

It is not permitted to wear phylacteries on the Sabbath. Surprised? Well, on the Sabbath, the distractions of the workday week are not supposed to exist; besides, the Sabbath is a day of holiness, and does not *need* the added sanctification of phylacteries.

See also DAVEN.

Thanks a lot

Yinglishmen prize this sardonic analogue from Yiddish: *A sheynem dank aykh*: "Pretty thanks to you."

An ironic inversion of "Thank you"—meaning "Thanks for nothing!" or "*That* you call a favor?"

This sarcastic response came into English in the late 1940s and 1950s, from comedy sketches on radio and television. "Thanks a *lot*!" became the paradigm of super-dry disagreement or irritated contradiction.

This caustic gibe relates to the ironic Yiddish phrases *A groysn dank dir* ("Huge thanks to you") or *A sheyner, reyner dank dir* ("A pretty, pure thank you"). The latter gains force from its echo of the age-old curse: *A sheynem, reynem kapore of zey* ("May a beautiful, purified plague befall them").

See also AGREEMENT DEPLOYED . . . , ANGER CONVERTED . . . , ASSENT ENTHUSIASTICALLY ENLARGED . . . , CONCURRENCE AS A VEHICLE FOR SARCASM, CONTEMPT BY NOMINAL CONCURRENCE, IS THE BRIDE TOO BEAUTIFUL?, SARCASM AMPLIFIED . . . , THAT'S ALL I NEED!, WHO NEEDS IT?

That's all I need!

A much-used favorite of Yinglishmen. From Yiddish: *Dos felt mir nokh*: "That's all I lack yet."

1. (By inversion) That's one thing I *don't* need!
2. *That's* all I need (yet).
3. On top of everything else, do I need *that*?

This gem of irony has become Yinglish with celerity—and deservedly, for it is a colorful variation of those hoary chestnuts, "from the frying pan into the fire" and "Are you kidding, mac?" Adding the intensifier *yet* ("*That's* all I need yet") raises the sarcasm to a brisker dimension.

"Her *son* is moving upstairs? That's all we need!"
"A broken filling? That's all I need yet."

WOMAN PATIENT (on couch): Oh, Doctor! If you would only—just once—kiss me!
PSYCHOANALYST: Kiss you? *That's* all I need yet! Why, I shouldn't even be lying here next to you!

An old Jew, riding on a subway, sat down next to a black—who (can you *imag*ine?!) was reading a Yiddish newspaper. The old Jew, unable to contain himself, exclaimed, "You should excuse me, Mister. But—are you Jewish?"

The black man slapped the paper in disgust. "*That's* all I need yet!"

See also CONCURRENCE AS A VEHICLE FOR SARCASM, SARCASM AMPLIFIED . . . , THANKS A LOT, WHO NEEDS IT?

That's for sure

This idiom has won such wide popularity in conversational English that it must be considered established Yinglish. From Yiddish: *Dos iz oyf zikher*.

"That's for sure" is quite serviceable for cheerful concurrence upon hearing such *aperçus* as these, say, from the folklore of the Jews:

"Out of snow, you can't make cheesecake."
"If you're doing something wrong, at least enjoy it."
"Never consult a coward about war, a salesman about a bargain or a woman about a rival."

———————

Father Terence Devanny, new to his parish, was walking down the street and saw a large sign over a hardware store:

GITTELMAN AND O'TOOLE
HOME APPLIANCES

In went Father Devanny.

An old man with a beard and a *yarmulka* came forward to him.

"I just came in to introduce myself," smiled Father Devanny, "and to say how wonderful it is to see Catholics and Jews joined in partnership. What a splendid surprise, Mr. Gittelman."

"A surprise it's for sure," said the old man. "A bigger surprise: *I'm* O'Toole."

See also AGREEMENT DEPLOYED . . . , THANKS A LOT, THAT'S ALL I NEED!

That should be . . .

Yiddish: *Zol dos zayn*: "That should be . . ." Equivalent to the English:

1. May that be.
2. That should only be.

Notice the inversion so dear to Yiddish:

"Your hair is too thick? *That* should be your biggest problem!"
"Your son didn't graduate first in his class? *That* should be the biggest setback in his career!"

See also IS THE BRIDE TOO BEAUTIFUL?

That's not chopped liver

A new locution that is racing through the ranks of Yinglish, especially in the world of entertainment.

1. "That ain't hay!"
2. "That's not peanuts!"

This declamatory judgment is favored by the natives of Broadway and Beverly Hills. It has often been uttered by Johnny Carson, doyen of television's *Tonight Show*.

"Did you know that she got fifty grand for one week in Las Vegas?"
"Man! That's not chopped liver!"

"How many people turned out for your concert?"
"Twenty-two *thousand*!"
"Hey . . . that's not chopped liver."

That's what *you* say

Yinglish—especially if you stress the pronoun. From Yiddish: *Azoy zugst du*: "So say *you*."

The sarcastic rendition of an otherwise matter-of-fact observation triggers contrasted meanings:

1. I don't believe you!
2. I take that with a grain of salt.
3. There is a more plausible explanation.
4. What a story! What an invention! What a lie!

See also SARCASM AMPLIFIED . . . , THANKS A LOT.

There's no one here to talk to!

See NO ONE HERE TO TALK TO.

Tisha Bov
Tisha B'av
Tisha B'ab

Pronounced TISH-*a-bawve* or to rhyme with "Misha dove." Hebrew: "the ninth day of the month Ab," or "Av."

The solemn day of fasting and mourning (usually in

August) that commemorates both the first (586 B.C.) and the second (A.D. 70) destructions of the Temple in Jerusalem: the Babylonians razed the first Temple, the Romans the second. Reform Jews do not observe this day of communal lamentation.

Down the gloomy centuries, Tisha Bov, known as "the blackest day in the Jewish calendar," has added disasters, catastrophes and horrors to the two separate destructions of the Temple: the slaughter of Bar Kochba's followers in 138, Hadrian's leveling of Jerusalem, the Holy Crusades and their unholy depredations, England's expulsion of Jews in 1290, the Spanish expulsion of the Jews in 1492 . . .

Tisha Bov climaxes nine days of mourning during which meat is not eaten and marriages are not performed. Cheerfulness, laughter, even smiles are considered inappropriate. Those who enter the synagogue do not even greet one another. They sit on the floor or on low benches. A black curtain is draped over the Ark.

The Book of Lamentations is recited by the cantor, in a low, depressing chant. Poems of suffering and dirges of sadness (some of which date from the Middle Ages) are intoned. But the day ends on a note of hope, with the reading of the *Zionide* of Judah ha-Levi (1085–1145).

T.L.

Code initials for "*tochis* [or *tuches*] *lekker*."
Vulgarism.

1. (Literally) Ass-licker.
2. Sycophant, shameless flatterer.

Among Londoners, A.K. is used—not to mean *alter kocker* (cf. A.K.), but exactly as T.L. is used: "ass-kisser."

3. T.L. is also used, especially among teenagers, to mean "trade last"—or, more completely, "I have a compliment I heard about you and I'll tell it to you—if you give me a T.L. [something nice said about me] first."

"Trade last" appears in F. Scott Fitzgerald's *This Side of Paradise*. The Yinglish T.L. is about as far from Fitzgerald's people and world as one can possibly get.

tochis
tuchis

Vulgar. Pronounced TUKH-*is*, to rhyme with "duck hiss," or TAWKH-*is*, to rhyme with "caucus." Remember to rattle that guttural *kh*. Hebrew: "under," "beneath." The meaning "buttocks" is entirely Yiddish, but has been adopted by Israelis.

1. (Vulgarly) The behind, buttocks. "Get off your *tochis*" means "Get off your tail," or "Get moving." *A potch in tochis* is a swat on the behind.
2. A "cold fish"; someone who has *a kalten tochis*, a "cold ass."

See also T.O.T.

Torah

I do not think much of any English dictionary that does not contain this momentous word. Pronounced TOY-*rah*, to rhyme with "Moira," or TOE-*rah*, to rhyme with "Bowra," or TAW-*ra*, to rhyme with "Nora." Hebrew: "doctrine," "teachings."

1. The Five Books of Moses: Genesis, Exodus, Leviticus, Numbers and Deuteronomy.
2. The scroll containing the Five Books of Moses, which is handwritten by a scribe on parchment and is read in the synagogue on *Shabbes (q.v.)*, on festivals and on Mondays and Thursdays.
3. One of the three central, commanding aspects of Judaism, as demonstrated in the ancient saying: "God, Torah, Israel."
4. All of Jewish law and religious studies. Torah *sheh-beal peh* refers to the oral teachings of the rabbis, as contrasted to *Torah sheh-bik-sav*, the written teachings of the Pentateuch, Prophets, and Hagiographa (Sacred Writings).

Torah, strictly speaking, does not mean "law," it means "teaching" or "instructions." The difference is significant. The Torah does not contain a complete codification of laws. It is meant to be a way of indicating God's values. The laws in the Torah are sometimes repeated and often do not even include moral injunctions one would expect to find in so important a document. The Torah is meant to be not a legal or judicial code but an instrument for instructing the Israelites in religion.

The Torah has always held a cardinal place in Jewish history, which bursts with tales of the martyrdom and sacrifices Jews endured in order to transmit "our holy Torah" from one generation to the next. A Torah scroll is considered priceless.

The highest ideal held before every believing Jew was the study of Torah. The Talmud is full of admonitions like this one: "How long is one required to study Torah? Till the day of his death . . ."

In order to enable even the least educated to learn Torah, a section (*parshah*) was read in the synagogue each Monday and Thursday morning (originally, these were market days in agricultural Palestine) and each Sabbath and holiday. By the end of the year, the cycle of Torah readings was completed—and immediately begun once more!

The word *Torah* is found in many epigrams and proverbs: "May you live to introduce [him] to study [Torah], marriage, and good deeds." This is the expression extended to parents at a son's *bris* (*q.v.*).

Hillel, noblest of the Pharisees, was once baited to condense the Torah into its briefest possible form. Hillel replied: "What is hateful to thee, never do to thy fellow man. That is the entire Torah; all else is commentary." (Another version: "Do unto others as you would have them do unto you.")

Gunther Plaut has edited *The Torah: A Modern Commentary*, giving the Hebrew text, English translation, and essays by distinguished Jewish and non-Jewish authorities.

T. H. Gaster's scholarly *Customs and Folkways of Jewish Life* offers many striking parallels between Israelite and earlier customs and beliefs.

The story of the Flood, for instance, appears to be a later version of an account in the Babylonian *Epic of Gilgamesh* (c. 2000 B.C.) that was probably based on the annual floods in the Euphrates Valley. In the Sumerian-Babylonian version, an Ark is constructed, the righteous are spared, birds are dispatched from the vessel to the shore, etc.

The model for the Tower of Babel is found in the ziggurat, the stepped temple of Babylon.

God's destruction of Leviathan (Psalm 74) seems to have roots in an earlier myth of the Canaanites—a myth reconstructed from newly discovered clay tablets excavated in North Syria. Isaiah's description of the Leviathan (27:1) as "the piercing serpent . . . the crooked serpent" repeats the exact words of an earlier text.

See also SIMCHATH TORAH.

T.O.T.

Yinglishmen love these code initials for *Tochis afn tish.*

1. *Tochis afn tish* does not mean "buttocks on the table," which is its literal translation, but—"Put up or shut up," "Let's get down to brass tacks," or "Lay all your cards on the table."
2. The phrase above is lusty but unquestionably improper, and because it is *infra dig*, the initials T.O.T. are often used as a genteel shorthand: "Let's stop evading the issue: *T.O.T.*, please."

Mr. Farkin came to a *shadchen*, sighing, "Maybe you have a good prospect for my Lily. . . . Such a fine girl! Educated. A good cook. A—"

"How old is your Lily?" asked the *shadchen*.

"Eh—twenty-nine."

"Twenty-*nine*?" echoed the *shadchen*. "Listen, Farkin, I'm no fool. To me, your daughter looks forty!"

"Looks, looks. Who goes by looks? My Lily would make such a wonderful wife—"

"Sure, sure. You say she's twenty-nine. *Tochis afn tish*: Is that *true*?"

Mr. Farkin cleared his throat. "Partly."

The attorney for the defense, famed for his skill in cross-examination, leaned close to the star witness for the prosecution, one Melvin Prosker, and, in the smoothest of voices, crooned: "Now, Mr. Prosker, you have testified that it was night—moreover, a very dark night—and that you were almost two blocks from the scene, yet you clearly

saw my client beat the plaintiff over the head with his cane
. . . Is that correct?"

"Yes, sir."

"Mr. Prosker," smiled the attorney, "please tell the
court: T.O.T.—How far can you see at night?"

Prosker leaned back. "I don't know for sure."

"You don't *know*?" sneered the attorney. "Well, make
a guess."

Prosker leaned forward. "How far is the moon?"

See also BOTTOM LINE.

tough tochis

Emphatic, vulgar Yinglish. Gargle the *ch* as *kh*.
  (Taboo) for: .

1. (Literal) Tough ass.
2. Tough luck.
3. Too bad.
4. Nothing can be done about it.
5. (Ironic) You'd better learn to like it.

"My wife won't budge a penny on the alimony!"
"Tough *tochis*."

———

"I'm so busy making money I can't take that Hawaiian
cruise."
(Ironically) "Oh, tough *tochis*."

See also ASSENT ENTHUSIASTICALLY ENLARGED . . . , CON-
CURRENCE AS A VEHICLE FOR SARCASM, GO FIGHT CITY
HALL.

trayf

Often encountered in writings by Jewish authors. Pronounced TRAYF, to rhyme with "safe." From the Hebrew: *teref*: "torn to pieces."

An animal not slain according to the ritual laws and
by an authorized *shochet (q.v.)*; any food which is not
kosher (q.v.).

Pork is *trayf*. Ham is *trayf*. Oysters and shrimp are
trayf.

See also KOSHER, PAREVEH.

trombenik
trombenyik

A juicy, colorful word, recommended for Yinglish. Pronounced TROM-*beh-nik*, to rhyme with "Brahma kick," or TRAUM-*beh-nik*, to rhyme with "brawn the pick." From the Polish, and/or Yiddish: *tromba*: "a trumpet," "a brass horn."

1. A blowhard, a braggart, a blower of one's own horn.
2. A lazy man or woman, a ne'er-do-well.
3. A parasite.
4. A fake, a phony, a four-flusher.
5. A *fonfer—plosher—shtarker—hoo-ha-nik*.

Any way you look at it, *trombenik* is not a word of praise. A *trombenik* is part of the raucous gallery of *nudniks, shleppers*, and *paskudnyaks*.

"Jenny," said a *trombenik*, "open the little case."
Inside the case was a thin gold ring, in the center of which was a tiny, tiny diamond.
"Jenny, it may *look* small, but there isn't a single flaw in it!" the *trombenik* boasted.
"Bernie, inside such a ring there's no *room* for a flaw."

See also BLUFFER, FIFER, NUDNIK, PASKUDNA, PLOSHER.

tsadaka

See TZEDAKA.

tsaddik

See TZADDIK.

tsatske

See TCHOTCHKE.

tsedoodelt   (adjective)
tsedoodelter   (noun, masculine)
tsedoodelteh   (noun, feminine)

The splendid echoic ring of this term recommends it to Yinglish, however many synonyms you may think already exist in English. Pronounced *tseh*-DOO-*delt*, to rhyme with "the zoo belt." Etymology: unknown.

1. Confused, mixed-up, pixilated.
2. Wacky, crazy, kooky.

A *tsedoodelter* said that if he found a million dollars in the street he would keep it—unless, of course, he discovered that it belonged to some poor man, in which case he would return it at once.

See also FARFUFKET, FARMISHT, MESHUGGE, TSEDRAYT, TSETUMMELT.

tsedrayt (adjective)
tsedrayter (noun, masculine)
tsedrayteh (noun, feminine)
tsedraydelt (adjective)

The qualifications cited for *tsedoodelt* (*q.v.*) apply with equal force to *tsedrayt*. Pronounced *tse*-DRAYT, to rhyme with "de-freight." From German: *zerdreht*: "twisted," "confused."

1. *Tsedrayt* or *tsedraydelt* means mixed-up, confused, wacky.
   "I can't make head or tail out of it; it's *tsedrayt*."
2. A *tsedrayter* is a man or boy who is all mixed-up, a kook, a crackpot.
   "Poor man, he's a hopeless *tsedrayter*."
3. A *tsedrayteh* is a woman or girl nut, a crank, a kook, a lunatic.
   "Who can believe her? She's a *tsedrayteh*."

Someone with a "*tsedrayter kop*" (deranged head) is pleasantly pixilated—or not so pleasantly demented.

See also FARFUFKET, FARMISHT, MESHUGGE, TSEDOODELT, TSETUMMELT.

tsetummelt (adjective)
tsetummelter (noun, masculine)
tsetummelteh (noun, feminine)

The sheer picturesqueness of this word urges itself upon Yinglish. Pronounced *tse*-TU-*m'lt*, to rhyme with "'ts tumult."

1. Confused, bewildered.
   "I've never been so *tsetummelt* in my life."
2. A confused, discombobulated man.
3. An eccentric man or woman.

Old Dr. Greengolder was notoriously absentminded. In fact, he was once so *tsetummelt* while presiding at a meeting of the Omaha Medical Society that he said, "Gentlemen, you have heard the resolution. All in favor—say 'Ah.'"

See also FARFUFKET, FARMISHT, MESHUGGE, TSEDRAYT, TUMMEL.

tsimmes

A truly priceless, versatile word, as useful in Yinglish as it is in Yiddish. Pronounced TSIM-*mess*, to rhyme with "Kim miss." From two German words: *zum*: "to the"; *essen*: "eating."

1. A side-dish of mixed cooked vegetables and fruits, slightly sweetened. The ingredients may be carrots and peas, prunes and potatoes, sweet potatoes, etc.
2. A dessert of stewed fruits.

Since making *tsimmes* took time, care and various mixings, the word, in time, came to mean:

3. An involved or prolonged procedure.
   "Keep it simple; don't make a *tsimmes* out of it!"
4. Troubles, irksome details, contretemps.
   "Within a week, their marriage was nothing but *tsimmes*."

A television commercial for interstate bus travel contained the inspired jingle:

Why not skip the fuss?
Leave the *tsimmes* to us!

See also MEGILLA, MISH-MOSH, SHTUSS.

tsitser (verb)

An echoic marvel of a word, waiting to be drafted into Yinglish. Pronounced TSI-*tzer*, to rhyme with "hits 'er." An onomatopoetic coinage.

1. One who is always going "Ts! Ts!" or "Tsk! Tsk!" or even "Tchk! Tchk!"
2. A habitual sympathizer and bystander, not a participant.
3. A *kibitzer* given to expressing his or her feelings with sibilant "tchk"-ings.

Shmerl saw his friend Toploff rushing down Cherry Street, mopping his brow and gasping.

"Hey, Toploff," called Shmerl. "What's going on?"

"Wh-what's going on is that all morning long I've been running around like a w-wild man, trying to get something for my wife!"

"Tchk, tchk," Shmerl sympathized. "Couldn't you get even *one* offer?"

See also DOPPESS, KIBITZER, SHMEGEGGE, TROMBENIK.

tsuris (noun)
tsouris
tsoris

Eloquent and expressive Yiddish. Pronounced TSOO-*riss*, or TSAW-*riss*, to rhyme with "juris" or "Boris." The plural of *tsorah* or *tsureh*. From Hebrew: *tsarah*: "trouble."

Troubles, woes, worries, suffering.

The singular is *tsorah* or *tsureh*—but trouble is rarely singular.

Tsuris has gained considerable vogue in theatrical and literary circles.

"Oh, have I got *tsuris*!"

"Her life these years has been one *tsorah* after another."

"All he adds up to is—*tsuris*."

The phrase "He's *auf tsuris*" means "He has real troubles," or "He's sick."

And when *tsuris* pass beyond the cozy realm of the ordinary, they are called *gehokteh* (chopped-up) *tsuris*. Why troubles are worsened when chopped up, like chicken liver, I do not know, but the phrase certainly *sounds* authoritative.

Tsuris are partial to wetness: to tears, and whiskey.
Bygone *tsuris* are good to discuss.

—Folk sayings

tuchis

See TOCHIS.

tummel   (noun)
tumel

Would serve most usefully in Yinglish: it telegraphs its
meanings. Pronounced TUM-*m'l*, to rhyme with "full
pull." From German: *Tummel*: "tumult."
    Noise, commotion, noisy disorder.

"He can drive a person crazy; everywhere he goes he
creates *tummel*."

Tummler (*q.v.*) is the exalted form of *tummel*.

See also MISH-MOSH, SHTUSS, TARARAM.

tummler

Yinglish. A primary, expressive and irreplaceable part
of Borsht Belt—and therefore, all show business—ter-
minology. Pronounced TOOM-*ler*, with the *oo* pronounced as in *took*.

1. The paid nonstop social director, entertainer and
   "fun-maker" in those Catskill resorts that constitute
   the "Borsht Belt" (*q.v.*).
2. One who creates a lot of noise (*tummel*) but accom-
   plishes little.
3. A fun-maker, a "live wire," a clown, a prankster,
   the "life of the party."

It is the *tummler*'s job to guarantee to the patrons of a
summer resort that most dubious of vacation boons:
"Never a dull moment!" The *tummler* jokes around all day
long and then performs every night: as a comic, singer,
actor, master of ceremonies. He acts, writes, directs, produces shows. He puts on vaudeville skits, minstrel shows,
amateur nights, ordeals-by-dance.

The *tummler* is a noisemaker and overall buffoon. He wears outlandish costumes, falls off diving boards. He leads songs like "Old MacDonald Had a Farm," and games like "Simon Says."

The peculiar tribulations of the *tummler* have been deftly described by Moss Hart in *Act One* and by Joey Adams and Henry Tobias in *The Borscht Belt*.

The *tummlers* of our time may not know of the historic tradition in which they function: the professional *badchen*, a jokester-M.C., engaged to make merry at Jewish weddings.

See also BADCHEN, BORSHT BELT, PLOSHER, TROMBENIK.

turkey

A linguistic digression of interest.
The fowl, not the country.

The translator whom Columbus took along on his first voyage, Luis de Torres, probably the first white man to set foot in the New World, wrote a letter in which he described some of the strange new fauna he had seen, among them "a peacock." He wrote in Hebrew, and the Hebrew word for peacock is *tukki*—which was readily transformed by Europeans into "turkey."

Every Thanksgiving, Americans far and wide feast on a misnamed bird.

tush (noun)
tushy (noun, diminutive and affectionate)

Already part of English slang, especially in the suburbs. Rhyme with "push" and "bushy." From Yiddish: *tochis*, "buttocks" *via* the Galician *tukhes*—which became a euphemism by softening the *kh* into a *sh*.

1. (Slang euphemism) Backside, buttocks, "ass."
2. Neologism used by people in show business for that on which comedians land when completing a pratfall.

This genteel nice-nellyism (as euphemisms were once called) is often used by American–Jewish mothers in talking to a child about its posterior.

"He fell down so hard he almost broke his *tush*."
"You know what, dolling? I think you have a rash on your *tushy*."

See also TOCHIS, T.O.T.

type ("of" omitted)

Has become (I regret to say) a firmly established feature of Yinglish. From Yiddish: *tip*, and German: *typ*.
Type (of).

The banishment of the preposition, creating such ungrammatical phrasings as "type book," "type friend," or even "type type," fills me with undiluted dismay. Yet this direct transfer of Yiddish to English usage has taken a firm foothold in the American vernacular. "That's the type English I find awful."

———————

Here's a type joke I love:

In the elegant suite of law offices, the telephone rings. It is answered: "Goldbaum, Goldbaum, Goldbaum and Goldbaum."

"Hello," comes a voice. "May I talk to Mr. Goldbaum, please?"

"I'm sorry, sir, but Mr. Goldbaum is out of the city."

"Then—let me speak to Mr. Goldbaum."

"Mr. Goldbaum is in court today."

"Oh. Well, suppose you connect me to Mr. Goldbaum."

"Mr. Goldbaum won't be back until seven."

A sigh. "Okay. Then can you connect me to Mr. Goldbaum?"

"*Spea*-king."

tzaddik
tsaddik

Pronounced TZOD-*dick*. Hebrew: "a righteous man." The plural is *tzaddikim*, pronounced *tzah*-DIK-*im*.

1. A most righteous man.
2. A holy man; a man of surpassing virtue and (possibly) supernatural powers.

3. (Used ironically) An unholy, wicked, cynical man.

Originally, *tzaddikim* were regarded as upright, honorable men who, by their example, brought others closer to righteousness. The medieval cabalists and, later, the Hasidim, attributed mirific powers to the *tzaddik*.

The famous legend of the Thirty-six Saints (*Lamed-vav Tzaddikim*) says that on earth there always live thirty-six saints—who do not know they are sainted. The world continues to exist, by God's favor, only because of these nameless thirty-six—and their unselfish ways and work. No one can tell who they are: one may be a pauper, one a grocer, a shoemaker. . . .

The legend holds that the *Lamed-vav* disclose their identity only on rare occasions—especially emergencies, when Jews are in danger. Then a *tzaddik* will do God's bidding in a sudden, magical rescue mission—and vanish, for he must never have his identity revealed. (That, apparently, would deplete his supernatural powers.) The departed saint is instantly replaced, by God, with another.

The idea of doing good secretly, without reward, fleeing from any recognition or gratitude, held great fascination for the men of the Talmud. A superb book about the angelic Thirty-six is André Schwartz-Bart's *The Last of the Just*.

A famous *tzaddik* was being extolled before a congregation, by a rabbi who waxed more eloquent by the second: ". . . Our beloved *tzaddik* is a man of such wisdom that even the most learned sit at his feet; of such kindness that young and old alike flock to him for advice; of such honesty that men and women are uplifted by his example; of such keen understanding of human problems that—"

At this point, the *tzaddik* tugged at the eulogist's sleeve and whispered, "Don't forget my humility."

For a week, the beloved *tzaddik* of Tarnapolchev had lain in a fever. The end was near.

A disciple leaned over the old saint's form and in the gentlest tone asked, "*Rebbe* . . . have you made your own peace with—*baruch ha-Shem*—the Lord?"

Wheezed the old man. "Eh—mnyeh . . . Who told you we ever quarreled?!"

———

Old Isadore Jacobson sought out a saintly *tzaddik*, who, so everyone asserted, could cast spells and commune with the angels . . .

Mr. Jacobson said, "Dear *Tzaddik*, my heart is sore—and my mood is one of fear . . ."

"And why is that?" the venerable *tzaddik* murmured.

"Because—I do not know what awaits me after death! If only I knew whether I shall be taken to paradise, and bask in the Divine Presence—or be sent to Gehenna—"

The *tzaddik* closed his eyes, began to hum, "*Bim-bom, ta-ra-ta-ra-rom* . . ." and slipped into a trance.

Mr. Jacobson held his breath and waited.

"*Bim-bom . . . bimbidy-be-bom.*" After a while, the old man's eyelids fluttered and opened. "So, my friend, I spoke to a fine angel, and I have the whole answer for you!"

"Tell me—"

"It's in two parts: good news and—eh—bad news. First, the good news! When you leave this world of travail, because you have been such a good man, a kind man, the angels will waft you to heaven! There you will forever remain, near the Golden Throne—"

"Oh, *Tzaddik!*" cried Mr. Jacobson. "How glorious! After that, how can any news be *bad*?"

The old wiseman murmured, "Tonight."

See also HASID.

tzedaka   (noun)
tsadaka

A remarkable word for a more remarkable concept. Pronounced *tze*-DOCK-*a*, to rhyme with "Malacca." Hebrew: from *tzedek*: "righteousness."

The obligation to establish justice by being righteous, upright, compassionate—and, above all, helping one's fellow man.

There is no separate word for "charity" in Hebrew or Yiddish. *Tzedaka* is a moral *obligation* of the highest, noblest order.

Jews are forbidden to ignore or turn away anyone who asks for help. Jews never separated charity from a *duty*, a moral and religious obligation. The poor and needy must, moreover, be spared embarrassment. Every Jewish community placed great stress on helping the poor, the sick, the handicapped—and refugees, who have always been a tragic part of the history of the Jews.

Maimonides set down variously rated forms of *tzedaka*. The highest form of charity, he said, is to help someone to help himself; after that, to help anonymously and secretly—so that the benefactor does not know whom he helps, and the benefactee does not know who helped him. Thus, the old story of the Jew who walked rapidly down the street in a poor neighborhood, one night, throwing little sacks full of coins into one doorway, then another—so that neither he, nor those he helped, knew each other's identity.

See also PUSHKE, SHNORRER.

U

---

underlining absurdity by holding a contrary mirror before it

Q: How would you like me to take you to a four-star French restaurant for dinner?

A: Oh, I'd rather have a hot dog and sauerkraut at a deli.

See also DEMOLISHING A STATEMENT . . . , EXPOSING THE UTTER ABSURDITY . . .

underlining the absurdity of a question simply by repeating it

Q: Would you like me to drive your mother-in-law to the doctor, dentist and supermarket?

A: (sardonically): Would I like you to drive my mother-in-law to the doctor, dentist and supermarket?

See also ACCENTUATING SCORN . . . , ADVERTISING ONE'S FORBEARANCE . . . , AGREEMENT DEPLOYED . . . SARCASM AMPLIFIED . . .

utz   (verb and noun)

This steely Bronxism has not, to my astonishment, caught on in English. I re-recommend it for consideration by ardent Yinglishmen. Rhymes with "foots." German: *uzen*: "to tease," "to fool."

As a verb
1. To needle someone.

2. To nag.
3. To give someone "the shaft."

As a noun

1. A verbal goading, pestering.
2. Prolonged scolding, hectoring.
3. A vitriolic verbal jab.

Old Yosher Baruch, a sour, dyspeptic man, took a chair in Koznitsky's Cheerful Barbershop.

Baruch slid into the empty chair before Koznitsky, the cheeriest of cheerful barbers—who whipped a cover across Baruch with a friendly "*Sholem aleichem.* So—a haircut, *hanh*?"

To which Baruch delivered this *utz*: "N-no, I just dropped in for an estimate."

———

Mr. Lovitz entered the gilded elevator of the posh department store. The *soigné* operator closed the door with insolent force. "And what floor," she asked with insolent sarcasm, "do *you* want?"

"Four," said Mr. Lovitz, then added this *utz*, "*if* it isn't out of your way."

———

"Excuse me, lady. Are you going to have a baby?"
"No. I'm just carrying it for a friend."

———

A New Yorker, in Israel, was boasting to his Israeli cousin, "Why, at Columbia University we have a professor who speaks thirteen languages!"

"My!" sighed the cousin, then unloosed as subtle an *utz* as ever I heard. "I don't think we have a hundred men in our local schools who can do that."

———

Charley Gans, a congenital wiseguy, visiting Israel, stopped at a vegetable stand. He picked up several large canteloupes, hefted them for weight, then *utz*ed the farmer, "Hey, can't you *sabras* grow bigger peaches than these?"

The farmer fixed Gans with an icy stare, *utz*ed back, "Do me a favor, mister; put down the two grapes and go away."

See also ACCENTUATING SCORN. . . , GUT SHABBES, MAZEL TOV!, SARCASM AMPLIFIED . . . , THANKS A LOT, THAT'S WHAT *you say*.

W

---

wear it in good health
wear it in the best of health

A harmless enough addition to Yinglish. Often introduced by the interjection *nu* or the conjunction "so." Thus: "So wear it in good health," or "*Nu*, wear it in the best of health."

This supplication is part of the litany of conditioned reflexes among Jews when giving a present or upon noticing a new article of clothing.

JOSIAH: My God, Les, what happened to you?
LES: I broke my arm in three places. I have to wear this cast for six weeks!
JOSIAH: So wear it in good health.

See also FUHR GEZUNDERHEIT!

What else?

A delicious Yinglish transmutation of the typically Yiddish *Vuden?* (Rhymes with "good Ben.")

1. What else (did you expect)?
2. Of course; naturally.
3. That's to be expected; I'm not surprised.
4. You mean to say you're *surprised*?

This many-layered expletive, seemingly interrogative, is actually a slash of scorn—or a shaft of superior disdain.

"What else?" is not only a question, for it answers itself with such absoluteness as to destroy the ego of the questioner.

1. "She left him for that rich auto dealer!"
   "*Vuden*?" ("What else?")
2. "Are you going to speak at the banquet?"
   "What else?" ("I'm not going for the *food*.")
3. "He never paid the bill!"
   "*Vuden*?" ("I'm not surprised.")
4. "They left the place looking like a pigsty!"
   "So? *Vuden*?" ("You mean that surprised you?")

What gives?

This is a stellar addition to the colloquial phrases of conversational Yinglish. From Yiddish: *Vi geyt's*?: "How goes it?" Via German: *Was gibt*?

1. What's going on there?
2. What's new?
3. What's the matter? What's wrong?
4. Tell me the whole story.

See also GIVE!, T.O.T.

What is, is
What was, was

Yinglish: crisp, fresh and philosophically definitive.

Mrs. Korngold greeted a newcomer to the canasta tables: "So welcome to our group. Let me give you a few of our rules. We *never* tell a lady how she *should* have played a hand. We don't discuss our husbands. We don't boast about our grandchildren. Finally, we never discuss S-E-X. The way we all feel is: what was, was."

what's to . . . ?

This deplorable metaphrase has, nevertheless, won great popularity in sports and show biz circles. From Yiddish: *Vos iz tsu . . .*

This elimination of "there" ("What is there—") is indubitable Yinglish, and thrives in popular phrasings like:

"What's to lose?"
"What's to celebrate?"
"What's to get all worked-up over?"

My only comment about such philistine diction is: "What's to comment?"

Mr. Shissel asked the tailor, "So how much do you charge to press a suit?"

"I charge four dollars," said the tailor.

"Four *dollars*? Why, in Miami Beach I can get a suit pressed A–Number One for only three dollars!"

The tailor shrugged. "What's to argue? . . . And how much is the plane fare?"

Old Sam Kessler had spent a dollar on a sweepstake ticket—and his number won ten million dollars!

Kessler's children did not know how to break the fantastic news to him. "He has such a bad heart," said his son. "The excitement could kill him!"

"Let's ask Dad's doctor," said Kessler's daughter.

They phoned the doctor, told him the news, and described their dilemma. Said the doctor, "Let me handle it. I'll come right over."

So Dr. Vallach dropped in and was shown to the old man's bedroom. He made casual conversation with Kessler for a bit and then, in the most offhand manner, asked, "By the way, Sam, I hear you bought a sweepstake ticket. What's the amount if—by some *miracle*—you should win?"

"Ten million dollars!"

Dr. Vallach laughed. "That certainly is a lot of money . . . Have you thought of what you'd do if—oh, I *know* the chance is very, very slim—you *won* that much money?"

"Doc, I sure have thought of that," Kessler nodded. "In fact, I put it in my legal will . . . If I win ten million dollars, half goes to you."

Dr. Vallach dropped dead.

(What's to explain?)

What was, was

See WHAT IS, IS.

Who knows?

> Pure and priceless Yinglish, for the reasons elucidated below.
>
> From Yiddish: *Ver veyst?*

1. *I* don't know!
2. Maybe someone, some*where*, knows the answer—but I doubt it.
3. You may search the whole *world* for an answer to that question, but—believe me!—there is none!

Any language contains the neutral interrogation "Who knows?" But as rendered in Yinglish ("*Who* knows?" or, with umbrage, "Who *knows*?"), the phrase is not interrogatory: it is declarative. It is also accusatory ("Why do you ask me for an answer to a question that is clearly unanswerable?") or sarcastic ("What a dope you are to think I can answer something like that!") or philosophical ("Beware the surface innocence of the question; to answer is to risk entrapment in epistemology").

The ironic ploy of "Who knows?" may be transferred to any number of pseudo-interrogative asseverations: "Who *cares*?" "Who could?" "Who should?"

4. It's Greek to me.
5. I see *you* don't know the answer either.

———————

DR. RIFKIND: God I'm so *tired*! All day long, day in and day out, all I hear are stories of pain, suffering, conflict. Sometimes, I really regret going into psychiatry. Hermie, how do you manage to look so *serene* after listening all day?

DR. HERSCH: *Who* listens?!

(Yes, I *know* you heard that one before.)

See also DO ME SOMETHING, GO FIGHT CITY HALL.

Who *needs* it?

Stressing the "needs" with force makes this fourteen-karat Yinglish. From Yiddish: *Ver darf es?*

1. Who needs it?
2. Who *needs* it?

The phrase comes directly from Yiddish—and, apart from being widely used, has given birth to an amusing covey of children:

"Who *wants* it?"
"With friends like I have, who needs enemies?"
"That's something I *need*?!"

Advertising and headline writers have seized upon the locution as a "grabber"; thus, the following tributes to the special linguistic attributes of Yinglish:

> *Insurance company ad, showing a smug smartguy:*
> Medical insurance? Who *needs* it?

> *Magazine ad for carpets:*
> This is Acrylan, so who needs wool?

> *Advertisement for a co-op on the Palisades, facing Manhattan:*
> With this view, who needs Palm Beach?

See also GUT SHABBES, THANKS A LOT, THAT'S ALL I NEED!

what's with . . . ?

Another favorite of denizens of the race track, the basketball courts, the movie studios. A vigorous, albeit unaesthetic, newcomer to Yinglish. From Yiddish: *Vos iz mit . . .?*

1. What's wrong with . . . ?
2. Why are you (he, she) acting this way?
3. Explain! Tell me more.

The proper English phrasing would be "What's the matter with . . . ?" or "What's wrong with . . . ?" or "What's bothering . . . ?" The syntax of "What's with . . . ?" is distinctly Yiddish; its popularity in American and British slang has made it Yinglish.

As the air-raid sirens began to shriek all over Haifa, Mr. and Mrs. Plachek leaped out of bed and toward the corridor and the air-raid shelter, when suddenly Mrs. Plachek cried, "Wait! My false teeth!"

"What's with the teeth?" cried Mr. Plachek. "You think the Arabs are going to drop *sand*wiches?"

See also DO ME SOMETHING.

𝒴

Yahrzeit

See YORTZEIT.

Yahveh
Yahweh

Pronounced YAH-*vay*. Presumably, the way the four "sacred letters," Y H V H or Y H W H, were pronounced. In German the letter *W* is pronounced like the English *V*. The vowel sounds for Y H V H were indicated by diacritical marks, to signify YeHoVaH.
Jehovah.

This name and pronunciation are unmistakably incorrect.

See also ADONAI, JEHOVAH, Y H V H.

yak (verb)
yak-yak
yakkety-yak

If ever a word won the hearts of Yinglishmen it is this one. Onomatopoeia. Not to be confused with *yok*. Origin: unknown.

1. To chatter, chatter, chatter.
2. To gossip.

Unlike *shmooze, yak* entirely lacks the idea of a warm, heart-to-heart exchange. *Yak* is derogatory; it describes talk that is of irritating length and trivial substance. And *yakkety-yak* is more so.

3. To laugh.

What makes *yak* appealing? Its phonology: the liquid *y* followed by the emphatic *k* is a sonic delight. The persistent use of *yak* in show business by Jewish comedians, writers, ad-libbers ensured its popularity.

See also HOCK A TCHYNIK, PLOSHER, SHMOOZE, TROMBE-NIK, YENTA.

yarmulka
yarmulke

Pronounced YAHR-*m'l-keh*, to rhyme with "bar culpa." From a Tartar word, via the Polish for "skullcap."
The caplet perched on the top of the head by observing Jewish males. Among Hasidim, a broad black hat sits over the caplet.

No religious edict I can uncover directs Jews to cover their heads (though Exodus prescribes head-covering for the Temple priests).

During the early Middle Ages, the rabbis instructed Jewish men not to go about bareheaded. Why? Because man should cover his head as a sign of respect before God. Covering the head as a sign of respect and reverence is a custom not restricted to Jews, of course; it is common among the peoples of the East, from Arabia to India.

Reform Jews, however, hold that in the Western world it is more appropriate to bare one's head as a sign of respect. Conservative Jews reply that baring the head is an imitation of a non-Jewish custom, and prefer to maintain the traditional head-covering during prayer.

The current custom seems to be:

1. Traditional, Orthodox males wear a *yarmulka* at home and at work, no less than in the synagogue, to remind them of whom they stand before at every moment.
2. Other religious males wear a *yarmulka* in the synagogue, while studying sacred texts, and while engaged in a religious ritual at home.
3. Reform Jews, in western Europe and in America, do not wear a *yarmulka*.

4. Nonreligious Jews may don a *yarmulka* for a *bris*, Bar Mitzva, wedding, funeral—as a concession to tradition, to please their elders, to add a note of ceremonial solemnity.

The most charming comment ever about the skullcap appeared in 1964 in a cartoon in a Tel Aviv newspaper. The cartoon showed the pope and the president of Israel, side by side, during the holy pontiff's history-making trip. The caption:

The Pope is the one wearing a *yarmulka*.

The sign on the door of the office on 37th Street read:

BYKOFSKI AND SHATZ
CORSETS, GIRDLES, BRASSIERES
(FOUNDED IN 1952)

Into this office one morning staggered Benny Shatz, red-faced, apoplectic, shouting, "Arty! Arty! We are *ruined*!"

Arty Bykofski leaped to his feet. "Benny, calm down! You'll have a stroke. What's the matter?"

"I just came from the stockroom, Arty. You'll never guess what *happened*! That crate of brassieres we sent to Smolinsky and Trilling in Omaha! Remember?"

"Of course I remember. All black—"

"*Returned*, Arty! Every single brassiere—returned! *Two hundred dozen* brassieres, Arty! *What can we do?*!"

It took Arty Shatz but a minute to groan, frown, think, grin—and snap his fingers. "What can we *do*, Benny? It's wonderful! We'll cut off the straps and sell them for *yarmulkas!*"

See also DAVEN.

yenta
yente

This word is one of the most popular and widely used Yiddish words in the Yinglish patois. Pronounced YEN-*ta*. From Italian, Spanish or French—maybe. Otherwise: derivation is unknown. *Yenta*, I am told, was a perfectly acceptable name for a lady, derived from the Italian *gentile*—until some ungracious *yenta* gave it a bad name. *Yenta* may be an ironic corruption of the French feminine for well-bred, *gentille*—but I doubt it.

1. A blabbermouth; a gossip.
2. A woman of low origins or vulgar manners.
3. A shrew; a shallow, coarse termagant.
   "She is the biggest *yenta* on the block."
4. A man who acts like one of the above.

Yenta Telebende was a famous character in a Yiddish newspaper published in New York; she was invented by the humorous writer "B. Kovner," the pen name of Jacob Adler.

————

Two *yentas* met in Miami.

"So tell me, Rivke, have you been through the menopause?"

"The menopause? I haven't even been through the *Fontainebleau* yet."

————

This happened years ago, when Americans traveled mostly by train.

Mr. Fortescue, tossing and turning in an upper Pullman berth, could not get to sleep because, from the berth below, came a woman's mournful muttering: "*Oy* . . . am I toisty . . . *Oy* . . . am I toisty . . ."

On and on went the lament, until Mr. Fortescue got out, crawled down the ladder, padded the length of the Pullman car, filled two paper cups with water, brought them back, and handed them through the curtains to the passenger in the lower berth. "Madam, here. Water!"

"God bless you, mister! Thank you . . ."

Fortescue crawled back into his berth.

He was on the very edge of somnolence when, from below, came the suspiration: "*Oy* . . . vas I toisty . . ."

See also KOCHLEFFL, PLOSHER, SHLEP, SHLUMP.

yentz (verb and noun)
yents

> Cheerfully used by Yinglishmen "in the know"—it is
> strictly taboo in proper circles. Rhymes with "rents."
> From German: *jenes* (see below).
>   (Vulgarism, taboo)

1. To copulate.
2. To cheat, to swindle, to defraud. In this usage, *yentz*
   is akin to the English slang "screw." Thus: "Don't
   trust him; he'll *yentz* you."

Yentz is a most coarse word, never used in the presence
of women or children. The Yiddish equivalent of the best-
known four-letter English word for sexual congress, *yentz*
has become a solid part of the vernacular of the American
underworld.

The origin of the word is extremely interesting. *Yentz*
comes from the German demonstrative pronoun *jenes*,
meaning "that," "that thing," "the other," "the other
thing." The German pronunciation is YAYN-*es*; the Yiddish
rendition became YENTS.

But how did "the other" or "that thing" become invested with carnal content? Quite simply, as a euphemism—*i.e.*, "that unmentionable thing." (In the United
States, the word "it" is used for copulation: "They did it";
"Does she—do it?")

I call your attention to the extraordinary fact that Hebrew contains no words for the sex organs: the male member is called "that organ" (*ever* or *gid*); the female
receptacle is called "that place" (*ossu mokum*). There once
were explicit Hebrew words for fornication, penis, vagina,
et alia—but it seems that they perished from disapproval
and disuse. So in Hebrew (and later Yiddish), the penis
became "that organ," testicles were identified as "eggs,"
and the vagina was briskly dubbed "that place."

With such a prudish tradition, it is not surprising that
Jews seized upon *jenes*—which, incidentally, is how gen-
teel ladies' maids, nurses, and governesses in Germany and
Austria and Hungary referred to you-know-whats.

Now comes a paradox. *Yenes* is a proper Yiddish word,
meaning "that thing" or "the other." But it also serves the

euphemism, in rabbinical literature, for a dozen "unmentionables": genitalia, urine, dung, a devil, a demon.

It is the ironic fate of euphemisms to replace the unacceptable—and themselves become taboo.

———

The attitude of Jews to sex is at once relaxed and repressive. The sexes were carefully segregated. In the old country, men never danced with women. The marriage canopy was a sacrosanct symbol. Illegitimacy was virtually unknown.

On the other hand, sex was no shameful thing and surely no *sin*. Indeed, the sexual aspect of marriage is celebrated in the Talmud and in rabbinical writings.

Rare among religions, Judaism recognized women's right to, and need for, sexual satisfaction! Rabbi Akiba called the Song of Songs the "holiest of holies."

———

A friend tells me that in the old country she shyly protested to her father that she did not want to marry the man chosen to be her husband. "Why not?" asked her father.

"B-because I don't *love* him!"

To which the old man bellowed, "You want to love him *before* you marry him?!"

See also SHMUCK, SHTUP, TCHOTCHKE.

yeshiva
yeshiba
yeshivot   (plural, Hebrew)
yeshivos   (plural, Yiddish)

Pronounced *yeh*-SHEE-*va*, to rhyme with "believe a." From Hebrew: *yeshov*: "to sit." (Students sat while studying, and the places where they so sat became known as *yeshivot*.)

1. A rabbinical college or seminary.
2. (In the United States) Also a secondary Hebrew school; an elementary school in which both religious and secular subjects are studied.

The *yeshiva* was the outgrowth of the *Bes Midrash* ("House of Study"), the place in every Jewish community where men met to discuss the Torah and the Talmud. The great Mishnah (*q.v.*) drew upon the vast accumulated body of knowledge, interpretations and debates of the innumerable, unending seminars in the innumerable "houses of study" where Jews carried on their unending discussions on God, faith, good, evil, responsibility.

The *yeshivas* were the creative source and critical laboratory of all Jewish theology, law, ethics and moral guidance. From the tenth century on, *yeshivas* spread wherever Jews lived or migrated—to North Africa, Spain, France, Italy, Germany, England, Holland and especially in eastern Europe.

It must be emphasized that the purpose of the *yeshiva* was *not* primarily to produce rabbis, but to produce Jews well versed in the Talmud, learned men, men who would dedicate themselves to live according to the Torah, men who would spend several hours a day for the rest of their lives studying the ever-discussable tractates of the Talmud.

In most *yeshivot* it was unheard of to read anything but the Bible and the Talmud. All secular works—philosophy, science, fiction, poetry—were strictly excluded. Religious Jews feared that secularization would follow if worldly influences were permitted to attract the Jewish young. (In the late nineteenth century, however, the *yeshiva* of Volozhin advocated the acquisition of secular knowledge.)

The first American *yeshiva, Etz Chayim* Talmudical Academy, was organized in New York City in 1886. It eventually grew into Yeshiva University, which (in addition to a rabbinical seminary) includes institutions ranging from high schools to its own medical school.

The first rabbinical college for Reform Jews was established in Cincinnati in 1875: Hebrew Union College.

The Jewish Theological Seminary was founded in New York in 1886 and reorganized in 1902; today it is the leading Conservative rabbinical training center.

See also BES MIDRASH, RABBI.

yeshiva bucher
bachurim (plural)

Pronounced ye-SHEE-*va* BOO-*kher* or BAW-*kher*, with a Scottish *kh*, not the voiced aspirate of "Chickamauga."

Hebrew: *yeshov*: "to sit"; *bachur*: literally, "chosen"; also "young man" or "bachelor." The plural of *bucher* is *bachurim*; but in English, usage is often *buchers*.

1. A young man who is a student at a *yeshiva* (college for Talmudic study).
2. A scholarly, shy, unworldly type.
   "He is as gentle as a *yeshiva bucher*."
3. (Used ironically) A naive, gullible type; an inexperienced and unrealistic sort.
   "Don't ask him for an opinion; he's a *yeshiva bucher*."

Study at a *yeshiva* was extremely demanding, beginning with early prayers and continuing all day, in rigorous cerebral discipline, until late at night. It took about seven years of *yeshiva* study to become a rabbi.

Students who came from far distances to a *yeshiva* were boarded and lodged with local families. It was considered an act of piety to feed and lodge a *yeshiva bucher*, many of whom went from home to home, eating and sleeping in a different place each night. Some slept on the benches in the *yeshiva*. The *yeshiva bucher* was a familiar figure in eastern Europe: his innocence, his asceticism, his gentleness became legendary.

A *yeshiva bucher* was a matrimonial prize. The Talmud (*Pesahim*) says: "If you must, sell everything and . . . marry your daughter to a scholar." The father of the bride would settle an amount on the scholarly groom as dowry, or would provide him with support.

———

Two *yeshiva bachurim* paused before a store, to examine a reproduction of a painting called *The Child in the Manger* in the window. "You know what this is about, Yussel?"

"N-no. I don't understand. Here is a family living in a *stable*, with animals, the floor covered with straw, and that poor little baby, stark naked . . ."

"So?"

"So, how could they afford to have their picture painted?"

See also LUFTMENSH, RABBI.

yet

A special gem in the diadem of Yinglish. Exceptional: brusque, yet ironic. From Yiddish: *nokh.*

Don't jump to conclusions: the adverb *yet* as used in Yinglish does not mean what it does in English. In Yinglish, *yet* is umbrageous, indignant, a cry against the unjust. It is an exceptionally forceful intensifier.

1. On top of everything else!
2. Even after all that!
3. Can you imagine such bad luck?

"—and for losing my whole investment, he wants to be *paid*, yet."
"It wasn't enough he borrowed my car for an hour and kept it a week: he burned a hole in the *seat*, yet."

———————

MAXIE: Papa, to help in all my schoolwork—will you buy me an encyclopedia?
FATHER: Are you *meshugge*? . . . You can walk to school, like all the other kids yet.

See also AGAIN . . . ?, ALRIGHT ALREADY, BIG DEAL, HOO-HA!, NOW—?

Y H V H

These four Hebrew letters, which appear no fewer than 6,823 times in the Old Testament, form the Hebrew name for God.

We do not know how Y H V H was pronounced by the ancients: there are no vowels in written (or printed) Hebrew. The vowel *sounds* are indicated by diacritical marks (points, dots, dashes) above or below the Hebrew letters.

Today, Y H V H is rendered vocally as "Yahveh."

"Jehovah," which first appeared in Christian texts in 1516, is simply incorrect—based on a German papal scribe's reading of Y H V H with the diacritical marks meant for *Adonai*, which had been added in the margins of a scroll, as aids to pronunciation; so Y H V H became a German's mistaken transliterated Latin: YeHoVaH.

The King James version of the Bible usually translates Y H V H as "Lord."

> Oh God: Do not inflict upon us all that You know we can endure.
> Oh, Lord, give me a good excuse.
> —Folk sayings
> God will forgive me: *c'est son métier* [it's his business].
> —Heinrich Heine

See also ADONAI, JEHOVAH, YAHVEH.

Yid

An offensive, demeaning, disagreeable way of referring to a Jew—if you pronounce this *Yid*, to rhyme with "kid," instead of YEED, to rhyme with "deed." Jews say "Yeed"—unless they want to characterize a Jew as a coarse, vulgar, ill-mannered, greedy, grubby (*et alia*) person. From the German: *Jude*: "Jew." And *Jude* is a truncated form of *Yehuda*, the name given to the Jewish Commonwealth in the period of the Second Temple. That name, in turn, was derived from the name of one of Jacob's sons, *Yehuda* (Judah, in English), whose descendants constituted one of the tribes of Israel.

1. A Jew, male or female—if you pronounce the word to rhyme with "deed": *Yeed*.
2. A word akin to *kike*—and just as offensive—if pronounced to rhyme with "did."

Permit me a brief sortie into linguistic self-indulgence. In Hebrew, *Yehudi* means an inhabitant of *Yehuda* (romanized: Judea). Jews have called themselves "Yehudi" in every language they were obliged to speak. But the word suffered syncopation, so to speak: *e.g.*, in the Talmud, Rabbi "Yuda" replaced "Yehuda," and "Yuda" became "Yudi." By the thirteenth century, says the most learned Dr. Nathan Susskind, every accented *u* that is followed by an *i* of the next syllable became an umlauted *ü* in German. In Yiddish, the umlauted *ü* was unrounded into an *i*. Hence the progression: Yehudi, Yudi, Yude, Yid. (Whew!)

So sensitive are Jews about racial aspersions, that when a Vassar girl told her father they were experimenting in the psychology lab with guinea pigs, he drew back in horror: "At college, haven't they told you *never* to say 'guinea' for Italian?"

Old Meyer Fritkin was waiting at a stop light, when a very *goyish* bruiser stopped, a large, sullen dog on his leash.

"My, my," said Mr. Fritkin. "That's a good dog you got there. What type is he?"

"He," sneered the bruiser, "is a cross between an ape and a Yid!"

"Tsk, tsk," said Mr. Fritkin. "Related to both of us."

Mrs. James Hale Rillington III telephoned the headquarters of the infantry base several miles from Forty Elms, her ancestral home. "This is Mrs. James Hale Rillington the Third. With Thanksgiving coming up," she said, "I would like to invite ten of your enlisted men to share our family feast at Forty Elms."

"That's wonderful, Mrs. Rillington."

"Only one thing. We—prefer not to have any Yids. I'm sure you understand."

"Madam, I *quite* understand."

When her bell rang on Thanksgiving Day, Mrs. Rillington hurried to the door herself. "Welcome to Forty—" She stopped. Under the great portico stood ten black soldiers. "My God!" she gasped. "There has been a terrible mistake!"

The black sergeant said, "Oh, no ma'am. Captain Kaminsky *never* makes a mistake."

(Of *course* I know I have used this parable elsewhere. Is it not worth repeating?)

See also ESKIMO, KIKE, MISHPOCHE, SHEENY.

Yiddish

From the German: *jüdisch*: "Jewish."

The language spoken and written by the Jews of eastern Europe, the Ashkenazim. (The comparable vernacular for the Sephardim is Ladino, also called Dzhudesmo or Judesmo.)

Yiddish is not Hebrew, which remains (with Aramaic) the Jews' language of prayer and religious ceremonies. Hebrew is the official language of Israel. "Jewish" refers to a people—"Yiddish" to a language.

Yiddish uses the *letters* of the Hebrew alphabet; it is written from right to left; its spelling is emphatically phonetic.

Please note: Jews do not speak "Jewish," any more than Methodists speak "Methodist" or Canadians speak "Canadish." *Jewish* is an adjective, not a noun. (But because "Yiddish" means "Jewish" *in* Yiddish itself, many use the words interchangeably.)

Yiddish uses the letters of the Hebrew, not the Roman, alphabet, and is written or printed from right to left:

ybab   eht   em   dnaH*

Hebrew and Yiddish are entirely independent languages. You may be a wizard in Hebrew and not understand a line of Yiddish; the same is true vice versa.

Experts differ considerably on this subject, but the vocabulary of Yiddish seems to be drawn from

German	72	percent
Hebrew	16	percent
Slavic tongues	12	percent
Romance languages (Latin/French/ Italian)	5.60	percent
English	3.55	percent

The fact that these numbers add up to more than 100 percent demonstrates the limitations of statistics: I *know* the figures are to be trusted: I made them up as approximates myself (but only after an exhausting analysis of the clashing estimates of philologists).

---

*I am sure this never happened, but how I wish it had: Abe Shpeisel, reporter for the *Jewish Daily Forward*, dashed into a phone booth, dropped his coins, dialed, barked "Managing Editor!" and cried, "Chief? Shpeisel. I've got a story that'll rip this town wide open! Hold the back page!"

Whatever the percentages, do not sniff with superior nostrils over a tongue once said to be "jargon." English draws 53.6 percent of its vocabulary from Latin–French–Italian–Spanish, 31.1 percent from German–Dutch–Scandinavian–Old English, and 10.8 percent from Greek. And *these* figures come from the editors of the *Concise Oxford Dictionary* (Preface).

In the dry, technical world of linguistics, *Yiddish* is classified as "Judeo-German." But it also contains what philologists call Loez—Jewish correlates of Old French and Old Italian.

Philologists identify three main types of Yiddish: Lithuanian, Polish, South Russian (Ukrainian). (Romanian Yiddish is close to Polish Yiddish; Austrian and Hungarian versions are close to Ukrainian.) In the newspapers and journals published in the United States, Lithuanian Yiddish predominates.

Yiddish uses Hebrew words for all references to the Bible, the Talmud, religious tenets, observances, rituals, etc. The Yiddish words are spelled as they are in Hebrew. But Hebrew words are pronounced differently in Yiddish than they are in Hebrew. Hebrew words accent the last syllable; Yiddish, usually the penultimate syllable. The Hebrew *th* is pronounced as *s* in Yiddish.

Believe it or not, Yiddish is not a "new" or even a "young" language. It is older than modern German, which may be said to have begun with Martin Luther's translation of the Bible; and Yiddish is older than modern English, which dates from 1475, according to the *Random House Dictionary*.

Over two hundred manuscripts in Old Yiddish (A.D 1200–1500) have to date been discovered. As long ago as 1534 a Hebrew–Yiddish dictionary of the Bible was published in Cracow.

As far back as the fifteenth century, Elijah Bochur, a Hebrew scholar, wrote and published poems in—Yiddish. In 1602 there appeared a Yiddish storybook, a collection of folktales and stories out of the Talmud. A book on morals and manners, meant for Jewish women, appeared in 1542. Much Yiddish poetry was published by Jews in Prague in the second half of the sixteenth century. Josephus' *Antiquities of the Jews* was adapted into Yiddish in Zurich, in 1546.

The first Yiddish newspaper in the world began publication (semi-weekly) in 1686–1687 in Amsterdam.

The significance of these data is sharply highlighted if you consider that modern Latin lexicography was born in a thesaurus first produced in 1531—and the first English dictionary (by Nathan Bailey) did not appear until 1721!

Around 4000 B.C., the ancient Israelites spoke Hebrew, a Semitic language of the Canaanite group, and they continued to do so until Solomon's Temple was destroyed (586 B.C.) and they were taken into captivity.

A hundred or so years later, when the Jews returned from Babylonia, they found the inhabitants of the Holy Land speaking Aramaic, the vernacular of the Near and Middle East. Aramaic crept into the prayers of the Jews (*e.g.*, *Kaddish*, *Kol Nidre*), despite strong resistance from the rabbis. But Hebrew was (as it still is) the language used in prayers and religious ceremonies.

After the rise of Islam, Arabic displaced Aramaic (and other tongues) as the oral language of Jews in the Arab world. Many scholars, physicians and poets wrote in Arabic (Maimonides, Saadia Gaon and others), often using Hebrew letters.

How and where did Yiddish begin? *The Standard Jewish Encyclopedia* offers the following chronology:

Initial Yiddish	A.D. 1000–1250
Old Yiddish	1250–1500
Medieval Yiddish	1500–1750
Modern Yiddish	1750 on . . .

About a thousand years ago, Jewish emigrants from the north of France began to settle in towns along the Rhine. These Jews spoke Hebrew and Old French, to which they now added the Germanic dialects of the Rhine. The Jews *wrote* the new vernacular with Hebrew characters (Jews had good reason to eschew Latin—*i.e.*, "monkish"—letters). Jews had always used the letters of the Hebrew alphabet—to write Persian, Greek, Latin, etc.

It was in the ghettos (begun by Lateran Councils in 1179 and 1215) that the new linguistic mélange took root and flourished. The terrible pogroms that accompanied the First

Crusade and the Black Plague drove Jews into South Germany, Austria, Bohemia and North Italy, and the Jews brought their languages along.

Yizkor

Pronounced YISS-*kor*, to rhyme with "disk oar." Hebrew: "May [God] remember."
Memorial service for the dead, held in a synagogue.

Yizkor is the shortened name for the memorial service, *Hazkarat Neshamot* (Remembrance of the Souls), which is recited on the eighth day of Pesach, the second day of Shevous, the eighth day of Succoth and on Yom Kippur.

The service opens with a reading that emphasizes the duties of the living more than the dead. Deceased kinsfolk and parents are recalled: "Their desire was to . . . teach us Thy statutes and commandments, and to instruct us to do justice and to love mercy." Those reciting *Yizkor* pledge themselves to perform "acts of charity and goodness" in honor of the deceased's memory. A congregational prayer, *El Maleh Rachamim*, petitions God to grant peace and eternal life to the departed souls.

Part of the *Yizkor* service is a memorial to the martyrs, of all generations, who died for the sanctification of God's name. Many synagogues recite a special memorial prayer for the six million victims of the Nazis. In Israel, a *Yizkor* prayer is said for the men and women who fell while defending Israel in its War of Independence and in the later wars to avoid annihilation.

See also KADDISH, SHIVA, YORTZEIT.

yok   (noun and verb)

A standby prized by Yinglishmen—especially those in the world of entertainment. Please do not confuse with *yak*. Derivation: probably echoic.

1. To laugh loudly.
2. A belly-laugh.

This neologism is theatrical argot, born in vaudeville, used by stage comedians, then by radio comics—and now by anyone who appreciates the tympanic force of this colorful and expressive word.

I first encountered *yok* in the 1930s in *Variety* and the *Hollywood Reporter*.

————————

Jack Benny drew many a *yok* when, accepting an award, he would say, "I really don't deserve this beautiful award. But I have arthritis, and I don't deserve *that* either!"

yold

Pronounced YULD, to rhyme with "gulled." Hebrew: *yeled*: "child," "boy."

1. A naive, gullible person.
2. A fool.
3. A simpleton.
4. A harmless yokel.

Yold is sometimes defined as a cross between a *schlemiel* and a *shmegegge*.

See also KNOW FROM NOTHING, NAYFISH, NEBECH, SHMEGEGGE, SHMENDRICK, SHMO, SHNOOK.

Yom Kippur

Extremely well known, especially since the historic Six-Day War.

In Yiddish, pronounced *yum-*KIP-*per*, to rhyme with "hum dipper." Hebrew: "Day of Atonement." (Some scholars trace *kippur* to the Babylonian for "purge," "wipe off.") But in Hebrew, the pronunciation is YOM-*kip-*POOR, to rhyme with "Tom Mature." The latter pronunciation, adopted by virtually all radio and television newscasters, discombobulated Jews everywhere—who did not know there was a Hebrew pronunciation.

The last of the annual Ten Days of Penitence and one of the two high Holy Days of the Jewish calendar, Yom Kippur is the day that has the strongest hold on the Jewish conscience.

Rosh Hashanah marks the first day of the Ten Days of Penitence. On that day, say the Orthodox, all men stand before God for judgment, but the Lord's decision is made on the *last* of the Ten Days—and that day is Yom Kippur.

The Mishnah instructs pious Jews not to eat or drink, wash or wear shoes on Yom Kippur. Because Jews hold that offenses against other men can only be forgiven by other men (and not by God!), Jews on Yom Kippur eve would hurry around to those they had offended (or been unfriendly to) during the year—and beg their pardon.

Pious families would gather and ask forgiveness of each other for any slights, insensitivities, or injustices they might have committed against each other in the preceding year. Husband and wife would ask each other's forgiveness; children would ask forgiveness of each parent and of each other; each parent would ask each child for forgiveness. I think this custom noble—and psychologically peerless.

Synagogue service begins just before nightfall the evening before Yom Kippur. In the synagogue, the cantor stands before the Ark; on each side of him stands an honored member of the congregation. Each carries a large scroll of the Torah. The cantor and the two worshipers act as spokespersons for the congregation:

> By the authority of the . . . Lord, blessed be He, and by the permission of this sacred congregation, we declare it lawful to pray with those who have transgressed.

This is thrice repeated; then the cantor begins to intone *Kol Nidre (q.v.)*.

Prayers on Yom Kippur continue, virtually without interruption, from morning until after sunset. Since purity of conscience is the *leitmotif* of the day, white predominates. The curtain of the Ark and the Torah covering are white (they may be of varied colors during the year). The rabbi and cantor wear white robes; many men in the congregation wear white *yarmulkas* instead of the traditional black.

The primary feature of Yom Kippur is the Confession, repeated several times during the day. It involves the confessing of no fewer than fifty-six categories of sin, accompanied by breast-beating. The confession of guilt is recited by a collective "we," not by an individual "I." On Yom Kippur, Jews "share" responsibility for the misdeeds and shortcomings of humankind.

As the long day of fasting, prayer and new resolve draws

to a close, the *Ne'ilah* service is held. This service begins the moment the setting sun is level with the treetops; and it is timed to end with the appearance of the first stars. Most congregants stand, to pay special honor:

Lord, though every power be Thine
And every deed tremendous,
Now, when heaven's gates are closing,
Let Thy grace defend us.

Yom Kippur ends with the call of the *shofar (q.v.)*, which Saul Lieberman has called "a prayer without words." A valuable source book is *The Yom Kippur Anthology*, edited by Philip Goodman.

———————

The operator in the law offices crooned, "Floyd, Horgan and Zytenheim."

A male voice said, "May I please speak to Mr. Zytenheim?"

"I'm sorry, sir. Mr. Zytenheim is out. This is Yom Kippur."

"Oh. Well, Miss Kippur, when he gets in, tell him his reading glasses are ready."

———————

The most memorable story I know:

On the eve of Yom Kippur, that most solemn and sacred day, an old Jew looked up to heaven and sighed: "Dear God, listen: the butcher in our village, Shepsel, is a good man, an honorable man, who never turns away the needy; yet Shepsel himself is so poor that he and his wife sometimes go without meat! . . . Or take Fishel, our shoemaker, a model of piety and kindness—yet his beloved mother is dying in terrible pain . . . And Reb Label, our *melamed* [teacher], who loves all the lads he teaches and is loved by all who know him—he just developed an eye disease that may leave him blind! . . . So, on the eve of this most holy night, I ask You directly, God: Is this *fair*? I repeat: *Is this fair*? . . . So, tomorrow, O Lord, on Yom Kippur—if You forgive us, we will forgive You!"

See also KOL NIDRE, ROSH HASHANAH, SHOFAR, YONTIF.

yontif (noun)
yontef
yom tov (Hebrew)
yontifdik (adjective)

Steadily working its way into Yinglish. Pronounced YUN-*tiff* in Yiddish, to rhyme with "bun miff." From Hebrew: *yom*: "day"; *tov*: "good."

1. Holiday. "The post office is closed; it's *yontif*." (Third generation Jews would say: "a *yontif*.") "Happy *yontif*!"
2. A celebration, a festivity. "I felt all *yontifdik* that day."
3. (Sarcastically) "Thanks a *lot*!" "Why don't we split the bill?" "Good *yontif*."

To say "Good *yontif*!" would seem redundant, like "a good good-day," except that *yontif* has been given its own meaning: "holiday." In Israel, people use the Hebrew phraseology: *chag sameyach*: "Happy holiday."

———————

A denizen of Flatbush, having seen the pope in one of the large, public, papal audiences, felt obliged to send His Holiness a Christmas greeting. It ran: "Good *yontif*, Pontiff."

Yortzeit
Yahrzeit

Pronounced either YAWR-*tzite*, to rhyme with "court site," or YAR-*tzite*, to rhyme with "dart site." The first pronunciation is Yiddish; the second, German. *Yahrzeit* is, of course, German: "year's time," or "anniversary."
The anniversary of someone's death.

Many observances are incumbent on religious Jews to commemorate the death of someone in the family. On the annual anniversary, a memorial candle or lamp is lighted in the home and another in the synagogue, where it burns from sunset to sunset. A burning light is connected with the idea of immortality—Proverbs 20:27: "The spirit of man is the candle of the Lord. . . ."

Orthodox Jews fast all day at *Yortzeit*. So do many others.

———————

I know no jokes about *Yortzeit*, and if I did, I would not put them here, for two candles burn in my mind—and will until I die, too.

See also KADDISH, SHIVA, YIZKOR.

You don't have to put a finger in his mouth

This is one of the most colorful and original entries in this lexicon. I hope it spreads into Yinglish.

More exactly, "Him, no one need put a finger in his mouth": *Im [aym] darf men keyn finger in moyl nit araynleygen.*

1. You don't have to explain it to *him*.
2. He can take a hint.
3. He's very smart and very quick.

This picturesque phrase provides an image that has haunted me ever since I heard it: a finger inserted into a mouth. Why? To arrange the unuttered letters into comprehensibilities.

———————

Hilda Mazer could not deny that her late husband, Benny, had been very unpopular. Friends he had none; critics he had everywhere. So it was with special feeling that she asked Rabbi Berman, "Doesn't even a *momzer* deserve a kind word after he dies?"

"Stop!" said the rabbi. "I'll make for your Benny a sermon no one will ever forget."

And he did. To a huge audience, Rabbi Berman declaimed: "We are here to say good-bye to a man known to us all as a no-good, a *paskudnyak* who never helped a friend, never paid a debt, never gave a *cent* to charity. But one thing I can tell you, with a full heart: compared to his brother Louie, Benny was an angel!"

(I think that you will agree that Rabbi Berman was a man who did not need anyone to put a finger in *his* mouth.)

See also A.M, AMERICA GONIF!, IT CANT HURT!, MACHER, MOMZER, PSSSSH!, SHTARKER, TUMMLER.

you should excuse the expression [me; my frankness]

Emphatically and indisputably Yinglish—unfortunately, in my judgment. From Yiddish: *Zolst mir antshuldigen*: "You should excuse me."
Please excuse . . .

"You should excuse" is synonymous with "If you'll excuse" or "If you'll pardon [the expression, my candor] . . ." Yes, it's substandard English.

This genteelism, long a feature of New Yorkese and of vaudeville/radio comedy, takes on a satirical note in conversation among the sophisticated:

"He is a Good Humor (you should excuse the expression) salesman."

Intramural aspersions are more easily expressed in this barbarism than in naked disdain:

"Professor Hepman is (you'll excuse the expression) a monetarist."
"He plays rock-and-roll (excuse the expression) 'music.' "

See also MOXEY, SARCASM AMPLIFIED. . .

You want to hear something?

A colloquial phatic opening in Yiddish—and now Yinglish. Yinglish for *Ir vilt eppes her'n*?

Do not mistake this proclamation for, say, "Do you want to hear what happened?" or "Do you want to hear how we got home?" These promise to convey precise information. But "You want to hear *something*?" is an invitation to the revelation of unsolicited information. The question is an offer, open-ended, bait.

One may answer the question "Do you want to hear

what we ate?'' with a polite ''Not really.'' But I cannot imagine anyone who is asked ''Do you want to hear something?'' replying, ''No.''

———————

Into an office of NASA came an old man in a *yarmulka*, hunched over a cane. To the receptionist, he handed a newspaper clipping:

WANTED

For training as Astronaut. Age: 21–26. Should have degree in science or engineering. Must be in perfect health. Write National Aeronautics and Space Agency.

The receptionist said, ''Excuse me, sir, but—for whom are you here?''

''For mineself. Hymie Gittelman.''

''Your*self*?! Do you—have a degree in science—?''

''No. Also no for engineer. Plus, I am over seventy-four years old.''

''Then why did you come—?''

''You want to hear something?'' said Mr. Gittelman. ''On *me*, you shouldn't depend!''

See also NU, SO.

zaftig
zaftik

Zaftig is totally at home in Yinglish. Pronounced ZOFF-tig. From German: "juicy."

1. Plump, buxom, well-rounded (of a female). This is the most frequent American usage.
2. Juicy. "What a *zaftig* plum."
3. Provocative, seminal, germinal. "The book is full of *zaftig* ideas."

Zaftig describes in one word what it takes two hands, outlining an hourglass figure, to do.

Two *zaftig* matrons talking:
"I think women like us should take a greater interest in politics . . . Tell me, what do you think of the Common Market?"
"I still prefer the A&P."

Mrs. Belferz was sitting in her husband's office, waiting for him to return from lunch, when a curvaceous, *zaftig* blonde sasheyed in and sat down behind the reception desk.
"I," said Mrs. Belferz, "am Mrs. Belferz."
"Please t' meet ya," said the blonde. "I am Mr. Belferz's secretary."
"Oh," Mrs. Belferz murmured, "*were* you?"

See also TCHOTCHKE, YENTA.

zayde
zeyde

> Often used in English by Jewish writers of fiction. Pronounced ZAY-*deh*, to rhyme with "fade a." Some American children accentuate affection by saying "*zaydee*." Probably of Slavic origin.
>
> 1. Grandfather. "My *bubbeh* and *zayde* came to visit yesterday."
> 2. An old man. You may say to any old Jew, "How are you, *zayde*?" just as a Chinese will affectionately greet an old man who is not his grandfather.

Zayde: "The press agent for his grandchildren."

Letter from a ten-year-old at a summer camp:

Dear Zaydie:
   Remember I told you if my parents made me go to camp, *something terrible would happen*?? Well, it did.
                                        Love,
                                        Maury

For months, Mrs. Pitzel had been nagging her husband to go with her to the séance parlor of Madame Froda. "Milty, she is a real gypsy—and she brings the voices of the dead—from the other world—we all *talk* to! Last week I talked with my mother, may she rest in peace . . . Milty, for twenty dollars you can talk to your *zayde* who you miss so much!"

Milton Pitzel could not resist her appeal. At the very next séance at Madame Froda's Séance Parlor, Milty sat under the colored light at the green table, holding hands with the pilgrim to his right and the mystic to his left. All were humming, "Ooooom . . . oooom . . . Tonka Tooom . . ."

Madame Froda, her eyes lost in trance, was making passes over a crystal ball. "My medium . . . Vashtri . . ." she keened. "Come in . . . Who is that with you? . . . Who? . . . Mr. Pitzel? . . . Milton Pitzel's *zayde*?"

Milty swallowed the lump in his throat and called, "Grampa? . . . *Zayde*?"

"Ah, *Mil*teleh?" a thin, thin voice quavered.

"Yes, yes!" cried Milty. "This is your Milty! *Zayde*, are you happy in the other world?"

"Milteleh . . . I am in bliss. With your *bawbe* together. . . . We laugh . . . we sing . . . we gaze upon the shining face of the Lord!"

A dozen more questions did Milty ask of his grandfather, and each question did his *zayde* answer, until: "So now, Milty, I have to go . . . The angels are calling . . . Just one more question I can answer . . . Ask . . . ask . . ."

"*Zayde*," sighed Milty, "when did you learn to speak English?"

See also BUBBE.

zetz

Used by Jewish stand-up comedians. Pronounced as spelled; rhymes with "gets." From German: *Zurück setzung*: literally, "a setting back."

1. A strong blow or punch.
   "He gave me a *zetz*—knocked out two teeth."
2. A setback, misfortune.
   "Have you ever played Peoria? That's a *zetz* to anyone's career."

zhlub (noun)
zhlob

Pronounce it ZHLAWB, to rhyme with "rub" or "daub." From Slavic: *zhlob*: "coarse fellow."

1. An insensitive, ill-mannered person.
   "He acts like a *zhlub*, that *zhlub*."
2. A clumsy, gauche, graceless person.
   "Vassar-Shmassar, the girl's still a *zhlub*."
3. An oaf, a yokel, a bumpkin.
   "What can you expect from such a *zhlub*?"

A Jew came running into a railway station, the perspiration pouring down his face, panting, crying, "Stop, train, stop!"

A *zhlub* said, "What's the matter?"

"I missed my train!" the man exclaimed. "By twenty measly seconds!"

"The way you're carrying on," said the *zhlub*, "one would think you had missed it by an hour!"

———

Yisroel Glotz was visiting his old friend Moishe (Moses) Yorkin. Both men were widowers. "Moishe, the most important thing at our age, alone—is to get an interesting hobby."

"I have a hobby," sighed Moishe.

"You do? What is it?"

"Bees. I keep bees."

Glotz looked out of the window. "So where is the hive?"

"I don't use a hive. I keep them in my bedroom."

"In your *bed*room? Don't the bees *sting* you?"

"How can they sting me? I keep them in the closet."

"In—migod, Moish, when you open the closet, don't the bees swarm out—?"

Yorkin shrugged. "They can't. I keep them in a box."

"Inside a *box*? . . . I suppose you punched a lot of holes in it?"

"What for should I punch holes in the box?"

"For air. For *oxygen*. If they don't get any air, the bees will die!"

"So?"

" 'So?' What's the matter with you, you *zhlub*? Don't you care if all your bees die?"

Cried Moishe Yorkin: "It's only a hobby!"

See also KLUTZ, PUTZ, YOLD.

Zion
Tziyon

An eternal word: Hebrew, Yiddish, English, Yinglish. Pronounced ZYE-*on* in English, TZEE-*yone* in Yiddish, to rhyme with "see bone." Hebrew: *Zion*.

The land of Israel; Jerusalem.

Since the first exile of the Jews to Babylonia, Zion has been synonymous with the idea of a reunited Jewish people in their original homeland. "By the rivers of Babylon, there

we sat down, yea, we wept when we remembered Zion"
(Psalm 137).

Wherever they have lived, traditional Jews have turned
in the direction of Zion when they prayed. Pious Jews long
to be buried there.

See also ISRAEL, JEW, MESHIACH.

Zohar

Pronounced ZOH-*harr*, to rhyme with "go far." From
Sefer ha Zohar: "Book of Splendor."
   The most important book of the cabalistic movement,
written in the thirteenth century (probably).

The *Zohar* is believed to have been written/assembled
by the Spanish rabbi Moses de Leon (who deliberately
attributed the work to a second-century rabbi, Simeon ben
Yohai).

The *Zohar* is a fantastic compendium of mysticism and
folklore, used to reveal "hidden" meanings in the Bible. It
is a hodgepodge of abstruse codes, dreams and symbols and
excursions into demonology (and angelology). It explains
ways of exorcising devils; it delves into the transmigration
of human souls; it is steeped in astrology.

The *Zohar* is especially beholden to a "science of numbers" that endows them with special meanings in a method
called *gematria: e.g.*, a numerical value is assigned to each
Hebrew letter, then a text from the Bible is analyzed, the
text arranged in every conceivable pattern—vertically, backwards, diagonally, upside down, in a triangle shape, as a
hexagon, a palindrome, an acronym, an acrostic, etc., etc.
One name—of a prophet, say—may be arranged in all the
possible permutations of its separate letters.

The *Zohar* also contains enchanting stories, ethical pro-
nouncements, and moving prayers.

The book exerted a significant influence on the Hasidim.
The rabbis often warned the laity not to hazard mental
danger by overly deep immersion in the *Zohar*'s occult
mysteries—and I can only agree with them.

See also CABALA, HASID.

TO MY READERS:
SHOLEM ALEICHEM!!

APPENDIX

A Guide to the English Spelling of Yiddish Words

Adapted from The Joys of Yiddish*

The authoritative YIVO Institute for Jewish Research has tried energetically to create a standard Yiddish orthography, and standard rules for the transcription of Yiddish into Roman letters. These were "established" in 1937—and have been rather widely ignored ever since.† Jewish philologists and editors, too, have attempted, not successfully, to set abiding standards and rules. In 1954 a publication, *The Field of Yiddish*, was established for this purpose, and in 1958 an international conference on the study of Yiddish was held in New York.

The American Jewish Press Association appointed a Committee on Transliteration in 1950. A report of that committee, some sixteen years later, confessed: "All were in agreement on the desirability of a uniform system of transliteration . . . but unfortunately there was no agreement on a specific plan." Part of the problem lay in the fact that certain linguistic rules, necessary for scholarly and scientific publications, are intensely resisted—by the popular press, by deeply ingrained habits, by the preferences of influential Jews to whom their own version of the vernacular remains sacrosanct.

Indecision continues to plague those who seek a uniform system for the transliteration of Yiddish. Accordingly,

*pp. 516–517.

†See *The Standard Jewish Encyclopedia*, ed. by Cecil Roth, Doubleday, 1966, p. 1943.

words like *Chanukah* and *Rosh Hashanah* have been spelled in some fifteen different ways. "Since there existed no authoritative guide, every writer was a law unto himself," said the American Jewish Press Association, which finally decided to sacrifice all for simplicity and uniformness, and agreed that its members would

1. set aside formal philological rules;
2. recognize the Israeli/Sephardic *pronunciation* of Hebrew words, which would be spelled phonetically in Yiddish;
3. write the Hebrew letter "het" (given in English as *ch* or *kh*) as "*h*";
4. omit the "*h*" letter where it is silent at the end of a word (Rosh Hashana);
5. write the Hebrew "tzadik" as "tz," not "ts."*

Certain variations of spelling in the present lexicon occurred however much I would have preferred uniformity: Quoted material contained variant ways of spelling Yiddish words in English, and my own transliterations changed—to satisfy contexts, niceties of print, or in behalf of clarity rather than consistency. Many compromises had to be made—sometimes simply to simplify pronunciational cues to readers unfamiliar with Yiddish or Hebrew. Finally, not ignorance but economics dictated the preservation of certain variations as they appeared in the galley proofs. Since many words may be spelled quite correctly in more than one way (*epg., Mishnah* or *Mishna*) I sometimes decided to allow either version, in a given passage of texts, depending on the other material that surrounded it.

Adapted from the Preface of Hooray *for* Yiddish

"Standard Yiddish," as prescribed and propagated by the YIVO Institute for Jewish Research, has been accepted by leading linguists, the Library of Congress, the *Encyclopedia Judaica*, and the continuing journal, *The Field of Yiddish*.†

*I have drawn all this material from an undated copy of a "copyrighted, 1966" one-page résumé by Leo H. Frisch, editor of the *Jewish World*, entitled "War of Words Is Peacefully Resolved," distributed by the American Jewish Press Association.

†The standard orthography follows the Northern (Lithuanian or

5. The long English *oo* undergoes a transformation to a short *u*; a "pool" becomes a *pull*—and vice versa. To say that a dumbbell is drunk, a virtuoso might declaim, "That full is fool *shnaps*!"

6. The rounded *ow* becomes *ah*: "how" is rendered as *hah*, "powder" as *podder*, and "louse" sounds exactly like the Spanish article *las*.

7. The *w* regularly becomes a *v*: "We went to Willie's wedding" is vivified into "Ve vent to Villie's vaddink."

8. The final *g* becomes a *k*; thus "walking the Muggs' pug dog" becomes "valkink the Muck's puck duck"—a most unholy metamorphosis.

9. The *ng* and *ngg* sounds are often confused; thus "Long Island" sounds like "Long Guyland."

10. Voiced final consonants tend to become unvoiced: in such a vagarious world, one eats corn on the *cop*, spreads butter on *brat*, and consumes potato chips by the *back*.

It should be noticed that some of these vowel shifts are consistent and others are not, and that pronunciational variations appear in the speech of people who can conform to accepted sounds. In Yiddish itself, for instance, the word for "bread" is pronounced not *Broht*, as in German, but as *broyt* or *brayt*. What accounts for the transposition of *a*'s for *e*'s, or the interchangeability of the short *i* and the short *e*, or the use of *v*'s for *w*'s, when—obviously—each can be enunciated with ease, is a mystery I cannot resolve.

For technical questions about Yiddish, its grammar, vocabulary, and syntax, see Uriel Weinreich, *College Yiddish*, YIVO Institute for Jewish Research, 1965 edition. This is the first English textbook on Yiddish grammar. The late Professor Weinreich also produced the first dictionary of Yiddish-English, English-Yiddish, since Alexander Harkavy's quixotic classic of 1981. Weinreich's dictionary was published by McGraw-Hill in 1968.

A Carnival of Vowels:
How Jewish Immigrants
Pronounced English Words

For several years, way back in the early 1930s, I taught elementary English at a night-school for adults at the Jewish Peoples Institute on the West Side of Chicago. (My adventures were later published in two books about H*Y*-M*A*N K*A*P*L*A*N.) Among the more startling surprises I encountered was the carnival of mispronunciation in which my students indulged. Their pronunciational "shifts," to use the technical name for their acrobatics in rendering English words according to their own dictates, have never ceased to astonish and (secretly) delight me.

I give you a résumé I wrote in an effort to systematize the ways in which my charges distorted the pronunciation of perfectly straightforward English words:

1. The short *a* becomes a short *e*: "cat" is pronounced *ket*, and "pat" becomes *pet*.
2. The short *e*, in turn, emerges as a short *a*: "pet" is rendered *pat*. (I hate to think of what occurred with "a bad bed.")
3. The short *i* becomes a long *e*—and vice versa. This means that "pill" is pronounced *peel* and "peel" comes out *pill*. An Ashkenazic dentist (his patients called him "dentnist") might well fall into this euphoric promise: "Rilex! I'll feel your cavity so you won't even fill it!"
4. The long *o* becomes *aw* or *u*, and the *aw* sound, in turn, becomes the long *o*: thus, "phone" becomes *fawn* or *fun*; "saw" becomes *so*.

4. To make sure that my readers, of whatever persuasion or complexion, do not pronounce a three-syllable word in two syllables (because of the English spelling) I employ blunt orthographic cues: *meshugge*, for instance, is clearly better for American vocal cords than the standard *meshuge*. This was driven home to me by a friend who displays his fondness for Yiddish by pronouncing the priceless adjective *m'shug*. (He knows from nothing about *mama-loshn*.)

5. I double consonants in certain words to squelch the possibility that the word will be pronounced with a long, rather than a short, vowel. Standard Yiddish orthography uses *rebe*. I would hate to have a rabbi addressed as "Reeb," a syllable obviously from Jabberwocky.

6. I use *sh* at the beginning of a word instead of the oft-encountered *sch*. The *sch* is German; in English it usually calls for the cluster *sk*. It is foolhardy to encourage the unwary into calling a shlepper a "sklepper."

7. I prefer to use *h* for the uvular fricative instead of *kh*, although I follow standard Yiddish by using *kh* where it seems feasible. But I cannot bring myself to inflict *khutzpe* (or even *hutspa*) upon *chutzpah*

8. Where a terminal *e* dictates the lengthening of the preceding vowel (*mat, mate*) I often checkmate the rule by adding a minatory *h*: thus, *opstairsekeh* escapes the fate of rhyming with "Mozambique."

On all of the above, I should warn you, I could not achieve complete consistency. I was, after all, raised in Southern (Polish) Yiddish. That was the language we spoke all through my childhood. It was the language used in the school where I learned to read and write the lovely tongue. It was the accent and cadence I heard in the marvelous Yiddish theater. There is no point in pedants lamenting my occasional lapses. For my part, I hold no grudge against the Humboldt Current.

Of one thing I am sure: Sholem Aleichem would understand, if for no other reason than that I refuse to change his pseudonym to Shol'm Aleykhem.

1. I shall respect the rules of standard Yiddish, *except* where a different spelling, in Roman characters, has already been well established. The contrast between the two is often startling:

Standard Yiddish	*Established in English*
b'yali	bialy
khale	challa
matse	matzo
meyvin	maven

To spell *shamus* as *shames*, which standard Yiddish urges upon me, is to suggest that iniquity attends even the most respectable detective.

2. I also depart from standard Yiddish where its spelling discombobulates the innocent reader. To give the name of the Sabbath as *Shabes*, instead of the almost universal *Shabbes*, is to cue a reader into making the holy day rhyme with "slaves" instead of "novice."

3. Wherever there are several ways of spelling a word, I list those ways in columnar form; the first spelling is the one that has so widely taken root in English periodicals and books that it must be given preference. Example:

> Chanuka
> Khaneke (standard)
> Channuka

I may add that I have also seen Chanuka Englished as Chanukah, Chanuke, Channukah, Khanuka, Khanuke, Hanuka, Hanuke, Hannuka, Hannuke, etc.

"Litvak") spelling and pronunciation—a somewhat surprising state of affairs, given the fact that the overwhelming majority of Jews who spoke or speak Yiddish (surely over 70 percent) did not follow the Litvak articulation but used the Polish, Galician, Czech, Ukrainian, Russian vocalizations. You will understand the dilemma YIVO presented to many Jews, including the writer of these words. The scholars of Vilna, that Jerusalem of Jewish learning, were commanding figures, to be sure. Unfortunately, they would not pronounce (I mean this literally) the *yi* that characterizes the speech of Polish Jews. They said "Idish" and "ingele" for "Yiddish" and "yingele." They have prevailed—at least in the spelling.